A **FALCON** GUIDE®

D0403818

DEC 3 1 2019

Birding Washington

Rob and Natalie McNair-Huff

FALCON®

GUILFORD, CONNECTICUT
HELENA, MONTANA

AN IMPRINT OF THE GLOBE PEQUOT PRESS

A FALCON GUIDE®

Maps created by XNR Productions, Inc. © The
Globe Pequot Press

Library of Congress Cataloging-in-Publication Data
is available.
ISBN 0-7627-2577-X

Manufactured in the United States of America
First Edition/Second Printing

The Globe Pequot Press assumes no liability for accidents happening to, or injuries
sustained by, readers who engage in the activities described in this book.

Contents

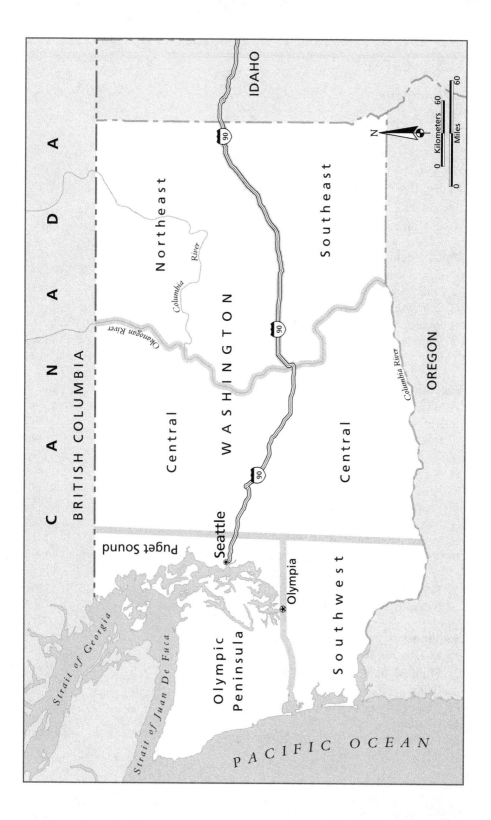

Central

Northeast

Southeast

Acknowledgments

While bird-watching can be a solo pursuit, writing about it requires the assistance of others. We never could have undertaken this project without the help of many people. From the depths of our bird-crazed hearts, we thank each person who helped us along the way, including countless bird-watchers we encountered.

Our friends and family kept us sane and reminded us about what is most important. In addition to much love and support, our parents opened our eyes to the richness of nature's tapestry when they spent countless hours with us camping in the desert, walking on the beach, hiking in the woods, and skiing in the mountains. Jana Wennstrom, Marie Stewart, the Mortburns, and many other friends kept us sane and laughing. Jason Wennstrom graciously tended to our eight-beast menagerie while we were on the road—they send licks and love nips. Special thanks to John Froschauer for offering his photographic expertise and Katrina Weihs, who was one of our original cheerleaders and coined the phrase "birding in context," which we use to describe this book.

Ken Brown, Idie Ulsh, and Mary Sue Gee each shared volumes of knowledge about birds, butterflies, native plants, and habitats through classes they taught at Tahoma Audubon Society (TAS). Many fellow birders shared their expertise, made suggestions, or read our work, including Matt Bartels, Vicki Biltz, Marv Breece, Ken Brown, Kelly Cassidy, Tim Cullinan, Mike Denny, Michael Hobbes, Ken Knittle, Kelly McAllister, Bob Morse, Rolan Nelson, Alan Richards, Marcus Roening, Carol Schulz, Andy Stepniewski, Patrick Sullivan, Ruth Sullivan, Ed Swan, Mike Walker, Thomas Weber, Diane Yorgason-Quinn, our TAS classmates, and the knowledgeable birders on the Tweeters and BirdYak e-mail lists. Our fellow TAS board members have encouraged us with their support and patience while we completed this book. All birders owe thanks to the park rangers and National Wildlife Refuge staff for the work they do, and we would like to thank those who spent time talking with us about their sites. Without the ornithologists and scientists, such as Diann MacRae, Dennis Paulson, Terry Wahl, Bud Anderson, and Art Kruckeberg, who have spent innumerable hours learning about the birds and ecosystems of our state and sharing that knowledge through their writings and records, we could not have undertaken this task.

We'd also like to thank a group of people who, in our estimation, can never be thanked enough for all of their stewardship—our nature-loving elders and predecessors who have fought long, hard battles to preserve, restore, and protect the animals and natural areas throughout state. Thanks especially to Thelma Gilmur, Mary Fries, and Helen Engle for teaching us that individuals can make a difference, and to writer, naturalist, and teacher Robert Michael Pyle, our idol and role model.

Without our fine editors and production team at the Globe Pequot Press, the book you now hold in your hands would still be a pile of notes. Thanks especially to Erin Turner, who stuck with us for the second time and patiently worked with us through many difficulties and delays.

Thank you everyone for what you have shared with us; we believe all of your efforts will help protect the many gifts of nature that we all love.

Map Legend

═══⟨90⟩═══	Interstate highway
═══⟨2⟩═══	U.S. highway
───⟨22⟩───	State highway
───[33]───	Forest road
───────	Other paved road
═══════	Gravel road
┝┿┿┿┿┿┿┥	Railroad
---------	Trail
···············	Ferry route
⊥⊥⊥⊥⊥⊥⊥⊥⊥	Cliff
✕	Airport
⊃⊂	Bridge
▲	Campground
—	Dam
●—●	Gate
◻	Overlook/viewpoint
🅿	Parking
▲	Peak/elevation
■	Point of interest
▮	Ranger/guard station
⚲	Spring
🚶	Trailhead
ℹ	Visitor information
∥	Waterfall

Introduction

Nature nurtures us in many ways. Even seasoned birders thrill at the site of a Bald Eagle flying along the Skagit River and smile at the incessant peeping of young sparrows on their nests. Nature teaches us about ourselves when we see a pair of American Crows preening each other on a branch. And based on the number of active birders we know who are beyond the age of eighty, we have seen how birding keeps us active and young.

Birds have always been important to the people of the Pacific Northwest. Many of the coastal tribes claim affiliation with the Eagle or the Raven clan, and in some mythologies Raven loosed humans on the earth and then gave us the gift of light. The first explorers describe the birds of the coast in their journals, and Lewis and Clark documented—and ate—many of the bird species in the state; they were, in fact, chased off an island by the never-ending, raucous noise of tens of thousands of migrating waterfowl in what is now Ridgefield National Wildlife Refuge. It's exciting to think about how the birds we love to watch link us with the rich cultural history of our state.

Washington State has a lot to offer resident and visiting birders. More than 480 bird species have been seen in the state since record keeping started. Of those 480, more than 350 are regular visitors. This abundance is due in part to the diverse habitats scattered across the state: Sitka spruce forests and rocky coast on the Olympic Peninsula, sandy beaches on the southern coast, the Palouse near the Idaho border, the shrub-steppe and grasslands of the Columbia Basin, and the mountains, riparian zones, and wetlands decorating the state like confetti. The geography of the state adds to this richness by funneling migrating birds down two primary flyways: one on the outer coast and along Puget Sound and the other down the center of the state east of the Cascades and through the Columbia Basin. Unfortunately, much of the prime bird habitat that once covered the state either is long lost due to agricultural development or is being currently lost due to urban sprawl, commercial development, and the ever-encroaching housing developments that are now beginning to spill into the valleys just east of the Cascade crest. With the efforts of many ecologists and conservationists and the cooperation of such organizations as the Nature Conservancy, Sierra Club, and the Audubon Society, some prime habitat is being protected and restored. Especially important to this effort is Audubon Washington's list of Important Bird Areas—sites that serve as important nesting, winter, or migratory habitat for many of the state's endangered and at-risk species.

While some people are content to watch nature on their televisions or with short, fifteen-minute forays to a viewpoint, Rob and I prefer to immerse ourselves in it. The time we spend watching birds is invaluable. For us, it is a gateway to learning more about our state and all of its inhabitants, from the bats, butterflies and other insects that share the gift of flight to the slugs and mosses that claim the forest floor. We hope that by sharing our passion for bird-watching with you, you too will learn more about all that the diverse habitats of our state offers to those who are willing to look for it. We also hope that as you explore these areas you do so with the respect it deserves so that the treasures we describe are preserved for future generations.

Regions

Birding Washington is organized around a regional approach to bird-watching, and as such we have divided the state into six major regions: the Olympic Peninsula, Puget Sound, Southwest Washington, Central Washington, Southeast Washington, and Northeast Washington.

Here is how we determined the artificial dividing lines between each region: The Olympic Peninsula is easy to single out as a distinct region. For the purposes of this book, Hood Canal defines the eastern edge of the region, the Strait of Juan de Fuca is the northern boundary, and the Pacific Ocean is the western boundary. We arbitrarily choose to use an imaginary line projecting due west from Olympia—roughly following State Route 8 and State Route 12—to define the southern boundary of the Olympic Peninsula region.

The Puget Sound region includes the area commonly referred to as the Puget Trough, from the Canadian border in the north to Olympia in the south and from Hood Canal in the west to the foothills of the Cascade Mountains in the east. Since this region includes the highest human population density in the state, it holds a distinct subset of the state's bird species and includes the largest number of urban bird-watching sites in this book.

The Southwest Washington region ranges from Olympia south to the Oregon border, with the Pacific Ocean as the western border and the foothills of the Cascade Mountains the eastern border. This region includes the southern Washington coast, with its publicly accessible beaches that offer the best shorebirding opportunities in the state.

The Central Washington Region covers a wide swath down the center of the state, from Canada in the north to the Columbia River in the south, and from the Cascade Mountains in the west to the Columbia River as its eastern border. This is the most mountainous region in the state, and it offers the largest number of parks and campgrounds in this book, as well as the widest range of habitat types of any one region. This region includes some of the best shrub-steppe habitat of eastern Washington as well as alpine and subalpine habitats in the Cascade Mountains.

The region of Southeast Washington covers the area from Interstate 90 in the north to the Oregon border in the south, with Idaho serving as the eastern border and the Columbia River serving as the western border. Included are thousands of acres of farm fields, much of the Lower Columbia Basin and its remnant shrub-steppe habitats, and the Blue Mountains in the far southeastern corner of the state.

The Northeast Washington Region covers the area from I–90 in the south to the Canadian border and from the Idaho border in the east to the western edges of the Okanogan Highlands in the west. This region also includes thousands of acres of farm fields and apple orchards, as well as the Okanogan area and the Selkirk Mountains in the far northeastern corner of the state.

The Sites

Choosing the sites for *Birding Washington* was one of the toughest tasks in the project. During 2001, 2002, and 2003, we visited roughly 200 potential birding sites across the state and narrowed the initial list of locations down to a more manageable 100 sites. We later whittled the list down to seventy sites.

The sites highlighted in this book are not being ranked as the seventy best sites in the state. Instead, the sites were chosen because they are seventy of the most representative sites for birding in Washington. They span the variety of habitats and regions across the state, and they offer an overview of Washington's 480 bird species. These sites are by no means the only good places to watch birds in Washington. We suggest you use these sites as a starting point for further exploration.

How to Use This Guide

Birding Washington is not a guide to help you identify the birds you see in your backyard or on trips around the state. Instead, *Birding Washington* is all about places and habitats—where to go and what you might find if you venture into the varied settings in our state. For this reason the book, and each of its seventy site overviews, focuses on habitats and the birds that may be found in them.

The first chapter of this book is about making the transition from being a backyard bird-watcher to exploring the wider world of birding on a statewide basis. We take a look at how backyard birding skills can be used in the field, and we offer some basic birding tips.

The second chapter offers tips for planning a bird-watching trip—what to take and when to go. We don't pretend to have a secret formula to guarantee a successful birding trip, but we boil down some of the things that have worked for us in our years of bird-watching and in the time we spent researching this book.

The third chapter explores and explains the habitats found in the state. One of the keys to locating and identifying birds is learning which species use which habitat.

The "Birds in the City" chapter offers tips about where to find good bird-watching in urban areas across the state, from city parks to open spaces and streamside riparian areas, and the "Pelagic Birding" chapter offers information about seabirds that can be seen only by taking a boat trip far off the Washington shores.

The rest of the book offers descriptions of the seventy birding sites, and each site description offers the following elements:

Habitats: Each of the major habitat types found on the site are noted in this section.

Specialty birds: We have selected a subset of the birds found in Washington that are either significant or hard-to-find species or birds that bird-watchers would especially come to Washington to see. In addition to the stock list of roughly one hundred bird species we chose as specialty birds for the state, we also include other birds from outside that list that are significant or special for individual sites. As an example, Bobolink is not on our specialty bird list for the entire state, but the unique birds can be found only in a limited number of places in Washington. As a result, if a site holds a known population of Bobolink, we include that species in our specialty bird list for that site.

Below is the list of specialty birds we have chosen for the state:

Common Loon
American White Pelican
Brown Pelican
Pelagic Cormorant
Brandt's Cormorant
Great Egret
Tundra Swan
Trumpeter Swan
Greater White-fronted
   Goose
Brant
Greater Scaup
Harlequin Duck
Barrow's Goldeneye
White-tailed Kite
Golden Eagle
Bald Eagle
Northern Goshawk
Swainson's Hawk
Ferruginous Hawk
Peregrine Falcon
Gyrfalcon
Chukar
Blue Grouse
White-tailed Ptarmigan
Sharp-tailed Grouse
Sandhill Crane
Black-bellied Plover
American Golden-Plover
Pacific Golden-Plover
Snowy Plover
Black Oystercatcher
American Avocet
Black-necked Stilt
Willet
Wandering Tattler

Solitary Sandpiper
Long-billed Curlew
Marbled Godwit
Bar-tailed Godwit
Ruddy Turnstone
Black Turnstone
Surfbird
Rock Sandpiper
Red Knot
Baird's Sandpiper
Pectoral Sandpiper
Short-billed Dowitcher
Wilson's Phalarope
Red-necked Phalarope
Red Phalarope
Heerman's Gull
Bonaparte's Gull
Little Gull
Mew Gull
Thayer's Gull
Western Gull
Forster's Tern
Common Tern
Common Murre
Pigeon Guillemot
Marbled Murrelet
Ancient Murrelet
Rhinoceros Auklet
Tufted Puffin
Band-tailed Pigeon
Short-eared Owl
Great Gray Owl
Spotted Owl
Snowy Owl
Flammulated Owl
Northern Pygmy-Owl

Burrowing Owl
Black Swift
Vaux's Swift
Black-chinned Hummingbird
Anna's Hummingbird
Calliope Hummingbird
Rufous Hummingbird
Acorn Woodpecker
White-headed Woodpecker
Lewis's Woodpecker
Black-backed Woodpecker
Pileated Woodpecker
Williamson's Sapsucker
Red-breasted Sapsucker
Red-naped Sapsucker
Least Flycatcher
Hammond's Flycatcher
Gray Flycatcher
Dusky Flycatcher
Pacific-slope Flycatcher
Hutton's Vireo
Cassin's Vireo
Gray Jay
Northwestern Crow
Purple Martin
Pygmy Nuthatch
Western Bluebird
Sage Thrasher
Bohemian Waxwing
Hermit Warbler
Northern Waterthrush
Sage Sparrow
Gray-crowned Rosy-finch
White-winged Crossbill
Pine Grosbeak
Common Redpoll

Best times to bird: This section offers a brief note about which seasons have the most bird variety at each site.

About the site: A full description of the site and some of the birds and plants you will find there makes up the bulk of each site description. In addition to birding highlights, many site descriptions offer notes about butterflies and animals that may be seen at the site, as well as details about the history and in some cases the geological history of the site.

Other key birds: This is a list of additional bird species that you may encounter while bird-watching at a particular site. The list of other key birds is not meant to encompass all of the species you may find, but it offers highlights of the birds expected to be seen on the site at various times of the year.

There are a number of bird species that are so common in their appropriate habitats everywhere in Washington that we have not listed them in either the specialty or key birds sections in most site descriptions. Below is the list of bird species that are listed only when the bird is indicative of a site.

Double-crested Cormorant	Great Horned Owl	Ruby-crowned Kinglet
Great Blue Heron	Belted Kingfisher	American Robin
Canada Goose	Northern Flicker	European Starling
Mallard	Steller's Jay	Cedar Waxwing
Northern Harrier	Common Raven	Yellow-rumped Warbler
Sharp-shinned Hawk	Black-billed Magpie	Song Sparrow
Cooper's Hawk	American Crow	White-crowned Sparrow
Red-tailed Hawk	Horned Lark	Dark-eyed Junco
American Kestrel	Tree Swallow	Western Meadowlark
Ring-necked Pheasant	Violet-green Swallow	Red-winged Blackbird
California Quail	Cliff Swallow	Brewer's Blackbird
American Coot	Northern Rough-winged	Brown-headed Cowbird
Killdeer	Swallow	House Finch
Glaucous-winged Gull	Barn Swallow	Pine Siskin
Rock Pigeon	Black-capped Chickadee	American Goldfinch
Mourning Dove	Red-breasted Nuthatch	House Sparrow
Barn Owl	Golden-crowned Kinglet	

Nearby opportunities: In addition to the seventy featured sites in this book, we also note good bird-watching areas that are near each of the featured sites. Including these nearby opportunities, this book includes notes about more than 150 sites across the state.

Directions: This section offers driving directions to help you find each of the sites in the book.

DeLorme Map Grid: Along with driving directions, we offer map coordinates from the well-known *Washington Atlas & Gazetteer* map books that are widely used by bird-watchers and other outdoors enthusiasts. The map grids given are meant to offer an additional aid in finding each site.

Elevation: We offer a rough estimate of the elevation of each site, including a range of elevation for those sites that rise or fall in elevation in the route described in the site description.

Access: If the site is wheelchair accessible, we offer notes about that in this section.

Bathrooms: Some of the more rugged bird-watching sites don't offer bathroom facilities or even pit toilets. We note if each site offers these basic amenities in this section. Be aware, however, that in some areas you may need to drive miles to find a public restroom. Also keep in mind that some toilets are offered only seasonally.

Hazards: Although most of the sites are easily accessible and hold no notable hazards, we do note those sites where rough roads or extreme weather conditions could pose a hazard as you go about your bird-watching.

Nearest food, gas, and lodging: Since many bird-watching sites are in far-flung locations around the state, we offer basic notes about where you can find a meal and a place to stay.

Nearest camping: If you feel more like roughing it and sleeping in a tent or under the stars, we offer notes about nearby camping sites for each birding site. Be aware that in the case of some urban bird-watching sites nearby camping can be hard to find, since most campgrounds are out in the wild rather than in the urban areas. Also be sure to check on campsite status and make reservations to stay at state parks in the busy summer months. The state has been busy closing some parks during the last few years due to budget shortfalls. Many parks are also closed during the winter.

For more information: This section offers links to Web sites and in some cases phone numbers and other contact information for each birding site.

Sidebar: In selected site descriptions we offer more in-depth notes about specific bird species, history, geology, or other natural history that is unique to that site.

Maps: All but one of the seventy sites described in *Birding Washington* has a basic map with details about trails and other interesting features at the site. The only exception is Protection Island, which can be reached only by boat.

In addition to the information in each site description, we also offer more general information about Washington bird-watching and birding resources in the appendices.

Appendix A offers a checklist of Washington bird species that is annotated with our Washington specialty birds noted in bold print, birds rarely seen in Washington in italics, and indications of bird species that are going to be found only on either the western or eastern side of the state. The checklist also lists the sites where specialty birds are most likely to be found. Appendix B offers details about how to report rare birds, and the last appendix notes a basic glossary of bird terminology used throughout this book and by bird-watchers in general.

The book concludes with a resources section that offers information about state and national birding organizations, including contact information for your local chapter of the Audubon Society, along with books that can serve as great references as you head out to explore Washington's natural areas. We also offer details about general birding Web sites that offer information about Washington birding, addresses for e-mail lists that are used extensively by the state's top bird-watchers, and details about bird-watching events held across the state each year.

We are offering corrections for any mistakes found in *Birding Washington* as well as a birding diary and other resources for Washington bird-watchers on our Web site, www.birdingwashington.com.

Becoming a Bird-watcher

How do you go from being someone who likes to look at birds at the beach or on a bird feeder to becoming a bird-watcher—someone who can name the birds she sees or hears, and knows the birds' life histories? Simple, you start with what you know.

Most people can tell the difference between an American Robin and a European Starling. The challenge comes when trying to tell the difference between a Fox and a Song Sparrow or Greater and Lesser Yellowlegs, and even the experts can become bamboozled detecting the difference between a Dusky and a Gray Flycatcher. Learning the differences between species often requires more than a long, close look. Birders who know which warblers feed at the top of a tree and which stick near the bottom center of a tree nail identifications more effectively. Discovering why shorebirds have bills of different lengths helps sort out the differences between all those sandpipers. You don't have to know any of these things to enjoy watching birds; however, when you understand a little more about the creatures you are looking at, you will find that what a bird does takes on a whole new meaning.

So, how exactly did those advanced bird-watchers learn to identify five different and seemingly identical flycatchers, and how can they tell that the speck in the sky is a Peregrine Falcon and not a Red-tailed Hawk? All birders started at the beginning: They picked up their field guides and their binoculars and hit the road to look at and listen to birds. Then they went home and read about birds. Some took classes taught by expert birders at their local Audubon Society chapters. Most keep notes and bird-watching journals. They learned the names of feather groups and anatomical features so they could better remember the field marks. They listened to birds in the field and took field trips with other birders. And, perhaps most importantly, they studied how birds behave: where they live, where they forage and hunt, when they migrate, and where they nest. They started with the birds they knew best from their time spent watching at feeders and local parks. They spent time watching a robin hunt for worms. They noted the subtle variation in streaking between the House Finches and Purple Finches that came to their bird feeders. They learned that on a cold day a Bushtit looks twice as bulky as on a hot summer day.

Anatomy and Field Marks

You won't learn field marks if you can't identify the parts of a bird's body. You need to know the difference between tertials and primaries, between undertail and wing coverts. If you are in the field with another bird-watcher and she tells you to see if a bird has a yellow supercilium and a pale median stripe, you won't want to waste time trying to remember where to look for those marks. Especially since the Savannah Sparrow sitting on top of that fence post may not stick around long enough. Take time to learn the anatomical markings. When I was first learning about anatomical features, I would concentrate on one section of the bird at a time. One week I would study heads, the next wings, the next would be tails, and so on. I'd sit with my book and my binoculars and talk myself through all the body parts from lores to undertail coverts. If you have a pet bird or know someone who does, study it as well. In *Birding Basics,* author David Sibley includes an excellent and detailed pictorial and written breakdown of all anatomical features.

Field marks are those visual features on a bird that distinguish it from similar species. Some field marks are easy to distinguish—a brief glimpse of the white head and tail of a mature Bald Eagle will let you name the bird. Others are subtle, such as the differences in scaling and coloration that help birders distinguish between Western and Least Sandpipers. Fortunately, with Western and Least Sandpipers, the two species often flock together so birders get a side-by-side look to compare height and the darker plumage and chest band of the Least Sandpiper to the more rufous plumage and arrow-shaped spots on the flanks of the Western Sandpiper. Most people automatically know to look at color and size. Birdwatchers tend to compare a bird's size to three well-known birds. When you first see a bird, try to determine whether it is longer, more bulky, or taller than a House Sparrow, an American Robin, or an American Crow. Determining that factor automatically excludes two-thirds of all birds. Add body shape and color and you may be able to narrow it down to family. Next look for more detailed field marks, including eye-rings/spectacles, wing-bars, streaking or barring, eye-lines or superciliums, median stripes, and other field marks. Add range and habitat considerations, and song and alert calls if you are lucky enough to hear them, to determine the species.

Birding by Ear

If you have ever walked through the woods with longtime bird-watchers, you were probably astounded by how many birds they identified without seeing a single feather. Don't despair—those birders did not wake up one day and magically know how to translate bird-speak. They, like all experts, spent time studying their craft. All spent time in the field matching bird to voice. Some went home and listened to tapes to help reinforce what they saw and heard in the field. Some birders take tape recorders into the field and go home to listen to the tapes again and again until they have the song or call note memorized. If you choose to use tapes to learn songs and calls, be aware that bird songs vary from region to region—almost like human dialects—and the sound on the tape may not match what you hear in the field. Additionally, some birds (starlings and mockingbirds are prime examples) change their songs or use several different tunes. Some bird-watchers take their own tape recorders into the field with them to create their own study tapes.

Most birds, especially songbirds, vocalize with songs and call notes. Songs are generally reserved for breeding season, when you'll see males sitting atop trees and shrubs, singing to their hearts' content. Some birds continue to sing beyond the breeding season, but their songs will commonly be abbreviated versions of their courting tunes. Raptors and waterfowl don't do anything that we would recognize as singing during breeding season; instead, they use different mating calls, which are often emitted during courting flights. Call notes, usually short chirps or buzzes, are used for in-flight contact to keep the flock together and to let flying companions know where a bird is, and to alert other birds to danger. Some species use a different alert call for each purpose, which can make learning them even more challenging. Take time to learn songs and calls, to be rewarded with the ability to identify birds based solely on their songs when you walk into the woods and name each sound you hear. You'll also be rewarded by long, leisurely sits and walks in the woods.

Migration Patterns and Range

Birds fly north to breed in the spring and then fly south for the winter in the fall to seek warmer weather and more prosperous foraging grounds. That's mostly true, but if you take that at face value, you'll miss the larger picture. Our definition of spring and fall is not shared by all birds. Some birds start their spring migration in February, and some don't begin their fall migration until November. In winter, birds such as Gray-crowned Rosy-Finches and Dark-eyed Juncoes engage in altitudinal migration by moving from higher to lower elevations based on temperature and the availability of food. While rare even in migration, if you want a chance of seeing a Pectoral Sandpiper in Washington, you'll need to know when they migrate.

Although a bird may be in the state at a given time, you'll increase your chances of seeing it if you take its range into consideration. Some birds, such as the Red-tailed Hawk, have a broad range and can be seen across the entire state, while others, such as the Hermit Warbler, have a narrow range and can be seen only in a handful of counties between the Cascade Mountains and the coastal range. Range and habitat are intrinsically linked. The Sage Sparrow has such a narrow range because it is a shrub-steppe obligate, which means it requires uncompromised sage lands for nesting. We write more about habitat in another chapter. Most guidebooks include range maps, and Seattle Audubon provides detailed maps for Washington State on its Web site at www.birdweb.org.

Ask a group of bird-watchers what their favorite time of year is and chances are they will say spring or fall migration. Rare birds and oddities show up during migration, and most birds are easier to see during migration due to the sheer numbers that pass through the state. Migration seems magical, especially when a site nearly devoid of birds one week is stuffed with migrants the next. You must head out to the field during migration if you want to see some of the state's rare and uncommon birds such as Baird's Sandpiper, Red-necked Phalarope, or Pacific Golden-Plover, since migration may be the only time of year they will be in the state. Occasionally, Eurasian species get "lost" and migrate with American species by tracking down the West Coast in a mirror migration, which can add even more highlights to the spring and fall migration seasons.

So if migration is such a great time to see birds, why don't you see them coming in droves to your backyard? Simply because, like people, birds are discriminating when it comes to where they choose to rest on their journeys. Birds become exhausted during their epic migratory flights and look for suitable stopovers where they may spend a day, a night, or a week recuperating and refueling before the next leg of their journeys. Sites that offer ample supplies of food and water as well as protection from the elements draw legions of migrants. These places are known as migratory hot spots. Most hot spots attract a variety of species from warblers to cranes. A visit to one of these hot spots on the right day, which is often due to pure luck, can put you in the front row for one of nature's spectacular shows: Thousands of shorebirds on the wing pursued by a solitary Peregrine Falcon at Bowerman Basin; a cyclone of incoming waterfowl circling with outgoing Sandhill Cranes at the Columbia National Wildlife Refuge; poplar trees decorated with colorful, singing warblers at Wanapum State Park.

Keeping Lists

If you read bird-watching magazines and books, or hang around bird-watchers at all, you will hear about life birds and life lists. Many bird-watchers keep lists. They list the birds they see in their yards and specific sites, the birds they see in a month, a season, a year. Life lists include all the birds a person has ever seen. Some people chase birds—hearing about and then immediately heading to where a specific bird was sighted—in order to add birds to their lists. While adding a rare life bird to a growing list can be exciting, we hate to see bird-watching shrink to a numbers game. Some bird-watchers don't keep any formal lists, preferring to start each journey with fresh eyes and a sense of adventure. We were list-less birders for years, and we still do not think that keeping a list is or should be the focus of bird-watching. However, we have found listing to be an excellent learning tool and an invaluable resource. Each year we can compare lists to see when the first swallows arrive in our neighborhood. We use our lists to remind us of habitat and seasonal changes for specific sites. Additionally, keeping accurate trip lists is important if you wish to contribute to the larger community of bird-watchers by posting sightings on bird-alert hotlines or e-mail lists. If you report a rare, uncommon, or out-of-place bird, other bird-watchers will want details for which you will want to refer to your list.

Listing can be as simple or as complicated as you want. A simple life list includes bird names, dates, and locations of each first sighting. Several journals are available that let bird-watchers keep a variety of lists (yard, site, season, year, life) in one place. Computer software is also available to help you cross-reference species, locations, and seasons. Some Web sites, such as enature.com, even let you keep online lists.

What to Wear

Birders head to the hills, beach, and sage desert no matter what the weather brings. While your day may start with fair skies and a good forecast, don't head out unprepared. The weather changes quickly. On any given spring day, you could suffer through torrential downpours, a brief snow flurry, and stinging pellets of hail carried horizontally on strong wind gusts before enjoying blue skies—all in one place and within two hours. With that fact in mind, wear the right clothes. In the wet Pacific Northwest, layered clothing is always a good idea; even in summer, winds can pick up and make a warm evening cool. While we tend to prefer natural fibers such as cotton and wool, we love our synthetic raincoats, fleece vests, and lightweight jackets.

Don't forget to think about your feet and the top of your head. Sturdy walking shoes and moisture-wicking socks are a must. Hiking boots allow you to dive deeper into the woods and sage brush, although for most sites, sturdy walking shoes will serve. Hats also make searching for birds easier and more comfortable. They keep the heat in when it's cold, and wide-brimmed hats shade your pate and your eyes when the sun comes out.

Veteran bird-watchers recommend wearing clothes that blend into the background. We also suggest that you think about how much noise your clothes make as you walk: rain gear can be especially loud if it's made out of the wrong material. When you pack your bird-watching kit, make sure you add (and don't forget to wear) sunscreen and sunglasses, and always pack a full bottle of water with you.

Ethics

It's a beautiful day, and you heard from other birders that they saw an Upland Sandpiper in a private meadow. You know how to get there. You know the only way to see this rare state bird is to take an uninvited walk through the meadow. What do you do? After all, it is an extremely rare bird for Washington State, and it would be a life bird for you.

If you are a responsible bird-watcher, the only way to answer this question is to say that you'll have to let this bird go. Chalk it up to bad luck, bad timing, and a responsible sense of what is right and wrong. Not all bird-watchers make the same decision, which is a detriment to those of us who do strive to act ethically. Acting responsibly helps maintain good relations with nonbirders. Acting irresponsibly encourages nonbirders to paint us all with the same brush, which can create some nasty friction. Take for example the normally quiet country road that becomes suddenly inundated with hundreds of bird-watchers seeking an uncommon bird that was reported on the local birding hotline. Try to put yourself in the place of the people who live on that road; people who may have little interest in winged creatures; people who prefer to pull out of their driveways without asking bird-watchers to move their cars; people who do not want to pick up the apple cores, banana peels, and cigarette butts left behind by "those thoughtless bird-watchers." This example is neither a pretty sight nor a good public relations campaign for bird-watchers or birds. With a little consideration, this type of mess can be avoided.

We encourage all bird-watchers to abide by the American Birding Association's Principles of Birding Ethics, which we have reprinted below. However, we consider this code to be the beginning of a larger code of ethics that extends to include educational outreach and conservation. Even new bird-watchers can teach others about birds by simply answering the questions of passersby who ask what it is you are looking at. Be specific if possible, and if you happen to have your scope on it or don't mind passing your binoculars, offer to let them take a look. On a group field trip to the Kitsap Peninsula, we were parked alongside the bay looking at Harlequin Ducks in the choppy water when a boy rode up on his bike and asked us what we were doing. It didn't take long for him to catch our enthusiasm for the birds that practically live in his backyard. When we head to Titlow Beach to monitor the Purple Martin boxes, we take our spotting scope with us and let people take a look at whatever happens to be in the scope at the time. While we love watching children get excited about seeing a baby gull, we get just as excited when we see an adult's expression change to one of keen interest when they really see a Pigeon Guillemot or a raft of Western Grebes or comprehend how fortunate we are to have an active martin colony at a popular park. We also help other bird-watchers when we can by pointing out the location of a bird we've sighted or by helping them with a sticky identification by pointing out field marks.

We feel that part of being a responsible bird-watcher involves protecting bird habitat. All birders can help by respecting ecologically sensitive areas. While it might be tempting to leave the trail and trek across the alpine prairie to get a closer glimpse of the White-tailed Ptarmigan chicks, doing so does years of damage with every footstep. Staying aware of how your decisions impact the environment is one step in the right direction, but if you value all of the pleasure that birds and nature bring to you, get even more involved. Anyone with a yard can create a haven for birds by creating a backyard wildlife sanctuary. You don't need to live next to a mountain, a stream, or a forest to attract wildlife. All you need to do is provide shelter, water, and plants that provide forage. For more information on creating such a spot in your yard, visit the Washington Department of Fish and Wildlife Web site, www.wa.gov/wdfw/, where you can order a guide. Local, state, and national conservation organizations will also welcome your participation. In addition to providing a place for bird-watchers to gather and learn from each other, your local Audubon Society also works to conserve and restore habitat through hands-on projects as well as advocacy. We list several similar organizations in the resources section at the end of the book.

If you need another reason to get involved in helping others learn about birds or in protecting habitat, think about this: doing so will make you a better bird-watcher. You will learn more about identifying birds and their habitats, and the natural world that surrounds you.

American Birding Association Principles of Birding Ethics

Everyone who enjoys birds and birding must always respect wildlife, its environment, and the rights of others. In any conflict of interest between birds and birders, the welfare of the birds and their environment comes first.

Code of Birding Ethics

1. Promote the welfare of birds and their environment.

1(a) Support the protection of important bird habitat.

1(b) To avoid stressing birds or exposing them to danger, exercise restraint and caution during observation, photography, sound recording, or filming.

Limit the use of recordings and other methods of attracting birds, and never use such methods in heavily birded areas, or for attracting any species that is threatened, endangered, or of special concern, or is rare in your local area.

Keep well back from nests and nesting colonies, roosts, display areas, and important feeding sites. In such sensitive areas, if there is a need for extended observation, photography, filming, or recording, try to use a blind or hide, and take advantage of natural cover.

Use artificial light sparingly for filming or photography, especially for close-ups.

1(c) Before advertising the presence of a rare bird, evaluate the potential for disturbance to the bird, its surroundings, and other people in the area, and proceed only if access can be controlled, disturbance minimized, and permission has been obtained from private landowners. The sites of rare nesting birds should be divulged only to the proper conservation authorities.

1(d) Stay on roads, trails, and paths where they exist; otherwise, keep habitat disturbance to a minimum.

2. Respect the law and the rights of others.

2(a) Do not enter private property without the owner's explicit permission.

2(b) Follow all laws, rules, and regulations governing use of roads and public areas, both at home and abroad.

2(c) Practice common courtesy in contacts with other people. Your exemplary behavior will generate goodwill with birders and nonbirders alike.

3. Ensure that feeders, nest structures, and other artificial bird environments are safe.

3(a) Keep dispensers, water, and food clean and free of decay or disease. It is important to feed birds continually during harsh weather.

3(b) Maintain and clean nest structures regularly.

3(c) If you are attracting birds to an area, ensure the birds are not exposed to predation from cats and other domestic animals, or dangers posed by artificial hazards.

4. Group birding, whether organized or impromptu, requires special care.

Each individual in the group, in addition to the obligations spelled out in Items #1 and #2, has responsibilities as a group member.

4(a) Respect the interests, rights, and skills of fellow birders, as well as people participating in other legitimate outdoor activities. Freely share your knowledge and experience, except where code 1(c) applies. Be especially helpful to beginning birders.

4(b) If you witness unethical birding behavior, assess the situation and intervene if you think it prudent. When interceding, inform the person(s) of the inappropriate action and attempt, within reason, to have it stopped. If the behavior continues, document it and notify appropriate individuals or organizations.

Group Leader Responsibilities (amateur and professional trips and tours).

4(c) Be an exemplary ethical role model for the group. Teach through word and example.

4(d) Keep groups to a size that limits impact on the environment and does not interfere with others using the same area.

4(e) Ensure everyone in the group knows of and practices this code.

4(f) Learn and inform the group of any special circumstances applicable to the areas being visited (e.g., no tape recorders allowed).

4(g) Acknowledge that professional tour companies bear a special responsibility to place the welfare of birds and the benefits of public knowledge ahead of the company's commercial interests. Ideally, leaders should keep track of tour sightings, document unusual occurrences, and submit records to appropriate organizations.

The American Birding Association offers more resources for birders as well as downloadable copies of this code of ethics on their Web site at www.American Birding.org.

HOW DO YOU SEE?

Joining other walkers taking advantage of the early warmth on a bright spring Sunday, we were walking along Ruston Way in Tacoma when we saw a Bald Eagle sitting on a piling about 20 feet from the sidewalk. Although seeing an eagle that close was a treat, we were more surprised by the fact that at least fifteen people walked right by it without seeing it. We are often surprised at what people do not see, but we have learned that many, if not most people, are entirely unaware of what goes on around them.

Seeing and hearing are the keys to bird-watching. If you neither see nor hear a bird, you are out of luck and might as well go back inside and turn on the Nature Channel. While most of us take our vision and hearing for granted, learning to use those abilities to observe the natural world is the most important skill a would-be birder needs to learn.

Have you ever heard silence? Silence is full of sound. Sitting in silence at Cape Flattery, I hear trees bending in the wind, the rustle of a chipmunk on the duff behind me, wind echoing in the caves below me, the pounding of the surf against the rock walls, a plane passing far overhead, the cry of sea lions floating over the water from Tatoosh Island, a chickadee calling behind me, gulls calling above me, and cormorants calling to each other as they cling to the cliffs all around me. While I may have heard some of these things while I was walking or talking, they all came at once when I took the time to sit and just listen. Do it now, wherever you are (take time to turn off the TV or radio if it is on). What do you hear? Nothing? Try again. Do you hear the sound of your own breathing? Your heartbeat? Do you hear a car or an airplane passing? Can you name all the sounds you hear? Practice hearing whenever you have a chance, especially when you are outside.

Good bird-watchers are good at recognizing subtle differences in patterns. That skill not only helps them see an olive-yellow-colored Orange-crowned Warbler in a willow tree but also helps them recognize the one Snowy Plover amidst a flock of Western Sandpipers.

Brilliant violet and green colors along the back of a Violet-green Swallow can make the mature birds easy to identify, along with the white that extends behind the bird's eyes.

Planning a Trip

Heading out to watch birds can be as simple as tossing your field guide and binoculars into the car and heading down to the local sewer pond, or as complicated as planning a weeklong field trip with a group of bird-watchers. Not much planning need go into the simple trips, but if you want to make the most out of longer trips, some strategic planning may make the difference between a safe and exciting trip and a miserable bust.

When to Go

You can go bird-watching any time and in any season. Go at midnight in September to look at the face of a full moon to see and hear migrating passerines. Go to the high desert of eastern Washington in the middle of winter to see a Snow Bunting or, in an irruptive year, a Snowy Owl. However, if you are trying to find that one, special bird, say a Baird's Sandpiper, you will want to head out in late summer for the early fall migration. A lot of Washingtonians, especially those of us on the west (or wet) side, are fond of saying we have two seasons: the wet season and the dry(er) season. But bird-watchers know that we have four distinct seasons, and each season brings a different collection of birds. Fall and spring migrations may be the most exciting times of year for bird-watchers. But don't let the names fool you. Some shorebirds start their fall migration in July, but the bulk of fall migrants pass through between mid-August and mid-October. The majority of spring migrants arrive between mid-March and mid-May.

I do not like getting up before the sun has risen, but birds simply don't have my predilection to sleep in. In summer, birds start their mornings before dawn. In June they start rustling and peeping at 4:30 A.M. They begin foraging in the twilight hours of the morning, and just as the sun is cresting, all are awake and busy working to fill the never-ending gullets of their young. You won't find us in the field at 4:30 A.M. (unless we've stayed up all night looking for owls), but we try to be in the field as close to dawn as possible. Arriving early increases your chances of seeing more birds with far less hunting. From midmorning to midafternoon, bird activity slows down: songbirds tuck themselves away and, depending on the tide, most shorebirds will have their heads tucked under their wings for a midday siesta. Activity picks up again about two hours before sunset. During the spring, summer, and fall months, we use the midday birding doldrums to watch butterflies and dragonflies, look at wildflowers, or draw, paint, and write in our nature journals. This allows us to remain in the field so we're already on-site when the birds begin their late-afternoon and early evening foraging. Raptors and crepuscular owls become active in the early evening, and if we aren't too cold or too tired, we'll stay out beyond sunset to look for nocturnal owls. On the east side of the state, we may drive back roads to look for Common Poorwills. However, if you aren't an early riser don't fret too much because no matter what time of day you go birding, if you pick the right habitat, you'll see something interesting: crows preening, Canada Geese herding their young, Snow Geese foraging on a field of green winter grass.

Concerned about the weather? Don't be. Unless a severe winter storm is blowing our way, the birds don't care if they get wet. And if a winter storm is approaching, song birds forage frenetically until just before the storm hits, and shorebirds and some pelagic birds head for the lee side of coves and protected bays. Some bird-watchers look forward to winter storms and head to the coast to see what pelagic birds have been blown in or sought shelter closer to shore. Winter storms offer exciting bird-watching opportunities, especially if you take the time to watch how the birds behave and track where they go. Blisteringly hot summer days quell bird activity far more than drenching rains. Like people do, birds seek shade when the sun comes out, but when evening arrives and the wind picks up, the birds come out again. If you want to see Sage or Brewer's Sparrows, Sage Thrashers, and bluebirds at the Quilomene Wildlife Area, don't expect to spot them between 11:00 A.M. and 3:00 P.M. First of all, you don't want to get sun stroke or heat exhaustion; furthermore, the birds won't be active. They'll be hiding deep in the sagebrush. Spend your afternoon instead driving the road between nearby Ginkgo State Park and Wanapum Dam. The high cliffs to the west provide afternoon shade for Canyon and Rock Wren, Chukar, Lark Sparrow, and Lazuli Bunting, while the river hosts waterfowl, American White Pelicans, and cooling breezes for songbirds that flit between the poplar trees that have been planted to break the winds and provide shade for the fruit orchards.

No matter what time of year you head to the mountains, keep an eye on the weather and take appropriate gear with you. A nice day can turn mean quickly in the Cascade range. Every year people get lost or caught in surprise whiteouts and snow storms. If you have your heart set on seeing White-tailed Ptarmigan, Boreal Owl, Mountain Chickadee, or White-winged Crossbill, you'll have to head into the mountains, and you may run into snow. Plan these trips carefully.

Where to Stay

Do you prefer comfort or adventure? If you look for a hot shower, a soft pillow, and heat or air-conditioning at the end of the day, we suggest you make reservations at a hotel, motel, or bed-and-breakfast inn. The Olympic Peninsula provides ample opportunity for extreme comfort combined with extreme birding if you elect to stay at one of its many bed-and-breakfast inns. You'll also find such inns scattered across the state, especially on the west side and around Spokane, Walla Walla, and Yakima. Innkeepers are usually happy to work with your schedule. They might not provide a multicourse, hot breakfast at 5:30 A.M., but they'll be happy to set out pastries, cereal, juice, tea, and coffee, even if you plan on hitting the road before they rise. If you plan on staying at a bed-and-breakfast inn, we suggest making reservations ahead of time. We rarely make reservations for hotels and motels unless we happen to be traveling with a large group or on a holiday or festival weekend.

We generally prefer to rough it. As long as nighttime temperatures don't drop too far below freezing, we pitch our tent or put the backseat down and sleep in the back of our station wagon. Sometimes we stay in state campgrounds, which cost between $15 and $20 per night. Don't plan on being able to drive into a state campground at the last minute to find a place. Make reservations at state campgrounds as far in advance as possible, especially during the height of summer camping season. State campgrounds fill quickly in the summer, and as campgrounds close due to state budget cuts, competition for the remaining spots is fierce. We have been fortunate to find a number of free Department of Natural Resources campgrounds scattered around the state, and some wildlife areas allow camping, although without any amenities such as on-site water or toilets. And, taking a cue from naturalist and author Robert Michael Pyle, we sometimes pull onto forest service roads and sleep in the car.

Be aware when you are in Central Washington during the summer concert season that you may have a hard time booking a hotel room or finding space at an established campground. Concertgoers from all over the state converge at the Gorge Ampitheater near George for weekend concerts. Most arrive a day ahead of time and stay overnight after the concert.

What to Take

Since we turn almost every trip we take into a nature study and research session, we have a crate of books we carry in our car with us: wildflower, butterfly, and insect field guides; geology and natural history texts; Washington state history books; and, of course, several field guides to birds. On top of that we include our cameras, computers, and camping gear. But you're in luck—you don't have to carry nearly that much with you for a successful birding trip. Most birders carry a few essentials in a pack along with their binoculars and field guides. Many also add a camera and a birding scope to their stash.

Use common sense if you plan a winter trip or intend to camp. It's better to be prepared and to take too much than it is to literally freeze in your car because it

Trip Essentials		Extras
This book	Pocket knife*	Field journal
Field guide to birds	Food*	Camera and film
Binoculars	Drinking water*	GPS or Compass*
Spotting scope	Toilet paper	
State map & DeLorme	Insect repellent	
Map book*	Sunscreen*	
Sunglasses*	Basic first-aid kit*	

has broken down on a backcountry road during a snow storm. Additionally, although you may think that short, 5-mile loop will be a quick and easy day hike, we recommend you always keep the ten essentials on hand, which include the starred items above as well as rain gear, waterproof matches, and a flashlight. Always take water with you when you leave your vehicle; it is as important to a successful birding trip as binoculars.

Field Hazards

People don't correlate bird-watching with danger but, depending on where you venture and when, you may be placing yourself in the path of an accident waiting to happen. More likely, however, your comfort will be more endangered than your life.

Sometimes bird-watchers seem to forget that they are watching wild animals. We all welcome close encounters with birds, but be aware of the other animals that may be nearby. Some of the areas we highlight are known to harbor cougar, elk, bear, and skunk. In fact, one night, we were reminded of how wild the wilds can be when a skunk sprayed near our car while we slept in the back with the windows open—luckily neither of us was outside when that skunk passed by.

Be wary of rattlesnakes east of the Cascade Mountains. While they will do their best to avoid you, they do blend into their surroundings. On warm days you'll find them hidden in the shade beneath rocks or tucked underneath the sage and rabbit brush. On cool mornings you'll find them sunbathing on top of dark rocks. If you hear the rattle, don't panic, find where the sound is coming from, and move away.

If you see a cougar, do not start running in the opposite direction. Cougars are big, fast cats, and if you run away from them, you trigger their chase instincts. Raise your arms over your head to make yourself look as big as possible and yell loudly. As for bears, the safest way to deal with them is to let them know you are in the woods, and, as Rob says, don't wear bacon. Any hiker knows that wearing a bear bell while on the trail is a good idea. If you do see a bear, back away, and make sure you don't put yourself between a mother and her cubs. If you are camping on a backcountry trail, follow good hiking practices and hang your food stores as high as possible in a tree. Do not keep food in your tent even if you are camping in an established campground, and if you want your food to be there in the morning, we also suggest putting your food in raccoon-safe containers. Zippers are not raccoon-safe, as we discovered one night when some marauding raccoons stole some of our stores after neatly manipulating the easy-to-open zipper and toggle closure on a backpack.

Other Hazards

Throughout the book we list known hazards, but there are some dangers that are hard to anticipate. Just as being aware of what is around you is one of the keys to becoming a good birder, it is equally important to staying safe. Beware when walking in the woods of precariously hanging branches caught in the canopy. When walking near talus slopes and below bluffs, keep your eyes and ears open for falling rocks, and please don't walk off the edge of a cliff or stand on what may well be an unsupported ledge. Hazards hide beneath your feet as well. Quicksand is not a myth, and it is difficult to detect until it is too late. If you do happen to get caught in quicksand, don't struggle to free yourself—you will only pull yourself deeper into the mire. Instead, lay back flat on the surface and coax your legs out slowly; then, roll to firmer ground.

Lest you believe hazards can always be easily seen, take a word of caution from us. One summer weekend we made the mistake of going into the field without putting on insect repellent. As we walked through the mowed grass field at Toppenish National Wildlife Refuge, we felt things crawling on our legs. To our horror, we had up to twenty ticks on our legs. We finished our trip with constant stops to brush off more ticks. We stripped and searched again when we got back to the car, but we still found a few more that night as we set up camp. Luckily none latched on and dug in, but the experience was far from pleasant. The trip was saved only by a close encounter with an adult Great Horned Owl and its fledgling. We have had similar experiences with mosquitoes, which are becoming more worrisome with the progress of West Nile virus. Anytime you are somewhere where insects could be a problem, keep insect repellent nearby.

Using a Map

Before setting out on your birding trip, be sure to check area maps, and bring the map along for the ride. We reference pages in the DeLorme *Washington Atlas & Gazatteer* in each site description. The DeLorme guide, or a similar map, is critical because it offers enough detail to show all major roads and some primitive and forest service roads that don't appear on less-detailed maps. If you have time to get them before your trip, county maps and U.S. Geological Survey (USGS) maps offer even greater detail, including contour and elevation information.

While maps are indispensable tools, they can be out of date, and the conditions in the field may be different from how they appear on even the most recent maps. Even if the map says that the road goes from point A to point B, be ready to change your plans to adjust for reality.

Birding with Children

Children love birds, and they quickly learn to recognize species by sight and song. Just as with adults, exposure is the key to recognition for children. All it takes is a little patience and help from a more experienced bird-watcher. Teach children to be quiet and listen when they are outside. Let them know that quick movements and loud sounds can scare birds and other critters away. Help them identify different plants and habitats, and let them figure out what birds might be there. Ask them questions about their surroundings, and answer their questions. When you plan trips that include children, keep in mind that many children have shorter attention spans than adults and plan accordingly. Schedule play breaks and snack times, and try not to plan an especially long hike or outing unless you know the children accompanying you are up for it.

We suggest that children carry their own binoculars and field guides, such as *Birds* (National Audubon Society First Field Guide). Don't underestimate a child's ability to use a standard guide, nor her ability to learn the real names of birds. It was an old, dog-eared, musty-smelling third edition of *Peterson's Field Guide to Western Birds* and my grandparents' birdfeeders in Gold Beach, Oregon, that introduced me to bird-watching. I would sit and flip the pages back and forth and try to memorize the Latin and common names of the birds as well as their field marks. Several young bird-watchers that we know excel at identification and bird lore. Many of the sites included in this book make kid-friendly trips. The following sites are especially kid-friendly due to habitat, special features, or accessibility.

Confluence State Park: Easy-to-walk trails along the water's edge as well as playing fields, picnic tables, and restrooms provide diversions when restlessness sets in. You will almost always find a raft of waterfowl on the river and songbirds in the shrubs along the trails.

McNary National Wildlife Refuge: Spotting scopes, an interpretive center, and a viewing blind stocked with bird food provide kid-friendly excitement. A close-up view of an American White Pelican's bill sluicing through the water goes a long way toward teaching children about how a bird's bill affects how it eats.

Nisqually National Wildlife Refuge: The interpretive center offers special programs just for kids as well as guided walks and activities throughout the year. A wheelchair-accessible boardwalk circles the pond near the visitor center and loops through the woods along the river. A longer, easy-to-walk 5-mile loop extends from the boardwalk and offers viewing platforms and a chance to get close to a variety of songbirds, herons, and waterfowl.

Dungeness National Wildlife Refuge: Five miles' worth of sand makes the Dungeness Spit a favorite destination for kids and adults. The 10-mile round-trip hike to the lighthouse at the end of the spit may be a bit much for most children, but luckily the long hike isn't necessary to find some great bird-watching. Look at the inner bay for dabbling ducks, hawks, and Bald Eagles. Flocks of shorebirds and gulls can be found on both sides of the spit, and alcids and sea ducks can be spotted in the Strait of Juan de Fuca. The walk down to the spit winds through mixed-coastal forest and features Brown Creepers, Common Ravens, nuthatches, and other songbirds.

Desert Wildlife Area: Two blinds located on the edge of shallow ponds offer a chance to see Great Egrets, Western and Eastern Kingbirds, Common Yellowthroat, and waterfowl as well as a handful of turtles. Interpretive signs provided by the Audubon Society teach about native and nonnative desert plants such as cheatgrass, rabbit brush, and big sagebrush.

Theler Wetlands: A hike through Theler Wetlands exposes children to a unique habitat where freshwater and saltwater marshes meet in an ever-changing transition zone. A floating boardwalk places you directly on top of the freshwater marsh while a longer 1.5-mile trail takes you through the transition zone to the edge of the river and the bay. The education center offers hands-on exploration and activities.

Blackbird Island: Blackbird Island sits in the middle of the Wenatchee River and the heart of Leavenworth's tribute to Bavaria. The island, the site of a former millpond, is now covered in black cottonwood, shrubs, and wildflowers. This island is located at the junction of two canyons and provides transitional habitat for a wide variety of birds (and butterflies) from California Quail to swallows to Gray Catbird to Nashville Warblers.

Ridgefield National Wildlife Refuge: A slow car trip around the River S unit might be too boring for kids, but a hike along the Oaks to Woodlands Trail and a stop at the bird blind along the S unit make nice places to take children to see Sandhill Cranes and waterfowl in the fall and songbirds in the spring and summer. Don't forget to check for turtles in Duck Lake and take time to watch the aerial fancy-dance of the swallows in the ghost trees on Boot Lake.

Padilla Bay: Tour Padilla Bay on foot or by bicycle. The 2.25-mile partially paved Padilla Bay Shore Trail hugs the shore and gives visitors a great chance to see Brant, Great Blue Heron, Northern Pintail, and other sea ducks, Western Sandpipers and other shorebirds, as well as grebes, loons, and alcids, Bald Eagles, and Peregrine Falcons. At the northern end of the trail, you can visit the Breazeale Padilla Bay Interpretive Center, part of the Padilla Bay National Estuarine Research Reserve, one of only twenty-five such research centers in the country. After that you can camp or picnic at nearby Bay View State Park.

Park and Wildlife Area Fees

Be sure to bring along some cash before you drive across the state to watch birds in your favorite state park or wildlife area, since many of these areas now require you either pay a fee on the spot or purchase a parking pass prior to your arrival. Many Washington Department of Fish and Wildlife sites require the purchase of an annual parking pass, and most developed state parks require either a yearly pass or a $5.00 entrance fee each time you enter a park. Mt. Rainier and Olympic National Parks also require an entrance fee or the purchase of an annual pass. Also be aware that many trailheads in national forest lands require daily or yearly parking passes. The fees can add up, so plan accordingly.

Finding Bird Habitat

To really explore the world of birds around your neighborhood or across the state, you need to spend time outside learning about the kinds of birds associated with different types of habitat. This makes it much easier to identify birds that you see and hear, as well as to predict what species could be at a given site based on its geology and plant life. Throughout this book we note the predominant habitats found at each site. Here is an overview of common habitats found in Washington.

Sandy Beach

The southern coast and inner portions of Grays Harbor contain the premiere sandy beaches in Washington. The beaches at Ocean Shores and areas north to Moclips, as well as the beaches along the Long Beach Peninsula, are all sandy beach habitat. On the upland side of the beaches, sandy dunes provide shelter and forage for passerines in the lupines, sedges, and grasses. Shorebirds such as Western and Least Sandpipers, Dunlin, Sanderling, and plovers are commonly found in this habitat, and the upland portions of this habitat are critical for endangered Snowy Plovers. Raptors such as Merlin and Peregrine Falcon target the birds on the beach while Northern Harriers hunt rodents on the dunes.

Rocky Beach and Rocky Shore

As opposed to the sandy beaches found in places such as Ocean Shores or on the Long Beach Peninsula, rocky beaches are predominate along the northern Washington coast, in the Olympic Peninsula region. The broad cobble beach at Rialto Beach on the mouth of the Quillayute River near Forks offers a prime example of this habitat. Rocky beaches cater to shorebirds such as Black and Ruddy Turnstone, Surfbird, and Rock Sandpiper—birds commonly referred to as "rock birds."

Rocky shores also attract Black Oystercatchers. You'll find rocky shore at the cliffs and on the rocks below Cape Flattery as well as along the eastern end of the Strait of Juan de Fuca and the San Juan Islands.

Jetty

Jetties are found in a few locations in Washington—at the mouth of the Columbia River, on the north and south edges of the entrance to Grays Harbor—and these heavy rock barriers put in place to hold the sea at bay also serve as bird habitat for rock birds and gulls. Jetties also provide high vantage points for viewing alcids, migrating seabirds such as Sooty Shearwater, and other species found only along the coast. Whatever you do, do not walk out onto a jetty during heavy surf conditions. These rock fingers that jut into the sea can be swept by huge waves that would give you no chance to hang on if you were caught in the wave's path.

Salt Marsh

Salt marshes are transitional habitats along the edges of saltwater beaches, and they commonly contain areas composed of grasses, sedges, and salicornia (short, stocky, leafless plants such as pickleweed) that are flooded by high tides and exposed during low tides. Examples of this habitat are found all along the Washington coast, such as in the upper tidal reaches at the Grays Harbor National Wildlife Refuge, in the Theler Wetlands near Belfair, and in North Cove on the northern edges of Willapa Bay near Tokeland. Salt marsh habitat is also present in tidal areas along Puget Sound, such as at the Nisqually National Wildlife Refuge. A variety of birds such as yellowlegs and sandpipers to Great Blue Herons and Great Egrets to a plethora of waterfowl and gulls use salt marsh.

Mudflat

In contrast to sandy beach habitats, mudflats are areas with largely stationary soils that don't shift with each incoming tide. Mudflats are often near sandy beach habitat, and the two types of shoreline habitat are often found alongside salt marshes to create an ecosystem that supports a wide range of birds and other wildlife. During low tides, eelgrass and seaweeds are often exposed. These areas attract Brant and some sea ducks and dabblers such as American and Eurasian Wigeon, sandpipers, plovers, and dowitchers, as well as the raptors that come to feast on the smaller birds. Bottle Beach on the shores of Grays Harbor and the Nisqually National Wildlife Refuge both offer examples of this habitat.

Marine

Washington owes a great part of its bird diversity to the immense amount of coastline provided along the outer coast, the Strait of Juan de Fuca, and Puget Sound. All of the salt water found off that coastline is marine water, but not all marine waters support the same birds. The coastal marine waters found on the westernmost edge of the state extend into the ocean, where birders find pelagic species such as albatrosses, fulmars, skuas, and pelagic gulls. The calmer waters of the Strait and the protected inland marine waters of the Sound host alcids, loons, grebes, gulls, and sea ducks.

Wetland/Freshwater Marsh

Wetlands include freshwater marshes, bogs, permanent riparian and estuarine wetlands, and seasonal shallows that fill with water for part of the year. Wetlands contain a mosaic of plant life consisting of sedges, rushes, and grasses bordered by water-loving shrubs and trees, including red alder, black cottonwood, water birch, quaking aspen, cascara, hardhack, willow and western red cedar. The shrubs and small trees surrounding wetlands provide shelter and nesting habitat for flycatchers, vireos, and warblers, including Common Yellowthroats and Yellow-breasted Chats. Often the grasses, sedges, and reeds such as cattail poke through the shallows in small islands of emergent vegetation, creating prime nesting habitat for many ducks and shorebirds as well as blackbirds and Marsh Wrens. All the plant life contributes decaying matter that feeds a rich stew of macroinvertabrates that attract waterfowl, shorebirds, and long-legged birds such as American Bittern, Sora, and Common Snipe. Larger, more stable wetlands in areas such as the Quincy Lakes

Wildlife Area and Turnbull National Wildlife Refuge in eastern Washington also offer nesting habitat for birds such as American Coot, Ruddy Duck, Wilson's Phalarope, and Black Terns. Wetland habitat can be found in all regions of the state—even in the arid Columbia Basin, where streams such as Crab Creek create wetland corridors along its edges. Trout Lake Marsh southwest of Mt. Adams and the Oak to Wetlands Trail on the Carty Unit of the Ridgefield National Wildlife Refuge exemplify the importance of the constantly flooded freshwater marsh to migrating and winter-resident waterfowl.

Ponds and Lakes

Freshwater ponds and lakes, and the margins of these open bodies of water—often transitioning into wetlands—are key habitat for nesting and migrating birds. Dabbling ducks, mergansers, Spotted Sandpipers, Belted Kingfishers, and other water-loving birds are commonly found on lakes or the emergent plant life along the shallow edges of lakes. Larger lakes also attract gulls, terns, Osprey, loons, and grebes.

Riparian

Riparian areas are found along the edges of creek and river corridors, lakes, and large ponds. Riparian plants include black cottonwood, Russian olive, black locust, and alder trees interspersed with salmon and thimbleberries, elderberry, and mock orange. These transitional habitats are often rimmed by mixed forests. Riparian habitats trace river edges across the state and can be found with varying plant communities from the subalpine zone all the way to the coastline and the creeks and potholes of the Columbia Basin. The Sunnyside Wildlife Area along the Yakima River oxbows in central Washington illustrates the habitat. Riparian zones attract a varying community of birds depending on what region of the state the zone is in. You can always count on a variety of passerines, including Song Sparrows, warblers such as Common Yellowthroat, wrens, and thrushes, as well as a variety of wood-peckers and hummingbirds, depending on the density of the canopy.

Meadow

Lowland meadows host wildflowers and grasses in a transitional zone between farm fields and other habitats and along the edges and in openings of forested habitat. Meadows are often a transitional habitat that is evolving into mixed-forest or wetland habitat. Large, grassy lowland meadows attract Savannah and other sparrows, bluebirds, American Robins, and crows and ravens.

Alpine meadows are more open, with low undergrowth and wildflowers that bloom each summer. Unlike lowland meadows, alpine meadows are more stable due to the effects of severe weather and elevation that stunt the growth of surrounding trees, keeping the trees from taking over the meadows. The meadows on Hurricane Ridge and at Sunrise on Mt. Rainier illustrate the typical alpine meadow, which attracts White-tailed Ptarmigan, American Pipit, and Blue Grouse, as well as a host of sparrows and finches.

Prairie

Native prairies used to cover much of the southern Puget Trough from south of Tacoma to Chehalis, but the Interstate 5 corridor swallowed the habitat. Two of the best examples of the remaining habitat are found at Mima Mounds Natural Area Preserve south of Olympia and on the grounds of the military base at Fort Lewis in western Washington. In eastern Washington, most areas that once held prairies have been converted to farming. Birds commonly found in grassy prairie land include Savannah and Vesper Sparrows, Western Meadowlark, Ring-necked Pheasant, Horned Lark, Western Bluebird, and Northern Harrier.

Farm Fields

Although much of western Washington's arable land has been covered by concrete, strip malls, and housing developments, farms remain at the edges of suburbia in such places as the Brady Loop near Satsop and the farms around Fir Island, which serve as important habitat for migrating and over-wintering birds. In eastern Washington, huge tracts of wheat, mint, corn, and other crops cover the irrigated portions of the Columbia Basin. The cornfields surrounding Othello draw thousands of migrating Sandhill Cranes, ducks, and geese each year to forage for dropped corn and to rest before moving north to their breeding territories. Agricultural fields and stockyards are magnets for blackbirds, and on occasion a stray Cattle Egret may show up among the livestock. Eastern Washington's farm fields are also key habitat for Long-billed Curlews and Bobolink.

Lawns and Parkland

Although this is largely an urban and unnatural habitat type, the expanses of mowed grasslands and lawns in state parks and urban neighborhoods serve as bird habitat. Unfortunately, in many cases the birds that love this kind of habitat are seen as nuisance species—European Starling, House Finches, and House Sparrows.

Shrub-steppe

Before the dams on the Columbia River converted much of the Columbia Basin into a vast series of farms, shrub-steppe habitat was predominate in the arid lands of eastern Washington. Small remnants of that original wealth of shrub-steppe and native steppe habitat remain in protected areas such as the Fitz Eberhardt Natural Ecology Reserve (much of which was devastated by fire a few of years ago) and to a lesser extent in wildlife areas in places such as the Hanford Reach and the Colockum and Quilomene Wildlife Areas. Although many people look at the shrub-steppe and see a wasteland of sage and dirt, the plant community that creates the habitat is much more diverse, and a complicated relationship has developed between the lichen/moss crust that is the understory of the sage forest and the grasses and wildflowers that emerge each spring. The plant community is composed of a variety of dry land shrubs, including Big, Stiff, and Three-tip Sagebrush, two species of rabbitbrush, bitterbrush, and greasewood, as well as a number of perennial and annual grasses, such as bluebunch wheatgrass, needle-and-thread grass, Sandberg's bluegrass, and the invasive, aptly named cheatgrass. Spring brings an explosion of flowers such as desert parsley, lupine, phlox, balsamroot, and bitterroot.

A number of birds depend on shrub-steppe habitat, including Greater Sage Grouse, Sage, Lark, Brewer's, Vesper, and Grasshopper Sparrows, Sage Thrasher, Loggerhead Shrike, and Ferruginous Hawks. Say's Phoebe, Burrowing Owls, and Long-billed Curlews also carve out homes in the habitat.

Mixed-coniferous Forest

Mixed-coniferous forests are found in the mountains of eastern Washington and in areas that have yet to be heavily logged and converted to urban space in western Washington. As its name implies, this habitat is covered with a mix of coniferous trees such as Douglas fir, hemlock, cedar, and pine. Western Washington's coniferous forests are dominated by Douglas fir with water-loving trees such as western red cedar and hemlock mixed in.

Rather than existing as a homogenous tract of unvarying trees, different regions and altitudinal zones feature different species. For instance, Sitka spruce claims much of the forest of the Olympic Peninsula, which gives way to Douglas fir along the Puget Trough, which then gives way to western hemlock. As the western slope of the Cascades climbs, mountain hemlock and silver fir increase and give way at the crest to subalpine fir and Engelmann spruce, which begin to trail down the east slope. A similar transition takes place on the east side of the crest but with heavy stands of grand fir and western larch mixed into the tapestry until the ponderosa-pine zone takes over and claims much of the midlevel forest lands in the central and eastern parts of the state up to the more densely forested regions of the northern-tier counties and the Okanogan. The ponderosa-pine zone is dominated by ponderosa, lodgepole, and white pines, with large tracts of larch mixed in throughout the mountainous areas. On both sides of the state, coniferous forests are home to a number of forest-dwelling birds, such as thrushes, woodpeckers, crossbills, Brown Creeper, Steller's and Gray Jays, Clark's Nutcracker, Common Raven, warblers, and other neotropical passerines such as Bullock's Oriole, Townsend's Solitaire, and most of the state's owl species, including Northern Pygmy, Northern Saw-whet, and Barred Owls. Various regions of the ponderosa-pine zone attract Common Poorwill, Flammulated Owl, Mountain Bluebird, a variety of flycatchers, and all three nuthatches, and White-headed Woodpeckers among other specialty birds.

Mixed-deciduous Forest

Mixed-deciduous forests are commonly found in riparian areas and river bottoms, where conifers are not as common. Trees found in this habitat include big-leaf maple, black cottonwood, aspen, birch, water birch, Oregon ash, and red alder, where you'll find vireos, warblers, Black-headed Grosbeak, House Wren, and Ruffed Grouse. A subset of this habitat is the Garry or Oregon white oak woodlands found in a few key locations around the state. Lewis's and Acorn Woodpeckers are found in stands of Oregon white oak in places such as the Oak Creek Wildlife Area and the Klickitat River canyon, where the sparse, grassy undergrowth hosts Wild Turkey, grouse, and pheasant, and Western Bluebirds and swallows nest in tree cavities.

Mixed Forest

Most forested areas are not dominated just by coniferous or deciduous trees. Instead, deciduous trees hug the creek and river bottoms along riparian corridors while coniferous trees populate the drier upland areas and mountains. This forest habitat has the widest distribution throughout the state, and it provides nesting and feeding areas for woodpeckers and sapsuckers, warblers, tanagers and grosbeaks, and other passerines, owls, and raptors.

Old-growth Forest

Old-growth forest habitat is limited and dwindling throughout the state as logging and sprawling development reduce the native forest areas to a smaller and smaller footprint each day. Old-growth forests are distinguished by their large, mature trees and stands of old snags and fallen trees that serve as nurse logs for plant life on the forest floor. These mature forests in places such as the Olympic National Park, the North Cascades National Park, and Mt. Rainier National Park provide key nesting and feeding areas for Vaux's Swift, Spotted Owls, Pileated Woodpeckers, Marbled Murrelet, and Northern Goshawk.

Rain Forest

There are a limited number of places in Washington that truly qualify as rain forests. The most famous is in Olympic National Park along the Hoh River, but there is also rain-forest habitat south of the Hoh River in the Queets River area of the national park and along the shores and upstream of Lake Quinault. The Lake Quinault Nature Trail site offers a prime example, with its moss-covered bigleaf maple trees and lush green understory of shrubs at a middle height and oxalis and trillium and other plants that love the damp and dark ground beneath the trees. A characteristic of the rain forest is that it features more biomass per square foot than any other habitat in the state, with mosses and lichens growing from the tree branches, and ferns growing out of the moss and on top of the branches as the trees rise toward the sky. Rain forests are key habitat for Swainson's and Hermit Thrushes, Winter Wren, warblers, and owls, including Spotted Owls that sometimes hunt in the dense, damp forest.

Subalpine

Subalpine habitat is where the tree line meets the snow zone in high elevation birding sites such as at Mt. Baker or Sunrise at Mt. Rainier. This habitat is notable for its limited amount of tree life, where subalpine fir and mountain hemlock grow in tight tree islands interspersed with low herbacious ground cover. Extravagant wildflower displays happen in June and July, after the snows finally melt away in subalpine habitats. A number of bird species rely on this mountain habitat, such as White-tailed Ptarmigan, Gray-crowned Rosy-Finch, Clark's Nutcracker, Common Raven, Mountain Chickadee, and Gray Jay. Subalpine areas can also host Boreal Owl, Boreal Chickadee, and Pine Grosbeak.

Alpine

The alpine zone is above the tree line, and examples of this habitat are found in the tallest of the state's mountain ranges in the Cascades and the Olympic Mountains. Just as the amount of plant life dwindles in the alpine zone, bird and animal life decreases with the rising elevation. Not many birds live in the alpine zone, but many species feed at and move through the alpine areas during migration.

Cliffs

Cliff habitat is found in a few key locations around the state, from the sandstone bluffs at Fort Flagler State Park and in Port Townsend to the rugged rocky cliffs in the Cascade Mountains and the endless cliffs that rim the Columbia River as it winds through the state. Cliffs are critical nesting habitat for many birds, ranging from raptors such as Peregrine and Prairie Falcons and Golden Eagles to smaller birds such as Cliff Swallows. In eastern Washington the cliffs along the Columbia River and in the scablands of the Columbia Basin also host White-throated Swifts, Common Poorwill, and Rock and Canyon Wrens.

SAVING BIRD HABITAT

As you get more involved in bird-watching and exploring the various bird habitats across Washington, we strongly urge you to consider joining one of the many advocacy organizations that works with local, state, and federal government agencies to protect critical wildlife habitat. A good place to start is to join your local Audubon Society chapter, and those chapters are listed in the Washington Birding Organizations section in the back of the book.

Joining an advocacy organization can also be a bridge to learning more about birds and their habitat through classes, seminars, and hands-on habitat restoration. You may also enjoy participating in annual citizen science projects such as the Christmas Bird Counts, also known as CBCs, held each year by local Audubon Society chapters. Citizen science projects also include programs such as the Cornell Lab of Ornithology's Feeder Watch program and the annual Backyard Bird Count that is held each spring. For more information on these events, check www.ebird.org.

Birds in the City

As I write, birds are feasting at our feeder. Today has been an exciting day for bird-watching out our window. For the first time, a Bewick's Wren visited our yard. Its bright, strong supercilium; clear, white breast and throat; downward-curved bill; and upright, subtly barred tail distinguished it from the usual visitors. During a thirty-minute period, late in the afternoon on an overcast early winter day, we were visited by House Finches; a Song Sparrow; House, White-crowned, and Golden-crowned Sparrows; Black-capped Chickadees; Dark-eyed Juncoes; Pine Siskins; an Anna's Hummingbird; and a Bewick's Wren. We don't have a big yard, and since our cascara tree blew down in a storm a few years ago, we don't have any large trees. Still, we see new birds in our yard every year. We have seen Cooper's and Sharp-shinned Hawks hunting in our snow ball bush, and we've seen Merlins tagging and feasting on European Starlings. While bird-watching at home doesn't replace our longer field trips, our observations keep us entertained and teach us more about how birds live. Watching from a warm living room with a cup of tea and a house-sized blind provides ample time for extended observation. Occasionally the birds, especially the young, curious Anna's Hummingbirds, watch us back through the glass, almost nose-to-nose with us—something we aren't likely to experience in the field.

We live in Tacoma, one of the three largest cities in Washington, but we don't have to leave the city limits to find great bird-watching opportunities. In fact, we don't even have to leave our neighborhood. A few blocks from our house, Mason Gulch is home to a variety of birds and animals. We take frequent walks to the gulch to look down on the maple- and fir-rich canopy. One evening we saw a Great Horned Owl fly out of the gulch around dusk. We've watched Peregrine Falcons chase songbirds and a Red-tailed Hawk teach its fledgling how to hunt. We've witnessed battles over nectar rights between hummingbirds and watched flocks of warblers flit from tree to tree before settling down for a break from their arduous spring migration.

You may not have such a spot in your neighborhood, but if you look around your town, you'll find plenty of places to watch birds without leaving the city limits. The key is to think like a bird and go where birds go. Again, this is where understanding habitats will help you uncover the bird-rich places in your city.

Most birds aren't attracted to fields of short, green, fertilized grass. You might find geese, crows, robins, and gulls. Look for parks with trees, shrubs, ponds and lakes; and if you can find one with a variety of habitats, you'll increase your chances of seeing a wider variety of birds. Since so many city parks consist of play toys and fields of grass, think beyond the local park. Get out of your car, walk through neighborhoods you haven't visited before, and, most of all, take time to look and listen. Below, we offer a few more suggestions of places to look for birds, but don't stop with our list.

College and School Campuses

At Tacoma Community College, trails crisscross a vacant lot that is overgrown with salal, Oregon grape, blackberry, and willow trees. The University of Washington arboretum hosts a variety of native and nonnative trees. We've also found that most of the community college campuses throughout the state have wooded areas with paved walkways or foot trails. Check the shrubs that grow along fence lines around the sports fields at your neighborhood schools as well.

Waterfronts

Whether they are on rivers, bays, or the coast, waterfronts always draw birds and bird-watchers. Off of Dickman Mill Park in Tacoma, we've seen rafts of Surf Scoters, Pigeon Guillemots, and Western Grebes, as well as Purple Martins, cormorants, gulls, ducks, Bald Eagles, herons, and resident Canada Geese. Through the winter we can almost always find a couple of Horned Grebes and loons, including a rare albino Yellow-billed Loon that wanders Commencement Bay. In Wenatchee, Confluence State Park marks the point where the Wenatchee River flows into the Columbia River. In winter and during migration, waterfowl float in great rafts on the rivers. Don't forget to check the shrubs that line the edges of rivers for songbirds.

Sewer Ponds

Don't wrinkle your nose until you try it. Some of our state's most interesting birds can be found at sewer ponds. The Hoquiam Sewer treatment ponds just outside of Bowerman Basin have become one of the most popular stops for birders heading to the coast. We find interesting birds there throughout the year: Pectoral Sandpiper, Heerman's Gulls, and Red-necked Phalaropes among others. The Kent Sewer ponds also draw quite a few bird-watchers. Of course, natural ponds and lakes should never be overlooked, no matter how small they are. When you are at a pond, don't forget to check the edges. You may find more birds in the shrubs than you will on the water, especially in summer when the waterfowl have headed north and the songbirds are breeding and migrating.

Greenbelts

As housing developments replace natural spaces, greenbelts are left behind to help soften the edges of urban sprawl. Some of these greenbelts are all that remain of once extensive forests that served as habitual pit stops for migrating songbirds. Some birds still elect to spend time in the diminished greenbelts since they are the only places the birds know. Nearly every time you find a greenbelt with coniferous trees, you'll find nuthatches, Black-capped Chickadees, Dark-eyed Juncoes, Cedar Waxwings, Northern Flickers, and possibly Brown Creepers and Hairy, Downy, and Pileated Woodpeckers. If the timing is right, you may also see warblers, flycatchers, and grosbeaks. Power line right-of-ways, the corridors along railroads, and golf courses also serve as default greenbelts.

Pay Attention

Bird-watchers see what other people don't see because we pay attention, and we don't take things for granted. If you want to find interesting birds in the city, you need to pay attention all the time. Rather than assuming that all of the geese on the golf course are Canada Geese, take a second look, and you might find a Greater White-fronted Goose. Look up in Seattle or Tacoma and you might see a Peregrine Falcon. Rob regularly says hello to a Red-tailed Hawk that he has nicknamed Gertie, who sits on the light poles above State Route 16 near the Tacoma Narrows Bridge. People have spotted Virginia Rails on the streets of downtown Seattle. East of the mountains, check neighborhood feeders for Calliope Hummingbirds and possibly Common Redpolls. Most bird-watchers who travel know about keeping raptor counts while driving on I–5. And don't forget to check the trees at the mall parking lot.

If you're only out to add a rare bird to your list, you might have an uphill battle in the city. Part of the allure of bird-watching in the city comes from being able to closely observe bird behavior. If you take the time to examine each bird you see, you'll learn the keys to identification more quickly. Soon you'll learn to identify a Northern Flicker based on the way it flies. You'll learn the difference between the alert calls and mating songs of passerines. And like the inner-city children involved in the Cornell School of Ornithology's pigeon project, you may learn that pigeons are far from boring when you notice the endless variations in plumage and watch their mating dances.

Because we want bird-watching to be accessible to everyone, we have included a number of urban sites in our book, including:

Confluence State Park in Wenatchee
Titlow Beach park in Tacoma
Blackbird Island in Leavenworth
Dishman Hills Natural Area in Spokane
Montlake Fill in Seattle
Marymoor Park in Redmond
Ridgefield Natural Wildlife Refuge just north of Vancouver
Bill's Spit in Ocean Shores

Other places you might check include:

Yakima River Trail
The Ballard Locks in Seattle
Moses Lake in Moses Lake
Columbia Point in the Tri-cities
Chuckanut Drive in Bellingham
Salt Lake State Park near Des Moines
Lake Sacajaweea in Longview
Kent Sewer Ponds

While going into the woods or driving back roads to find birds is certainly a rewarding pursuit, you simply may not have time, nor the energy to plan the trip. Add to that the fact that a day's worth of bad timing can make for a miserable long weekend. Fortunately, timing doesn't matter as much when you bird in the place where you live. You learn where the birds will be and when they will be there. Even if you do miss seeing the flock of migrating songbirds, the time, money, and energy you invested in the short afternoon trip won't hurt as much. Plus, you can always go back tomorrow, whereas finding the time to drive across the state may not happen for another month or two. Explore the place you live. Enjoy the wildlife that shares your city. Learn the song of the melodious House Finch in your backyard.

Pelagic Birding

If you want to see the oceangoing birds of literary fame—the albatrosses, petrels, jaegers, and kittiwakes—you have to hop on board a pelagic bird-watching trip. A new world of birding opens up as pelagic boat tours depart from Westport, Neah Bay, and Ilwaco on trips that venture dozens of miles out onto the open ocean in search of these birds that normally cannot be seen from shore.

Which Birds Are Pelagic?

The Washington Ornithological Society lists sixteen species that are considered the pelagic birds most likely to be seen in Washington's waters—Laysan and Black-footed and Short-tailed Albatross; Northern Fulmar; Pink-footed, Flesh-footed, Buller's and Sooty Shearwater; Fork-tailed and Leach's Storm-Petrel; South Polar Skua; Pomarine and Parasitic Jaeger; and Black-legged Kittiwake. Other pelagic birds can be seen off the coast from time to time, but not every year—Shy Albatross; Murphy's and Cook's Petrel; Wedge-tailed, Short-tailed, and Manx Shearwater; Wilson's Storm-Petrel; Red-legged Kittiwake, and others such as Sabine's Gull. What all of these birds have in common is that they spend nearly all of their time flying, feeding, sleeping, and living far out at sea.

Some of the pelagic birds can be seen from land, but only in the right conditions and from select locations along the Washington coast (detailed below). To get the best look at pelagic birds, book a trip on an oceangoing bird tour.

Pelagic Birding Tours

A trio of vendors offer pelagic birding opportunities, with the largest number of trips leaving Westport in the spring, summer, and fall months and a very limited number of trips leaving from Ilwaco near the mouth of the Columbia River and from Neah Bay on the far northwestern tip of the state.

Before you book your voyage, read through the Web site for the pelagic tour you plan to take and be sure to check any pre-trip tips offered on the sites. In general terms, there are a few birding tools that you should leave behind before stepping onto the boat. Forget about bringing a spotting scope, and be sure that your binoculars are up to the challenge of getting wet and salty from sea spray. Also wear layers of clothes and sturdy, slip-resistant shoes. Bring along motion sickness medication and be sure to take it at least thirty minutes before starting your trip.

Westport Seabirds

(www.westportseabirds.com)

The most consistent pelagic birding trips on the coast depart from Westport, home base for the 50-foot *Monte Carlo,* the boat used for birding trips each year between February and October. Terry Wahl started doing pelagic trips from Westport on a regular basis in 1966, and he started maintaining a census of seabirds along Grays Canyon in 1971. Now the database of seabird records maintained by Westport Seabirds is believed to be the longest running database of its type in the world.

Most of Westport Seabirds' trips go to Grays Canyon, a submarine canyon about 35 miles off the coast that sits on the edge of the North American continental shelf. A few trips go even farther, either hitting Grays Canyon as well as Quinault Canyon to the north in an all-day trip or venturing out over deeper water in search of rarities such as Murphy's or Mottled Petrels and Parakeet Auklets.

Westport Seabirds' Web site offers a trip-by-trip history of what birds are commonly seen from the boat throughout the season, and the species range from fairly common pelagic birds such as Black-footed Albatross and Fork-tailed Storm-Petrels to seasonal specialties. Check with Westport Seabirds for pricing information for its pelagic trips and for the company's tips on how to come prepared for a pelagic birding trip. The service's phone number is (360) 268–5222.

Olympic Park Institute

(www.yni.org/opi)

The Olympic Park Institute offers a wide range of seminars and excursions on the Olympic Peninsula, and over the last few years one of those excursions has included a five-hour pelagic bird-watching trip that departs from Neah Bay and explores up to 20 miles off the northern Washington coast in the area encompassed in the Pacific Northwest Marine Sanctuary. The trips, which have an educational focus, include a class about Pacific Northwest pelagic birds and marine animals on Friday followed by the trip that goes out past Tatoosh Island, along Swiftsure Bank, and out to the "headwaters" of the Juan de Fuca canyon. The attraction of the trip is that it ventures into an area not frequented by most bird-watchers.

Check the Olympic Park Institute Web site to see when trips are scheduled and for pricing and reservation information. In 2003 the trips were held in September and October.

The Bird Guide Inc.

(www.thebirdguide.com/pelagics)

With ten years of experience leading pelagic trips along the Oregon coast, Greg Gillison's The Bird Guide Inc. has branched out to offer a trip off the mouth of the Columbia River. The inaugural trip departed from Ilwaco in the fall of 2003, and Gillison hopes to offer another trip along the same area, crossing back and forth between Washington and Oregon waters off the mouth of the river. Check The Bird Guide Inc. Web site for information about upcoming trips.

Pelagic Birding from the Shore

There are a handful of key locations where a small subset of Washington's pelagic birds can be seen from the shore. The most well-known site is at the Brown Point

Jetty in Ocean Shores, but a couple of locations near Cape Disappointment—the North Head Lighthouse, the North Jetty along the Columbia River, and the bluff that houses the Lewis & Clark Interpretive Center—as well as the jetty at Westport, the far reaches of Leadbetter Point, and even the end of the Cape Flattery Trail near Neah Bay offer decent opportunities to see pelagic birds that venture close to the shore. Headlands along the portion of the coast encompassed in the Olympic National Park could also offer glimpses of pelagic birds for hardy hikers willing to tote binoculars and a spotting scope.

As much as location and luck are key ingredients to seeing pelagic birds from shore, paying close attention to the weather, especially in the winter, are important elements. During the winter months when vigorous storms blow in from the Pacific Ocean, the storm can also push pelagic birds in to the shore, where they can be seen by hardy bird-watchers. Besides being seen along the coastal headlands, many veteran birders know that if they venture to a place such as Grays Harbor or Willapa Bay on the day after a big storm, there is always the chance of finding a pelagic bird species outside of its normal range.

Olympic Peninsula

From rain forests to alpine mountain tops, the Olympic Peninsula region offers a variety of habitats in a compact area. The peninsula is bound by the fjord of Hood Canal in the east, the Strait of Juan de Fuca in the north, and the Pacific Ocean in the west. For the purposes of this book, we chose State Route 8 and U.S. Highway 12 as the southern boundary of the region.

The extreme topography of the Olympic Peninsula creates niche habitats that cater to birds that are not commonly seen in the rest of western Washington. The rain forest and old growth stands along the west side of the Olympic Mountains cater to reclusive birds, such as Northern Spotted-Owls and nesting Marbled Murrelets, while the rain shadow and open fields north of the mountains around Sequim draw such out-of-place birds as Chipping Sparrows.

Highlights in this region include Black Oystercatchers, Tufted Puffins, and Long-tailed Ducks, as well as pelagic birds that venture near the shore along the coast. The steep mountainous center of the region within Olympic National Park and along the shores of Hood Canal offer chances to see Golden Eagles, which are rare throughout the rest of western Washington.

There are four unique sites on the peninsula, all focused in the northern and western end of the region—Protection Island, the Dungeness Spit, Cape Flattery, and the rainforests in the Hoh River valley and the Lake Quinault area.

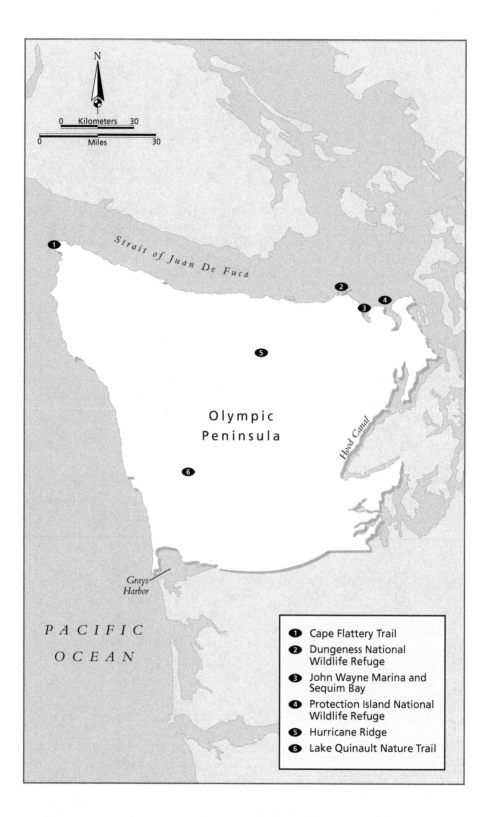

N

0   Kilometers   30

0   Miles   30

Strait of Juan De Fuca

❶

❷

❸   ❹

❺

Olympic
Peninsula

Hood Canal

❻

*Grays
Harbor*

PACIFIC

OCEAN

❶ Cape Flattery Trail
❷ Dungeness National
    Wildlife Refuge
❸ John Wayne Marina and
    Sequim Bay
❹ Protection Island National
    Wildlife Refuge
❺ Hurricane Ridge
❻ Lake Quinault Nature Trail

1 Cape Flattery Trail

Habitats: Cliffs, mixed forest.

Specialty birds: Common Loon; Pelagic and Brandt's Cormorants; Harlequin Duck; Bald Eagle; Peregrine Falcon; Blue Grouse; Black Oystercatcher; Ruddy and Black Turnstones; Rock Sandpiper; Heerman's, Bonaparte's, Mew, Thayer's, and Western Gulls; Common Murre; Pigeon Guillemot; Marbled and Ancient Murrelets; Rhinoceros Auklet; Tufted Puffin; Spotted and Northern Pygmy-Owls; Anna's and Rufous Hummingbirds; Pileated Woodpecker; Red-breasted Sapsucker; Pacific-slope Flycatcher; Hutton's Vireo; Northwestern Crow.

Best times to bird: Spring and fall for migrants and summer for nesting birds, but this trail is also a treat in winter, depending on the weather.

Sandstone caves at the end of the Cape Flattery Trail, such as these on the Strait of Juan de Fuca side of the trail, are used by nesting and feeding birds such as cormorants and Pigeon Guillemots. Tufted Puffin can be seen offshore here in the summer.

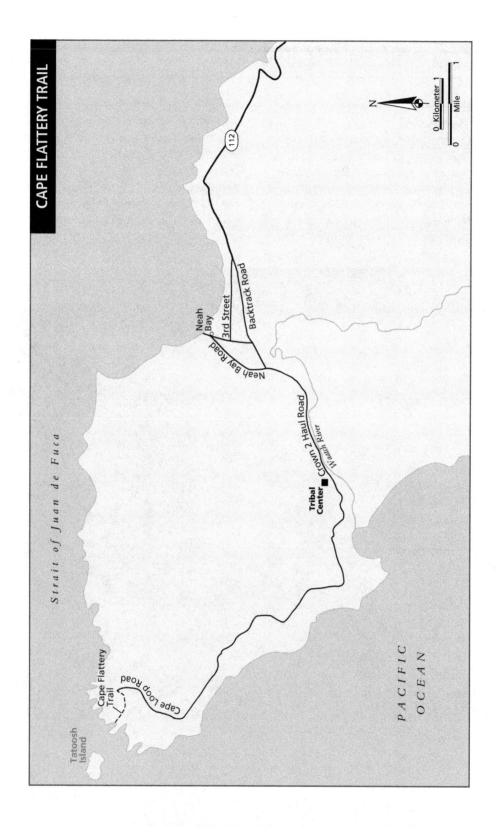

CAPE FLATTERY TRAIL

Strait of Juan de Fuca

Tatoosh
Island

Cape Flattery
Trail

Cape Loop Road

PACIFIC
OCEAN

Tribal
Center

Crown 2 Haul Road

Waatch River

Neah Bay Road

Neah
Bay

3rd Street

Backtrack Road

112

N

0 Kilometer 1
0   Mile   1

About the site:

Perched at the farthest northwestern tip of the Lower 48, Cape Flattery is a habitat of rain-drenched and windswept woodlands. Thanks to a 0.75-mile trail that spans wetlands on wooden boardwalks, it is easy to reach the five viewing platforms on land owned and administered by the Makah Tribe in Neah Bay. This is a great spot to catch a glimpse of rugged sea stacks, Tatoosh Island, and caves carved in the rock alongside the viewing platforms that host nesting cormorants in the summer. It is also a prime location to see such birds as Tufted Puffin without the need to jump in a boat for a pelagic birding trip.

The most open habitat near the trail is at the trailhead, where you may be able to see a Bald Eagle soaring over the hill to the north of the parking area before starting to walk the trail. The trail leaves the parking area and winds downhill through a dense wooded area full of fir, cedar, maple, and hemlock trees before turning to start the boardwalk section. Even in the dog days of summer, the hillside portion of the trail is a great place to watch for woodland passerines, and if you look closely you could find a Great Horned Owl sitting in one of the Sitka spruce trees. Cape Flattery holds one of the largest remaining Sitka spruce stands on the Olympic Peninsula.

The boardwalk starts just after you walk past a large blown-down tree. Check the underside of the root ball for the tiny ecosystem of ferns, mushrooms, and small wildflowers during summer. This area is riddled with mushrooms, and if you look down you are likely to find a sample of the Pacific Northwest's native monopod, the Banana Slug.

Birding starts to get really interesting near the end of the boardwalk, where side trails lead to each of the five platforms that look out over the Pacific Ocean and the Strait of Juan de Fuca. The habitat is more rocky here on ground that sits over the top of caves carved by waves slamming against the edge of the continent. If the surf is strong, you can feel the waves ramming against the rocks underneath the viewing platforms and feel the sea spray in the air.

Spring, summer, and fall offer the best birding at the end of the trail. Late July and early August are the best time for spotting a Tufted Puffin in the sea between the cape and Tatoosh Island, and you will see nesting Pelagic and Brandt's Cormorant flying in and out of the caves to the north of the viewing platforms in summer. Look closely and you are also likely to see Rhinoceros Auklet, Marbled Murrelet, Pigeon Guillemot, Harlequin Duck, and Common Murre in the waters off either of the viewing platforms. In recent years as many as 5,000 Common Murre nested on Tatoosh Island; though according to studies done by biologists at the University of Washington, the population is declining.

Before turning back for the uphill trek to your car, be sure to train your binoculars on the rocky shores at the foot of Tatoosh Island, where you can see California Sea Lions and Northern Fur Seals that have hauled out of the sea to sun themselves on the rocks.

A TRIBAL GIFT

Cape Flattery wasn't always so easy to reach. What is now a 0.75-mile hike along a boardwalk was a muddy trudge through wetlands until a few years ago when the Makah Indian Tribe created the current trail. Be sure to tread lightly on these lands that are offered for public use by the tribe, and if you are lucky you may encounter a Makah elder walking the trail as he plays his flute, as we did on a summer day a few years ago on a trip to the Cape Flattery Trail during the Makah Days festival.

Other key birds: Red-throated and Pacific Loons; Pied-billed, Red-necked, and Western Grebes; Northern Fulmar; Sooty Shearwater; White-winged and Surf Scoters; Long-tailed Duck; Common and Red-breasted Mergansers; Merlin; Ruffed Grouse; Pomarine and Parasitic Jaegers; Ring-billed and California Gulls; Western Screech- and Northern Saw-whet Owls; Downy and Hairy Woodpeckers; Western Wood-Pewee; Willow Flycatcher; Warbling Vireo; Chestnut-backed Chickadee; Bushtit; Brown Creeper; Winter and Bewick's Wrens; Swainson's, Hermit, and Varied Thrushes; Orange-crowned, Black-throated Gray, Townsend's, Yellow, MacGillivray's, and Wilson's Warblers; Fox and Golden-crowned Sparrows; Red Crossbill.

Nearby opportunities: Hobuck Beach is south of the Cape Flattery Trail on the other side of the Waatch River. Also check Lake Ozette off Washington Highway 112 east of Neah Bay at the end of Hoko-Ozette Road.

Directions: After taking State Route 112 into Neah Bay, continue to the end of the highway and take a left, following the signs for the Cape Flattery Trail and the Makah Tribal Center. Continue past the tribal center and the road changes from paved to gravel. Continue another 4 miles until you see signs for the Cape Flattery Trail. There is ample parking at the trailhead.

DeLorme map grid: Page 90, A3.

Elevation: 40 feet.

Access: The trail is rugged and steep in places, and it is not wheelchair accessible.

Bathrooms: Portable toilets are located at the trailhead, but these are not always open.

Hazards: Beware when walking the boardwalk in rain, as the boards can get slick. Also stay away from steep cliffsides at the end of the trail.

Nearest food, gas, and lodging: Neah Bay.

Nearest camping: Ozette or Pillar Point.

For more information: Check www.northolympic.com/capeflatterytrail or www.makah.com. You can also call the Makah Cultural Center at (360) 645-2711.

Dungeness National Wildlife Refuge

Habitats: Mixed forest; sand and cobble beach; tideflats; marine

Specialty birds: Common Loon; Pelagic and Brandt's Cormorants; Greater White-fronted Goose; Brant; Greater Scaup; Harlequin Duck; Barrow's Goldeneye; Bald Eagle; Peregrine Falcon; Black-bellied Plover; American Golden-Plover; Black Oystercatcher; Solitary Sandpiper; Ruddy and Black Turnstones; Surfbird; Red Knot; Baird's and Pectoral Sandpipers; Short-billed Dowitcher; Red-necked and Red Phalaropes; Heerman's, Bonaparte's, Mew, Thayer's, and Western Gulls; Common Tern; Common Murre; Pigeon Guillemot; Marbled and Ancient Murrelets; Rhinoceros Auklet; Tufted Puffin; Band-tailed Pigeon; Short-eared and Snowy Owls; Vaux's Swift; Rufous Hummingbird; Pileated Woodpecker; Red-breasted Sapsucker; Hammond's and Pacific-slope Flycatchers; Hutton's Vireo; Northwestern Crow.

Best times to bird: Fall through spring.

A Dunlin probes the sand along the edge of Dungeness Bay near the Three Crabs Restaurant.

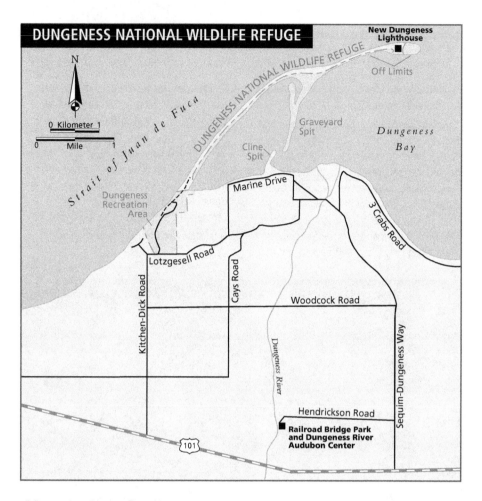

DUNGENESS NATIONAL WILDLIFE REFUGE

New Dungeness Lighthouse

Off Limits

N

0 Kilometer 1

0 Mile 1

Strait of Juan de Fuca

DUNGENESS NATIONAL WILDLIFE REFUGE

Graveyard Spit

Dungeness Bay

Cline Spit

Marine Drive

Dungeness Recreation Area

3 Crabs Road

Lotzgesell Road

Kitchen-Dick Road

Cays Road

Woodcock Road

Dungeness River

Sequim-Dungeness Way

Hendrickson Road

Railroad Bridge Park and Dungeness River Audubon Center

101

About the site:

During migration, Dungeness Spit and the surrounding landscapes are paradise for bird-watchers. The crest of the Dungeness Spit divides a protected inner harbor from the open waters of the Strait of Juan de Fuca. After crossing the strait, birds seek the spit for shelter and forage. Alcids, shorebirds, and waterfowl congregate along the spit while songbirds and raptors settle into the woods and onto the open fields of the reserve and recreation area above. More than 250 bird species have been recorded on the reserve, and more than 90 species have bred here.

In addition to being the most popular place to bird on the Olympic Peninsula, the Dungeness Spit is also the longest sand spit in the United States. The spit, first established as a wild bird reserve in 1915, is the star of the 631-acre refuge, but we encourage birders to take time to check the open fields of the adjoining 216-acre county-run Dungeness Recreation Area as well as the mixed-wood forest above the spit on the wildlife refuge. To get to the spit, visitors drive through the recreation area, but get out of your car to walk along the shrubby edges and trails of the open fields to add Savannah and Lincoln's Sparrows, other sparrows, other songbirds, and raptors to your site list. Short-eared Owls have been known to hunt in these rodent-rich fields. Be warned however that these fields are popular hunting destinations in fall during duck hunting season.

An easy 3/8-mile hike through mixed woods leads to a steep downhill climb to the spit. Enjoy the walk by checking the trees—fir, hemlock, and cedar interspersed with broadleaf alder, willow, and maple—for Brown Creepers, chickadees, kinglets, nuthatches, and wrens as well as flycatchers and warblers. At the caretaker's cabin take time to check the bird feeders and shrubs, where in the past we have seen Song, Fox, White and Golden-crowned Sparrow, Varied Thrush, California Quail, Mourning Dove, warblers, and flycatchers.

Most bird-watchers come to walk at least part of the 10-mile round-trip trek to the lighthouse at the end of the spit. Carry your spotting scope if you have one and want to improve your chances of seeing grebes, loons, and alcids such as Marbled and Ancient Murrelets, Tufted Puffin, auklets, and Common Murres that you may find in the strait on the north side of the spit. Some lucky birders have spotted infrequent visitors such as Yellow-billed Loons and Red Phalaropes near the spit. Eelgrass beds draw Brant, which overwinter here with numbers peaking at up to 8,000 during the spring migration in April. Sea ducks such as Harlequin and Long-tailed Duck, all three scoters, and Barrow's and Common Goldeneye also can be found through the winter. Oftentimes visitors find a wider variety of gulls here than are commonly found around the sound, including Heerman's, Thayer's, Mew, Bonaparte's, California, and Western.

As you walk along the spit, look ahead for flocks of shorebirds. Likewise, turn your scopes and binoculars to the shoreline of the inner harbor for more shorebirds. A scope is important here if you want to identify the birds in the inner harbor, since the south side of the spit is off-limits to all visitors. Scopes also will be useful for examining individuals in the flocks of shorebirds. If you take time to do this, you may find a few rarities or occasional visitors, such as an American Golden-Plover, Baird's or Solitary Sandpipers, or Short-billed Dowitchers. A different set of waterfowl favor the inner harbor. These include Northern Pintail, Northern Shoveler, Green-winged Teal, American and Eurasian Wigeon, and the occasional Ruddy Duck.

Because we see Bald Eagle so often, we tend to take them for granted, but each time we have visited the spit, we've been treated to impressive displays of their hunting skills. Check the trees and driftwood surrounding the inner harbor for perching and roosting eagles, and keep your eyes on them for a chance to see them dive into the water for a quick meal: salmon and steelhead fingerlings use the inner harbor as safe forage. For gulls and eagles it's like taking candy from a baby. The inner harbor can also hold other surprises for the patient and diligent birder. Sora, Virginia Rail, and American Bittern have been heard or spotted skulking along the mudflats, and on occasion Cinnamon and Blue-winged Teal have visited the refuge. And while it wouldn't be much of a surprise to see Canada Geese anywhere in the state, it is possible to see some of the less common sub-species such as cackling, dusky, and a handful of resting Aleutian.

If you plan to hike all the way to the lighthouse, where volunteer lighthouse keepers offer tours, make sure you check the tide table. Being trapped at the wrong end of the spit and waiting for the tide to go out could very well spoil a perfect day. Keep in mind that the harbor (south) side of the spit (except for a short section near the beginning of the spit that is open to foot traffic from May 15 to September 30) as well as Graveyard Spit and the tip of the main spit beyond the lighthouse are all closed to the public in order to protect the area and the animals such as the birds and harbor seals that breed here. Visitors can also explore the spit by boat as long as they observe the 100-foot buffer in the inner harbor. The area between the Graveyard and Dungeness Spits is closed even to boat traffic from October 1 to May 14. The $3.00 per-family per-day fee charged to visit the spit is a bargain when you consider all that you can find on a good day with some patience and a good eye.

On your way to or from the spit, check the ponds along Kitchen-Dick Road for more ducks, including Blue-winged and Cinnamon Teal. Additionally, while Chipping Sparrows are common east of the Cascade Crest, the Sequim-Dungeness area is one of the few places on the west side where they can be found. While bird-watching in the area is always a pleasure, what you see will depend on the season and on a good dose of lucky timing when it comes to finding those uncommon alcids, gulls, shorebirds, and migrant songbirds.

SANDS OF TIME

At 5.5 miles long, the Dungeness Spit is the longest in the United States, and it keeps growing. Every year between 5 and 15 feet of sand, gravel, and driftwood are added to the spit in a complicated geological process called littoral drift, which involves sandstone bluffs, tidal currents, and seasonal winds. Waves from the incoming tide constantly erode the steep sandstone bluffs. In fact, you can stand on the overlook at the edge of the bluff at the Dungeness Recreation Area at high tide and feel the impact of the waves. Each wave carves sand away from the cliff and carries it into the strait. The summer winds, winter storms, and prevailing currents carry the sediments and silts from the west and deposit them along the spit. Aerial views of the spit show more wave action carrying sand farther east, where it is deposited at the end of the spit. Cline and Graveyard Spits—so named because of the eighteen T'simshian that were buried there after a massacre—were created by reverse seasonal winds and currents moving material from the end of the spit as well as sediments deposited by the Dungeness River. Driftwood carried by high tides and plants that grow along the spits hold the sands in place. Nevertheless, high tides and stormy weather occasionally combine to breach the spit. In time, the breach is mended by more littoral drift.

As intriguing as the spit is, it is also a danger to nautical navigation. As a result, the New Dungeness Lighthouse, one of the first lighthouses in Washington, was built at the tip of the spit in 1857. At that time, it was situated ⅛ of a mile from the end of the spit; today, due to the growth of the spit, it sits .5 of a mile from the end. Until 1994 the Coast Guard staffed and operated the lighthouse, but due to funding cuts, the lighthouse was slated to be automated. Local residents and lighthouse fanatics formed the New Dungeness Chapter of the U.S. Lighthouse Society and have maintained the lighthouse with volunteer keepers since the last Coast Guard keeper said goodbye to the spit.

Other key birds: Red-throated and Pacific Loons; Horned, Pied-billed, Red-necked, and Western Grebes; Northern Fulmar; Wood Duck; Gadwall; Green-winged Teal; American and Eurasian Wigeons; Northern Pintail; Northern Shoveler; Ring-necked Duck; Lesser Scaup; Black, White-winged, and Surf Scoters; Long-tailed Duck; Common Goldeneye; Bufflehead; Common, Red-breasted, and Hooded Mergansers; Merlin; Ruffed Grouse; Sanderling; Dunlin; Semipalmated, Western, and Least Sandpipers; Long-billed Dowitcher; Wilson's Snipe; Parasitic Jaeger; Ring-billed, California, and Herring Gulls; Caspian Tern; Barred, Western Screech-, and Northern Saw-whet Owls; Downy and Hairy Woodpeckers; Olive-sided Flycatcher; Western Wood-Pewee; Willow Flycatcher; Northern Shrike; Warbling Vireo; Chestnut-backed Chickadee; Bushtit; Brown Creeper; House, Winter, Bewick's, and Marsh Wrens; Townsend's Solitaire; Swainson's, Hermit, and Varied Thrushes; American Pipit; Orange-crowned, Black-throated Gray, Townsend's, Yellow, MacGillivray's, and Wilson's Warblers; Common Yellowthroat; Western Tan-ager; Fox, Savannah, Lincoln's, and Golden-crowned Sparrows; Black-headed Grosbeak; Purple Finch; Red Crossbill; Evening Grosbeak.

Nearby opportunities: Dungeness Bay and John Wayne Marina; Railroad Bridge State Park.

Directions: From U.S. Highway 101, turn north onto Kitchen-Dick Road. Stay on Kitchen-Dick Road for 3 miles until it ends where it meets Lotzgesell Road and the entrance to the Dungeness Recreation Area. The parking area for the spit is at the end of the recreation area road.

DeLorme map grid: Page 93, C7.

Elevation: Sea level.

Access: Not wheelchair accessible. The hike down to the spit is steep.

Bathrooms: Near parking lot at top of bluff.

Hazards: Keep an eye on the tide: People have been trapped on the spit by high tides.

Nearest food, gas, and lodging: Sequim.

Nearest camping: Dungeness Recreation Area.

For more information: Call (350) 457-8451 or visit www.dungeness.com/refuge/index.htm.

John Wayne Marina and Sequim Bay

Habitats: Cobble beach, mudflats, marine

Specialty birds: Common Loon; Pelagic and Brandt's Cormorants; Greater White-fronted Goose; Brant; Greater Scaup; Harlequin Duck; Barrow's Goldeneye; Bald Eagle; Peregrine Falcon; Black-bellied and American Golden-Plover; Black Oystercatcher; Ruddy and Black Turnstones; Surfbird; Red Knot; Baird's and Pectoral Sandpipers; Short-billed Dowitcher; Heerman's, Bonaparte's, Mew, and Western Gulls; Common Tern; Common Murre; Pigeon Guillemot; Marbled Murrelet; Rhinoceros Auklet; Tufted Puffin.

Best times to bird: Fall through spring

About the site:

Yes, that's John Wayne, as in the movie star. He too loved Sequim Bay and bequeathed the land that has become the marina. Maybe the striking Common Loons, comical Black Oystercatchers, and impressive Bald Eagles that grace the bay influenced him. They certainly influence area birdwatchers, who rarely pass up a chance to take the short detour off of U.S. Highway 101 to check the bay. The highway skirts the bay, and if headed west, you can first take a look from Blyn, but you'll get closer to the birds if you go to the marina.

This is another spot where birders will benefit from bringing a good scope since alcids often float just beyond binocular range. One winter afternoon we stopped here with a birding buddy of ours. I kept trying to convince him that the alcid we were seeing was a Pigeon Guillemot. He kept saying that it had to be a Common Murre. I described the completely pigeonlike head and mottled sides, but he saw mostly black on top and white below, and it was too big, in his opinion, to be a guillemot. Taking a quick peek into his scope, I discovered that it was indeed a Common Murre. Back at my scope I confirmed that it was indeed a Pigeon Guillemot. We laughed at the discovery that we were looking at two different birds, his murre just beyond and in direct line with where my scope was focused tight on the guillemot.

Johnson Creek empties into the bay between the picnic tables and marina building, providing a good freshwater source for the birds that frequent the bay. We have found this to be one of the most reliable places for spotting Black Oyster-catchers. They like to forage along the pebbled beach at the edge of the creek. The area also attracts shorebirds such as Short-billed Dowitchers, Black and Ruddy Turnstones, and plovers. The protected and calm waters of the bay seem to encourage Barrow's and Common Goldeneyes to break into courtship behavior—eating at the picnic tables while watching goldeneyes throw back their heads to flirt with each other makes a nice lunch break.

Walk past the building and the boats to the north parking lot for views out to the strait. Check the water toward the strait for more alcids, loons, grebes, and gulls. Scoters also float in small flocks in the open water. Bufflehead and mer-

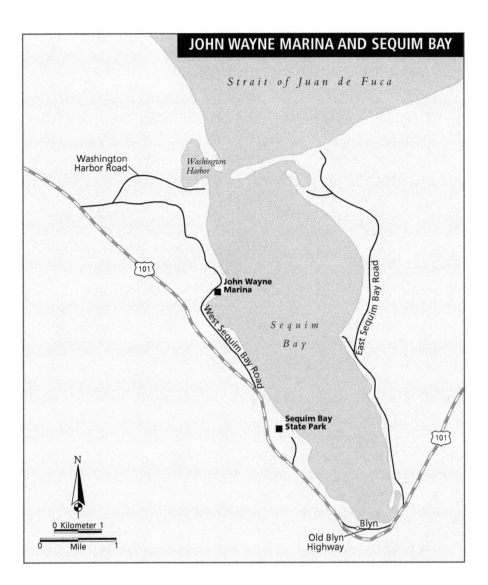

Strait of Juan de Fuca

Washington Harbor Road

Washington Harbor

John Wayne Marina

Sequim Bay

West Sequim Bay Road

East Sequim Bay Road

Sequim Bay State Park

101

101

N

0 Kilometer 1

0 Mile 1

Blyn

Old Blyn Highway

gansers dive for tidbits close to the rocks at the north end of the parking lot, and Great Blue Herons wade along the shore. The plethora of winter waterfowl attracts Peregrine Falcon, while the plentiful fish feast draws Bald Eagle and Osprey. Check the trees surrounding the bay to find these raptors perched and looking for prey.

To further explore the bay, continue north and east on West Sequim Bay Road and turn north onto Washington Harbor Road. Washington Harbor's mudflats provide ample habitat at proper tides for shorebirds, and eelgrass beds attract Brant. Waterfowl fill the small harbor during the winter months, including small flocks of Harlequin Duck. Cinnamon, Blue-winged, and Green-winged Teal also visit the shallow waters. Farther north on the bay, you can also walk the beach at Port Williams. To get to Port Williams, take Schmuck Road north from Port Washington Road, then head east on Port Williams Road.

COASTAL CLOWNS: BLACK OYSTERCATCHERS

Black Oystercatchers look a little bit clownish with their pink legs, long, red-orange cigar-shaped bills, and yellow eye surrounded by a bright eye-ring, all contrasting against their dark, black-brown bodies. They dart along the wave line on rocky beaches, jabbing into the foam with their sturdy, specially designed bills. While their jabbing and darting may look haphazard, these specialized feeders know exactly what they are doing. Shellfish tend to open their shells more when waves wash over them, which is exactly what the oystercatchers look for. When they see an open bivalve, they dart over and quickly jab their bills between the open shells. After severing the adductor muscle that holds the shells together, they pull or shake the flesh loose and gulp it down. Contrary to their names, however, Black Oyster-catchers rarely eat oysters, depending instead on other bivalves such as mussels and clams, as well as barnacles, isopods, and crab.

Black Oystercatchers tend to prefer the rocky beaches of the outer coast and the San Juans and are not often seen along the Strait of Juan de Fuca east of Port Angeles, but the conditions at Sequim Bay and the nearby Dungeness Spit attract breeding pairs, which return year after year to the same area to nest. More often than not, birders see oystercatchers in breeding pairs or small family groups, except in winter when the birds may form small flocks. Unlike most shorebirds, oystercatchers are attentive parents and continue to feed their young weeks after fledging, perhaps due to the specialized method of foraging that certainly takes time to master, even if it is mostly instinctual. Some captive-bred birds at zoos never perfect the techniques needed to feed on live shellfish and survive instead on shelled bivalves provided by their human keepers.

Oystercatchers can be cryptic, especially when their bright bills are buried in their back feathers during afternoon siestas. Their shiny black plumage blends in perfectly with the dark, wet, seaweed-covered rocks they are found on. One oystercatcher had us convinced it was just another wet rock on a tidal outcrop until it was startled and flashed its bill before emitting a high, keen-whistled alarm. These are fun birds to watch—if you can find them.

Other key birds: Red-throated Loon; Horned, Eared, Red-necked, and Western Grebes; Wood Duck; Gadwall; Green-winged Teal; American and Eurasian Wigeons; Northern Pintail; Northern Shoveler; Ring-necked Duck; Lesser Scaup; Black, White-winged, and Surf Scoters; Long-tailed Duck; Common Golden-eye; Bufflehead; Common, Red-breasted, and Hooded Mergansers; Turkey Vulture; Osprey; Semipalmated Plover; Greater and Lesser Yellowlegs; Spotted Sandpiper; Whimbrel; Sanderling; Dunlin; Semipalmated, Western, and Least Sandpipers; Long-billed Dowitcher; Ring-billed, California, and Herring Gulls; Bewick's Wren; Fox and Golden-crowned Sparrows.

Nearby opportunities: Dungeness Spit; Railroad Bridge State Park; Sequim Bay State Park.

Directions: From U.S. Highway 101, follow the signs to the marina by taking Whitefeather Road until it meets West Sequim Bay Road at the edge of the bay. Turn left until you reach the entrance to John Wayne Marina, approximately .2 miles.

DeLorme map grid: Page 93, D8.

Elevation: Sea level.

Access: Paved path, restrooms, and service building are ADA compliant.

Bathrooms: On-site.

Hazards: None.

Nearest food, gas, and lodging: Sequim; restaurant on-site.

Nearest camping: Dungeness Recreation Area.

For more information: Contact the Sequim Chamber of Commerce, P.O. Box 907, Sequim, WA 98382-0907; (800) 737-8462; www.cityofsequim.com.

Protection Island National Wildlife Refuge

Habitats: Sandy Beach, cliffs, mixed forest, prairie.

Specialty birds: Common Loon; Pelagic and Brandt's Cormorants; Brant; Harlequin Duck; Barrow's Goldeneye; Bald Eagle; Peregrine Falcon; Black-bellied Plover; Black Oystercatcher; Heerman's, Bonaparte's, Mew, and Western Gulls; Common Tern; Common Murre; Pigeon Guillemot; Marbled and Ancient Murrelet; Rhinoceros Auklet; Tufted Puffin; Northwestern Crow.

Best times to bird: Spring, summer, and fall. Especially good during spring breeding season.

Although it is just 3.5-miles long, Protection Island offers habitat for 70 percent of the nesting sea birds in Puget Sound and the Strait of Juan de Fuca.

About the site:

Looking at Protection Island from Port Townsend or Sequim gives no inkling of what the island holds. Only when you get close to the sandy beaches and steep slopes of the island does its role in the biodiversity of this corner of the state become clear. The 3.5-mile-long island is the largest nesting ground for birds in Puget Sound and the Strait of Juan De Fuca. Nearly 70 percent of all nesting seabirds in the two regions, from Rhinoceros Auklet to Glaucous-winged Gulls, spend the breeding and rearing season on the island.

There is only one way to see the Protection Island National Wildlife Refuge—by boat. The Port Townsend Marine Science Center offers cruises to the island from spring through fall each year, and private boat owners can investigate the area as well, as long as they don't land on the island and they stay at least 500 feet off the shore at all times.

For the best bird-watching, arrange a trip to Protection Island in summer, when the island is alive with breeding birds. Tufted Puffin dive and feed near the island's shores, along with Rhinoceros Auklet, grebes, and the ubiquitous Pigeon Guillemot. Working the southern shores of the island, look for Bald Eagle perched along the shore and scouting as well as feeding on fish and shellfish. The shore can also hold occasional shorebirds, including Black Oystercatcher.

Look up to the top of the cliff to see a Double-crested Cormorant condo that grows to new heights each year. The cormorants nest here at the top of the cliff, where they are building homes from twigs, grasses, and guano. Below the nests in holes in the sandstone and sand are the burrows of thousands of Rhinoceros Auklet.

Farther along the shore a spit of sand reaches toward Discovery Bay; try to count all of the seals hauled out onto the beach for a bit of sun. During our visit in midsummer, there were dozens dozing on the shore. Just past the spit the shallow waters hold an eelgrass bed right below the water's surface. The eelgrass bed was obvious on the citizen science cruise we took with The Menzies Project, which offers cruises during the summer months in conjunction with the Port Townsend Marine Science Center. Named after George Vancouver's botanist Archibald Menzies, the project is cataloging the water quality, plant life, and aquatic life around Protection Island and in the nearby bays.

ADVOCACY PAYS OFF

If not for the efforts of Zella Schultz and Eleanor Stopps, Protection Island might have been the site of a resort rather than the home of thousands of birds. After studying the colony of Glaucous-winged Gull on the island in the 1970s, the two women started an effort to protect the island from a series of development schemes. Forty-eight-acre Zella Schultz Seabird Sanctuary was established in 1974, just after the death of Schultz and, after years of lobbying efforts and work to establish the Port Townsend Audubon Society,

Stopps helped lead the way to the final establishment of the wildlife refuge in 1982. In exchange for the prospect of a few vacation homes, the Port Townsend area now holds one of the largest concentrations of breeding seabirds in Washington.

Other key birds: Red-throated and Pacific Loons; Horned, Red-necked, and Western Grebes; Black, White-winged, and Surf Scoters; Long-tailed Duck; Common Goldeneye; Bufflehead; Common, Red-breasted, and Hooded Mergansers; Sanderling; Dunlin; Western Sandpiper; Parasitic Jaeger.
Nearby opportunities: Sequim and Discovery Bays, and the Strait of Juan de Fuca.
Directions: Protection Island can be reached only by boat. Arrange a boat trip through the Marine Science Center in Port Townsend.

DeLorme map grid: Page 94, D1.
Elevation: Sea level.
Access: None.
Bathrooms: None.
Hazards: Rough seas.
Nearest food, gas, and lodging: Port Townsend.
Nearest camping: Fort Worden State Park.
For more information: Port Townsend Marine Science Center at (360) 385-5582, www.ptmsc.org; The Menzies Project at (800) 566-3932 or (360) 385-5582, www.menzies project.org.

5 Hurricane Ridge

Habitats: Subalpine meadow, fir stands.

Specialty birds: Golden and Bald Eagles; Northern Goshawk; Blue Grouse; Northern Pygmy-Owl; Vaux's Swift; Rufous Hummingbird; Pacific-slope Flycatcher; Gray Jay.

Best times to bird: Summer and early fall.

Even during the summer months, snow fields linger along the north side of the mountains near Hurricane Ridge, providing a dramatic backdrop for high elevation wildflowers.

About the site:

Olympic Peninsula tourists visit Hurricane Ridge for its panoramic views of the Olympic Mountains to the south and the Strait of Juan de Fuca to the north. More than one million people visit the area each year, which means you'll need to plan your bird-watching trip to avoid the masses. The majority of the tourists visit the park between June and August, which happens to be prime bird-watching season on the ridge. However, most people visit between 10:00 A.M. and 3:00 P.M., which, fortunately for bird-watchers, coincides with the time that most birds take a midday break from foraging. If you arrive early and stay late, you'll see more birds with fewer noisy interruptions. We like to visit in September, when the weather is still pleasant, the tourists have left for the season, and migration is in full swing.

Start your visit with a walk around the Meadow Loop Trails near the visitor center. The paved trails are easy to walk and offer views of Port Angeles far below and across the strait to Vancouver Island on clear days. The meadows and subalpine fir tree islands host sparrows, finches, and woodpeckers, including Red-breasted Sapsuckers. Many tourists never venture beyond the visitor center, which benefits bird-watchers who drive a mile beyond the lodge and walk the more challenging 1.5-mile (3 miles out and back) Hurricane Hill Trail along a ridge that is interspersed with steep cliffs and stands of subalpine fir.

Take your time while birding Hurricane Ridge. Rushing through may mean you will miss seeing what it has to offer. Find a quiet spot and sit for a while— hopefully away from the crowd—then listen and watch the tree line to see what flits about. If you do this at the picnic tables near the Hurricane Hill Trail, you'll likely gather a few Gray Jays around you. Sit on the rock wall in front of the visitor center and watch the slope for the movement of Blue Grouse that nest in the meadows below. Watch carefully though because Blue Grouse, especially the nestlings, are perfectly camouflaged to blend in with the beige, brown, and green high-mountain meadows. While listening is always a key to finding birds, that skill is often lost on the ridge when the high winds kick up and whistle past your ears. Birds hunker down and nestle close to the ground or close to tree trunks in such weather. Head for the opposite side of the ridge when these winds pick up, because that is where you will hear and see birds.

Although they are uncommon, it is possible to see Northern Goshawk and Golden Eagle flying along the ridges. The heart of the Olympic Peninsula is the only place in western Washington that you can regularly see Golden Eagle and Pine Grosbeak, both more common eastside residents. If you plan your trip for late summer, you will find more species on the ridge since some birds arrive only during migration or as part of the post-breeding dispersal, including Violet-green and Barn Swallow, Ruby-crowned Kinglet, Cedar Waxwing, and Western Tanager.

Life is not easy in the subalpine zone, as the ancient, snow- and wind-sculpted trees attest. A hundred-year-old subalpine fir may look no larger than a fifteen-

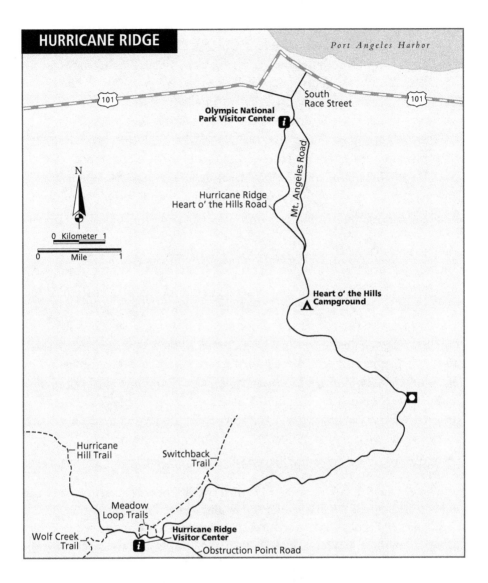

HURRICANE RIDGE

Port Angeles Harbor

101

South Race Street

Olympic National Park Visitor Center *i*

Mt. Angeles Road

101

N

Hurricane Ridge Heart o' the Hills Road

0 Kilometer 1

0 Mile 1

Heart o' the Hills Campground

Hurricane Hill Trail

Switchback Trail

Meadow Loop Trails

Wolf Creek Trail

Hurricane Ridge Visitor Center

i

Obstruction Point Road

year-old Douglas fir found in the lowland forests. The growing season is short, and the landscape is seldom free of snow. Few animals can survive the brutal winters here, and those that do, such as the endemic Olympic marmot, hibernate. While the snow-covered winter landscape looks beautiful, except for the humans who ascend the mountain to cross-country ski or strap on show shoes, animals and birds are seldom seen. Nearly all of the birds and the black-tailed deer that are ever-present during the summer retreat down to the lowlands. However, as the avalanche lilies push their way through the crust of snow to announce spring, the birds, insects, and mammals begin their journey back. From the time the lilies push their way through the snow, the subalpine zone sports a multicolored mantle of

ON THE OCEAN FLOOR, 1 MILE UP

Imagine, if you will, standing on top of Hurricane Ridge 25 million years ago. Instead of trees and panoramic views of jagged mountains with the Strait of Juan de Fuca far below, imagine hundreds of feet of water over your head and the ocean floor beneath your feet. The Olympic Mountain range is one of the unique and puzzling geological features in the world. Most mountain ranges were formed as the result of volcanic action—like the Cascade Range—or were formed when the continental plates pushed into each other and one of the plates buckled, creating mountains such as the Himalayas. However, something else happened with the land of the Puget lowlands and that surrounding the Olympic range. For some reason—and that reason is still under debate by geologists—after eons of normal tectonic activity, where oceanic plates sink below lighter continental plates, the oceanic plate began sliding over and crumpling against the continental plate when tectonic forces smashed them into each other. Later, the debris that had accreted in the trench where the continental plate scraped over the oceanic plate floated up and broke through the old ocean floor to create the high sharp ridge of the Olympic formation. Then came the ice ages, and along with them came the immense glaciers that dug great divots of earth to create Puget Sound and the Strait of Juan de Fuca. The glaciers also carved into the old oceanic plate to create the jagged peaks and deep valleys of the Olympic Mountains. At least that's the current theory.

---

wildflowers, the first link in the aerial food chain: flies, bees, beetles, butterflies, and some birds come for the flowers, then other birds come for the insects.

Summer ends just as quickly as it began, so birds do not have the luxury of lingering fall warmth. As a result, birds on the ridge lead life at a hectic pace. As soon as they arrive, they begin nesting, and from that point on, it's one frantic race to find enough food to fill the gaping maws of their young, get them safely out of the nest, and ready to migrate before the fall snows freeze the landscape to silence again.

Don't restrict your bird-watching to the top of the ridge, or you will miss the neo-tropical passerines that prefer the alder, big-leaf maple, Pacific yew, and western red cedar of the mixed forest below. Stop at the Klahhane Ridge Trail to add some easy-to-see butterflies to your trip. Water collects at the base of the trail and attracts puddling butterflies that sit on the seeps and puddles to suck up much-needed minerals. Stopping at the various turnouts and trailheads on your way up to the ridge will give you a chance to see how habitat changes as the elevation rises. The birds you find in the lower elevation mixed forest, such as Brown Creeper, Spotted Towhee, Downy Woodpecker, and Cooper's Hawk, don't fly to the 1-mile-high mark of the ridge.

A seven-day pass to the Olympic National Park costs $10 per car. With this in mind, you may want to plan a trip that includes other sites in the park, such as the Elwha River. Or, if you are a frequent visitor, pick up an annual National Parks Pass, which covers entrance fees to all national parks.

Other key birds: Merlin; Ruffed Grouse; Northern Saw-whet Owl; Downy and Hairy Woodpeckers; Western Wood-Pewee; Chestnut-backed Chickadee; Hermit and Varied Thrushes; American Pipit; Orange-crowned, Black-throated Gray, Townsend's, Yellow, MacGillivray's, and Wilson's Warblers; Western Tanager; Fox, Savannah, Lincoln's, and Golden-crowned Sparrows; Purple Finch; Evening Grosbeak.

Nearby opportunities: Ediz Hook; Deer Creek.

Directions: Follow U.S. Highway 101 to Port Angeles. Go south on South Race Street approximately .75 mile until it takes a slight left to become Heart o' The Hills Road, which becomes Mt. Angeles Road. At the Y intersection where Mt. Angeles Road becomes South Mt. Angeles Road, veer right onto Hurricane Ridge Road. Continue up the road to the visitor center and beyond, stopping where fancy strikes.

DeLorme map grid: Page 76, A4.

Elevation: 5,200 feet.

Access: Restrooms and lower loop trail are wheelchair accessible.

Bathrooms: On-site at the visitor center.

Hazards: Watch the weather if you are hiking. Call (360) 565-3131 to check on weather conditions at the ridge. Note that conditions on the ridge often will not be the same as those found in Port Angeles.

Nearest food, gas, and lodging: Food is available at the visitor center. All are available in Port Angeles.

Nearest camping: Heart o' the Hills Campground.

For more information: Call (360) 565-3131 or visit www.nps.gov/olym.

6 Lake Quinault Nature Trail

Habitats: Mixed forest, riparian, freshwater marsh.

Specialty birds: Bald Eagle; Peregrine Falcon; Band-tailed Pigeon; Northern Pygmy-Owl; Rufous Hummingbird; Pileated Woodpecker; Red-breasted Sapsucker; Hammond's and Pacific-slope Flycatchers; Hutton's Vireo.

Best times to bird: Spring and fall migrations, summer.

The lush rain forest habitat around Lake Quinault is open year-round to bird-watchers near the Lake Quinault Ranger Station on the north side of the lake.

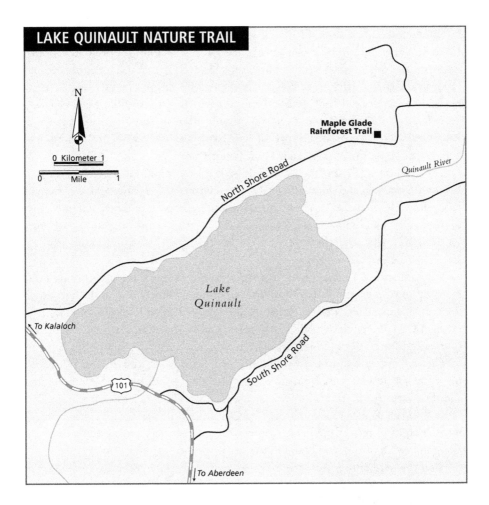

LAKE QUINAULT NATURE TRAIL

N

0 Kilometer 1

0 Mile 1

Maple Glade
Rainforest Trail ■

North Shore Road

Quinault River

Lake
Quinault

To Kalaloch

South Shore Road

101

To Aberdeen

About the site:

Water defines the environment along the Maple Glade Rain Forest Trail. Nestled in one of the three rain-forest areas on the west side of the Olympic Peninsula, you cannot escape the sounds of water, the water's sculpting of the forest floor, and the small streams that split off in a thousand places only to merge again on their rush downstream to Lake Quinault. Birds and signs of recently passed elk add to the deep greens of Douglas fir, hemlock, maple, and vine maple above and salmon-berry, ferns, oxalis, mosses, and lichen below.

The Maple Glade Rain Forest Trail is half a mile of easy walking among the trees and alongside Kestner Creek. For more birding opportunities walk the Homestead Trail, which breaks off from the shorter trail and covers about 1.5 miles through more varied habitat, including a section along farm fields and an old orchard that offers a look at birds that stay in more open habitat.

Good birds appear along these trails as soon as you leave the parking area. Crossing the bridge over Kestner Creek, be sure to stop and scan the waters both upstream and downstream in the riffles for American Dipper and listen for the rattling calls of Belted Kingfisher flying over the creek. On the opposite side of the bridge, the Homestead Trail turns left and winds farther west of the Maple Glade Trail. If you want to walk the shorter interpretive trail, be sure to check at the ranger station for the brochure that offers information about each of the numbered stops along the Maple Glade Rain Forest Trail.

The Homestead Trail branches off into an even more lush green environment laced with bracken and deer fern, oxalis, and long hanging mosses and lichen that droop from the branches of the maple trees in stereotypical rainforest fashion. It is in the midlevel and upper canopy that you can see passerines working the woods for food. Remember to check the tree trunks for Brown Creeper and the brushy areas near the ground for wrens.

The Homestead Trail makes its first major turn in a short distance, turning to the right into an area mixed with more conifer trees. During one of our visits to the trail, it was in this area that we heard the low, guttural hooting of a Great Horned Owl. We never actually saw the owl, but hearing it was a great reminder to stay alert for all signs of birds and not just the obvious visual signs.

The trail emerges from the woods into small farm fields with an orchard off to the right side. Just stick to the main road, which cuts a path between the buildings and then turns to the right along a fence-lined lane. The birding opportunities in these fields add the chance to see such species as hawks, Bald Eagle, jays, and warblers along the edges of the fields. Also watch for sapsuckers and woodpeckers along the edges of the woods and in the orchard.

After the road crosses a bridge over the creek, turn right and back onto the trail as it borders Kestner Creek on its way back to the parking lot and the ranger station. Again, check the small rapids in the creek for dippers and check the salmonberry and snowberry thickets for warblers and other songbirds.

IN THE LAND OF BIG TREES

The Lake Quinault area and the rest of the west side of the Olympic Peninsula are noted for the number of record-setting tall trees. At the time we were writing this book, the Quinault Valley held six record-setting trees, including the world's largest Douglas fir and largest Sitka spruce. Stop by the Quinault Rainforest Ranger Station during the summer months to ask about record trees in the area, as well as for tips about any notable bird sightings in the area. Due to its location, the area around Lake Quinault is not frequented by a lot of birders, so be on the lookout for out-of-place bird species.

Other key birds: Turkey Vulture; Merlin; Ruffed Grouse; Western Screech- and Northern Saw-whet Owls; Downy and Hairy Woodpeckers; Olive-sided Flycatcher; Western Wood-Pewee; Willow Flycatcher; Warbling Vireo; Chestnut-backed Chickadee; Brown Creeper; Winter and Bewick's Wrens; American Dipper; Swainson's, Hermit, and Varied Thrushes; Orange-crowned, Black-throated Gray, Townsend's, Yellow, and Wilson's Warblers; Western Tanager; Fox, Savannah, Lincoln's, and Golden-crowned Sparrows; Red Crossbill; Evening Grosbeak.

Nearby opportunities: Follow U.S. Highway 101 north to investigate the birding along the Queets River on Queets River Road or a bit farther north to see shorebirds and gulls at Kalaloch Beach. Also check the trails along South Shore Road, including the 4-mile Lake Quinault Loop trail that winds through huge fir, hemlock, spruce, and cedar trees.

Directions: From US 101, take North Shore Road east along the northern shore of Lake Quinault. Pass the July Creek campground and continue another couple of miles and then follow the signs for the Lake Quinault Rainforest Ranger Station.

DeLorme map grid: Page 76, D2.

Elevation: 175 feet.

Access: Not wheelchair accessible.

Bathrooms: Yes—at the ranger station/trailhead.

Hazards: Slippery trails. Watch for water across either the trails or the access roads leading into the site, and be aware that in winter North Shore Road can be closed by slides.

Nearest food, gas, and lodging: Amanda Park.

Nearest camping: July Creek campground.

For more information: For information about the record-setting trees in the area, check the map at www.quinaultrainforest.com/html/quinault_trail_map.html.

Puget Sound

From the shores of Birch Bay in the north to the Nisqually River delta and its national wildlife refuge in the south, the Puget Sound region offers a unique subset of western Washington birds. The majority of the state's human population lives in this region but nestled among the developments and artificial habitats are some wonderful birding sites.

Puget Sound is a region of lowlands bounded by the Canadian border in the north, by the western foothills of the Cascade Mountains in the east, by the southern reach of Puget Sound at Olympia in the south, and by Hood Canal in the west. The bird-watching opportunities it offers are diverse, from winter raptor viewing on the Skagit River delta to one of the state's oldest Purple Martin colonies at Titlow Beach Park in Tacoma.

Birds that highlight the Puget Sound region include Common Terns and the Parasitic Jaegers that chase them in the fall at Point No Point, alcids such as Rhinocerous Auklets, and the widest variety of gull species in western Washington. Despite the fact that this region offers the highest number of urban birding sites in the state, it also holds large concentrations of Bald Eagles and nesting Peregrine Falcons in Tacoma and Seattle.

Due to the sheer number of bird-watchers concentrated in this region, some sites such as the Montlake Fill in Seattle, Marymoor Park in Redmond, and the Nisqually National Wildlife Refuge north of Olympia are among the most extensively birded sites in the state. Rare birds are still seen seasonally at each of these sites.

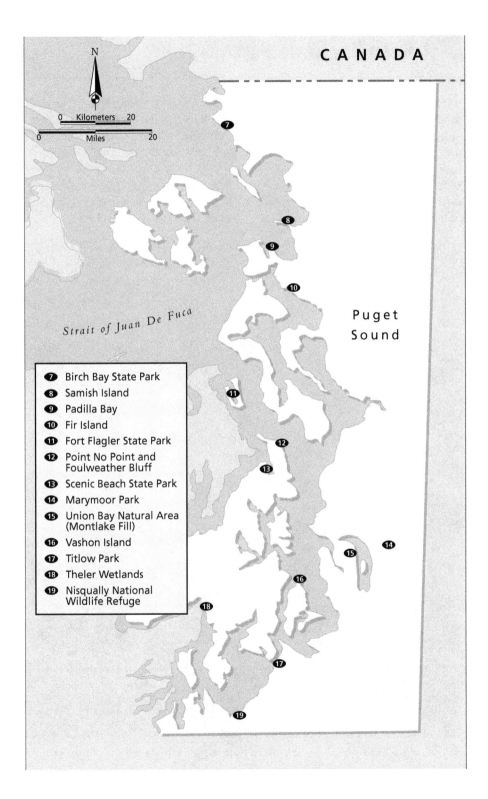

CANADA

N

0   Kilometers   20
0   Miles   20

Strait of Juan De Fuca

Puget
Sound

7   Birch Bay State Park
8   Samish Island
9   Padilla Bay
10   Fir Island
11   Fort Flagler State Park
12   Point No Point and
     Foulweather Bluff
13   Scenic Beach State Park
14   Marymoor Park
15   Union Bay Natural Area
     (Montlake Fill)
16   Vashon Island
17   Titlow Park
18   Theler Wetlands
19   Nisqually National
     Wildlife Refuge

Birch Bay State Park

Habitats: Sandy beach, mixed forest, freshwater marsh, wetland.

Specialty birds: Common Loon; Pelagic and Brandt's Cormorants; Brant; Greater Scaup; Harlequin Duck; Barrow's Goldeneye; Bald Eagle; Peregrine Falcon; Black-bellied Plover; Black Turnstone; Surfbird; Heerman's, Bonaparte's, and Mew Gulls; Common Murre; Pigeon Guillemot; Marbled Murrelet; Rhinoceros Auklet; Band-tailed Pigeon; Vaux's Swift; Rufous Hummingbird; Pileated Woodpecker; Red-breasted Sapsucker; Pacific-slope Flycatcher; Hutton's Vireo; Northwestern Crow.

Best times to bird: Year-round, but birding is best in spring and fall for migrating waterfowl. Winter is best for loons and Brant.

A broad eelgrass- and clam-shell-covered beach greets visitors during low tide at Birch Bay State Park.

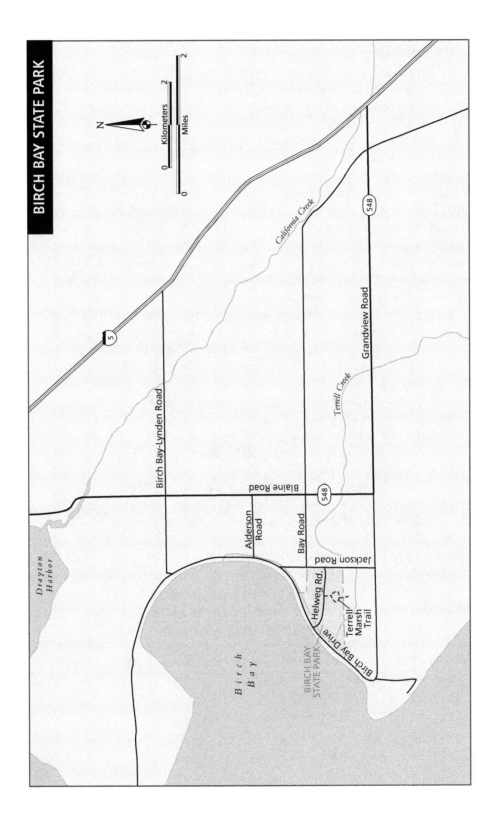

BIRCH BAY STATE PARK

About the site:

Noted as one of the first U.S. stopovers for migrating fall waterfowl, the waters of Birch Bay can be brimming with ducks, geese, and loons. But there is more to 194-acre Birch Bay State Park than the 8,000 feet of saltwater shoreline. Wetlands and more than 14,000 feet of freshwater shoreline on Terrell Creek combine with the mixed forest of the upper park and campgrounds to make this a great site for a wide variety of birds.

To glimpse the best birding in the mixed-forest habitat, plan a walk along the .5-mile Terrell Marsh Trail. Pick up a brochure at the entrance to the interpretive trail, located just past the entrance to the park on the left-hand side of the road. During a summer visit we saw and heard many Swainson's Thrush, as well as Golden-crowned Kinglet in the tree canopy high above and a House Wren singing on top of a stump. The forest is a mix of fir, cedar, black birch, and both vine and big-leaf maple, with an understory of lily of the valley, bleeding heart, fern, osoberry, star flower, and native shrubs.

The midpoint of the trail offers a great look at the wetlands of Terrell Creek. These wetlands cover more than forty acres, and they are noted as one of the few remaining freshwater/saltwater estuaries in northern Puget Sound. The wetlands are home to Red-winged Blackbirds, American Bittern, Marsh Wren, and swallows, among other birds.

The most well-known part of the park is the nearly 2 miles of waterfront along Birch Bay. The sand and pebbled beach is known for its wide variety of shellfish, and as a result it is home to many gulls and terns during low tide. If you walk the beach, watch your head to avoid being hit by falling shells as the gulls carry the shellfish up into the air and then drop them on the rocks below to break them open. Beyond the beach, Birch Bay is known for hosting all three types of loons—Red-throated, Common, and Pacific—as well as Double-crested and Brandt's Cormorant, grebes, scoters, alcids, and the occasional Pigeon Guillemot. Also watch overhead for Bald Eagle and Osprey. The park also has hosted a festival to celebrate the Brant that can be found feeding along the shore.

While along Birch Bay Drive, be sure to spend some time checking the freshwater shoreline of Terrell Creek, just opposite the bay. We watched nine Belted Kingfisher, including quite a few young, feeding and interacting along the slow-moving creek during a summer visit. And the grasslands in this marshy area are great habitat for Savannah and White-crowned Sparrow, as well as a host of butterfly species. The creek also can hold quite a variety of ducks—American Wigeon, Green-winged Teal, and Blue-winged Teal, and others.

A PARK SOAKED IN HISTORY

Birch Bay earned its name in 1792 when the George Vancouver expedition ventured into the bay and botanist Archibald Menzies noted the large number of black birch trees lining the bay. Prior to the arrival of white settlers, the shellfish and the bounty of game along the shoreline drew Native Americans from the Semiahmoo, Lummi, and Nooksack Tribes.

Today Birch Bay holds one the largest eelgrass beds in Puget Sound. Eelgrass is a key habitat for salmon as well as other fish, and it is one of the main reasons that the bay hosts large flocks of migrating Brant in the spring.

Other key birds: Red-throated and Pacific Loon; Horned, Pied-billed, Red-necked, and Western Grebes; Green Heron; Wood Duck; American and Eurasian Wigeons; Black, White-winged, and Surf Scoters; Long-tailed Duck; Common Goldeneye; Bufflehead; Common, Red-breasted, and Hooded Mergansers; Osprey; Merlin; Virginia Rail; Sora; Greater and Lesser Yellowlegs; Dunlin; Wilson's Snipe; Ring-billed and California Gulls; Barred, Western Screech-, and Northern Saw-whet Owls; Downy and Hairy Woodpeckers; Olive-sided Flycatcher; Western Wood-Pewee; Willow Flycatcher; Red-eyed and Warbling Vireos; Chestnut-backed Chickadee; Bushtit; Brown Creeper; House, Winter, Bewick's, and Marsh Wrens; Swainson's, Hermit, and Varied Thrushes; American Pipit; Orange-crowned, Black-throated Gray, Townsend's, Yellow, MacGillivray's, and Wilson's Warblers; Common Yellowthroat; Western Tanager; Fox, Savannah, and Golden-crowned Sparrows; Black-headed Grosbeak; Bullock's Oriole; Purple Finch; Evening Grosbeak.

Nearby opportunities: Lake Terrell Wildlife Area is managed by the Washington Department of Fish and Wildlife as a habitat reserve for migrating waterfowl. It is also a breeding area for Canada Goose. Lummi Flats is to the south of Birch Bay and home to the Lummi Indian Tribe. The farm fields along Slater Road are full of raptors in the fall and winter.

Directions: From I–5, take the exit for Grandview Road. Signs for the park are plentiful along the route west on Grandview Road to Jackson Road. Turn right onto Jackson and then left onto Helweg Road for the park entrance.

DeLorme map grid: Page 108, A2.

Elevation: 10 feet.

Access: Wheelchair-accessible restrooms and many paved trails. Terrel Marsh Trail is not wheelchair accessible.

Bathrooms: Restrooms are scattered throughout the park and campgrounds, and along Birch Bay Drive.

Hazards: None.

Nearest food, gas, and lodging: Ferndale.

Nearest camping: Birch Bay State Park has more than 140 standard campsites and 20 hookup sites.

For more information: Birch Bay State Park, (360) 371–2800, or Washington State Parks Information Center, (360) 902–8844. There is a $5.00 fee for visiting a state park. Also see www.parks.wa.gov.

Samish Island

Habitats: Saltwater marsh, freshwater marsh, wetland, mixed forest.

Specialty birds: Common Loon; Pelagic and Brandt's Cormorants; Greater White-fronted Goose; Brant; Greater Scaup; Harlequin Duck; Barrow's Goldeneye; Bald Eagle; Peregrine Falcon; Gyrfalcon; Black-bellied Plover; Solitary and Pectoral Sandpipers; Short-billed Dow-

itcher; Heerman's, Bonaparte's, Mew, Thayer's, and Western Gulls; Common Murre; Pigeon Guillemot; Marbled Murrelet; Rhinceros Auklet; Band-tailed Pigeon; Short-eared Owl; Vaux's Swift; Anna's and Rufous Hummingbirds.

Best times to bird: Year-round, but best in fall, winter, and spring.

About the site:

Samish Island and the surrounding area known as the Samish Flats are a paradise for raptor watchers. Bring together wide-open country, water-logged fields that draw hundreds of shorebirds, and a location close enough to Canada to draw species from the far north and you have the perfect formula for seeing Prairie Falcons, Peregrine Falcons, Bald Eagles, and even the occasional Gyrfalcon competing at the top of the food chain. It is all a matter of timing and luck.

Although the Welts-Samish Restoration Site, better known to area bird-watchers at the West 90, is just a few miles from Bay View State Park and other sites along Padilla Bay, the unique habitats and bird-viewing opportunities in the Samish Flats are enough to make the area stand out as one of the best birding locations in the northwest corner of the state. In short, you bird along Padilla Bay for waterfowl, but you would come to the Samish Flats for close-up views of falcons, Short-eared Owls, and shorebirds that gather by the hundreds in the farm fields along Samish Island Road.

The West 90 is a small hundred-plus-acre site with a few rough trails leading from the parking lot that is maintained by the Washington Department of Fish and Wildlife to a dike that keeps the salt water of Padilla Bay and the northern reaches of Puget Sound from intruding into the surrounding farm fields. A few small trees and shrubs are the tallest plants on the site. The rest of the vegetation is reeds and marsh grass that forms a dense, tangled habitat perfect for Marsh Wrens and other marsh birds, as well as voles and field mice, which are dinner for Northern Harriers and Short-eared Owls.

To start exploring the site, park in the large parking area and pull out your binoculars and spotting scope to take long-distance looks across the surrounding habitat. First scan the farm fields to the east of the parking lot on the other side of Samish Island Road. These fields are where Dunlin, sandpipers, and other shorebirds often can be seen feeding during winter. If the shorebirds are there you can bet that the nearby treetops or telephone poles will be occupied by Bald Eagles or falcons. After checking the scene east of the site, turn around and scan the pastures

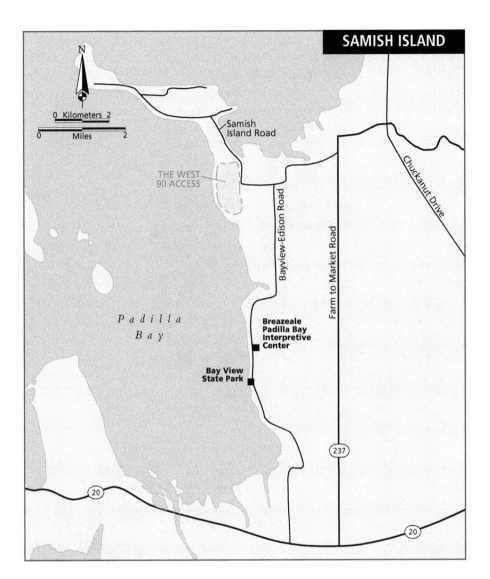

N

0 Kilometers 2

0 Miles 2

Samish Island Road

THE WEST 90 ACCESS

Bayview-Edison Road

Chuckanut Drive

Farm to Market Road

Padilla Bay

Breazeale Padilla Bay Interpretive Center

Bay View State Park

237

20

20

to the north and across the marsh to the west and south of the parking lot. Along with the harriers and owls that can be seen over the marsh, check the ground in open areas for other raptors, such as Rough-legged Hawks. If there is a place for close study of raptors and their habits in western Washington, this is it.

Depending on water levels and how prepared you are to get wet, you can venture out onto rough trails that lead across the fields toward the dike. Walking these trails offers much closer views of raptors and even better chances to see the owls that hunt along the edges of the dike and perch in the driftwood and logs on the dike's saltwater side. Once at the dike, you also have chances to see waterfowl that gather in the area between Samish Island and Guemes Island to the west.

Once you have exhausted the bird-watching opportunities at the main site, hop in your vehicle and return to Samish Island Road. Turn left to head north toward the island. Watch the brush alongside the road in the winter months for Northern Shrike and other species, and always keep an eye on the sky in case a Gyrfalcon or other raptor suddenly takes flight in pursuit of prey or to steal of a meal from another raptor. Samish Island offers few bird-watching sites, since the island is mostly privately owned land. Just turn around on the island and venture back along the main road, watching for new birds as you go.

SHORT-EARED OWLS

One of the best places in Washington to see Short-eared Owls is in the wetland habitat at the West 90 area along Samish Island Road. If you time your visit just right, you have a chance to see the elusive owls hunting over the marsh grasses in the open fields between the parking area and the dike that separates the land from Puget Sound and Padilla Bay. The key is making your visit during the winter months and staying around the site until dusk, when the owls can be seen hunting alongside the vast numbers of Northern Harrier that also hunt over these fields.

It is pretty easy to tell the Short-eared Owls apart from the harriers. The owls have a much more erratic flight pattern as they hunt, and they are about 3 inches smaller than the Northern Harriers. The owls also don't have the harrier's white rump patch.

Short-eared Owls are one of the most convenient owl species to view because they are crepuscular, meaning they start flying right around dusk rather than waiting to emerge under the cover of darkness like most owls.

Short-eared Owls spend the winter months in grassy fields and open areas, where they can hunt the small mammals that make up their diet. These owls used to commonly nest in western Washington, but they now are viewed mainly as winter visitors from the north. Short-eared Owls are widely distributed throughout eastern Washington, where they do continue to nest in appropriate habitats.

Other key birds: Red-throated Loon; Horned, Red-necked, and Western Grebes; American Bittern; Snow Goose; Wood Duck; Green-winged Teal; American and Eurasian Wigeons; Northern Pintail; Northern Shoveler; Canvas-back; Ring-necked Duck; Lesser Scaup; Black, White-winged, and Surf Scoters; Common Goldeneye; Bufflehead; Common, Red-breasted, and Hooded Mergansers; Ruddy Duck; Turkey Vulture; Osprey; Rough-legged Hawk; Merlin; Prairie Falcon; Virginia Rail; Sora; Greater and Lesser Yellowlegs; Spotted Sandpiper; Sanderling; Dunlin; Western and Least Sandpipers; Long-billed Dowitcher; Wilson's Snipe; Ring-billed and California Gulls; Caspian Tern; Northern Shrike; Warbling Vireo; Winter, Bewick's, and Marsh Wrens; American Pipit; Western Tanager; Fox, Savannah, Lincoln's, and Golden-crowned Sparrows; Bullock's Oriole; Evening Grosbeak.

Nearby opportunities: Chuckanut Drive also known as State Route 11 heads north from the Samish Island area toward Bellingham, with great views of Samish and Bellingham Bays as well as a stopover option at Larrabee State Park.

Directions: From I–5, take State Route 20 west from the Burlington exit until you reach Bayview-Edison Road. Turn right onto Bayview-Edison Road and drive north, past Bay View State Park and the Breazeale Interpretive Center to the intersection with Samish Island Road. Turn left onto Samish Island Road and park in the wildlife area parking lot where the road curves sharply to the right.

DeLorme map grid: Page 109, D5.

Elevation: Sea level to 30 feet.

Access: Not wheelchair accessible.

Bathrooms: None.

Hazards: High tides and waves along the dike trails.

Nearest food, gas, and lodging: Burlington.

Nearest camping: Bay View State Park.

For more information: The site is managed by the Washington Department of Fish and Wildlife (WDFW), and as such, visitors are required to have valid Vehicle Access Permits to park at the site. Check the WDFW Web site for more info at www.wa.gov/wdfw/.

9 Padilla Bay

Habitats: Saltwater marsh, freshwater marsh, sandy beach, mixed forest.

Specialty birds: Common Loon; Pelagic and Brandt's Cormorants; Brant; Greater Scaup; Harlequin Duck; Barrow's Goldeneye; Bald Eagle; Peregrine Falcon; Black-bellied Plover; Solitary and Pectoral Sandpipers; Short-billed Dowitcher; Heerman's, Bonaparte's, Mew, Thayer's, and Western Gulls; Common Murre; Pigeon Guillemot; Marbled Murrelet; Rhinoceros Auklet; Band-tailed Pigeon; Vaux's Swift; Rufous Hummingbird; Pileated Woodpecker; Red-breasted Sapsucker; Hammond's and Pacific-slope Flycatchers; Hutton's and Cassin's Vireos.

Best times to bird: Year-round.

Bald Eagles are commonplace in Padilla Bay and throughout the Skagit Flats. They are seen most often in the spring, fall, and winter months.

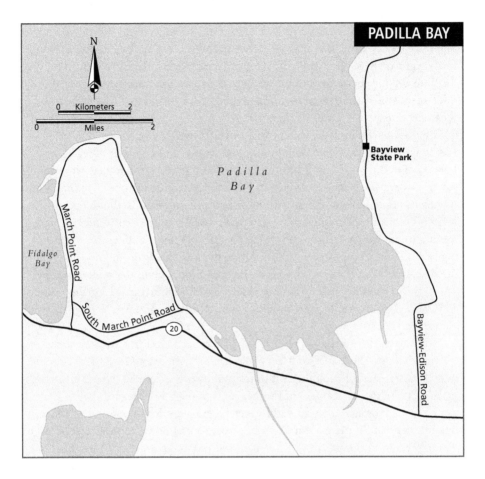

Padilla Bay

Fidalgo Bay

March Point Road

South March Point Road

20

Bayview State Park

Bayview-Edison Road

N

0 Kilometers 2

0 Miles 2

About the site:

Life comes and goes with the tides in Padilla Bay. When the tide rises, the bay fills with waterfowl, Great Blue Heron, and Bald Eagles that sit in fir trees along the shores, keeping at eye out for a meal. When the tide falls, shorebirds flood onto the mudflats to feed on invertebrates in the mud and on the blades of the extensive eelgrass beds in the 8-mile-long by 3-mile-wide bay.

Padilla Bay offers plenty of viewing choices for bird-watchers, with at least four major areas to pull out the binoculars and start watching—on the western edge of the bay off March Point, from the 2.25-mile Padilla Bay Shore Trail, from Bay View State Park, or from the upland areas around the Breazeale Interpretive Center. Each location offers a different glimpse of the bay and its surrounding wetland and mixed-forest habitats.

March Point is a slice of land that juts into Padilla Bay just north of State Route 20, with Fidalgo Bay to the west and the deepest waters of Padilla Bay to the north and east of the point. Although the presence of industrial oil refineries dominates the inland areas of March Point, the real bird-watching is along the shore, where shorebirds such as Black Turnstone, sandpipers, and others feed on the rocky shores when the tides are down and where sea ducks and other waterfowl can be seen north of the point in the deeper waters. Bald Eagle sit in the small trees along the shore and on piling that reaches out into the bay, and all three species of cormorant are commonly seen here. Just follow March Point Road north from SR 20 to explore the area.

For a less hectic bird-watching experience, try walking or biking the 2.25-mile Padilla Bay Shore Trail. The trail departs from two different locations along Bayview-Edison Road and it hugs the shoreline on top of a dike that separates the bay from farm fields. The trail makes a great destination for families looking for a way to combine bird-watching with more active exercise. Walk the trail in the winter months to see thousands of waterfowl that spend the season floating and feeding in the bay, or walk in the spring to spot shorebirds as they stop over during low tides to feed on the mudflats. Along the farm fields on the other side of the dike, watch for raptors that feed in the area. Especially in the winter months, this is one of the best raptor-watching locations in Washington. Peregrine Falcons and Prairie Falcons battle for food, along with Northern Harriers, Rough-legged Hawks, and other raptors.

North of the trail is Bay View State Park, another location with great views of the mudflats and the bay, as well as upland habitat with mixed forest and large fir trees. Besides offering camping, restrooms, and picnic tables, the twenty-five-acre park has more than 1,200 feet of shoreline. All of the 240-plus bird species that can be seen along the edges of Padilla Bay can be seen from these shores. During one research trip in the park, it was a huge concentration of common Great Blue Heron feeding in the bay just off the park shores that amazed us. More than 150 herons, many from a nearby rookery on Samish Island, gathered and danced in the falling tides as they fed in the eelgrass beds.

Although the bay is the highlight at the park, be sure to spend some time exploring the upland sections of the property. Songbirds are found here year-round, including some species such as Pileated Woodpeckers that rely on more mature forest habitats.

The Breazeale Interpretive Center just .5-mile north of Bay View State Park offers another opportunity for families and anyone curious about how the bay functions. The center is the public face for the 11,000-acre Padilla Bay National Estuarine Research Reserve, one of twenty-five national marine reserves in the United States and the only reserve of its kind in Washington. The Padilla Bay Reserve is managed by the National Oceanic and Atmospheric Administration and the Washington State Department of Ecology, and exhibits at the interpretive center explain the value of the bay and its habitats along with offering hands-on learning opportunities for kids and adults. The center grounds also hold a paved trail with views of the farmland where the center is located. The interpretive center is open Wednesday through Sunday from 10:00 A.M. to 5:00 P.M.; it is closed on holidays.

Another way to get an even closer view of the waterfowl that call Padilla Bay home throughout the year is to venture onto the bay in a sea kayak. The bay is a popular destination for paddlers, and nearby Anacortes offers a community of paddlers and kayak shops to support this interest.

EELGRASS AND BIRDS

As one of the best-preserved estuaries in Puget Sound, Padilla Bay offers unique habitat for birds as well as invertebrates that rely on eelgrass to live in the bay. Scientists estimate that more than 8,000 acres of eelgrass beds are located in Padilla Bay, which is the perfect habitat for the plants since it is a shallow, silt-filled bay that nearly drains completely during low tide to expose vast mudflats. Eelgrass is a critical plant for Brant, which feed on the plants, but, even more importantly, eelgrass is critical for salmon, other fish, and a rich web of aquatic life. Eelgrass provides a place to hide for young salmon that are making the transition from freshwater to saltwater habitats early in their life cycle, and since eelgrass holds other creatures such as crustaceans, it helps draw birds that feed on them.

To get a good look at the eelgrass beds in Padilla Bay, venture to the shoreline during low tide and use binoculars or a spotting scope to look out over the bay for the bright green strands of eelgrass. There are two predominant types of eelgrass in the bay, interspersed with mudflats formed from silt flowing out of the Skagit River. There are eelgrass beds in other birding locations around the state, including at Dungeness Bay, off the shores of Birch Bay State Park and off the shores of Titlow Beach Park in Tacoma.

Other key birds: Red-throated Loon; Horned, Pied-billed; Red-necked, and Western Grebes; Snow Goose; Wood Duck; Gadwall; Green-winged Teal; American and Eurasian Wigeons; Northern Pintail; Northern Shoveler; Canvasback; Ring-necked Duck; Lesser Scaup; Black, White-winged, and Surf Scoters; Common Goldeneye; Bufflehead; Common, Red-breasted, and Hooded Mergansers; Ruddy Duck; Turkey Vulture; Osprey; Rough-legged Hawk; Merlin; Virginia Rail; Sora; Greater and Lesser Yellowlegs; Spotted Sandpiper; Sanderling; Dunlin; Western and Least Sandpipers; Long-billed Dowitcher; Wilson's Snipe; Ring-billed and California Gulls; Caspian Tern; Western Screech- and Northern Saw-whet Owls; Downy and Hairy Woodpeckers; Olive-sided Flycatcher; Western Wood-Pewee; Willow Flycatcher; Northern Shrike; Red-eyed and Warbling Vireos; Chestnut-backed Chickadee; Bushtit; Brown Creeper; House, Winter, Bewick's, and Marsh Wrens; Swainson's, Hermit, and Varied Thrushes; American Pipit; Orange-crowned, Black-throated Gray, Townsend's, Yellow, MacGillivray's, and Wilson's Warblers; Common Yellowthroat; Western Tanager; Fox, Savannah, Lincoln's, and Golden-crowned Sparrows; Black-headed Grosbeak; Bullock's Oriole; Red Crossbill; Evening Grosbeak.

Nearby opportunities: Fidalgo Bay is farther west along SR 20, accessible from March Point Road before you reach Anacortes.

Directions: From I-5, take the exit for SR 20 at Burlington and drive west. Turn right onto Bayview-Edison Road, which has a stoplight on the highway. Stay on Bayview-Edison Road and watch for parking first for Bay View State Park and then Padilla Bay National Estuarine Research Reserve along the right side of the road.

DeLorme map grid: Page 95, A5.

Elevation: Sea level to 50 feet.

Access: Wheelchair access to the Breazeale Interpretive Center as well as to the Padilla Bay Shore Trail.

Bathrooms: The research center offers restrooms during operating hours. Bathrooms are also available at Bay View State Park.

Hazards: None.

Nearest food, gas, and lodging: Mt. Vernon.

Nearest camping: Bay View State Park.

For more information: The Padilla Bay National Estuarine Research Reserve offers information at inlet.geol.sc.edu/PDB. For information about Bay View State Park, check www.parks.wa.gov/parks/. For information about the Padilla Bay Shore Trail, check www.skagitparksfoundation.com/padilla.htm.

10 Fir Island

Habitats: Mixed forest, riparian, freshwater wetland, agricultural fields.

Specialty birds: Common Loon; Pelagic and Brandt's Cormorants; Tundra and Trumpeter Swans; Greater Scaup; Barrow's Goldeneye; Bald Eagle; Peregrine Falcon; Heerman's, Bonaparte's, Mew, and Western Gulls; Band-tailed Pigeon; Short-eared Owl; Vaux's Swift; Rufous Hummingbird; Pileated Woodpecker; Red-breasted Sapsucker; Hutton's and Cassin's Vireos.

Best times to bird: Year-round.

A Great Blue Heron hunkers down alongside a ditch on Fir Island. Although Snow Geese and raptors are the main winter highlights on Fir Island, herons are among the birds commonly seen at the site all year.

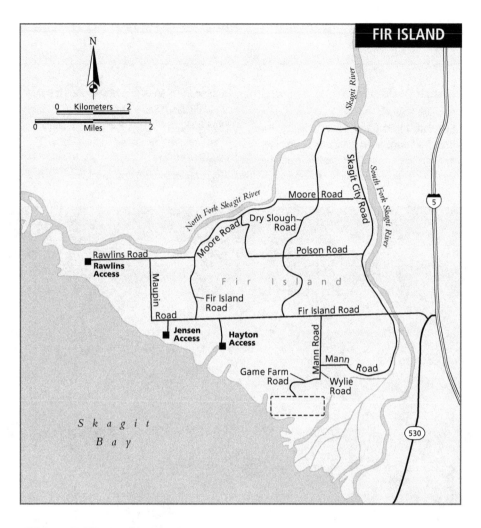

About the site:

Fir Island is a land laced with water, where the North and South forks of the Skagit River rush to Skagit Bay to meet in marshy fields, along riparian areas, and in tideflats that are teeming with birdlife year-round. In the spring and fall, this is a great location for observing shorebirds and songbirds in migration, and in winter it hosts thousands of Snow Geese and lesser numbers of Tundra and Trumpeter Swans.

To start exploring Fir Island, travel the bridge over the South Fork of the Skagit River just off I–5 at Conway and take an immediate left onto Mann Road. The farm fields here just inside the towering dike that separates them from the river are prime bird habitat. In the winter months these fields host Snow Geese, Tundra Swans, and Trumpeter Swans, and the trees along the river are often dotted with raptors. In fact, this is one of the best places to watch raptors in western

Thousands of Snow Geese gather in farm fields in the Skagit Valley each winter, and if you watch long enough you may see the entire flock rise as one in response to the fly-by of a Bald Eagle.

Washington during winter. Have your binoculars and scope ready to spy Peregrine Falcon, the occasional Rough-legged Hawk, and if you are lucky maybe even a glimpse of a Red-shouldered Hawk that was seen in the area in the first couple years of the new millennium.

Keep following Mann Road heading west until the road makes a sharp turn to the right. Go left at this intersection and follow the signs to enter the Skagit Wildlife Area (SWA)—a large riparian and marsh area managed by the state for hunting as well as for bird habitat. As with most wildlife areas managed by the Department of Natural Resources and the Department of Fish and Wildlife, you need to purchase a parking pass before parking at the Skagit WA. Once you park near the wildlife area management offices, check the bushes along the sloughs and the wires overhead. They can hold flocks of Brewer's and Red-winged Blackbird, Brown-headed Cowbird, and maybe even a Rusty Blackbird among hundreds of European Starling. The best bird-watching here is offered on the trail on top of a dike that leads west alongside fields and a slough. During one winter visit, we watched a pair of Wilson's Snipe fly overhead, followed a few minutes later by Northern Harrier hunting over the corn stubble in a nearby field as an immature Bald Eagle surveyed the scene from the top of a distant tree.

If you walk the dike trail, be sure to take the spur trails that lead to footbridges over the sloughs. Even if you don't wander into the fields, you can see different birds from the bridges than you would normally see from the dike trail. The dike trail offers a great feel for the habitat and plant life in this reclaimed land. The area is dotted with willow, alder, spruce, and fir, with a few cottonwood added to the mix. The understory holds blackberry brambles, Nootka rose, snowberry, and spirea, along with a host of grasses.

When you finish exploring the grounds around the Skagit Wildlife Area head-quarters, hop back in the car, drive back out to Mann Road, and go straight north to the intersection with Fir Island Road. Turn left, heading west on Fir Island Road, and continue west until reaching the intersection with Maupin Road. Rather than veering right and continuing on Fir Island Road, go left and then straight on Maupin Road to enter a farming area. Drive slowly here to scan the fields for raptors and shorebirds. At the point where Maupin Road veers right, go left down a short road and park at the end of the road. You can get out and walk around the gate to view the tideflats from the top of yet another dike. This partic-ular area is great in winter months for viewing Short-eared Owls around nightfall as they hunt among the logs blown up along the shoreline and the tidal wetlands.

RAPTOR CENTRAL

One the best reasons to visit Fir Island during the winter months is to view the raptors that gather here to feed through the cold months. Besides the year-round raptors—Bald Eagles, Northern Harriers, and Red-tailed Hawks among others—the Skagit Flats area commonly hosts Rough-legged Hawks, the occasional Gyrfalcon, and even sought-after owl species such as Snowy and Great Gray Owls, which have made rare appearances in the area. The combination of plentiful food sources, moderate temperatures, and the proximity of Skagit Flats and Samish Flats to the north country in Canada is a great draw for winter raptors. Add the fact that the Skagit River is well-known as a major draw for Bald Eagles, and this corner of the state is a raptor magnet.

Other key birds: Horned, Pied-billed, Red-necked, and Western Grebes; American Bit-tern; Black-crowned Night Heron; Green Heron; Snow Goose; Wood Duck; Gadwall; Green-winged Teal; American and Eurasian Wigeons; Northern Pintail; Northern Shoveler; Canvasback; Ring-necked Duck; Lesser Scaup; Common Goldeneye; Bufflehead; Common, Red-breasted, and Hooded Mergansers; Ruddy Duck; Turkey Vulture; Osprey; Rough-legged Hawk; Merlin; Virginia Rail; Sora; Greater and Lesser Yellowlegs; Wilson's Snipe; Ring-billed and California Gulls; Barred, Western Screech, and Northern Saw-whet Owls; Downy and Hairy Woodpeckers; Olive-sided Flycatcher; Western Wood-Pewee; Willow Flycatcher; Northern Shrike; Red-eyed and Warbling Vireos; Chestnut-backed Chickadee; Bushtit; Brown Creeper; House, Winter, Bewick's, and Marsh Wrens; Swainson's, Hermit, and Varied Thrushes; Orange-crowned, Black-throated Gray, Townsend's, Yellow, MacGillivray's, and Wilson's Warblers; Common Yellowthroat; Western Tanager; Fox, Savannah, Lincoln's, and Golden-crowned Sparrows; Black-headed Grosbeak; Bullock's Oriole; Red Crossbill; Evening Grosbeak.

Nearby opportunities: The farm fields south of Conway, near Stanwood, are also excellent for watching overwintering Snow Geese as they interact with Bald Eagles and other winter birds.

Directions: Take the Conway exit off I-5 and turn west toward the gas stations. Proceed across the bridge over the South Fork of the Skagit River, then take an immediate left onto Mann Road. The sign for the Skagit Wildlife Area is at the end of Mann Road.

DeLorme map grid: Page 95, B5.

Elevation: 20 feet.

Access: Not wheelchair accessible.

Bathrooms: Portable toilets.

Hazards: None.

Nearest food, gas, and lodging: Conway.

Nearest camping: Bay View State Park, www.parks.wa.gov/parkpage.asp?selected park=Bay%20View&pageno=1.

For more information: Washington Department of Natural Resources, (800) 527-3305 or www.wa.gov/dnr/base/dnrhome.html.

Fort Flagler State Park

Habitats: Sandy beach, salt marsh, mixed forest, prairie, parkland.

Specialty birds: Common Loon; Pelagic and Brandt's Cormorants; Brant; Greater Scaup; Harlequin Duck; Barrow's Goldeneye; Bald Eagle; Peregrine Falcon; Black-bellied Plover; Black Turnstone; Heerman's, Bonaparte's, Mew, Thayer's, and Western Gulls; Common Tern; Common Murre; Pigeon Guillemot; Marbled Murrelet; Rhinoceros Auklet; Tufted Puffin; Band-tailed Pigeon; Vaux's Swift; Anna's and Rufous Hummingbirds; Pileated Woodpecker; Red-breasted Sapsucker; Hammond's and Pacific-slope Flycatchers; Hutton's and Cassin's Vireos; Northwestern Crow; Western Bluebird.

Best times to bird: Year-round.

Dunlin and Sanderling launch into the air before an approaching wave licks the sand at Fort Flagler State Park.

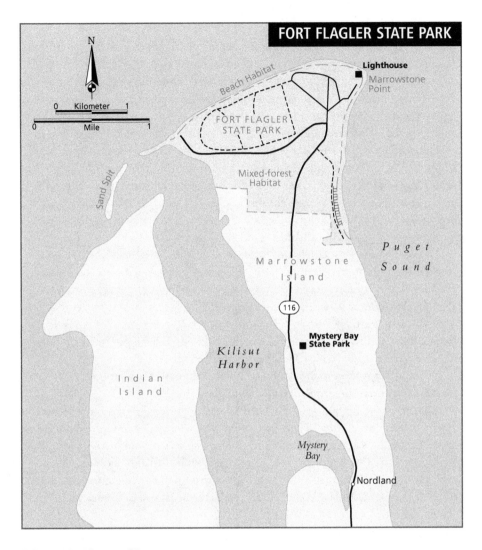

Lighthouse
Marrowstone Point

Beach Habitat

FORT FLAGLER STATE PARK

Sand Spit

Mixed-forest Habitat

Puget Sound

Marrowstone Island

116

Mystery Bay State Park

Kilisut Harbor

Indian Island

Mystery Bay

Nordland

About the site:

Fort Flagler State Park is one of those rare, northern Puget Sound birding locations that offers shorebird-watching along sandy beach habitat just a few feet from mixed-forest uplands that cater to songbirds and forest-loving raptors. The 784-acre park also features sandstone bluffs, open grassy habitat that can attract species such as Savannah Sparrows and Western Bluebirds, and shrubby thickets that appeal to a wide range of sparrows, wrens, and thrushes.

State Route 116 leads directly into the park, after passing a couple of other decent bird-watching sites along the way on Kilisut Harbor, near the town of Nordland, and at Mystery Bay State Park. When you enter the park, your best bet is to systematically take each of the routes from the entrance to experience the varied habitats. There are two main shoreline areas—one near the lighthouse and outbuildings in the northeastern corner of the park and another with a sand spit that is exposed at low tide in the northwestern corner of the park. In between are upland areas with prairie habitat and mixed forest.

Dunlin and Sanderling can often be seen feeding along the sand spit that juts into Kilisut Harbor during the winter months, and Long-tailed Ducks can be seen floating on the harbor in the background in the northwestern corner of the park. The same area also offers views of open water to the north, where alcids and gulls feed.

The northeastern corner of the park at Marrowstone Point offers more sandy beach habitat, but the stronger offshore current makes this a better place to watch for feeding alcids that flock to the area where the water churns. This corner of the park is also a good spot to watch for small flocks of Common Terns being pursued by Parasitic Jaegers in the fall. Also look over the waters from both beaches in winter for loons—Common, Red-throated, and Pacific Loons are possible off the shore.

The core of the park consists of large tracts of mixed woodlands with typical western Washington undergrowth of salal, Oregon grape, elderberry, and kinnick kinnick. This portion of the park offers the best opportunities to see Pileated Woodpecker, Winter Wrens, and other forest-loving species. Take time to walk some of the more than 5 miles of trails in the park to get an up-close look at the forest habitat and its edges against the prairie and beach habitats. Watch for hummingbirds, vireos, and Band-tailed Pigeons in this area as well.

As you explore the grounds of Fort Flagler State Park, keep an eye on the sky for Bald Eagles and other raptors, including Peregrine Falcon.

Aside from the birding, Fort Flagler offers an interesting glimpse at state history. The park was one of three major forts fitted with cannons set up to defend against any invading ships and to keep them from reaching Puget Sound. Along with Fort Worden in Port Townsend and Fort Casey on Whidbey Island—both of which are great birding sites—construction of the fort began in 1897 and continued off and on until the fort was closed in 1953. The property became a state park in 1955.

Other key birds: Red-throated and Pacific Loons; Horned, Eared, Red-necked, and Western Grebes; Gadwall; Green-winged Teal; American and Eurasian Wigeons; Northern Pintail; Northern Shoveler; Ring-necked Duck; Lesser Scaup; Black, White-winged, and Surf Scoters; Long-tailed Duck; Common Goldeneye; Bufflehead; Common, Red-breasted, and Hooded Mergansers; Ruddy Duck; Turkey Vulture; Osprey; Merlin; Ruffed Grouse; Greater Yellowlegs; Sanderling; Dunlin; Western and Least Sandpipers; Long-billed Dowitcher; Wilson's Snipe; Parasitic Jaeger; Ring-billed, California, and Herring Gulls; Caspian Tern; Northern Saw-whet Owl; Downy and Hairy Woodpeckers; Western Wood-Pewee; Northern Shrike; Red-eyed and Warbling Vireos; Chestnut-backed Chickadee; Bushtit; Brown Creeper; Winter, Bewick's, and Marsh Wrens; Townsend's Solitaire; Swainson's, Hermit, and Varied Thrushes; American Pipit; Orange-crowned, Black-throated Gray, Townsend's, and Wilson's Warblers; Western Tanager; Fox, Savannah, Lincoln's, and Golden-crowned Sparrows; Black-headed Grosbeak; Purple Finch; Red Crossbill.

Nearby opportunities: Mystery Bay State Park is along the drive out to Fort Flagler, and it often offers winter views of Long-tailed Ducks that gather in Kilisut Harbor.

Directions: From State Route 19 driving northbound toward Port Townsend, turn right onto Ness' Corner Road in Hadlock. At the four-way stop, go straight onto Oak Bay Road. In approximately a mile, turn left onto SR 116 and stay on this road until it ends at the state park.

DeLorme map grid: Page 94, D3.

Elevation: Sea level to 90 feet.

Access: Some wheelchair-accessible trails.

Bathrooms: Yes, in the northwest corner of the park.

Hazards: None.

Nearest food, gas, and lodging: Port Townsend.

Nearest camping: On-site.

For more information: Check the Web site for the park at www.parks.wa.gov/parkpage .asp?selectedpark=Fort%20Flagler&pageno=1.

Point No Point and Foulweather Bluff

Habitats: Sandy beach, tidal marsh, mixed forest.

Specialty birds: Common Loon; Pelagic and Brandt's Cormorants; Brant; Greater Scaup; Harlequin Duck; Barrow's Goldeneye; Bald Eagle; Peregrine Falcon; Red-necked Phalarope; Heerman's, Bonaparte's, Little, Mew, Thayer's, and Western Gulls; Common Tern; Common Murre; Pigeon Guillemot; Marbled and Ancient Murrelets; Rhinoceros Auklet; Band-tailed Pigeon; Vaux's Swift; Anna's and Rufous Hummingbirds; Pileated Woodpecker; Red-breasted Sapsucker; Hammond's and Pacific-slope Flycatchers; Hutton's Vireo; Northwestern Crow.

Best times to bird: Fall through spring.

From the beach at Point No Point, you can see Mt. Baker to the north and Mt. Rainier and the Seattle skyline in the southeast. The real highlight at the point is the chance to see Rhinocerous Auklets in their breeding plumage and Brant foraging in the eelgrass on the eastern side of the point.

About the site:

The combination of two sites at the tip of the Kitsap Peninsula, Point No Point and Foulweather Bluff, make a long drive worth the effort, especially when the alcids, gulls, and sea ducks that breed in Alaska and on the Yukon return for the winter.

At Point No Point, the convergence of several tidal zones from the Strait of Juan de Fuca to the north and Puget Sound to the south creates a food-rich zone that attracts rare vagrants in addition to the normal winter residents. Past reports have included Franklin's and Little Gulls. If you head to the point around September during the fall migration, you'll join hosts of gulls, including Mew, Bonaparte's, and Heerman's, as well as Common Tern, with Parasitic Jaeger hounding all of them to drop their catches. The area is so attractive to birds that Audubon Washington has named it as one of the state's Important Birding Areas.

We like to walk around the point and sit on driftwood with our scopes aimed at the water. Stormy days make birding the point more challenging since you have to watch between the swells, but the wind and waves can actually drive the birds to the lee side of the spit. While sea ducks such as Harlequin Duck and scoters and alcids abandon the southern reaches of Puget Sound during the summer months, you may still be able to spot them around Point No Point, which is not too distant from the nesting colonies on Protection Island. Through the winter you can count on seeing a number of sea ducks, including scoters, goldeneyes, Long-tailed Duck and alcids such as Common Murre, Marbled and Ancient Murrelet, and Pigeon Guillemot. All of Washington's alcids have been seen off the point, although Tufted Puffin and Cassin's Auklet are rare visitors. Sometimes Brant touch down to forage around the eelgrass beds located near the creek outlet on the east side of the point, and Horned, Red-necked, and Western Grebe bob on the water. Common and Red-throated Loon often join the grebes. Although most people visit the point to see what floats in the water, passerines, including finches, sparrows, Bushtit, and Red-winged Blackbird can be heard singing in the wetland and fields behind the lighthouse. Osprey and eagles that nest on the hill behind the point often fly down to make spectacular plunges into the water for fish.

After walking around the point, be sure to wander into the brush beyond the beach to reach a wooden viewing platform that overlooks a freshwater marsh south of the lighthouse. This viewpoint offers glimpses of winter waterfowl, Great Blue Herons, and closer views of Bald Eagles in the fir trees along the edge of the marsh.

To reach Foulweather Bluff and the Twin Spits, drive north through Hansville. You may drive right by the access to Foulweather Bluff if you don't watch carefully for the two signs that say NO PARKING BETWEEN DUSK AND DAWN and the small Nature Conservancy sign. As the sign denotes, Foulweather Bluff is a protected area totaling 101 acres and including 3,800 linear feet of beachfront in a protected cove. Protected largely due to the marsh, the land was donated to the

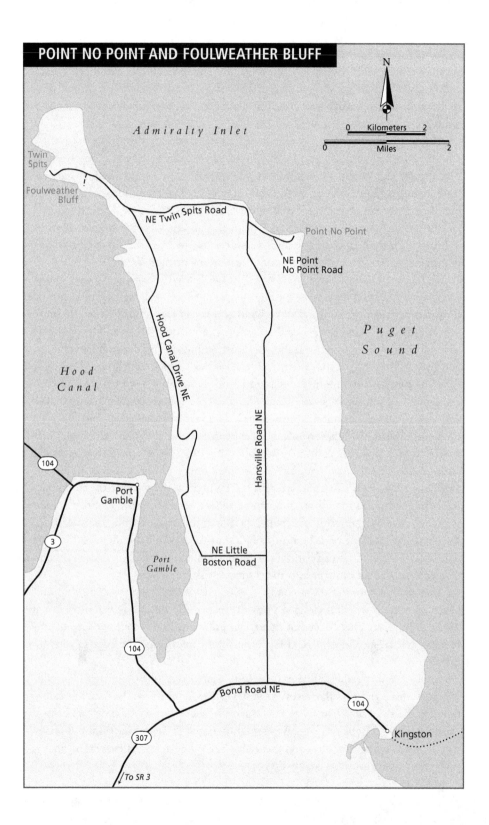

POINT NO POINT AND FOULWEATHER BLUFF

N

0 Kilometers 2

0 Miles 2

Admiralty Inlet

Twin
Spits

Foulweather
Bluff

NE Twin Spits Road

Point No Point

NE Point
No Point Road

Hood Canal Drive NE

*Puget
Sound*

*Hood
Canal*

Hansville Road NE

104

Port
Gamble

3

NE Little
Boston Road

*Port
Gamble*

104

Bond Road NE

104

307

Kingston

/To SR 3

conservancy by two brothers who originally bought eighty-six acres in order to prevent the mature second-growth forest in the uplands from being sold to lumber companies.

The combination of open beach, protected marsh, and wooded uplands makes this site another example of the riches found in edge habitats. Before you speed down to the beach to look for more ducks, walk slowly through the woods and listen for Winter and Bewick's Wren, kinglets, Red-breasted Nuthatch, and woodpeckers, including Red-breasted Sapsucker. The willow-edged marsh offers the laughing song of Marsh Wren and the cryptic calls of Willow Flycatcher, while the transition zone between the forest and the swamp features Pacific-slope Flycatcher and glimpses of warblers and other passerines, including Common Yellowthroat, Bullock's Oriol, and Western Tanager. On the water you'll find more alcids and more ducks, including American Wigeon, Green-winged Teal, Ring-necked Duck, Common Merganser, and large flotillas of Lesser Scaup. Shorebirds feed along the edge of the marsh and tideline. Because the tip of the peninsula offers the first and last landfall during migratory journeys, Foulweather Bluff's protected cove often attracts some of the less-common shorebirds in the flocks, including Baird's, Least, and Pectoral Sandpiper. Nearby Peregrine Falcon swoop down on the peeps to pluck a meal while eagles and Osprey, which nest near the bluff, dive for fish. The marsh and protected beach attract a handful of shorebirds, including Greater and Lesser Yellowleg, Semipalmated Plover, dowitchers, and a few annual sightings of Least, Baird's, and Pectoral Sandpiper. Depending on the tide, you may want to visit the Twin Spits, located at the end of the road. This bay is popular with anglers and crabbers. The beaches here are privately owned, so please respect that fact when you visit.

Other key birds: Red-throated and Pacific Loons; Horned, Eared, Pied-billed, Red-necked, and Western Grebes; Green Heron; Wood Duck; Gadwall; Green-winged Teal; American and Eurasian Wigeons; Northern Shoveler; Ring-necked Duck; Lesser Scaup; Black, White-winged, and Surf Scoters; Long-tailed Duck; Common Goldeneye; Bufflehead; Common, Red-breasted, and Hooded Mergansers; Ruddy Duck; Osprey; Merlin; Virginia Rail; Greater Yellowlegs; Spotted Sandpiper; Sanderling; Dunlin; Western and Least Sandpipers; Long-billed Dowitcher; Wilson's Snipe; Parasitic Jaeger; Ring-billed, California, and Herring Gulls; Caspian Tern; Western Screech- and Northern Saw-whet Owls; Downy and Hairy Woodpeckers; Olive-sided Flycatcher; Western Wood-Pewee; Willow Flycatcher; War- bling Vireo; Chestnut-backed Chickadee; Bushtit; Brown Creeper; Winter, Bewick's, and Marsh Wrens; Swainson's, Hermit, and Varied Thrushes; American Pipit; Orange-crowned, Black-throated Gray, Townsend's, Yellow, MacGillivray's, and Wilson's Warblers; Common Yellowthroat; Western Tanager; Fox, Savannah, Lincoln's, and Golden-crowned Sparrows; Black-headed Grosbeak; Bullock's Oriole; Purple Finch; Red Crossbill.

Nearby opportunities: Bainbridge Island offers a variety of habitats, including beaches and wetlands. Port Gamble is alongside a quiet, protected bay that hosts waterfowl throughout the winter and during migration.

Directions: From Bainbridge Island, take State Route 305 across Agate Pass. Turn right immediately onto Suquamish Way and continue through Suquamish to Hansville. From Hansville, proceed 2.8 miles on Twin Spits Road. The preserve is on the left. Look for the trail access between two NO PARKING DUSK TO DAWN signs.

DeLorme map grid: Page 78, A4.

Elevation: 5 feet.

Access: Not wheelchair accessible.

Bathrooms: None.

Hazards: None.

Nearest food, gas, and lodging: Poulsbo.

Nearest camping: Scenic Beach State Park.

For more information: Visit the Nature Conservancy Web site for more information about Foulweather Bluff, nature.org/wherewework/ northamerica/states/washington/preserves/ art6363.html.

⑬ Scenic Beach State Park

Habitats: Coniferous forest, cobble beach.

Specialty birds: Common Loon; Pelagic and Brandt's Cormorants; Greater Scaup; Harlequin Duck; Barrow's Goldeneye; Bald Eagle; Peregrine Falcon; Black Turnstone; Surfbird; Heerman's, Bonaparte's, Mew, and Western Gulls; Common Murre; Pigeon Guillemot; Marbled Murrelet; Rhinoceros Auklet; Vaux's Swift; Anna's and Rufous Hummingbirds; Pileated Woodpecker; Red-breasted Sapsucker; Pacific-slope Flycatcher; Hutton's Vireo.

Best times to bird: Fall through spring.

About the site:

Scenic Beach State Park is situated in a narrow fjord on Hood Canal, with 1,500 feet of beachfront and breathtaking views of the Olympic Peninsula and the rugged profile of the Olympic Mountain range to the west. The narrow channel provides a prime spot for viewing alcids such as Common Murre, Pigeon Guillemot, and Marbled Murrelet, for which a scope may be needed for the best views. Flocks of waterfowl and gulls sometimes form large flotillas in the channel or off the tip of the park, while others, including mergansers, forage along the shore. We spent an afternoon watching goldeneye and Bufflehead dive along the shore for morsels during one visit. Our observation spot about 20 feet above the deep, clear water let us see them "flying" beneath the water's surface as they darted after the small fish they chased. Although you won't always find shorebirds here, when the tide is out and a flock is migrating through, you might find a handful of Black Turnstone and Surfbird working over the cobbled beach.

Birding here can be a hit-or-miss venture, but a good day during migration will allow you to spot a variety of songbirds in the mixed coniferous forest that offers cedar, Douglas fir, hemlock, and yew. Listen carefully for the sound of woodpeckers as well as for wrens and thrush scratching in the litter below the trees. Keep a keen eye out for the movement of the cryptic Brown Creeper as they work their way up a tree looking for their next meal. Look for warblers, Black-headed and Evening Grosbeak, and flycatchers among maples and alders scattered throughout the picnic area, and look for hummingbirds, Fox Sparrow, Ruby-crowned Kinglet, and Hutton's Vireo among the rhododendrons and shrubby salmonberry patches fringing the open areas and around the Emel House. Anna's and Rufous Hummingbird competed for our attention during one visit to the park as they nectared on the blooms of Nootka rose on the embankment along Hood Canal.

When we venture out to Scenic Beach State Park, we always make a stop at Seabeck Bay to check the water for loons, grebes, Great Blue Heron, and other ducks as we pass through. Scan the waters on both sides of the road and watch the shoreline for any birds that might be sticking closer to land.

The beach at Scenic Beach is a popular summer swimming and camping destination, which is one of the reasons we avoid it from June to August, and even

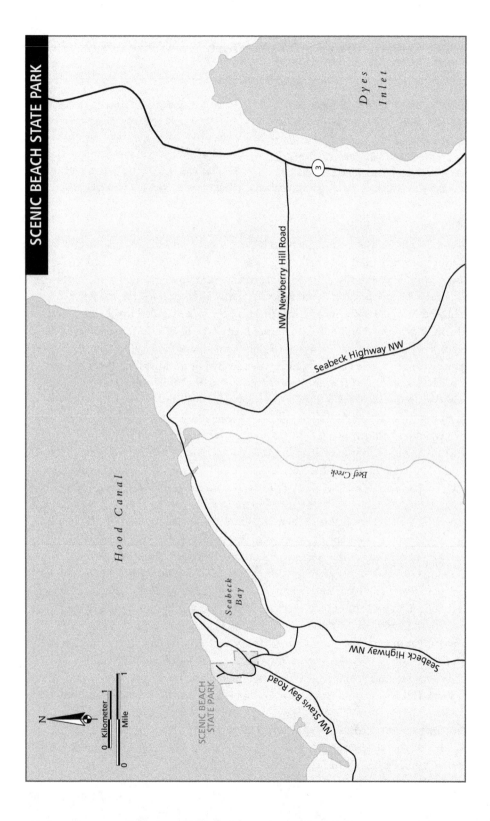

SCENIC BEACH STATE PARK

though it's also a popular place for people to gather crab and oysters, they have never interrupted our bird-watching. If shellfishers get too close to the waterfowl, the birds just move a few yards down the beach. The park is closed to camping from September 30 to April 9, but the rest of the park, including the picnic shelter and tables, remains open until dusk all year. Keep in mind that you will need to pay a $5.00 parking fee for day use.

Other key birds: Red-throated and Pacific Loon; Horned, Red-necked, and Western Grebes; Gadwall; Green-winged Teal; American and Eurasian Wigeons; Northern Shoveler; Lesser Scaup; Black, White-winged, and Surf Scoters; Common Goldeneye; Bufflehead; Common and Red-breasted Mergansers; Osprey; Spotted Sandpiper; Ring-billed and California Gulls; Western Screech- and Northern Saw-whet Owls; Downy and Hairy Woodpeckers; Western Wood-Pewee; Warbling Vireo; Chestnut-backed Chickadee; Bushtit; Brown Creeper; Winter and Bewick's Wrens; Swainson's and Varied Thrushes; Orange-crowned and Wilson's Warblers; Fox Sparrow; Purple Finch.

Nearby opportunities: Seabeck Bay, Shine Tidelands State Park, and Kitsap Memorial State Park.

Directions: From State Route 3 take the Scenic Beach exit and head west on Newberry Hill Road until it meets Seabeck Highway NW. Turn right and continue as it takes a sharp left past the small town of Seabeck and becomes Beach Road Northwest and curves around Seabeck Bay. Stay on this road until it leads you into the park.

DeLorme map grid: Page 78, C2.

Elevation: Sea level.

Access: Wheelchair-accessible paths and restrooms.

Bathrooms: On-site from April 10 to September 29; year-round at Kitsap Memorial State Park.

Hazards: None.

Nearest food, gas, and lodging: Silverdale.

Nearest camping: On-site.

For more information: Check the Web site for Scenic Beach State Park at www.parks.wa. gov/parkpage.asp?selectedpark=Scenic+Beach &pageno=1.

Marymoor Park

Habitats: Riparian, wetland, parkland.

Specialty birds: Common Loon; Greater White-fronted Goose; Greater Scaup; Barrow's Goldeneye; Bald Eagle; Peregrine Falcon; Mew and Western Gulls; Band-tailed Pigeon; Short-eared Owl; Black and Vaux's Swifts; Anna's and Rufous Hummingbirds; Pileated Woodpecker; Red-breasted Sapsucker; Pacific-slope Flycatcher; Hutton's and Cassin's Vireos; Purple Martin.

Best times to bird: Year-round.

The interpretive nature trail at Marymoor Park in Redmond offers a break from the urban landscape around Lake Sammamish. This section of the boardwalk shows the thickets on each side of the trail just before the view opens up to offer glimpses of the lake.

About the site:

Marymoor Park has many edges where differing habitats meet. Birds like edges and that makes this park a fun place to go birding, no matter what the season. Spring and fall trips feature neotropical migrants, summer stars include the nesting residents, and in winter waterfowl steal the show. Located at the north end of Lake Sammamish, on the east side of Seattle, the park is more than 600 acres. We used to spend lunch hours here and watch birds in the trees near the parking lots. While our time and the distance we covered was limited, we were able to build a nice list, including Bald Eagle, Osprey, Wilson's Warbler, Red-breasted Sapsucker, and Black-headed Grosbeak. Michael Hobbs, a dedicated Marymoor birder, regularly sees at least fifty bird species on his weekly walks, and he has created a site list that includes nearly 170 birds, including some west-side rarities such as Mountain Bluebird and kingbirds. Much of the park is dedicated to grassy monocultures and sports fields, but an off-leash dog-walking trail and the adjoining 1.5-mile interpretive trail on the nature reserve creep along the Sammamish River to the edge of the lake and provide a flat and easy birding route.

Walking the out-and-back interpretive trail is a good option, but starting in the dog park by the river creates a loop. Although the river actually looks more like a slough than a salmon-bearing stream, the grassy, willow and cattail-rich edges hide herons, including Green Heron; as well as American Bittern; Virginia Rail; and Willow Flycatcher. In summer, Spotted Sandpipers forage along the river's edge and pick among the lily pads. The scattered stands of cottonwood trees on the other side of the trail rustle with birds. Warblers love cottonwoods, and Sharp-shinned Hawks love warblers—interesting interactions abound. Look in the river at the accessible sections for coots and dabblers such as Northern Shoveler. We recommend you avoid the leash-free area on the weekends if you want to see birds. If you like dogs, a weekend trip is a blast. No dog lover could avoid smiling at the joyous frolic of hundreds of dogs playing chase, wrestling, and swimming. But the Sharp-shinned Hawk that we saw perched in a tree looked down upon them with certain disdain before flying off to a more peaceful part of the park. Even if you visit on a weekend and brave the canine maze, once you pass the last swimming hole, the dogs and people thin out, and the trail becomes a boardwalk where it crosses through a section of wetland.

Once past the gate that separates the interpretive trail from the dog park, you may well be alone on the trail. Low mixed shrubs soon give way to a tall, well-established cottonwood forest. Look for Red-eyed, Warbling, and Cassin's Vireos through here. Check the undergrowth for Swainson's Thrush and Spotted Towhee as well as other skulkers. Closer to the lake, the trail again turns to boardwalk. If you brought a spotting scope with you and lugged it all this way, set it down and scan the lake to see what is beyond the range of the naked eye. On a good day you'll add birds to your raptor count when Bald Eagle and Osprey dive into the water before your eyes to pluck out a meal. Depending on the season, you may

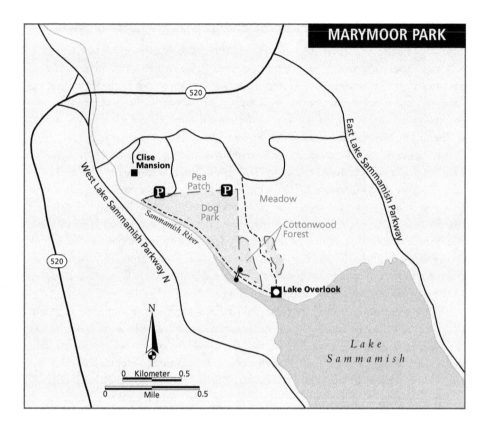

Clise
Mansion

Pea
Patch

Meadow

Dog
Park

Cottonwood
Forest

Lake Overlook

Lake
Sammamish

West Lake Sammamish Parkway

Sammamish River

Sammamish Parkway N

East Lake Sammamish Parkway

520

520

N

0   Kilometer   0.5

0   Mile   0.5

also see Common Loon, Horned and Western Grebe, as well as rafts of Canada
Geese and more ducks, including Common and Hooded Merganser, Common
Goldeneye, and both scaups.

The boardwalk angles back through the overgrown hardhack and willow. In
spring watch for male Rufous Hummingbird zooming by only inches away. Listen
for Common Yellowthroat and look up for swallows, including the Purple Martins
that nest in boxes installed for them nearby. When the clouds lower, you can also
see Black and Vaux's Swifts. When the trail reaches firm land, it again enters the
cottonwood forest. Let the sounds of the birds foraging guide your eyes. One day
we heard the pecking of a woodpecker. We quickly located the contrasting black-
and-white back of a female Downy Woodpecker. As soon as we spotted her, she
rounded the back of the tree. A few yards up the trail, we heard another. Thinking
that it was perhaps her mate, we looked and instead found a Bewick's Wren pecking on a cottonwood tree. In the same spot we saw a Brown Creeper, a handful of
Chestnut-backed Chickadee, Ruby-crowned Kinglet, Yellow-rumped Warbler, and a
single Orange-crowned Warbler. Unfortunately, that day we did not spot one of the
Black-headed Grosbeak or Red-breasted Sapsucker that can also be found here.

The forest gives way rather abruptly to low shrubs, and unfortunately a thicket
of invasive purple loosestrife. Across the footbridge the shrubs give way gradually

to a meadow. Near the stream look for Marsh Wren—or listen for their laughing, mocking chortle as they laugh and hide from sight. In the meadow look for field birds, including Savannah Sparrow and Western Meadowlark. Short-eared Owl have also been seen here, as have Northern Harrier, but you'll need luck and perfect timing on your side to see them. To get back to your car, you either can backtrack through the leash-free area or walk along the community garden, where you may see more sparrows.

If you have time and want to try to add a few more birds to your day, head back to the park entrance and check the trees near Clise Mansion. The twenty-eight-room mansion was the crowning jewel on a city banker's country farm. The conifers that surround it are some of the few remaining in the park. They and the cottonwood snags left behind after some severe "trimming" offer holes to house woodpeckers, creepers, and Red-breasted Nuthatch. The ponds near the rowing club on the lake also warrant a visit. Marymoor Park, though well-populated by us bipeds, gives bird-watchers a good reason to brave traffic jams . . . a couple of peaceful hours of birding at the end of the drive.

Other key birds: Horned, Pied-billed, and Western Grebes; American Bittern; Green Heron; Wood Duck; Gadwall; Green-winged Teal; American Wigeon; Northern Pintail; Northern Shoveler; Canvasback; Ring-necked Duck; Lesser Scaup; Common Goldeneye; Bufflehead; Common, Red-breasted, and Hooded Mergansers; Ruddy Duck; Osprey; Merlin; Virginia Rail; Sora; Spotted Sandpiper; Wilson's Snipe; Ring-billed and California Gulls; Downy and Hairy Woodpeckers; Western Wood-Pewee; Willow Flycatcher; Northern Shrike; Red-eyed and Warbling Vireos; Chestnut-backed Chickadee; Bushtit; Brown Creeper; Winter, Bewick's, and Marsh Wrens; Swainson's, Hermit, and Varied Thrushes; American Pipit; Orange-crowned, Black-throated Gray, Townsend's, Yellow, and Wilson's Warblers; Common Yellowthroat; Western Tanager; Fox, Savannah, Lincoln's, and Golden-crowned Sparrows; Black-headed Grosbeak; Bullock's Oriole; Purple Finch; Red Crossbill; Evening Grosbeak.

Nearby opportunities: Bridal Trails State Park, St. Edward's State Park, and Lake Sammamish State Park are all nearby.

Directions: From State Route 520 take the West Lake Sammamish Parkway exit and drive south onto West Lake Sammamish Parkway NE until you reach NE Marymoor Way, also the entrance to the park. Park in Lot G or in the lot for the off-leash dog area.

DeLorme map grid: Page 79, C7.

Elevation: 20 feet.

Access: Wheelchair-accessible restrooms are on-site; however, the trails are not ADA compliant.

Bathrooms: Wheelchair accessible.

Hazards: Rambunctious off-leash dogs.

Nearest food, gas, and lodging: Redmond.

Nearest camping: None

For more information: For general information about the park, visit the county parks page at www.metrokc.gov/parks/rentals/pomjun99 .htm, or to keep track of what is happening (and to avoid the crowds), visit the Friends of Marymoor Park Web site www.scn.org/fomp.

SIT A SPELL

It's like magic. You find a small stand of cottonwood trees on the shores of a lake, typical riparian habitat with cattails and willows, perhaps some spirea as well. You cruise the site quickly; nothing much catches your eye or ear, so you head back to your car and pull out your thermos, pour yourself a cup of tea, and sit there while the sun follows its course. Soon you see something flicker out of the corner of your eye, and you hear soft call notes. Down goes the tea, and you concentrate on the stand of cottonwoods. There it is again, a small bird flitting out and then back to a perch on a lower branch, then you hear the *seet* of a Pacific-slope Flycatcher. You begin to bring the binoculars up when you hear light tapping in another tree. Looking quickly, you spot a Downy Woodpecker. You look back at the first tree and see more birds moving about the upper branches. There, a Black-throated Gray Warbler, a flock of Yellow-rumped Warblers above, and an American Robin hiding on the other side of the tree. You sit and watch the warblers for a while and then notice more activity in the shrubs at the base of the tree, when a Song Sparrow lets loose with a fit of trills. You see a wren's tail twitching from side to side; you keep an eye on it, until it climbs up the side of the tree and your suspicions are confirmed when you discern the distinctive white supercilium of the Bewick's Wren. Next you hear the alert call of a Black-capped Chickadee. You start to look for it but get distracted when a Sharp-shinned Hawk streams in from stage right. The hawk twists and turns through the branches of the tree, but the blur of feathers it was chasing darts into the shrubs and is lost. All activity in the tree ceases. The hawk lands. After a long look at its beautiful plumage and long, squared-off tail, you take a look at your watch. One small stand of cottonwood trees has consumed all of your attention for half an hour.

So often bird-watchers seem on a mission to speed through multiple sites in a set amount of time. They allocate thirty minutes here, an hour there, forty-five minutes at the next site, all separated by an hour of driving. In all that rush, we wonder what birds they miss. We wonder what birds we miss when we do the same thing, and it's torture to hear that ten minutes after you left a site, the rare bird of the year flew in. Our most enlightening, enjoyable, and educational birding moments have taken place when we were "just watching for anything." So we suggest you pour yourself a cuppa and sit a spell.

15 Union Bay Natural Area (Montlake Fill)

Habitats: Lowland riparian, freshwater marsh, wetland.

Specialty birds: Common Loon; Greater White-fronted Goose; Greater Scaup; Barrow's Goldeneye; Bald Eagle; Peregrine Falcon; Western Gull; Vaux's Swift; Anna's and Rufous Hummingbirds; Red-breasted Sapsucker; Hutton's Vireo; Purple Martin.

Best times to bird: Year-round.

A pair of Canada Geese feed in front of a marshy section of the Union Bay Natural Area, better known to area bird-watchers as the Montlake Fill. The site sits on top of a former landfill alongside the University of Washington campus.

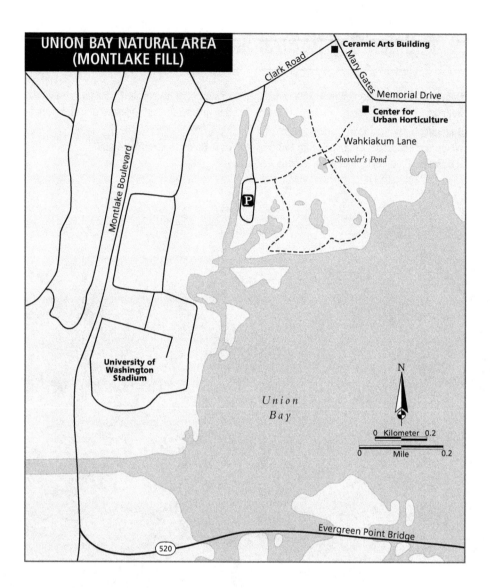

UNION BAY NATURAL AREA (MONTLAKE FILL)

Ceramic Arts Building

Clark Road

Mary Gates Memorial Drive

Center for Urban Horticulture

Wahkiakum Lane

Shoveler's Pond

Montlake Boulevard

P

University of Washington Stadium

Union Bay

N

| 0 | Kilometer | 0.2 |
| 0 | Mile | 0.2 |

Evergreen Point Bridge

520

About the site:

If you are looking for a way to let your life go to the birds in Washington's biggest city, the Union Bay Natural Area, better known as the Montlake Fill or simply The Fill to area birders, is the place to be. More than 180 species of birds have been seen in this reclaimed natural area that nestles up against the bustling University of Washington (UW) campus on one side and Union Bay on the other. Throughout the years the site has hosted some local bird rarities that stay around the grassy meadow and small ponds before moving on in their migration routes.

To start exploring the site, find a parking spot somewhere nearby and wander in along the gravel paths that bisect the site, cutting from the meadows to the treed areas and the shrubs along the edges of several ponds that make The Fill such an attraction. Starting from the UW parking lot E5, walk into the site and travel a counterclockwise route, heading south toward Union Bay Slough and alongside the first of the ponds. Waterfowl join with nonnative turtle species in this first pond, and you can see the turtles basking in the sun if the weather is right. Be sure to check the fields opposite the pond before you reach the water's edge and turn left to continue the walk.

Just south of The Fill is the State Route 520 floating bridge, and the open water of Union Bay between The Fill and the highway offers glimpses of birds such as Common Merganser, Bufflehead, Pied-billed Grebe, and Greater and Lesser Scaup. Be sure to check the edges of the cattails and reeds along the small islands and the other side of the slough for blackbirds and American Coot. This is also a great area to listen for Marsh Wrens.

The real star of The Fill is a series of low-lying, shallow ponds at the center of the natural area. The edges of these ponds and the grassy shorelines are well-known to area birders as places to watch for shorebirds in the spring and fall migration season. While the ponds themselves hold a host of waterfowl species— Northern Shoveler, American Wigeon, Green-winged Teal, and more—the shores of the ponds commonly see small numbers of sandpipers, plovers, and other shore-birds. Meanwhile, in the shrubs along the shores it is not uncommon to find at out-of-place Western Kingbird or American Pipit. The problem is, these birds don't tend to stay at The Fill very long, so often a bird seen one day and reported on a birding e-mail list will be long gone the next day. That is just the nature of the Montlake Fill.

A bird-watcher looks at waterfowl on one of the ponds at the Union Bay Natural Area. The site is a favorite for Seattle-area birders, and it has a reputation for hosting a wide variety of bird species during spring and fall migrations.

One final tip about The Fill: If you are planning a spring weekend trip to the site, keep in mind that sunny days will mean more people on the trails in such an urban birding site. If you can manage it, weekday visits and even overcast days will decrease the number of people using the site and increase your chances of seeing skittish birds. And if you happen to show up at The Fill on the weekend of the annual plant sale at the adjacent Center for Urban Horticulture, expect throngs of people walking the paths with plants in hand.

FROM LANDFILL TO NATURAL AREA

The Montlake Fill may seem like an odd name for one of the only open prairie habitats in Seattle, but the name belies the history of the property that was originally part of Lake Union, then became a wetland area full of cattails and other wetland plants, and then was used as a landfill from 1926-1966. The Union Bay Natural Area was set aside in 1972 with the goal of creating a natural habitat on top of the old landfill. While the area grows with new plant life, signs of the site's past as a landfill still can be seen through careful observation. Look down at mud puddles along the trails and there is an oily film that rises from the rotting landfill underneath the site, and the size of the ponds and wetlands at The Fill change as the debris underneath subsides.

Other key birds: Horned and Pied-billed Grebes; American Bittern; Green Heron; Wood Duck; Gadwall; Green-winged, Blue-winged, and Cinnamon Teals; American Wigeon; Northern Pintail; Northern Shoveler; Canvasback; Ring-necked Duck; Lesser Scaup; Common Goldeneye; Bufflehead; Common and Hooded Mergansers; Ruddy Duck; Turkey Vulture; Osprey; Merlin; Virginia Rail; Greater Yellowlegs; Spotted, Western, and Least Sandpipers; Wilson's Snipe; Ring-billed and California Gulls; Common Nighthawk; Downy and Hairy Woodpeckers; Olive-sided Flycatcher; Western Wood-Pewee; Willow Flycatcher; Chestnut-backed Chickadee; Bushtit; Brown Creeper; Winter, Bewick's, and Marsh Wrens; Swainson's and Varied Thrushes; American Pipit; Orange-crowned, Black-throated Gray, Yellow, and Wilson's Warblers; Common Yellowthroat; Western Tanager; Fox, Savannah, Lincoln's, White-throated, and Golden-crowned Sparrows; Black-headed Grosbeak; Bullock's Oriole; Red Crossbill; Evening Grosbeak.

Nearby opportunities: Washington Park Auboretum.

Directions: From I-5, exit onto Northeast 45th Street and drive east toward the University of Washington campus. Continue past the campus and down the hill, then straight through the light to pass by University Village. Turn right at the stoplight onto Mary Gates Memorial Drive and drive south before turning right onto Clark Road. Turn onto the side road to parking lot E5 to access the trails.

DeLorme map grid: Page 79, C6.

Elevation: 50 feet.

Access: None.

Bathrooms: None.

Hazards: None.

Nearest food, gas, and lodging: Seattle.

Nearest camping: Saltwater State Park, Des Moines.

For more information: On the Internet, the Union Bay Natural Area site has background info at depts.washington.edu/ubna/. The Washington Ornithological Society has info about sightings at the Montlake Fill from 1972 to 1989 at www.wos.org/WB01A 02.htm.

16 Vashon Island

Habitats: Saltwater marsh, sandy beach, rocky beach, mixed forest.

Specialty birds: Common Loon; Pelagic and Brandt's Cormorants; Greater White-fronted Goose; Greater Scaup; Barrow's Goldeneye; Bald Eagle; Peregrine Falcon; Black-bellied Plover; Solitary, Baird's, and Pectoral Sandpipers; Red-necked Phalarope; Heerman's, Bonaparte's, Mew, Thayer's, and Western Gulls; Common Tern; Common Murre; Pigeon Guillemot; Marbled Murrelet; Rhinoceros Auklet; Band-tailed Pigeon; Northern Pygmy-Owl; Vaux's Swift; Anna's and Rufous Hummingbirds; Pileated Woodpecker; Red-breasted Sapsucker; Hammond's and Pacific-slope Flycatchers; Hutton's Vireo; Purple Martin.

Best times to bird: Year-round.

Lisabuela Park on the west side of the island is a great location for watching waterfowl in the fall and winter and shorebirds and Purple Martin in the late summer.

About the site:

Bird-watching on Vashon Island can be as easy as riding the ferry to the island from Seattle or Tacoma and simply driving around and exploring the 12-mile-long and 8-mile-wide island complex. Extensive saltwater shorelines coupled with a handful of well-placed parks offer intriguing on-island opportunities. Add the birding from the ferry on the way to the island and you'll have one of the simplest ways to spend the day watching birds within easy reach of the Puget Sound's urban centers.

The area known as Vashon Island is really a complex of two islands—the larger Vashon Island and the smaller, hilly Maury Island, which is joined to the main island by a narrow strip of land at Portage.

The best way to get a feel for the island and its bird habitats is to drive around its outer edges, making stops at public beaches along the way. We start our description on the southern end of the main island, where madrona trees cascade down the steep hillsides toward Commencement Bay to the south and Quartermaster Harbor, which separates Vashon Island from Maury Island to the east. Quartermaster Harbor is designated by Audubon Washington as an Important Bird Area, most notably for its importance as overwintering habitat for thousands of Western Grebe. Roughly 8 percent of all Western Grebe found in Washington make their way to the harbor to feed on fish and ride out the winter weather.

After climbing the hill from the ferry dock on the south end of the island, follow Vashon Island Highway, which runs north and south along the middle of the island. The highway eventually drops down alongside Quartermaster Harbor, with views of the shoreline and a few wide spots in the road before it reaches the small town of Burton. Check these protected shores for waterfowl as well as straggling shorebirds. At Burton, turn right onto 240th Street and drive to the intersection with Bay View Road. Turn right and in a short while the road will pass Jensen Point Park on the right side of the road—the first park offering views of the harbor and its protected waters that can hold thousands of waterfowl during the winter months. This small park offers a boat ramp and is an easy put-in location for kayaking. It also features picnic tables that offer good views of the harbor.

Return to Vashon Island Highway at Burton and turn right to follow the road a short distance, crossing a bridge that spans Judd Creek, and then turn right onto SW Quartermaster Drive to start the trek out to Maury Island. The road comes to a Y after a few turns. Continue toward the right, and the road skirts the north end of Quartermaster Harbor before reaching a stop sign. Turn right at the sign onto Dockton Road SW, and then follow the signs toward the small town of Dockton. Dockton Park is on the right side of the road before you reach the town. It is a more-developed park with views across the harbor as well as public docks for area boaters. The park offers public restrooms as well as access to the dock, where you can get closer views of waterfowl in the harbor.

The second birding location on Maury Island may be the best of the bunch—Point Robinson Park, with its lighthouse built in 1885 and views to the east of

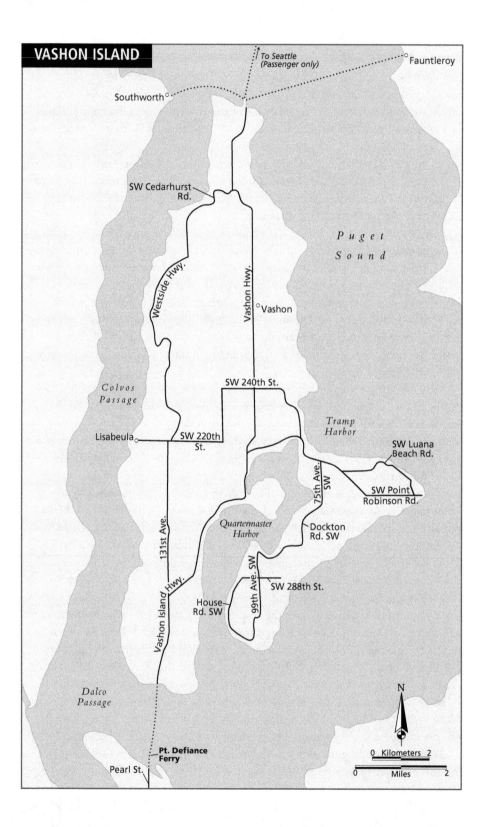

VASHON ISLAND

To Seattle
(Passenger only)

Fauntleroy

Southworth

*Puget
Sound*

SW Cedarhurst
Rd.

Westside Hwy.

Vashon Hwy.

Vashon

*Colvos
Passage*

SW 240th St.

Tramp
Harbor

Lisabeula

SW 220th
St.

SW Luana
Beach Rd.

75th Ave. SW

SW Point
Robinson Rd.

131st Ave.

*Quartermaster
Harbor*

Dockton
Rd. SW

Vashon Island Hwy.

99th Ave. SW

SW 288th St.

House
Rd. SW

N

*Dalco
Passage*

Pt. Defiance
Ferry

Pearl St.

0   Kilometers   2

0   Miles   2

Seattle, Des Moines, and Mt. Rainier in the distance. To get to the park, backtrack along Dockton Road to Southwest 240th Street and turn right next to the Vashon Country Club onto 240th Street. Continue straight on this road and it will lead to Point Robinson, which juts into Puget Sound and can offer views of shorebirds, alcids, and waterfowl, as well as songbirds in the open field behind the lighthouse. Local birders consider this location a must-see because it can offer surprise birds that are normally not seen on the rest of the island.

Another bird-watching spot along the east side of the main island is known to locals as KVI beach. The beach is located near the Ellisport area at Heyer Point. Just continue straight on SW Dockton Road as you leave Maury Island, drive along the shores of Tramp Harbor to Ellisport, and go right onto Chataqua Beach Road. Continue along the shoreline and find parking to view KVI beach, which is a sandy beach that is one of the better shorebird-watching locations on the island during the spring and fall migrations.

The less-sheltered west side of Vashon Island has its bird-watching highlights as well, most notably Lisabuela Park, alongside Christianson Cove, and Colvos Passage, which separates Vashon Island from Kitsap County on the opposite shore. Depending on the tide levels and season, Lisabuela Park can hold shorebirds as well as a wealth of waterfowl. During one late summer visit, we watched a pair of Spotted Sandpipers fly into the cove and begin feeding while Purple Martins called and circled overhead and a Belted Kingfisher chattered as it flew across the cove. The best time for birding at this park is in winter, when the cove can hold

Local bird-watchers know to check the shores and waters at Point Robinson Park for uncommon Vashon Island birds. The point reaches into Puget Sound on the east side of the island.

dozens of waterfowl species. To get to Lisabuella Park, take SW 204th Street toward the west side of the island from Vashon Island Highway. Turn left onto 111th Avenue SW and then right onto SW 220th Street. Just follow this road to its end and it will drop down into the day-use only park.

There are other shore-side bird-watching locations on Vashon Island—Spring Beach and Fern Cove among them—as well as isolated parklands and open space in the upland areas of the islands. Just spend time crisscrossing the island and watching and listening, and you never know what can turn up.

Other key birds: Red-throated Loon; Horned, Pied-billed, Red-necked, and Western Grebes; American Bittern; Green Heron; Wood Duck; Gadwall; Green-winged, Blue-winged, and Cinnamon Teals; American and Eurasian Wigeons; Northern Pintail; Northern Shoveler; Canvasback; Ring-necked Duck; Lesser Scaup; Black, White-winged, and Surf Scoters; Common Goldeneye; Bufflehead; Common, Red-breasted, and Hooded Mergansers; Ruddy Duck; Turkey Vulture; Osprey; Merlin; Virginia Rail; Sora; Greater and Lesser Yellowlegs; Spotted Sandpiper; Sanderling; Dunlin; Western and Least Sandpipers; Wilson's Snipe; Parasitic Jaeger; Ring-billed and California Gulls; Caspian Tern; Western Screech- and Northern Saw-whet Owls; Downy and Hairy Woodpeckers; Olive-sided Flycatcher; Western Wood-Pewee; Willow Flycatcher; Northern Shrike; Red-eyed and Warbling Vireos; Western Scrub-Jay; Chestnut-backed Chickadee; Bushtit; Brown Creeper; House, Winter, Bewick's, and Marsh Wrens; Townsend's Solitaire; Swainson's, Hermit, and Varied Thrushes; American Pipit; Orange-crowned, Black-throated Gray, Townsend's, Yellow, MacGillivray's, and Wilson's Warblers; Common Yellowthroat; Western Tanager; Fox, Savannah, Lincoln's, and Golden-crowned Sparrows; Black-headed Grosbeak; Bullock's Oriole; Purple Finch; Red Crossbill; Evening Grosbeak.

Nearby opportunities: Birding from the ferries.

Directions: From Seattle, drive to West Seattle and take the Fauntleroy to Vashon Island ferry run and explore the island starting in the north. From Southworth, take the short ferry ride to the north end of the island. From State Route 16 in Tacoma, take the Pearl Street exit and follow the signs toward Point Defiance Park. The ferry terminal adjoins the park.

DeLorme map grid: Page 63, A5.

Elevation: 15 feet.

Access: Varies with each site.

Bathrooms: At Dockton Park and portable toilets in season at Point Robinson Park.

Hazards: None.

Nearest food, gas, and lodging: Vashon.

Nearest camping: Manchester State Park (take the Southworth ferry from the north end of Vashon Island to drive to Manchester).

For more information: The Vashon-Maury Island Chamber of Commerce offers information at www.vashonchamber.com or by phone at (206) 463-6217.

 # Titlow Park

Habitats: Parkland, lowland riparian, mixed forest, wetland, ponds, cobble beach.

Specialty birds: Common Loon; Pelagic Cormorant; Barrow's Goldeneye; Bald Eagle; Bonaparte's, Mew, Thayer's, and Western Gulls; Common Murre; Pigeon Guillemot; Rhinoceros Auklet; Anna's and Rufous Hummingbirds; Pileated Woodpecker; Red-breasted Sapsucker; Pacific-slope Flycatcher; Purple Martin.

Best times to bird: Year-round.

A Double-crested Cormorant for every piling is not an unusual sight at Titlow Park in Tacoma. This small urban park is well known for its colony of nesting Purple Martin that return to the site each spring.

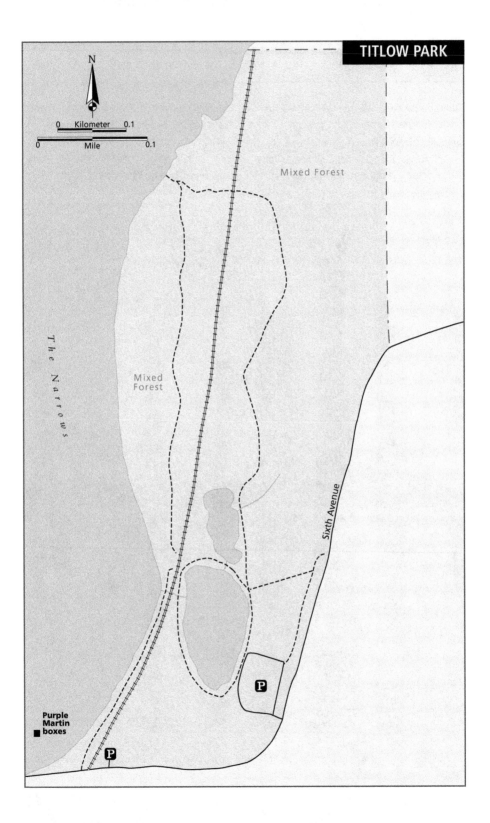

N

0 — Kilometer — 0.1

0 — Mile — 0.1

TITLOW PARK

Mixed Forest

The Narrows

Mixed Forest

Sixth Avenue

P

P

Purple
Martin
boxes

About the site:

Accessible urban birding doesn't get much easier than from the paved walkways with views of the Tacoma Narrows at Titlow Park in Tacoma. The fifty-four-acre park is one of the most reliable places in the state to see nesting Purple Martin from April through September, and as the seasons pass, the site also features views of Bonaparte's Gulls feeding in flocks on the narrows, close-up looks at Common Loons, large flocks of American Wigeon, and Western Grebes gathered on the swift waters between the park and Fox Island.

Besides the views of the Tacoma Narrows Bridge—and its twin, which was slowly rising from the waterline when this book was written—Titlow Park offers a great combination of habitats that maximize the chances for bird variety in such a small site. Saltwater and a cobble beach teeming with sea life define the west side of the park, while freshwater ponds fed by a stream and a tidal area where the saltwater and freshwater mix offer habitat for a wide range of gulls and dabbling ducks. Mixed-forest habitat in the northern end of the park rounds out the bird-watching areas.

When you arrive at Titlow Park, it's best to start by checking the saltwater and beach. Bring your spotting scope or binoculars to check for gulls and grebes far out in the narrows, and look among the pilings just offshore for Pigeon Guillemot, Common Murre, all of the site's gulls, and ever-present Double-crested Cormorants. The Purple Martin boxes that were home to sixteen birds in 2003 are mounted on some of the pilings close to shore.

Once you finish birding from the picnic area overlooking the old pilings, walk north along the paved walkway that parallels the railroad tracks. At the end of the pavement, if you continue north along the side of the railroad tracks and then follow a trail into the trees to the left, you will enter the mixed-forest habitat and have the chance to see Red-breasted Sapsucker, Pileated and Downy Woodpeckers, and other forest birds. Check the low shrubs for warblers during the summer, and watch the trees for Chestnut-backed Chickadees. The elderberry, snowberry, and Indian plum also can hold sparrows. Although it isn't a sure bet, it could pay to check the area for White-throated Sparrow in late fall and winter.

The third major habitat area at Titlow Park is the freshwater pond and intertidal area inside the grassy main section of the park. Belted Kingfisher are a common sight in this area, as are dabbling ducks—Northern Shoveler, Mallards, and others.

Given its easy-to-reach location, Titlow Park is a convenient spot to visit at different seasons throughout the year. Stop by in early summer to watch the arrival of Purple Martin, visit in fall to watch the Horned and Western Grebes return from their nesting season in other parts of the state, or check the waters over the narrows in winter to see hundreds of Bonaparte's Gulls flocking and feeding over the salt water.

PURPLE MARTINS

Once a commonly seen bird species in Washington, the deep purple and black hues of the Purple Martin are not as easily seen today. A series of well-known sites, such as Titlow Park, offer artificial nesting boxes that house many of the roughly 1,000 Purple Martins that come to Washington each spring. Titlow Beach is one of the state's oldest Purple Martin sites where nest boxes have been set up and maintained to encourage the largest of Washington's swallows to return each year after their long migration from South America.

During the last fifty to sixty years Purple Martin numbers have declined in Washington, mainly due to the competition from nonnative cavity nesting birds, especially European Starling and House Sparrows. The starling and sparrows set up nests in traditional Purple Martin nesting holes prior to the arrival of the martins in April and May. For this reason, volunteers coordinated by the Washington Department of Fish and Wildlife install and maintain nesting boxes along the shores of Puget Sound and on the shores of the Columbia River for Purple Martins. Besides the colony at Titlow Park, there are colonies on Vashon Island, on Shilshole Bay and the Duwamish River in Seattle, on Lake Sammamish, and at other locations northward in Puget Sound. Purple Martins still nest in natural nesting cavities on Fort Lewis and in the San Juan Islands.

Other key birds: Red-throated Loon; Horned, Pied-billed, Red-necked, and Western Grebes; Green Heron; Wood Duck; Gadwall; Green-winged, Blue-winged, and Cinnamon Teals; American and Eurasian Wigeons; Northern Pintail; Northern Shoveler; Lesser Scaup; Surf Scoter; Common Goldeneye; Bufflehead; Common, Red-breasted, and Hooded Mergansers; Turkey Vulture; Osprey; Merlin; Dunlin; Ring-billed and California Gulls; Caspian Tern; Downy and Hairy Woodpeckers; Olive-sided Flycatcher; Western Wood-Pewee; Warbling Vireo; Chestnut-backed Chickadee; Bushtit; Brown Creeper; Winter and Bewick's Wrens; Orange-crowned, Townsend's, Yellow, and Wilson's Warblers; Western Tanager; Fox, Savannah, Lincoln's, and Golden-crowned Sparrows; Black-headed Grosbeak.

Nearby opportunities: The Tacoma area offers a host of birding locations. Try Point Defiance Park in the north end of town for forest birds and Bald Eagle, or drive along Ruston Way at the south end of Commencement Bay in winter and early spring for waterfowl and gulls. Other possibilities include Swan Creek and the West Hylebos Wetlands State Park in nearby Federal Way.

Directions: From I-5, take the State Route 16 exit and head toward the Tacoma Narrows Bridge. Exit SR 16 at the Jackson Street exit and turn left at the end of the ramp, crossing back over the highway. In about a quarter of a mile, turn right onto Sixth Avenue. Follow this street to its conclusion at Titlow Beach.

DeLorme map grid: Page 62, C4.

Elevation: 20 feet.

Access: Some wheelchair-accessible trails.

Bathrooms: Yes.

Hazards: None.

Nearest food, gas, and lodging: Tacoma.

Nearest camping: Dash Point State Park.

For more information: Metro Parks Tacoma offers a Web site about Titlow Park at www.discoverparks.org/ns/index.cfm?fuse action=parkdetails&park_id=80.

Theler Wetlands

Habitats: Freshwater and tidal marshes, wetland, mixed forest, riparian, mudflats.

Specialty birds: Brant; Greater Scaup; Barrow's Goldeneye; Golden and Bald Eagles; Peregrine Falcon; Bonaparte's, Mew, and Western Gulls; Band-tailed Pigeon; Vaux's Swift; Anna's and Rufous Hummingbirds; Pileated Woodpecker; Red-breasted Sapsucker; Pacific-slope Flycatcher; Hutton's Vireo; Purple Martin.

Best times to bird: Year-round.

The Theler Wetlands area at the northeastern end of Hood Canal offers a mix of mudflats, lowland riparian, and wetland habitats. Walk the trails or venture onto the long boardwalk over the mudflats for views of Marsh Wrens, Great Blue Heron, and Northern Harriers hunting over the marsh.

About the site:

Water defines the Theler Wetlands. Bounded on two sides by the Union River and Hood Canal, the area is threaded with a combination freshwater ponds and forested wetlands on the upland side, tidal wetlands in the salt marsh, and an estuary at the mouth of the river. Artistic touches, including native plant gardens, carved totems, and other sculptures, enhance the wildlife experience. Interpretive trails and interactive displays offered at the educational center make Theler Wetlands one of the best places to introduce children to birding.

After passing through the arches of "Nature's Gate," the trail, flanked by a hand-built rock wall, winds down to a short expanse of boardwalk. This trail leads to the educational complex, which is surrounded with interpretive signs. You can pick up a trail guide and interpretive materials here and explore the hands-on exhibits, which are fun for adults as well as kids. The native gardens might inspire you to add some bird friendly plants to your garden. The remaining trails radiate from the center.

To avoid retracing your steps, start your tour by taking the Alder/Cedar Swamp Trail. You'll literally walk on top of the wetland on the innovative floating boardwalk. Forested wetlands like this are the closest things to the bayous of the south that we have in Washington, which reveals the real nature of our western red cedar trees—a true, water-loving cypress. The thick canopy of the tall cedars creates a quiet, dim atmosphere where birds are easily heard, even the scratching of Brown Creepers and wrens working around the trees. You can also find Hairy and Pileated Woodpeckers. The trail exits the woods at the dike that holds the salt water of the tidal marsh back from the freshwater marshes and forest.

Turn right to take the 1.5-mile one-way Union River Estuary Trail, the longest of the trails. Ponds created by the man-made dike host waterfowl, including Green-winged and Cinnamon Teal, Gadwalls, and Pied-Billed Grebes. Mallard ducklings trail behind their parents in the spring and summer, and Red-winged Blackbirds, Song Sparrows, and Marsh Wrens nest in the cattails. If you visit early in the morning, listen for Virginia Rails and look carefully among the reeds for Sora. Green Herons also visit the edges of the ponds. The trail passes by some old prune trees, where sparrows and finches typically hang out, and turns north at the mouth of the Union River. Check the river for mergansers and otters. On the other side of the trail, ducks, geese, and gulls sometimes roost on the private family farm. The trail splits near the end. One path ends in the woods, the other ends at an archaeological dig in a meadow.

Return to the dike trail and continue walking to the South Tidal Marsh Trail, a boardwalk that leads to the center of the tidal marsh near the edge of Hood Canal. On your way out, check the trees, willows, and other shrubs at the edge of the freshwater wetland for Evening Grosbeaks, Western Tanagers, and warblers, including Black-throated Gray Warblers and Common Yellowthroats. In the spring and summer, three types of swallows swoop and dive for insects; sometimes they fly so low here that they just skim the tips of the sedges. Great Blue Herons hunt

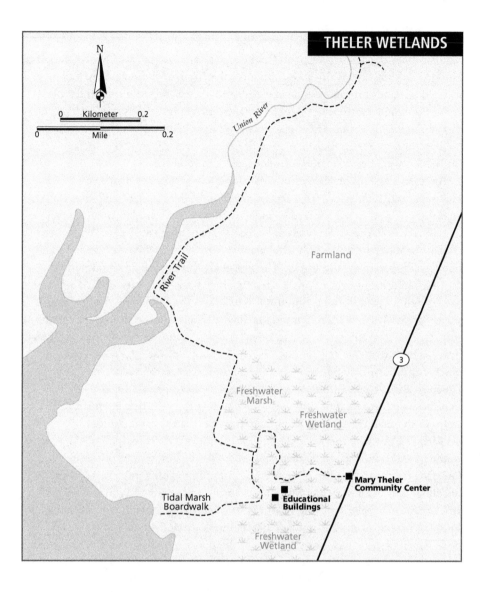

N

| 0 | Kilometer | 0.2 |
| 0 | Mile | 0.2 |

Union River

River Trail

Farmland

3

Freshwater
Marsh

Freshwater
Wetland

Mary Theler
Community Center

Tidal Marsh
Boardwalk

**Educational
Buildings**

Freshwater
Wetland

between the clumps of green, mousing at low tide and fishing at high tide, and Canada Geese nest in the drier portions. During migration and in the winter months, the end of the boardwalk as well as at the curve of river trail near the mouth of the river are the best places for you to set up your scope if you have one. Shorebirds, including yellowlegs, dowitchers, and a few species of sandpipers, forage on the mudflats of the bay and in the tidal marsh, while Brant, Horned and Western Grebes, all three scoters, and both goldeneyes and more ducks dive and forage on the bay.

A fourth trail, the short Sweetwater Creek Trail, displays the typical riparian habitat of the region with alders, sword ferns, and salmonberry. Walk quietly and listen for the scratching of wrens and thrushes nearby. To add to your experience, find out when you can join one of the summertime bat walks. The wetlands are open daily from dawn to dusk, and admission is free.

Other key birds: Horned, Pied-billed, and Western Grebes; Green Heron; Wood Duck; Gadwall; Green-winged Teal; American and Eurasian Wigeons; Northern Pintail; Northern Shoveler; Ring-necked Duck; Lesser Scaup; Black, White-winged, and Surf Scoters; Common Goldeneye; Bufflehead; Common, Red-breasted, and Hooded Mergansers; Turkey Vulture; Osprey; Merlin; Virginia Rail; Sora; Greater Yellowlegs; Dunlin; Western Sandpiper; Wilson's Snipe; Ring-billed and California Gulls; Caspian Tern; Northern Saw-whet Owl; Downy and Hairy Woodpeckers; Willow Flycatcher; Northern Shrike; Warbling Vireo; Chestnut-backed Chickadee; Bushtit; Brown Creeper; Winter, Bewick's, and Marsh Wrens; Swainson's, Hermit, and Varied Thrushes; Orange-crowned, Black-throated Gray, Townsend's, Yellow, MacGillivray's, and Wilson's Warblers; Common Yellowthroat; Western Tanager; Fox, Savannah, Lincoln's, White-throated, and Golden-crowned Sparrows; Black-headed Grosbeak; Purple Finch; Red Crossbill; Evening Grosbeak.

Nearby opportunities: Visit nearby Twanoh State Park, on the edge of Hood Canal, to see more waterbirds, gulls, and shorebirds. Tahuya State Forest hosts a rare blue butterfly as well as more woodland and neotropical passerines.

Directions: Take State Route 3 north from Shelton or south from the Kitsap Peninsula. Turn into the Theler Community Center parking lot, which is across the highway from Belfair Elementary School.

DeLorme map grid: Page 62, A2.

Elevation: 5 feet.

Access: Wheelchair-accessible trails and restrooms.

Bathrooms: At the education center.

Hazards: None.

Nearest food, gas, and lodging: Belfair.

Nearest camping: Belfair or Twanoh State Parks.

For more information: To download trail maps or find out what activities are taking place at the wetlands, visit the Hood Canal Project Center Web site at www.hctc.com/~hcwater.

19 Nisqually National Wildlife Refuge

Habitats: Mixed forest, riparian, mudflat, salt marsh, wetland.

Specialty birds: Common Loon; Pelagic and Brandt's Cormorants; Greater White-fronted Goose; Brant; Greater Scaup; Barrow's Goldeneye; Bald Eagle; Peregrine Falcon; Sandhill Crane; Black-bellied Plover; Baird's and Pectoral Sandpipers; Short-billed Dowitcher; Red-necked Phalarope; Bonaparte's, Mew, Thayer's, and Western Gulls; Common Murre; Pigeon Guillemot; Band-tailed Pigeon; Short-eared Owl; Vaux's Swift; Anna's and Rufous Hummingbirds; Pileated Woodpecker; Red-breasted Sapsucker; Pacific-slope Flycatcher; Hutton's and Cassin's Vireos; Purple Martin.

Best times to bird: Year-round.

The snow- and glacier-capped slopes of Mt. Rainier in the distance give life to the Nisqually River, which flows through the Nisqually National Wildlife Refuge to the largest estuary in the southern reaches of Puget Sound.

About the site:

As one of western Washington's most accessible wildlife refuges, the Nisqually National Wildlife Refuge is as close to a sure bet for good birding as you can get. The varied habitats along the Nisqually River and the tideflats host more than 200 bird species and, depending on the season, the refuge offers everything from waterfowl to glimpses of some of the west side's hard-to-find shorebirds.

All you need is a little knowledge and good walking shoes to bird along more than 7 miles of trails at the refuge, including boardwalks and dirt trails that top dikes that ring the refuge.

A wheelchair-accessible 1-mile boardwalk trail departs from the visitor center and offers looks at freshwater ponds, riparian areas alongside the ponds, and a viewing platform at the Twin Barns, which offers panoramic views of wetlands and open grassy fields. In spring and summer, be sure to watch the swallows that nest inside and under the eaves of the barns, and Band-tailed Pigeon can commonly be seen around the barns as well. Also spend some time looking over the fields to watch Northern Harrier and other raptors hunting.

This trail is a great opening act for exploring the refuge. Watch Wood Duck and Mallard with their young in the summer along the shores of the inner ponds, or look skyward for numerous Tree, Violet-green, Barn, and Northern Rough-winged Swallows that are common sights. Swainson's Thrush and many warblers and flycatchers can frequently be seen in the trees along the boardwalk as well. The boardwalk makes a loop back to the visitor center, with the option to depart and explore along the shore of the Nisqually River midway around the loop. If you have only a short time to explore Nisqually, this is a good introduction to the site.

To get the most of the birding opportunities at Nisqually, come prepared for more walking. From spring through early fall, the 5.5-mile Brown Farm Dike Trail offers the best the Nisqually Delta has to offer—extensive views of freshwater ponds, former farm fields, and berry brambles on the inner portion of the dike, and tidal lands, open beach, and saltwater marsh on the outer portions of the dike. Add views of the tideflats from a platform that overlooks Puget Sound and the waters leading north to Anderson Island and the Olympic Mountains and this is a must-see birding opportunity.

There are two starting points for the dike trail—either walk clockwise from the parking lot heading west toward McCallister Creek or walk counterclockwise toward the cottonwood-filled forest along the banks of the Nisqually River. Since the biggest birding highlights are often in the shallow ponds and wetlands between the visitor center and the creek, take a clockwise route—especially if there is standing water in the wetlands just west of the parking lot.

As you leave the parking lot, pay close attention to the sparrows and other birds along the edges of the brush. Savannah Sparrows are common here in spring, when they call from the tops of cattails and grasses. Farther down the gravel road

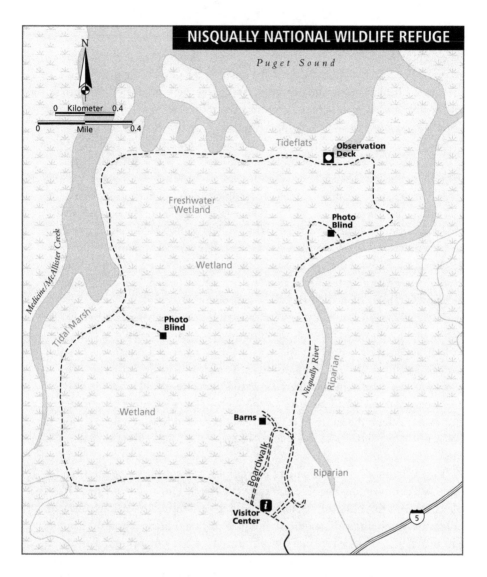

toward the creek, be sure to check the grass and any water remaining in the wetlands. In past years this area has hosted Wilson's Phalarope, Solitary and Baird's Sandpiper, and other hard-to-find shorebird species. On rare occasions these wetland ponds have also held bird species more common to eastern Washington, such as Black-necked Stilt. It pays to use a spotting scope to check all of the birds along these wetlands.

As the trail reaches the banks of McAllister Creek, it offers views of different habitat, a muddy area of saltwater tideflats where the creek empties into Puget Sound. This far-southern section of the refuge commonly offers great views of Great Blue Heron hunting and Bald Eagle perching in the Douglas fir trees that line the steep hillsides on the west bank of the creek.

The payoff for the long walk along the dike trail is a section closest to Puget Sound, where tideflats offer seasonal views of shorebirds during their spring and fall migrations. These tideflats offer glimpses of dowitchers, sandpipers, and plovers, and they can on rare occasions offer views of Long-billed Curlew and other shorebirds normally associated with the Washington coast. Also be sure to use a spotting scope to scan the waters of Puget Sound for sea ducks and alcids, as well as loons. The viewing platform helps you get a longer view over the tideflats and waters, so waiting for a turn to access the platform is worth the effort.

The last part of the trail loops back toward the visitor center, cutting across a dike that separates the Nisqually River from the inner wetlands. The cottonwood, alder, and willow trees can hold songbirds, and during a fall visit to the refuge we walked underneath a Great Horned Owl that patiently posed for photos along this section of the trail. During the spring and fall fish runs, you often can see salmon caught in Native American fishing nets in the river, and don't be surprised if you see a mink or other small mammals along the banks of the river. Just take your time and you never know what nature will unveil for your visit.

Before setting out on the 5.5-mile dike trail walk, make sure to have clothes, water, and food to stay comfortable during the long hike. Also keep in mind that there are no restrooms along the route. (Restrooms are at the visitor center only.)

The open fields at the Nisqually National Wildlife Refuge offer inviting habitat for Savannah Sparrows.

FROM TIDEFLATS TO FARM AND BACK AGAIN

After serving for centuries as a gathering place for Native American tribes at the mouth of the Nisqually River, settlers moved into the Nisqually tide-flats area and converted huge tracts of the land from saltwater marsh to seasonal farm fields. Throughout much of the twentieth century, the Nisqually National Wildlife Refuge was the site of a series of farms, culminating with Brown Farm, which sent produce and milk to growing communities in the surrounding area, including Olympia and Tacoma. In the 1960s and 1970s, conservationists rallied to preserve the Nisqually tideflats area, which led to the establishment of the refuge in 1974. Since that time the old farming dikes that kept saltwater from Puget Sound from infiltrating into the freshwater wetlands and farm fields have been left largely intact. That is about to change, with a new management plan for the refuge calling for breaking a number of dikes and allowing the tideflats to return to a more natural state that would benefit salmon with more intertidal habitat. The plan was still in transition as we went to press with this book.

Besides the history of the Nisqually flats as a farming area, it is also the site of a major happening in Washington state history—the signing of the Medicine Creek Treaty in 1854. The treaty, promoted by territorial governor and superintendent of Indian Affairs Isaac Stevens, stated that the heads of the Nisqually, Puyallup, Steilacoom, Squawksin, S'Homamish, Stehchass, T'Peeksin, Squi-aitl, and Sa-heh-wamish Tribes would relinquish huge tracks of land—more than 2.5 million acres—to the United States while retaining fishing and hunting rights in all of their accustomed grounds. The treaty was signed along the shores of Medicine Creek, which has since been renamed as McCallister Creek.

Other key birds: Red-throated Loon; Horned, Eared, Pied-billed, Red-necked, and Western Grebes; American Bittern; Green Heron; Wood Duck; Gadwall; Green-winged, Blue-winged, and Cinnamon Teals; American and Eurasian Wigeons; Northern Pintail; Northern Shoveler; Canvasback; Ring-necked Duck; Lesser Scaup; White-winged and Surf Scoters; Common Goldeneye; Bufflehead; Common, Red-breasted, and Hooded Mergansers; Ruddy Duck; Turkey Vulture; Osprey; Rough-legged Hawk; Merlin; Virgina Rail; Sora; Semi-palmated Plover; Greater and Lesser Yel-lowlegs; Spotted Sandpiper; Sanderling; Dunlin; Western and Least Sandpipers; Long-billed Dowitcher; Wilson's Snipe; Ring-billed and California Gulls; Caspian Tern; Western Screech-Owl; Common Nighthawk; Downy and Hairy Woodpeckers; Olive-sided Flycatcher; Western Wood-Pewee; Willow Flycatcher; Northern Shrike; Warbling Vireo; Chestnut-backed Chickadee; Bushtit; Brown Creeper; House, Winter, Bewick's, and Marsh Wrens; Townsend's Solitaire; Swainson's, Hermit, and Varied Thrushes; American Pipit; Orange-crowned, Black-throated Gray, Townsend's,

Yellow, MacGillivray's, and Wilson's Warblers; Common Yellowthroat; Western Tanager; Chipping, Fox, Savannah, Lincoln's, White-throated, and Golden-crowned Sparrows; Black-headed Grosbeak; Lazuli Bunting; Bullock's Oriole; Purple Finch; Red Crossbill; Evening Grosbeak.

Nearby opportunities: Tolmie State Park.

Directions: From Interstate 5, take the Nisqually exit 114 and follow the signs to Brown Farm Road for the Nisqually National Wildlife Refuge, which is just north of the highway.

DeLorme map grid: Page 62, D3.

Elevation: 20 feet.

Access: Portions of the boardwalk trail are wheelchair accessible.

Bathrooms: Wheelchair-accessible restrooms at the visitors center.

Hazards: None.

Nearest food, gas, and lodging: Nisqually for food and gas, and Lacey for lodging.

Nearest camping: Millersylvania State Park off the Maytown exit south of Olympia.

For more information: Check the refuge's official Web site at nisqually.fws.gov, or you can call (360) 753-9467. Written inquiries can be sent to the Nisqually NWR, 100 Brown Farm Road, Olympia, WA 98516. Admission to the Nisqually NWR costs $3.00 per family for each visit.

Southwest

The Southwest Region of Washington features some of the most popular birding sites in the state, from the sandy beaches at the Willapa Bay National Wildlife Refuge to the easily accessible auto tour route at the Ridgefield National Wildlife Refuge near Vancouver. Like much of western Washington, water defines this region, which features one of the major stopovers for migrating shorebirds in Grays Harbor.

The northern edge of Grays Harbor marks the northern boundary of the region, the Pacific Ocean marks the western boundary, and the Columbia River marks the southern boundary. The western foothills of the Cascade Mountains are the eastern edge of the region. In between these boundaries are rolling second-growth forests in the Capitol Forest and the Willapa Hills, and one of the few remaining prairie habitats in western Washington at the Mima Mounds Natural Area Preserve south of Olympia.

Southwest Washington offers some of the best chances to see bird species that are more common to the south in Oregon. Among the recent arrivals are Black Phoebes, White-tailed Kites, and Red-shouldered Hawks. This region also offers viewing large numbers of impressive migrating birds such as Sandhill Cranes in the spring and fall.

The southwest is also the land of Lewis and Clark. This duo and their Corps of Discovery made stops near many of the sites on the Columbia River, including Ridgefield National Wildlife Refuge, the Julia Butler Hansen Refuge for the Columbian White-tailed Deer, and Cape Disappointment.

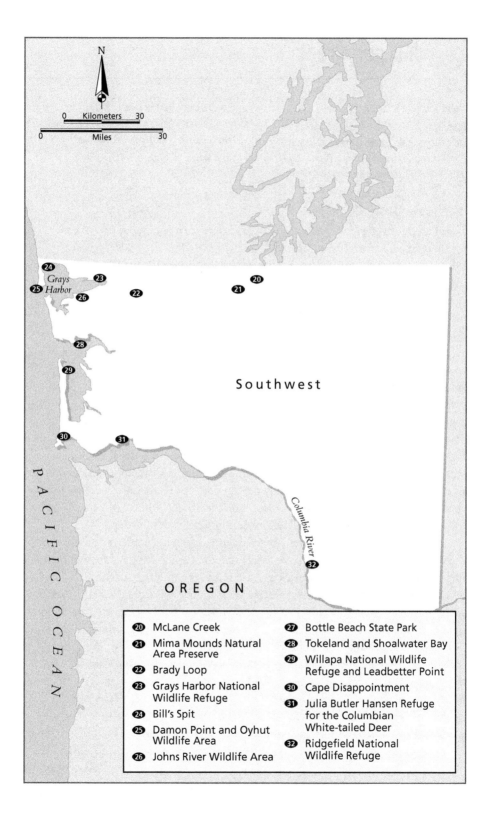

N

0 Kilometers 30
0 Miles 30

24 Grays
25 Harbor
26
23
22
20
21

28

29

Southwest

30
31

Columbia River

32

PACIFIC OCEAN

OREGON

20 McLane Creek		**27** Bottle Beach State Park
21 Mima Mounds Natural Area Preserve		**28** Tokeland and Shoalwater Bay
22 Brady Loop		**29** Willapa National Wildlife Refuge and Leadbetter Point
23 Grays Harbor National Wildlife Refuge		**30** Cape Disappointment
24 Bill's Spit		**31** Julia Butler Hansen Refuge for the Columbian White-tailed Deer
25 Damon Point and Oyhut Wildlife Area		**32** Ridgefield National Wildlife Refuge
26 Johns River Wildlife Area		

20 McLane Creek

Habitats: Mixed forest, riparian.

Specialty birds: Greater Scaup; Barrow's Goldeneye; Bald Eagle; Peregrine Falcon; Band-tailed Pigeon; Northern Pygmy-Owl; Vaux's Swift; Rufous Hummingbird; Pileated Woodpecker; Red-breasted Sapsucker; Hammond's and Pacific-slope Flycatchers; Hutton's and Cassin's Vireos; Hermit Warbler.

Best times to bird: Year-round.

About the site:

If you are looking for a way to combine birding with a family outing, McLane Creek is an attractive place to make the most of both. The site on the outskirts of Olympia offers a 1.1-mile and a .5-mile, wheelchair-accessible trail along with viewing platforms that reach out across beaver ponds that cater not only to birds but also to turtles, rough-skinned newts, and frogs. Add a tunnel that cuts underneath the roots of a cedar tree in the middle of the 1.1-mile trail and this is a natural playground for kids and adults.

Two loop trails start from the parking lot. Walk west toward the site's restrooms and follow the signs as the trails start by dropping down toward the largest of the site's beaver ponds. As you explore from the pair of viewing platforms that jut out over the pond, watch for ducks and listen for Red-winged Blackbirds. The pond also can hold geese and mergansers, and during the spring migration and nesting season you often can see Common Yellowthroat and other warblers hunting for bugs in the low-lying brush at the pond's edge. Watch for movement in the tops of the trees, where Red-breasted Sapsuckers can be seen feeding on insects and pecking sap holes in tree trunks. Also be sure to look down and under the pond's surface to see rough-skinned newts swimming along the bottom and leaving telltale bubbles gurgling to the pond's surface as they forage. The newts are most active in spring.

After crossing a boardwalk over part of the pond, the trail comes to a fork, with the 0.6-mile trail veering right along a flat path and the longer 1.1-mile trail continuing straight on a narrow boardwalk that leads into the fir and hemlock forest along a hillside. The shorter trail follows the path of a logging railroad that ran through the McLane Creek site in the early 1900s. The railroad was built by the Mud Bay Logging Company, and it carried logs from logging camps in the ghost town of Bordeaux to the south and from another camp higher in the hills west of the nature trails, deep in the heart of what today is the Capitol Forest. McLane Creek is part of the Capitol Forest, maintained by the Washington Department of Natural Resources. Today the railroad grade offers a shortcut to the other side of the beaver pond.

For the best birding opportunities, take the boardwalk for the 1.1-mile trail and start exploring among the second-growth cedar, fir, maple, and hemlock trees that have grown up since the area was logged. Notice how trees have taken root and risen from the stumps of older trees, and in some areas how the cedar trees have sent roots

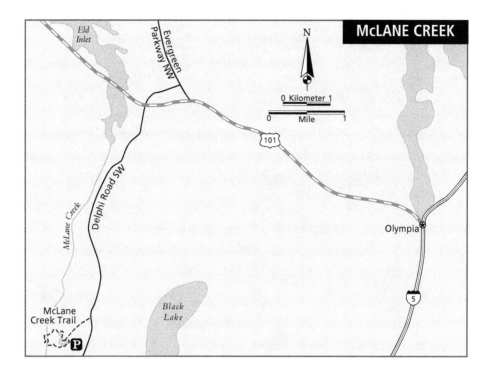

down the sides of the old stump and into the surrounding soil. This is how the natural tunnel underneath a cedar tree farther along the trail was formed.

The trail leaves the flat, grassy areas in the lowlands along the ponds for a mixed-forest habitat that offers glimpses of Winter Wren, Spotted Towhee, Varied Thrush, and woodpeckers. Stop every now and then along the trail to listen for bird calls and movement, since you are more likely to hear a bird in this habitat than to suddenly see it. Also look at the sides of tree trunks for Brown Creeper, chickadees, and nuthatches. As the trail approaches McLane Creek, be sure to avoid bumping into Devil's club—the tall, formidable-looking thorny plant that can reach up to 8 feet tall in this part of the undergrowth. Closer to the ground, ferns—bracken, maiden, deer, and licorice—are common, and during the spring there are violets, bleeding heart, wild lily of the valley, and fringe cup blooming wherever enough sunlight reaches the ground.

As the trail continues, twice crossing the creek and going under the natural tree tunnel before starting to head back downhill to the beaver ponds, pay close attention to dead trees and snags that are prime feeding areas for Downy and Pileated Woodpecker. Depending on the time of year, you also may see a number of butterflies working the blooms in the undergrowth.

The two trails merge again at a bridge that spans one of the site's beaver dams. This is a turnaround point for wheelchair users who took the 0.6-mile trail, and others can continue along the north side of the beaver ponds and back toward the parking lot.

SO THAT'S WHY THEY CALL THEM BUSY BEAVERS

The creation of the ponds at the McLane Creek Nature Trail can be credited to a family of beaver that spends its nights building and rebuilding dams with tree branches, grasses, and mud. Signs of the beavers' work are obvious around the pond—recently fallen trees that have been chewed down by their sharp teeth, and the beaver dams themselves that can be seen in the northwest corner of the main pond where one dam is right alongside the trail and a secondary dam is just below on the other side of the wooden boardwalk.

Although signs of the beaver are all around the site, don't expect to see a beaver unless you visit early in the morning or around dusk. Beaver are nocturnal, so much of their handiwork takes place under the cover of darkness. Luckily for birders, the times when beaver are most likely to be seen each day are right before the birds wake and become most active in the morning and right after the birds settle down in their nightly perches for the night. Beaver ponds can be found in other locations around southwest Washington, including a number of dams on streams elsewhere in the Capitol Forest.

Other key birds: Pied-billed Grebe; Green Heron; Wood Duck; Gadwall; Green-winged Teal; American Wigeon; Northern Shoveler; Ring-necked Duck; Lesser Scaup; Common and Hooded Mergansers; Turkey Vulture; Osprey; Merlin; Virginia Rail; Sora; Western Screech- and Northern Saw-whet Owls; Downy and Hairy Woodpeckers; Olive-sided Flycatcher; Western Wood-Pewee; Willow Flycatcher; Warbling Vireo; Chestnut-backed Chickadee; Bushtit; Brown Creeper; Winter, Bewick's, and Marsh Wrens; Townsend's Solitaire; Swainson's, Hermit, and Varied Thrushes; Orange-crowned, Black-throated Gray, Yellow, MacGillivray's, and Wilson's Warblers; Common Yellowthroat; Western Tanager; Fox, Lincoln's, and Golden-crowned Sparrows; Black-headed Grosbeak; Bullock's Oriole; Purple Finch; Red Crossbill; Evening Grosbeak.

Nearby opportunities: Black Lake holds a wealth of ducks, geese, and other waterfowl.

Directions: From I-5, take U.S. Highway 101 west to the Mud Bay exit. At the end of the off-ramp, turn left and head southbound on Delphi Road for 3.3 miles. The entrance to the site is on the right. Drive 0.4 mile to the end of the road to park at the trailhead.

DeLorme map grid: Page 61, D8.

Elevation: 150 feet.

Access: Portions of the boardwalk trail are wheelchair accessible.

Bathrooms: Wheelchair accessible restrooms at the trailhead.

Hazards: Slippery boardwalk in some areas during the rainy season. Also avoid walking the trails in strong winds to avoid falling limbs.

Nearest food, gas, and lodging: Olympia or Tumwater.

Nearest camping: Multiple seasonal campgrounds in the Capitol Forest, or Black Lake RV Park.

For more information: Washington Department of Natural Resources, (800) 527-3305 or www.wa.gov/dnr/base/dnrhome.html.

Mima Mounds Natural Area Preserve

Habitats: Prairie, coniferous forest.

Specialty birds: White-tailed Kite; Bald Eagle; Peregrine Falcon; Band-tailed Pigeon; Short-eared and Northern Pgymy-Owls; Vaux's Swift; Rufous Hummingbird; Pileated Woodpecker; Red-breasted Sapsucker; Pacific-slope Fly-catcher; Hutton's and Cassin's Vireos; Western Bluebird; Hermit Warbler.

Best times to bird: Spring and fall migrations, winter for raptors. Summer months are best for wildflowers and butterflies.

The odd terrain at the Mima Mounds Natural Area near Olympia is most pronounced in the evening sunshine. Watch for Northern Harriers flying among the mounds or a glimpse of a White-tailed Kite hunting in the distance as the day fades to night.

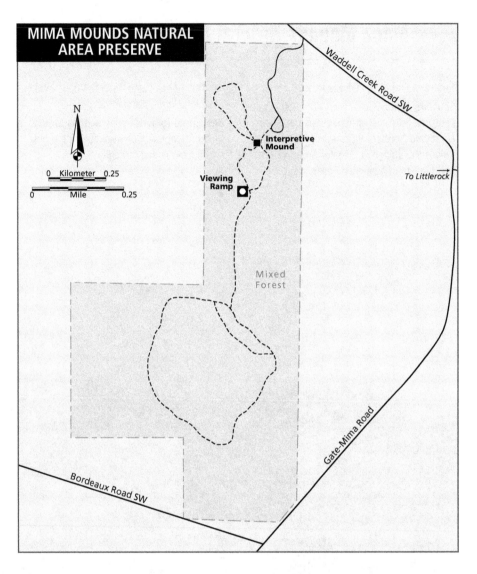

MIMA MOUNDS NATURAL
AREA PRESERVE

N

0   Kilometer   0.25

0   Mile   0.25

Waddell Creek Road SW

Interpretive
Mound

Viewing
Ramp

To Littlerock

Mixed
Forest

Gate-Mima Road

Bordeaux Road SW

About the site:

One of the few native grassland prairies left in western Washington is contained in the 445-acre Mima Mounds Natural Area Preserve. This prairie and the mysterious origins of the roughly 6-foot-tall mounds are enough to draw thousands of annual visitors to this small preserve, but it also holds some of the best birding, butterfly-watching, and wildflower gazing in the southern reaches of the Puget Trough. You'll find interesting birding year-round at the Mima Mounds, though the interest peaks in the late spring and early summer when migrating passerines make their way through the area and the wildflowers start to open in all of their glory. For a quick visit to the preserve, park at the end of the access road and walk through the Douglas fir and vine maple forested area at the eastern edge of the preserve. Listen carefully in this wooded area to see if you can locate woodpeckers and flickers as well as nuthatches, chickadees, and Brown Creeper. After a short walk through the wooded area, the trail leads to a large man-made concrete mound that offers information about the site as well as a viewing platform at the top of the stairs. Scanning the prairie from the top of the stairs will give a good indication of what birds are around before you set out on either the 0.5-mile interpretive trail or one of the longer and more rustic trails into the prairie.

Another good place to scan the terrain for interesting birds is from the viewing ramp (wheelchair-accessible) at the midpoint of the interpretive trail. During a spring visit to the preserve, we watched a relatively rare White-tailed Kite hunting over the mounds at the western edge of the preserve while we were on the viewing platform. Small birds can be hard to see on this pimpled prairie, so be sure to listen carefully and use all of your senses to locate birds. The metallic rattling call of a Ring-necked Pheasant or the piercing cry of a Red-tailed Hawk can turn a slow day at the preserve into a much more interesting one.

From the viewing platform, the interpretive trail turns back into the woods while a more rustic route winds off to the south among the mounds. If you have time, be sure to take one of these side trails, which offer a chance to get away from other people and to fully experience the Mima Mounds environment with its wildflowers such as the protected White Camas, native prairie grasses, and wide variety of mosses and lichens that grow on the sides of the rocky mounds. And for a special treat, time your visit to be among the mounds just before dusk for a chance to see a Northern Harrier pass just a few feet overhead as it hunts and winds in between the mounds.

THE PIMPLED PRAIRIE

Mounded prairies around the world are known as Mima Mounds. The prairie was first spotted by European eyes during the Charles Wilkes expedition in 1841, and it has been a source of constant debate since its discovery. Explanations for the origin of the mounds vary from myths of giant pocket gophers to Native American burial grounds and even to seismic reasons for the formation of the mounds. Geologists still cannot agree on the mechanism that caused the rocky mounds that sit on a glacial outwash plain.

The Mima Mounds Natural Area Preserve is listed by the Washington State Audubon Society as an Important Birding Area.

Other key birds: Turkey Vulture; Merlin; Ruffed Grouse; Western Screech- and Northern Saw-whet Owls; Downy and Hairy Woodpeckers; Western Wood-Pewee; Willow Flycatcher; Northern Shrike; Warbling Vireo; Western Scrub-Jay; Brown Creeper; House, Winter, and Bewick's Wrens; Townsend's Solitaire; Swainson's, Hermit, and Varied Thrushes; Orange-crowned, Black-throated Gray, Yellow, MacGillivray's, and Wilson's Warblers; Western Tanager; Chipping, Fox, Savannah, Lincoln's, and Golden-crowned Sparrows; Black-headed Grosbeak; Lazuli Bunting; Bullock's Oriole; Purple Finch; Red Crossbill; Evening Grosbeak.

Nearby opportunities: Scatter Creek is an area managed by the Washington Department of Fisheries and Wildlife for hunting alongside I-5, but it also offers birding opportunities as well as glimpses of more prairie butterfly species. Also nearby are the Black River wetlands, part of a yet-to-be-developed national wildlife refuge.

Directions: From I-5, take the Maytown exit and drive west, following the signs to Littlerock. Continue straight on Gate-Mima Road through Littlerock, then turn right onto Waddell Creek Road at the top of a small hill west of town. The entrance to the natural area is on the left in 1 mile.

DeLorme map grid: Page 45, A8.

Elevation: 10 feet.

Access: Loop trail and ramp to an observation deck, as well as accessible bathrooms.

Bathrooms: Yes.

Hazards: None.

Nearest food, gas, and lodging: Littlerock (food and gas), Tumwater (lodging).

Nearest camping: Capitol State Forest, Mima Falls Campground.

For more information: Washington Department of Natural Resources, (800) 527-3305 or www.wa.gov/dnr/base/dnrhome.html.

Brady Loop

Habitats: Lowland riparian, wetlands, agricultural fields.

Specialty birds: Tundra and Trumpeter Swans; Greater White-fronted Goose; White-tailed Kite; Bald Eagle; Peregrine Falcon; Sandhill Crane; Black-bellied, American, and Pacific Golden-Plovers; Willet; Short-billed Dowitcher; Bonaparte's, Mew, and Western Gulls; Band-tailed Pigeon; Short-eared Owl; Vaux's Swift; Anna's and Rufous Hummingbirds; Pileated Woodpecker; Red-breasted Sapsucker; Hutton's Vireo.

Best times to bird: Spring and fall for migrating waterfowl, winter for overwintering waterfowl

About the site:

To the uneducated eye, the land circled by Brady Loop looks like yet another typical series of agricultural fields. To the bird-watcher, however, the area around Brady Loop is a big playground, especially during fall migration, winter, and early spring. This valley was once inundated with water as the glacial floods of the last ice age sped toward the Pacific Ocean. Since then, the rivers that bound the valley have repeatedly deposited silt as they cut across it. When farmers began settling the area, they turned riparian wetlands into agricultural fields edged with shrubby riparian habitat. During the winter months, the fields turn into a giant, seasonal wetland. The rains that start in fall and carry on through spring chase the farmers inside as their fields flood. Shallow pools and ponds created by the gathering rainwater and the mucky stubble left in the fields attract waterfowl and shorebirds. Hedgerows, shrubs, and riparian habitat edging the Chehalis River attract migrating songbirds. The birds, of course, attract bird-watchers.

Brady Loop Road takes a circuitous loop through farmland that sits in a narrow valley bounded by three rivers—the Satsop to the east, the Chehalis to the south, and the Wynoochee to the west. The seven-mile loop is easily accessible from State Route 23, which leads to the coast. The convenience makes this a must-see side-trip for anyone heading to Grays Harbor, Ocean Shores, or the Olympic Peninsula. We generally travel the loop in a clockwise direction by heading south on Monte-Brady Road, which turns into Brady Loop Road, after exiting the highway.

Early spring visitors will be greeted by rows of blooming daffodils and tulips, which give way to rows of potatoes, field corn, and other vegetables as the season progresses. Keep a look out along the hedgerows for grouse and ring-necked pheasant. On fence posts, utility poles, and the edges of the trees often serve as perches for raptors, Short-eared Owls, and Northern Shrikes. Western Meadowlark occasionally sing in these fields and draw the attention of birders. Calling American Pipits also draw birdwatcher's eyes to the skies as small flocks of these sometimes winter residents and migrants fly overhead.

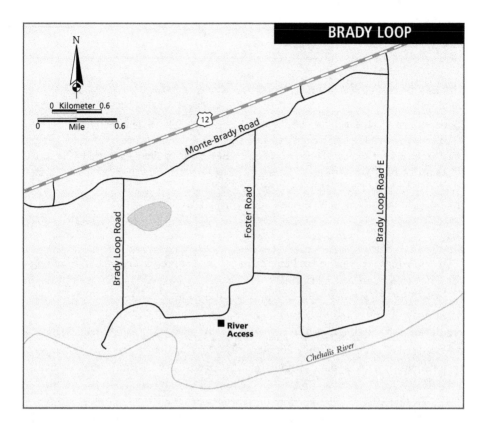

Take a detour from the loop by driving along Foster Road, halfway around the loop, for an opportunity to see more raptors, possibly even Peregrine Falcons that come for the ducks. Depending on the day, you'll find everything from Northern Shoveler, Canvasback, and Green-winged and Cinnamon Teals to Bufflehead, Northern Pintail, and American and Eurasian Wigeons. Check the edges of the ponds, the shallow mud, and wet grasses for the shorebirds. If you check the flocks carefully, you might find a surprise or two. Scopes are a must on the loop if you want to distinguish the brownish back of the handful of Pacific Golden-Plovers hidden in the larger flock of Black-bellied Plovers or the occasional Short-billed Dowitcher among the Long-billed. You'll also find a plethora of Western Sandpipers mixed with Least Sandpipers and Dunlin, with, perhaps a Whimbrel thrown in for spice. Look along the edges of the fields and in the emergent vegetation around the ponds, and listen carefully, to spot skulking Green Heron, American Bittern, Sora, Virginia Rail, and Wilson's Snipe.

Take sturdy shoes or hiking boots if you plan to walk to the edge of the Chehalis River. The trail is not marked but starts behind the pit toilet and runs along a fence line. We advise caution as the trail can be slippery with sucking mud after a few good rains. During migration, you'll have a good chance of seeing migrating warblers, including Black-throated Gray Warblers. Spotted Towhees and thrushes also like the thick shrubs here. At the loop's southwest corner, the road curves around Moo Slough and a thick stand of alder and willow. Pull well off the road here to check the trees for more songbirds and woodpeckers. If you're timing is good, you may be able to see Hairy, Downy, and Pileated Woodpeckers practically within spitting distance of each other. Check this area as well as the trees along the river access for Red-breasted Sapsucker, Western Wood-Peewee, Bewick's Wren, Fox Sparrow, and flycatchers.

The west end of the loop is one of the few places in the state where the Red-shouldered Hawk has been glimpsed. You will be more likely to see other hawks as well as Bald Eagles hunting amidst the trees to the west side of the road at this end of the loop. In winter, look to the wetland and pond on the east side of the road for Tundra and Trumpeter Swans as well as the ubiquitous flock of Canada Geese. Evening Grosbeak have been seen regularly in the fir and alder trees on the north side of the loop, and Scrub Jays sometimes sit on the wires near the farmhouses on the loop. During spring and fall migration, keep your ears open for the *whoop* of passing Sandhill Cranes and the *krek* of Caspian Terns. Osprey nest around Winslow slough and the surrounding area and hunt in the rivers and slough, and the alert birder will see them flying over the fields on their way to fish for dinner.

Locals are used to seeing bird-watchers pulled off to the side of the road armed with binoculars and spotting scopes, however, remember to respect their privacy and to stay off the fields unless given permission. Some of the fields are open to hunting during the season.

Other key birds: American Bittern; Green Heron; Wood Duck; Gadwall; Green-winged Teal; American and Eurasian Wigeons; Northern Pintail; Northern Shoveler; Canvasback; Ring-necked Duck; Common Goldeneye; Bufflehead; Common and Hooded Mergansers; Turkey Vulture; Osprey; Rough-legged Hawk; Merlin; Virginia Rail; Semipalmated Plover; Greater and Lesser Yellowlegs; Dunlin; Western and Least Sandpipers; Long-billed Dowitcher; Wilson's Snipe; Ring-billed, California, and Herring Gulls; Caspian Tern; Downy and Hairy Woodpeckers; Olive-sided Flycatcher; Western Wood-Pewee; Willow Flycatcher; Northern Shrike; Warbling Vireo; Western Scrub-Jay; Chestnut-backed Chickadee; Bushtit; Brown Creeper; Winter and Bewick's Wrens; Swainson's, Hermit, and Varied Thrushes; American Pipit; Orange-crowned, Black-throated Gray, Yellow, and Wilson's Warblers; Common Yellowthroat; Western Tanager; Fox, Savannah, Lincoln's, and Golden-crowned Sparrows; Lapland Longspur; Black-headed Grosbeak; Bullock's Oriole; Purple Finch; Evening Grosbeak.

Nearby opportunities: Lake Sylvia State Park.

Directions: From State Road 12, turn south onto Middle Satsop Road, opposite the sign for Lake Sylvia State Park. Follow Middle Satsop Road the short distance to Monte Brady Road, where you will see a wood sign marking the loop. Turn left onto Monte Brady Road and follow it until it curves to the south and turns into Brady Loop Road. Brady Loop Road more or less parallels the Chehalis River. You can truncate the loop by turning north onto Foster Road, which will lead you back to Monte Brady Road, but we suggest you stay on Brady Loop Road as it turns north and meets Monte

Brady Road. Turn right onto Monte Brady Road. At this point you may want to extend your trip by turning south onto Foster Road and then backtracking along Brady Loop Road, or you may choose to simply close the loop and head back along Monte Brady Road to Middle Satsop Road and SR 12.

DeLorme map grid: Page 44, A3.

Elevation: 10 feet.

Access: The river trail is not wheelchair acces-

sible, but the loop is best seen by car.

Bathrooms: Outhouse at river access.

Hazards: Water over the road; watch for farm machinery and cyclists.

Nearest food, gas, and lodging: Montesano or Aberdeen.

Nearest camping: Lake Sylvia State Park.

For more information: Grays Harbor Audubon Society at www.ghas.org.

Grays Harbor National Wildlife Refuge

Habitats: Mixed forest, mudflat, salt marsh.

Specialty birds: Common Loon; Brown Pelican; Pelagic and Brandt's Cormorants; Greater White-fronted Goose; Greater Scaup; Barrow's Goldeneye; Bald Eagle; Peregrine Falcon; Black-bellied Plover; Willet; Wandering Tattler; Marbled Godwit; Red Knot; Baird's and Pectoral Sandpipers; Short-billed Dowitcher; Red-necked Phalarope; Heerman's, Bonaparte's, Mew, and Western Gulls; Common Murre; Band-tailed Pigeon; Vaux's Swift; Anna's and Rufous Hummingbirds; Pileated Woodpecker; Red-breasted Sapsucker; Hutton's Vireo.

Best times to bird: Year-round.

About the site:

Despite its stature as one of the four largest shorebird staging areas in North America, the Grays Harbor National Wildlife Refuge wasn't established until 1990. The refuge designation saved nearly 1,500 acres of the best tidal feeding areas on the West Coast from potential development as an industrial park, much to the benefit of hundreds of thousands of shorebirds and thousands of birders who flock to the area each spring to view the migration.

The refuge on Bowerman Basin features a number of habitats—mudflats that serve as the last area flooded at high tide and the first exposed to hungry shorebirds as the tide recedes, freshwater wetlands and a salt marsh that cater to dabbling ducks, and a grove of red alder that caters to songbirds. And right next door to the refuge is one of the most productive sewage-treatment ponds in the state, where rare shorebirds and hard-to-find waterfowl settle for days at a time before moving on in their migrations.

The best way to get an overview of the refuge is to find a parking spot near the airport cafe and walk around the gate on Airport Way en route to the Sandpiper Trail boardwalk. The walk from the parking area to the farthest tip of the trail is 2 miles round-trip, and along the way you get some of the best views of shorebird habitat on the West Coast.

As you walk along the paved roadway that is part of the Bowerman Airfield, pay close attention to the low-lying shrubs to the north where hummingbirds, vireos, and flycatchers can be seen in the late spring and summer. We also have seen warblers and Northern Flicker working the bushes for insects.

After walking through the airport property, you reach the payoff for the paved walk—a wide boardwalk with viewing platforms and outdoor binoculars that offer close-up views of shorebirds when the tide pushes them up into the shallow mudflats. The Sandpiper Trail heads west alongside the airstrip and toward the end of the peninsula that separates the refuge from the open bay, then turns north to make a loop with even closer views of the tideflats. The key to seeing shorebirds here is timing—for the best birding, note the time of the high tide and plan your trip for the two hours before and the two hours after high tide. When the migration

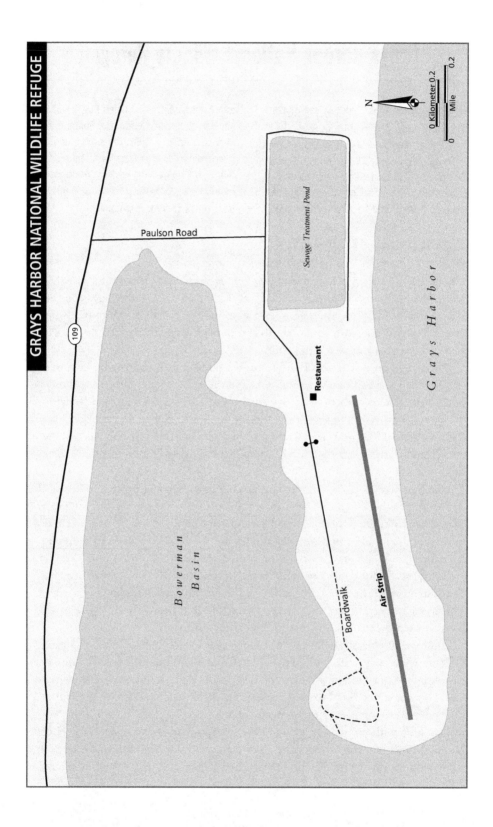

GRAYS HARBOR NATIONAL WILDLIFE REFUGE

109

Paulson Road

Bowerman Basin

Sewage Treatment Pond

Restaurant

Boardwalk

Air Strip

Grays Harbor

N

0 Kilometer 0.2

0 Mile 0.2

is at its peak, that timing will bring hundreds and sometimes thousands of Western Sandpiper, fewer numbers of Least Sandpiper, and many of the Dunlin and Sanderling up into the mudflats for close viewing. As an added bonus, the presence of the shorebirds also draws raptors—Peregrine Falcon, Bald Eagle, and Merlin among other birds of prey—to take their best shot at catching a well-fed shorebird. When the raptors arrive, the real spectacle of shorebird-watching happens as shorebirds of all species rise in one mass and form tight, undulating formations as they work together to fend off their hunters. If the raptor isn't initially successful, it will usually fly away dejectedly to a nearby perch to try again later, leaving the shorebirds to settle down to feed.

Red-breasted Sapsucker and other woodpeckers are most likely to be seen in the section of the boardwalk that winds between an alder grove; also pay close attention to what is blooming in this area. Elderberry and salmonberry are prevalent and could be great candidates for hummingbirds looking to feed on an early spring afternoon. Also watch the trees for tiny moss- and lichen-laden nests created by the hummingbirds.

If you don't happen to time your visit to the refuge around the tides, the next best bet is to bird the area around the Hoquiam Sewer Ponds. The large pond is known to hold some of the best birds in the state from time to time, offering glimpses of Pectoral and Solitary Sandpipers, Long-billed Curlew, and other shorebirds in addition to providing some of the best duck-watching habitat in the state. Especially in the fall and winter months, the pond is a great stop for duck-watching. Just drive Airport Way alongside the north side of the pond, stopping now and then to view ducks and any shorebirds gathered in the grass in the west end of the pond. Also be sure to drive the road on the other side of the pond, which offers views with Grays Harbor on the south side and the sewer pond on the north side. It is advisable to get out of the car and use a spotting scope to look at the reeds in the west end of the pond for any secretive shorebirds, but be sure to stay outside any fenced areas unless you obtain permission to venture onto the site.

Other key birds: Red-throated Loon; Horned, Eared, Pied-billed, Red-necked, and Western Grebes; American Bittern; Green Heron; Wood Duck; Gadwall; Green-winged, Blue-winged, and Cinnamon Teals; American and Eurasian Wigeons; Northern Pintail; Northern Shoveler; Canvasback; Ring-necked Duck; Lesser Scaup; Black, White-winged, and Surf Scoters; Common Goldeneye; Bufflehead; Common, Red-breasted, and Hooded Mergansers; Ruddy Duck; Turkey Vulture; Osprey; Merlin; Semipalmated Plover; Greater Yellowlegs; Spotted Sandpiper; Whimbrel; Sanderling; Dunlin; Western and Least Sandpipers; Parasitic Jaeger; Ring-billed, California, and Herring Gulls; Caspian Tern; Downy and Hairy Woodpeckers; Willow Flycatcher; Northern Shrike; Warbling Vireo; Chestnut-backed Chickadee; Bushtit; Brown Creeper; Winter, Bewick's, and Marsh Wrens; Orange-crowned, Black-throated Gray, Yellow, and Wilson's Warblers; Common Yellowthroat; Western Tanager; Fox, Savannah, Lincoln's, White-throated, and Golden-crowned Sparrows; Lapland Longspur; Black-headed Grosbeak; Bullock's Oriole; Red Crossbill; Evening Grosbeak.

Nearby opportunities: The Olympic Wildlife Area north of Aberdeen and Hoquiam on Wishkah Road.

Directions: Take State Route 109 west out of Hoquiam until you reach Paulson Road. A large refuge sign offers a cue to turn left onto Paulson Road. The refuge is to the right of the road. Take a right turn at the end of Paulson Road onto Airport Way and find parking near the gate and interpretive sign. Walk around the gate to the Sandpiper Trail. You can bird around the Hoquiam Sewer Pond as well at the end of Paulson Road. Pay attention to NO TRESPASSING signs.

DeLorme map grid: Page 44, A1.

Elevation: 14 feet.

Access: The boardwalk is wheelchair accessible.

Bathrooms: None.

Hazards: None.

Nearest food, gas, and lodging: Hoquiam.

Nearest camping: Ocean City State Park near Ocean Shores.

For more information: On the Internet check graysharbor.fws.gov. You can write the refuge at Grays Harbor National Wildlife Refuge, c/o Nisqually National Wildlife Refuge, 100 Brown Farm Road, Olympia, WA 98516. Call (360) 753-9467.

CELEBRATING THE SPRING MIGRATION

Every spring in late April, just as hundreds of thousands of shorebirds descend to feed on the tideflats along Grays Harbor, the Grays Harbor Audubon Society hosts the annual Grays Harbor Shorebird Festival. The festival offers lectures, field trips, and vendors gathered in a central location at what is normally the peak of the spring migration. The festival Web site can be found at graysharbor.fws.gov/events.html.

The real stars of the weekend are the birds. Western and Least Sandpipers, dowitchers, Dunlin, Sanderling, and other shorebirds flock to the tideflats to feed and build their energy stores for their long flight north to breeding grounds. Besides the refuge on Bowerman Basin, other great places to witness the migration include Bottle Beach State Park, Bill's Spit, and other locations with views of Grays Harbor tidelands.

Bill's Spit

Habitats: Sandy beach, salt marsh.

Specialty birds: Common Loon; Brown Pelican; Pelagic and Brandt's Cormorants; Bald Eagle; Peregrine Falcon; Black-bellied Plover; Willet; Long-billed Curlew; Marbled Godwit; Red Knot; Baird's and Pectoral Sandpipers; Short-billed Dowitcher; Red-necked Phalarope; Heerman's, Bonaparte's, Mew, and Western Gulls; Common Murre; Pigeon Guillemot; Marbled Murrelet; Rhinoceros Auklet; Vaux's Swift; Rufous Hummingbird.

Best times to bird: Year-round.

A deer wanders close to the authors as they watch the birds at Bill's Spit in Ocean Shores.

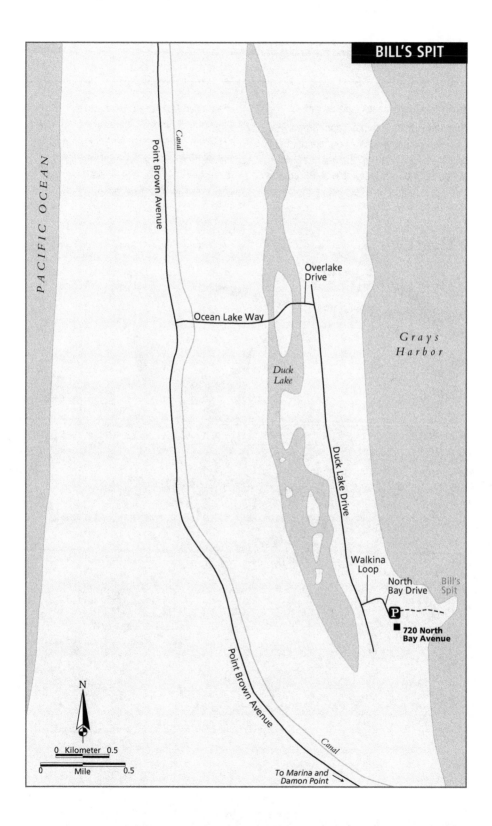

BILL'S SPIT

PACIFIC OCEAN

Point Brown Avenue

Canal

Overlake Drive

Ocean Lake Way

Grays Harbor

Duck Lake

Duck Lake Drive

Walkina Loop

North Bay Drive

Bill's Spit

P

■ **720 North Bay Avenue**

Point Brown Avenue

Canal

N

0 Kilometer 0.5
0   Mile   0.5

To Marina and Damon Point

About the site:

Bill's Spit is one of those small birding spots that can be gold when the timing is right and leave you shaking your head when the timing is wrong. As with many of the birding sites on the inner Grays Harbor during the migration season, if you watch the birds in the two hours before or the two hours after the high tide you are in for a treat. But show up at low tide and you will see little more than tiny dots on the sand that might be birds hundreds of yards from the spit.

The trickiest part about birding Bill's Spit is finding the place. Once you arrive at the small parking area and start the short walk through tall grass and low-lying shrubs, birding the site is simple. The spit itself is a sandbar that sticks out into Grays Harbor that can fill with shorebirds and gulls as the waters rise near high tide and recede following the high tide. Sandpipers, dowitchers, Long-billed Curlew, and godwits are among the shorebirds that frequent the spit during the migration season—April and May in the spring and July through October in the fall. Be sure to bring a spotting scope or powerful binoculars not only to distinguish between the shorebirds in the foreground, but also to look out at islands of sand far out in the North Bay section of the harbor. Pilings anchored in the sand far offshore also can hold Bald Eagles, which watch over the gathering shorebirds.

Besides the obvious gatherings of shorebirds that can be on the spit during the right tidal conditions, be sure to check the sand in the foreground for probing feeders such as Semipalmated Sandpiper. And look skyward now and then for passing Brown Pelicans that effortlessly fly overhead in long, silent lines as they hunt for fish. Just offshore there are also chances to see Brant, loons, geese, and ducks.

To expand the birding possibilities at Bill's Spit, take some time to walk along the beach and scan the shoreline to the south toward Damon Point, and also remember to check the Marsh Wren and sparrows in the salt marsh and grass above the tideline. Be alert to other wildlife in the area. On one visit we were engrossed with watching godwits along the shoreline and when we looked behind us we saw two deer just about 8 feet away, looking like they were waiting for a turn at the spotting scope. Be careful or such close encounters could end up trumping the birding, even if you do time the tides correctly!

Other key birds: Red-throated and Pacific Loons; Horned, Red-necked, and Western Grebes; Gadwall; Green-winged Teal; Black, White-winged, and Surf Scoters; Common Goldeneye; Bufflehead; Common and Red-breasted Mergansers; Turkey Vulture; Osprey; Merlin; Semipalmated Plover; Greater Yellowlegs; Whimbrel; Sanderling; Dunlin; Western and Least Sandpipers; Parasitic Jaeger; Ring-billed, California, and Herring Gulls; Caspian Tern; Northern Shrike; Warbling Vireo; Lapland Longspur.

Nearby opportunities: Damon Point.

Directions: From downtown Ocean Shores on Point Brown Avenue, take Ocean Lake Way to the left and drive east to Overlake Drive. Take Overlake Drive and cross Duck Lake on a bridge before turning right onto Duck Lake Drive. Go south on Duck Lake Drive before turning right onto Wakina Street and then right again onto North Bay Drive. Park in the two-car parking area in an empty lot labeled as a wildlife viewing area. The trail to the spit begins at the head of the parking area.

DeLorme map grid: Page 58, A2.

Elevation: 11 feet.

Access: None.

Bathrooms: None.

Hazards: None.

Nearest food, gas, and lodging: Ocean Shores.

Nearest camping: Ocean City State Park.

For more information: Check with the Ocean Shores Chamber of Commerce at www.ocean shores.org/about.htm or by calling (800) 76–BEACH, or check the Grays Harbor Audubon Society Web site at www.ghas.org.

Damon Point and Oyhut Wildlife Area

Habitats: Sandy beach, prairie, salt marsh.

Specialty birds: Common Loon; Brown Pelican; Pelagic and Brandt's Cormorants; Greater Scaup; Barrow's Goldeneye; Bald Eagle; Peregrine Falcon; Black-bellied, Pacific Golden-, and Snowy Plovers; Willet; Wandering Tattler; Solitary Sandpiper; Long-billed Curlew; Marbled Godwit; Red Knot; Baird's and Pectoral Sandpipers; Short-billed Dowitcher; Red-necked Phalarope; Heerman's, Bonaparte's, Mew, Thayer's, and Western Gulls; Common Tern; Common Murre; Pigeon Guillemot; Marbled Murrelet; Rhinoceros Auklet; Short-eared Owl; Vaux's Swift; Western Bluebird.

Best times to bird: Year-round.

About the site:

If there is a magnet that draws birders to Ocean Shores, then Damon Point State Park and the Oyhut Wildlife Area are the main attractions. Throughout the years the two areas have combined to serve as migrant traps, where rare and out-of-place species have stopped for a short time before continuing their migration. Even though the habitat on Damon Point has changed over the years, it remains a great site for birders to dig out interesting coastal birds.

Damon Point State Park is a 61-acre day-use site with a small parking area on the north side of the park and an old road—Damon Point Road—running down the middle of the mile-long sandbar. About a half a mile across, Damon Point combines with the adjacent wildlife area to provide some of the best natural beach and salt marsh habitat on the Ocean Shores peninsula. And since the only way to access the sites is on foot, the number of people plodding through the fields and over the sand dunes is minimal—perfect for seeing more birds.

Start your birding at Damon Point State Park by looking at the inner harbor side of Damon Point Road, once you go around the gate that keeps cars from driving down the middle of the site. By looking to the left you are viewing birds in Grays Harbor—Brown Pelicans, grebes, cormorants, and ducks, among others. Be sure to look along the shore for any shorebirds, and look at the tops of driftwood on the beach to see if any raptors are sitting and devouring a meal. We had great views of a female Merlin just inside the gate on one fall visit.

As you continue walking east on Damon Point Road, be sure to look in the brush on either side of the road for sparrows and other songbirds. Northern Harrier are commonly seen flying low over the rolling sand dunes. The habitat here includes lupine, native grasses, moss, and lichens, against a backdrop of wind-stunted small spruce trees.

A short distance down Damon Point Road there is a salt marsh and lagoon on the right-hand side of the road. A few years ago this was a freshwater pond that was a birding hot spot for migrating birds, but over the last few winters the waters from Grays Harbor cut a path across the road and to the former pond, converting

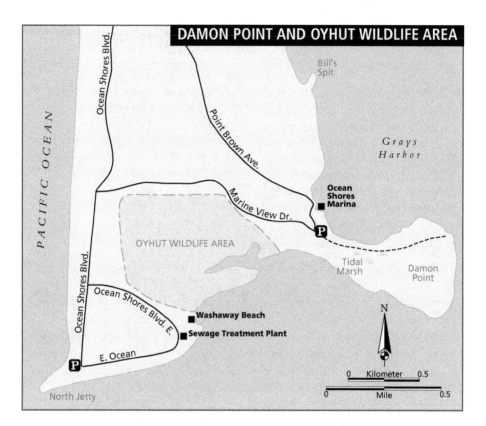

it into a tidal lagoon favored by shorebirds and the occasional influx of fish that can be seen jumping wildly in the shallow waters when conditions are right. Take one of the paths down to the sides of this lagoon to maximize your chances of seeing Short-billed Dowitchers, Western and Least Sandpipers, Semipalmated Plovers, and other shorebirds that gather in the protected area.

After walking around the lagoon and carefully viewing any shorebirds, another good option is to walk south toward the ocean side of the point, where Grays Harbor opens its mouth to the Pacific Ocean and waves crash up against a steep beach. Depending on the tide and surf conditions, you could find more shorebirds here. Be careful when walking along the ocean side of Damon Point, staying alert for heavy surf conditions and the possibility of sneaker waves, which can send logs high onto the beach.

Stay on the lookout throughout the entire site for rare sightings of Snowy Plover, which have nested at Damon Point in the past and continue to nest in small numbers along the coast to the south of Grays Harbor. Damon Point is the northernmost nesting location for Snowy Plover in North America. Also watch for any movement in the thick beach vegetation, where a Lapland Longspur may emerge from its feeding area.

By walking west again, picking your way among the driftwood on the southern side of Damon Point, you can spend time watching the shoreline as well as scanning the ocean for views of gulls and any movements of migrating seabirds. This location and the Ocean Shores jetty site nearby offer the best chances to see shearwaters, petrels, and jaegers that are normally seen only from boats on pelagic birding trips. Time your visit for the early fall and you might see thousands of Sooty Shearwaters streaming past the mouth of Grays Harbor, and sometimes by timing a birding trip just after a strong wind-storm you can see less-common pelagic species, such as petrels.

Also check the waters just offshore for murrelet, loons, and scoters. Three loon species—Common, Pacific, and Red-throated—can be seen along this part of the Ocean Shores Peninsula, along with White-winged and Surf Scoters.

Once you reach a point where you are about even with the parking area at the north end of Damon Point, follow a rugged path back across the point toward Damon Point Road to complete the walking tour.

Access to the Oyhut Wildlife Area, or the Ocean Shores Game Range as it is known to many locals and birders, is pretty limited. You can access the area on foot from Damon Point, or leave the park and drive west to reach other access points. Depart from Damon Point State Park and turn left onto Marine View Drive, and the wildlife area is on the left-hand side of the road as it winds toward the Ocean Shores jetty. You can bird the wildlife area from the road, paying close attention to the tops of the grasses and prevalent Scotch broom for Horned Larks, sparrows, and songbirds. Another access point is beside the Ocean Shores sewer treatment plant on Ocean Shores Boulevard East. Park outside the fenced treatment plant and walk along the fence line to the south and then head left at the end of the fence to work your way to Washaway Beach, an area that can be loaded with shorebirds in the foreground and loons and scoters in the background when the conditions and seasons are right.

Take some time to explore all of the areas on this southern tip of Ocean Shores and you are sure to find interesting coastal birding.

CREDIT ACCRETION FOR DAMON POINT

Damon Point is cited as a prime example of the process of accretion—a natural process that is the opposite of erosion—where water and wind currents cause sand to accumulate over many years to form new land. While erosion is a concern along the Washington coast, the sandbar at Damon Point benefits from sand and silt flowing down the Chehalis River and into Grays Harbor, as well as sand thrown onto the sandbar by tidal action.

Other key birds: Red-throated and Pacific Loons; Horned, Red-necked, and Western Grebes; Sooty Shearwater; Gadwall; Green-winged Teal; American and Eurasian Wigeons; Black, White-winged, and Surf Scoters; Common Goldeneye; Bufflehead; Common and Red-breasted Mergansers; Turkey Vulture; Merlin; Semipalmated Plover; Greater and Lesser Yellowlegs; Spotted Sandpiper; Whimbrel; Sanderling; Dunlin; Western and Least Sandpipers; Parasitic Jaeger; Ring-billed, California, and Herring Gulls; Caspian Tern; Northern Shrike; Warbling Vireo; House, Bewick's, and Marsh Wrens; American Pipit, Orange-crowned and Wilson's Warblers; Common Yellowthroat; Fox, Savannah, and Golden-crowned Sparrows; Lapland Longspur; Snow Bunting.

Nearby opportunities: The North Jetty at Point Brown on the southern end of Ocean Shores Boulevard offers more bird-viewing.

Directions: From downtown Ocean Shores, follow the main drag on Point Brown Avenue south to the end of the road. Turn right onto Marine View Drive and drive a short distance before turning left into a small driveway and parking area for Damon Point and the Oyhut Wildlife Area.

DeLorme map grid: Page 58, A2.

Elevation: 15 feet.

Access: None.

Bathrooms: Portable toilets.

Hazards: None.

Nearest food, gas, and lodging: Ocean Shores.

Nearest camping: Ocean City State Park.

For more information: Check with the Ocean Shores Chamber of Commerce at www.ocean shores.org/about.htm or by calling (800) 76-BEACH, or check the Grays Harbor Audubon Society Web site at www.ghas.org. Parking at Damon Point State Park now requires a $5.00 parking pass, available on the site.

Habitats: Lowland riparian, freshwater marsh, saltwater marsh, sandy beach.

Specialty birds: Common Loon; Pelagic and Brandt's Cormorants; Great Egret; Greater White-fronted Goose; Greater Scaup; Barrow's Goldeneye; Bald Eagle; Peregrine Falcon; Solitary, Baird's, and Pectoral Sandpipers; Heerman's, Bonaparte's, Mew, Herring, and Western Gulls; Band-tailed Pigeon; Short-eared and Northern Pygmy-Owls; Vaux's Swift; Rufous Hummingbird; Pileated Woodpecker; Red-breasted Sapsucker; Pacific-slope Flycatcher; Hutton's Vireo; Purple Martin; Western Bluebird.

Best times to bird: Year-round.

A creek joins with Johns River and nearby wetlands and marshes to provide a host of damp habitats at the Johns River Wildlife Area.

About the site:

If you are looking to add variety to a birding trip in Grays Harbor country, a stop at the Johns River Wildlife Area offers a departure from shorebirds and salt water. The 1,500-acre wildlife area features a half-mile-long paved trail on the south side of Johns River, with a bird blind for views of migrating waterfowl and resident Roosevelt elk. But the paved trail is just the start of what you can do and find on the site. By taking some time to explore off the main path, you can wander red alder stands in search of sapsuckers and woodpeckers or walk along the top of a dike to find waterfowl and occasional shorebirds in the extensive mudflats that are exposed during low tide.

The easiest way to start exploring at Johns River is from the half-mile paved trail that ends with access to a photo blind alongside the river. Walk south from the parking area, watching the mudflats on the left side of the trail for wading birds—Great Blue Heron, dowitchers, and yellowlegs, among others. During low

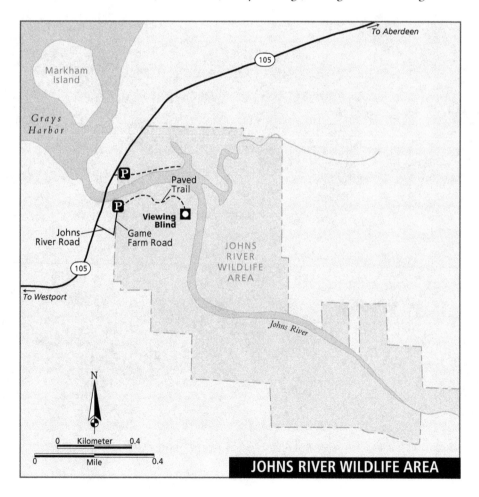

JOHNS RIVER WILDLIFE AREA

tide check the muddy edges of the river for shorebirds, especially those such as Solitary and Pectoral Sandpiper that tend to stay away from large gatherings of shorebirds. On the right side of the trail, an open field with streams running toward the river offers views of ducks and geese, Pied-billed Grebe, and other waterfowl in the foreground, while elk often can be seen feeding along the back edge of the fields. Visitors are allowed to walk on these fields and off the main trail in this wildlife area, which could be a boon for birders who want to expand their opportunities. Whether you walk across the fields or not, be sure to scan the tree-tops along the western edge of the field to see raptors perched between dives at their prey.

Another area to watch closely from the paved trail is the series of snags that stick up from the saltwater marsh and freshwater wetlands across the plain that holds Johns River. These snags can be prime hunting grounds for Pileated Wood-pecker and sapsuckers, and they can be popular perches for raptors.

Besides the obvious birding on the west side of Johns River, an access road just norh of the river offers even more opportunities. Park in the dirt parking area and walk around the gate to hike along the road and trails that meander through maple and birch and along the edges of a swampy section of the wildlife area. This habitat is suited to songbirds and sapsuckers and offers the chance to see more wetland species such as Green Heron.

If you have access to a canoe, Johns River also offers great birding opportunities from small boats, including birding along the river and just offshore from the river's mouth on and around Markham Island, which is a marshy island that is part of the wildlife area. Keep in mind that the Johns River Wildlife Area is a popular destination for hunters, so timing your visits around the hunting schedule will maximize your birding chances.

Other key birds: Horned and Pied-billed Grebes; American Bittern; Green Heron; Wood Duck; Gadwall; Green-winged and Blue-winged Teals; Common Goldeneye; Bufflehead; Common, Red-breasted, and Hooded Mergansers; Turkey Vulture; Osprey; Merlin; Ruffed Grouse; Virginia Rail; Sora; Greater and Lesser Yellowlegs; Spotted Sandpiper; Sanderling; Dunlin; Western and Least Sandpipers; Wilson's Snipe; Ring-billed, California, and Herring Gulls; Caspian Tern; Western Screech- and Northern Saw-whet Owls; Downy and Hairy Woodpeckers; Olive-sided Flycatcher; Western Wood-Pewee; Willow Flycatcher; Northern Shrike; Warbling Vireo; Western Scrub-Jay; Chestnut-backed Chickadee; Brown Creeper; House, Winter, Bewick's, and Marsh Wrens; Swainson's, Hermit, and Varied Thrushes; American Pipit; Orange-crowned, Black-throated Gray, Yellow, MacGillivray's, and Wilson's Warblers; Common Yellowthroat; Western Tanager; Fox, Savannah, Lincoln's, and Golden-crowned Sparrows; Lapland Longspur; Black-headed Grosbeak; Bullock's Oriole; Purple Finch; Red Crossbill; Evening Grosbeak.

Nearby opportunities: Bottle Beach State Park is just a few miles to the west on State Route 105.

Directions: From Aberdeen, follow U.S. Highway 101 across the Chehalis River bridge, then veer right onto SR 105, heading toward Westport. The entrance to the wildlife area is on the left, just past the Johns River bridge. Turn left onto Johns River Road, then left again onto Game Farm Road. Follow the road down a hill to a gravel parking lot.

DeLorme map grid: Page 44, A1.

Elevation: 30 feet.

Access: Wheelchair-accessible, paved trail.

Bathrooms: Portable toilets.

Hazards: None.

Nearest food, gas, and lodging: Aberdeen or Westport.

Nearest camping: Twin Harbors Beach State Park along SR 105.

For more information: On the Internet, check www.wdfw.wa.gov/lands/r6john5.htm. This is a Washington Department of Fish and Wildlife site and parking requires that you have the $10 vehicle-use permit.

27 Bottle Beach State Park

Habitats: Lowland riparian, freshwater marsh, sandy beach, mudflats.

Specialty birds: Common Loon; Brown Pelican; Pelagic and Brandt's Cormorants; Greater Scaup; Barrow's Goldeneye; Bald Eagle; Peregrine Falcon; Black-bellied, American Golden-, and Pacific Golden-Plovers; Solitary Sandpiper; Red Knot; Baird's and Pectoral Sandpipers; Short-billed Dowitcher; Heerman's, Bonaparte's, Mew, and Western Gulls; Band-tailed Pigeon; Vaux's Swift; Rufous Hummingbird; Hutton's Vireo.

Best times to bird: Year-round.

A Western Sandpiper probes for food along Bottle Beach while another sandpiper and a Dunlin rest on the mudflats.

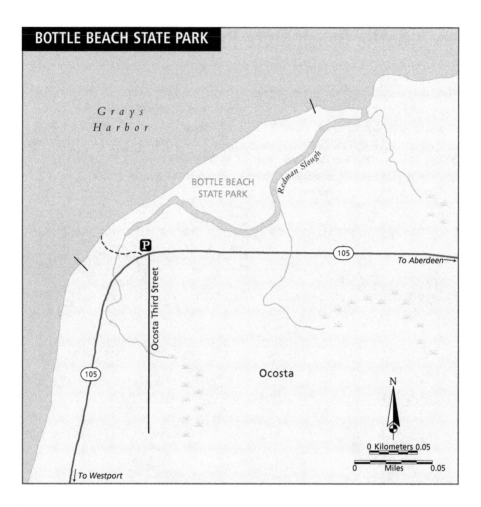

BOTTLE BEACH STATE PARK

Grays Harbor

BOTTLE BEACH
STATE PARK

Redman Slough

105

To Aberdeen →

Ocosta Third Street

P

105

Ocosta

N

To Westport

0 Kilometers 0.05

0   Miles   0.05

About the site:

Although Bottle Beach is a state park, it may be the least-developed and the easiest-to-miss park in Washington. This doesn't bother the thousands of shorebirds that flock to the gradually sloping sandy shores as the tide rises in Grays Harbor. When the tidal conditions are right—during a two- or three-hour window around each high tide—this can be one of the best shorebird-watching locations in the state. And when the tide is out, bird-watching across the highway in the water-logged fields along Ocosta Third Street offers more bird diversity than can be found at most shorebird locations.

The birding at Bottle Beach starts before you even reach the beach. The path that leads to the beach cuts through a freshwater marsh filled with cattails, sedges, and other marsh plants, and depending on the season, you may see Marsh Wren or Common Yellowthroat flitting between the foliage. Short trees and shrubs rising along the sides of the creek that forms the marsh can also hold flycatchers and vireo, as well as many sparrow species. Also watch for wading birds such as Virginia Rail on the edges of the marsh.

The trail is little more than 100 yards long before it reaches the shallow, sloping beach. Be careful as you walk out onto the beach, because some of the most skittish birds can be startled into flight. In the spring migration season, especially late in April, when the tide is rising to fill the harbor it is possible to see thousands of shorebirds—Western and Least Sandpiper, Dunlin, Black-bellied Plover, and the occasional Red Knot—as they feed and rest along the shoreline. This offers a great opportunity for close viewing and study of bird plumages and identification skills. Be sure to bring your guidebook if you are unfamiliar with many shorebirds.

Bottle Beach State Park encompasses just a small strip of shoreline, but you can make the most of a visit by walking east along the shore and using a spotting scope or binoculars to look out across Grays Harbor for ducks feeding in the foreground and Bald Eagles sitting on piling well out into the harbor. Also be sure to turn around now and then to check the brush along the beach and to scan the fir trees that grow right up against the beach. During one spring visit we had long looks at a Merlin sitting in a fir tree after it made an unsuccessful attempt to catch a shorebird among the hundreds that rose as one when it swooped over the shore.

After you have thoroughly explored Bottle Beach, be sure to check the birding along Ocosta Third Street, right across the highway from the parking area for the park. Especially when rains have freshwater levels running high, the fields on either

A Black-bellied Plover and a Short-billed Dowitcher along Bottle Beach during spring migration.

side of Ocosta Third Street flood and offer excellent habitat for waterfowl and even a few shorebirds—yellowlegs, dowitchers, and others that spill over to the freshwater habitat when the tide rises in the harbor. Virginia Rail are commonly heard and sometimes seen running across the road, and Sora are fairly common, though hard to see as always. You can bird this area on foot, but we have had great luck birding from inside our car, where the car acts as a blind and doesn't spook the birds. Birding from your car is also a great courtesy to other bird-watchers, since this area can be a popular destination, especially during the height of the spring and fall migrations.

YELLOWLEGS

If you happen to visit Bottle Beach outside of the prime shorebird-viewing times around the high tide, you still may have the chance to see a few birds, including Greater and Lesser Yellowlegs. Greater Yellowlegs have long, slightly upturned bills and are most likely to be seen on the mudflats in Grays Harbor as the tide recedes, while Lesser Yellowlegs are more likely to be seen in the fields along Octosta Third Street, where freshwater often rises and threatens to cover the road. The number of Greater Yellowlegs peaks in mid- to late-April, although the birds are around the area all year. Lesser Yellowlegs are seen more commonly in the fall migration, especially in eastern Washington, but they can be seen in the spring migration, with more birds in Washington in May than in April. Lesser Yellowlegs leave the state in the winter months.

Since the two gangly shorebirds are hard to tell apart, one of the best ways to identify them is to listen for their calls. The taller Greater Yellowlegs make a loud *tu-tu-tu* call while the shorter Lesser Yellowlegs are not quite as loud in their shorter *tu-tu* call.

Other key birds: Horned and Western Grebes; American Bittern; Green Heron; Wood Duck; Gadwall; Green-winged and Blue-winged Teals; American and Eurasian Wigeons; Northern Pintail; Northern Shoveler; Canvasback; Ring-necked Duck; Lesser Scaup; Common Goldeneye; Bufflehead; Common, Red-breasted, and Hooded Mergansers; Turkey Vulture; Osprey; Merlin; Virginia Rail; Sora; Greater and Lesser Yellowlegs; Spotted Sandpiper; Sanderling; Dunlin; Western and Least Sandpipers; Wilson's Snipe; Ring-billed, California, and Herring Gulls; Caspian Tern; Willow Flycatcher; Northern Shrike; Warbling Vireo; Western Scrub-Jay; House, Winter, Bewick's, and Marsh Wrens; American Pipit; Orange-crowned, Yellow, and Wilson's Warblers; Common Yellowthroat; Western Tanager; Fox, Savannah, Lincoln's, and Golden-crowned Sparrows; Lapland Longspur.

Nearby opportunities: Westhaven State Park and the Westport waterfront.

Directions: From Aberdeen, follow U.S. Highway 101 across the Chehalis River bridge, then veer right onto State Route 105, heading toward Westport. Shortly after passing the Johns River Wildlife Area, SR 105 comes to a sharp left-hand turn at Ocosta Third Street. There is a small parking area for two cars right on the corner, where a path and a sign mark the park entrance.

DeLorme map grid: Page 58, A3.

Elevation: Sea level to 15 feet.

Access: None.

Bathrooms: None.

Hazards: None.

Nearest food, gas, and lodging: Aberdeen or Westport.

Nearest camping: Twin Harbors Beach State Park along SR 105.

For more information: Although this is a state park, Bottle Beach has not been developed in any way. As such, there is no parking fee for this site.

Tokeland and Shoalwater Bay

Habitats: Saltwater marsh, sandy beach, rocky beach.

Specialty birds: Common Loon; Brown Pelican; Peagic and Brandt's Cormorant; Great Egret; Greater Scaup; Bald Eagle; Peregrine Falcon; Black-bellied Plover; Marbled and Bar-tailed Godwits; Ruddy and Black Turnstones; Red Knot; Baird's Sandpiper; Heerman's, Bonaparte's, Mew, Thayer's, and Western Gulls; Band-tailed Pigeon; Vaux's Swift; Rufous Hummingbird; Hutton's Vireo.

Best times to bird: Year-round.

About the site:

Many birders make their way to Ocean Shores and Westport for views of migrating shorebirds, but for those with an eye for less-crowded birding and the chance to see large congregations of Marbled Godwits and Willet, the quiet banks of Shoalwater Bay and the northern reaches of Willapa Bay at Tokeland are worthy destinations.

Tokeland is a tiny Native American village on a piece of land that juts into Willapa Bay, with a broad cove and estuarine habitat west of town toward Graveyard Spit and Cape Shoalwater and a shallow harbor on Willapa Bay that reaches to the south and east. The area is home to the Shoalwater Bay Indian Tribe and is a long-time destination for shellfish gathering and fishing. During the spring and fall migrations and throughout the winter months, shorebirds stick to the relatively sheltered harbor.

Birding in Tokeland is an easy affair. Follow the main road through a residential area and to the end of Toke Point. The road ends near the Tokeland Marina, and this is the area that can be full of shorebirds when the tides rise to fill the bay. During one visit in 2003 we found a dozen Marbled Godwits walking around the grassy lots near the marina. After parking near a dock and wandering close to the embankment, we found 150 godwits and Western Sandpiper, Dunlin, and a single Willet gathered on the sandy beach alongside the piers and buildings at the marina. Other species that can be seen from the end of Toke Point include Whimbrel, Long-billed Dowitcher, and large congregations of cormorant, as well as grebes, loons, and other waterfowl.

One thing to keep in mind while birding at the Tokeland Marina is to try to lessen the impact of your presence in order to avoid scaring away the skittish shorebirds. As more people visit the site, everyone will benefit from making slow and careful movements on the embankment overlooking the shoreline.

Besides the birding offered at the marina, be sure to find a parking spot along the road leading to the marina and walk along the west side of the road with a spotting scope or binoculars to look over North Cove, a protected saltwater estuary and marsh. This cove can hold migrating waterfowl and other species, but the quality of the birding will depend on the tide, with better birding around high tide.

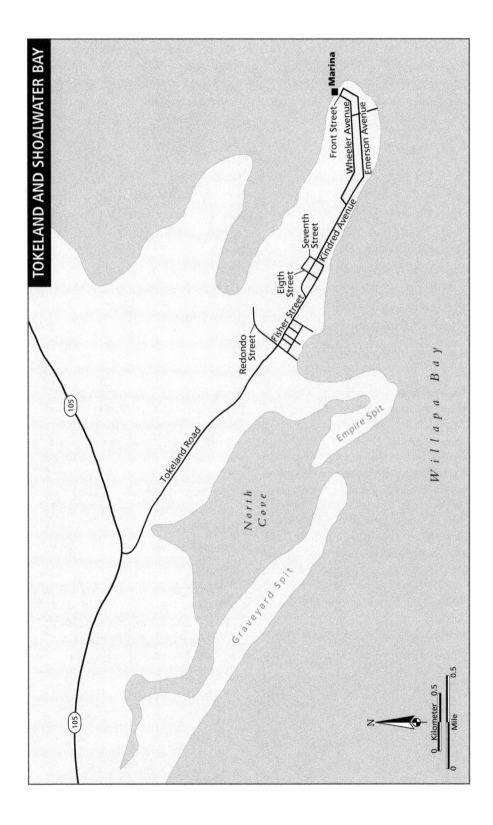

TOKELAND AND SHOALWATER BAY

Marina

Front Street

Wheeler Avenue

Emerson Avenue

Kindred Avenue

Seventh Street

Eigth Street

Fisher Street

Redondo Street

Tokeland Road

105

105

Willapa Bay

North Cove

Empire Spit

Graveyard Spit

N

0   Kilometer   0.5

0   Mile   0.5

As you leave Tokeland, consider turning left and continuing the drive toward Cape Shoalwater—a small shoulder of sandstone and clay that juts into the Pacific Ocean at the northern mouth of Willapa Bay. A pullout along the highway offers access to the beach and the opportunity to look out over the bay and the Pacific Ocean for migrating birds—Sooty Shearwaters, shorebirds, and others.

GODWITS GALORE

More than any other place on the Washington coast, Tokeland is known as an area to see godwits. Marbled Godwit are commonplace at the harbor when the tide rises to fill the bay, and a small flock commonly spends the winter along the shores of Willapa Bay. During 2002 an influx of Bar-tailed Godwits drew bird-watchers to Tokeland and Ocean Shores, and those with the shorebird identification skills may be able to key out a Bar-tailed Godwit during the fall and spring migrations—April through early May in the spring and July through October in the fall. A much less common Hudsonian Godwit was seen in Tokeland in 2002, so if you are looking for godwits, the tiny marina is a magnet for the large shorebirds.

Other key birds: Red-throated and Pacific Loons; Horned, Pied-billed, Red-necked, and Western Grebes; Gadwall; Green-winged Teal; American and Eurasian Wigeons; White-winged and Surf Scoters; Common Goldeneye; Bufflehead; Common, Red-breasted, and Hooded Mergansers; Turkey Vulture; Osprey; Merlin; Greater and Lesser Yellowlegs; Spotted Sandpiper; Whimbrel; Sanderling; Dunlin; Western and Least Sandpipers; Ring-billed, California, and Herring Gulls; Caspian Tern; Bewick's and Marsh Wrens; Orange-crowned, Yellow, and Wilson's Warblers; Common Yellowthroat; Fox, Savannah, Lincoln's, and Golden-crowned Sparrows.

Nearby opportunities: Johns River Wildlife Area along North River.

Directions: From Aberdeen, go south on U.S. Highway 101 to Raymond and turn left onto State Route 105. Turn left onto Tokeland Road and continue on this main road as it skirts North Cove to the west. Tokeland Road changes in name to Kindred Avenue. Just continue following this main road to reach the end of Toke Point and the Tokeland Marina.

DeLorme map grid: Page 44, C1.

Elevation: 15 feet.

Access: None.

Bathrooms: None.

Hazards: None.

Nearest food, gas, and lodging: Raymond.

Nearest camping: Grayland Beach State Park.

For more information: Check the Web site for the Tokeland Chamber of Commerce at www.geocities.com/tokelandwa or call (360) 267-0606.

Willapa National Wildlife Refuge and Leadbetter Point

Habitats: Lowland riparian, mixed forest, old-growth forest, wetland, salt marsh, mudflats, sandy beach.

Specialty birds: Common Loon; Brown Pelican; Pelagic and Brandt's Cormorants; Great Egret; Trumpeter Swan; Greater White-fronted Goose; Brant; Greater Scaup; White-tailed Kite; Bald Eagle; Peregrine Falcon; Black-bellied, American Golden-, and Snowy Plovers; Willet; Long-billed Curlew; Marbled Godwit; Black Turnstone; Red Knot; Baird's and Pectoral Sandpipers; Short-billed Dowitcher; Red-necked and Red Phalaropes; Heerman's, Bonaparte's, Mew, Thayer's, and Western Gulls; Common Tern; Common Murre; Pigeon Guillemot; Marbled Murrelet; Rhinoceros Auklet; Band-tailed Pigeon; Short-eared and Spotted Owls; Vaux's Swift; Anna's and Rufous Hummingbirds; Pileated Woodpecker; Red-breasted Sapsucker; Pacific-slope Flycatcher; Hutton's Vireo; Western Bluebird.

Best times to bird: Year-round.

A male Wood Duck hides among the reeds in a small pond, standing guard over his mate and young.

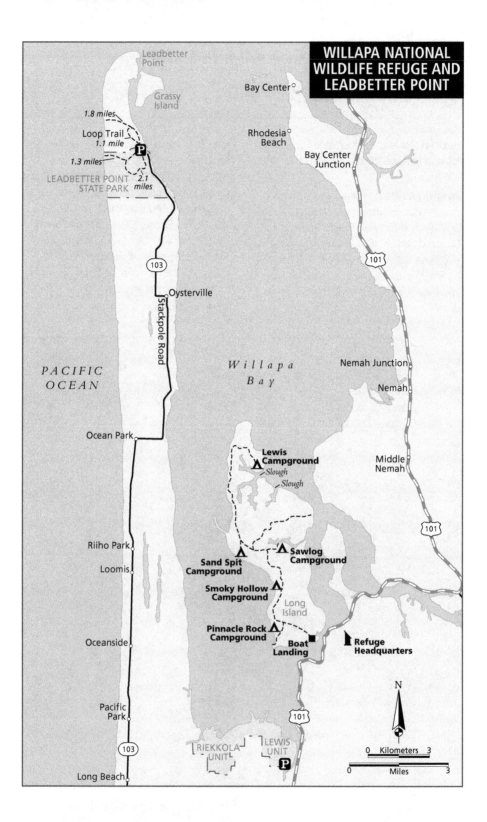

WILLAPA NATIONAL
WILDLIFE REFUGE AND
LEADBETTER POINT

Leadbetter
Point

Bay Center

Grassy
Island

Rhodesia
Beach

1.8 miles

Loop Trail
1.1 mile

Bay Center
Junction

1.3 miles

LEADBETTER POINT
STATE PARK

2.1
miles

103

Oysterville

101

PACIFIC
OCEAN

Willapa
Bay

Nemah Junction

Nemah

Stackpole Road

Ocean Park

Lewis
Campground

Slough

Slough

Middle
Nemah

101

Riiho Park

Loomis

Sand Spit
Campground

Sawlog
Campground

Smoky Hollow
Campground

Long
Island

Oceanside

Pinnacle Rock
Campground

Boat
Landing

Refuge
Headquarters

N

Pacific
Park

101

RIEKKOLA
UNIT

LEWIS
UNIT

0   Kilometers   3

0   Miles   3

Long Beach

103

About the site:

From the time it was established as the Willapa Migratory Waterfowl Refuge in 1937, local and national wildlife fans have recognized the importance of Willapa Bay for migrating and nesting birds. The bay and the shores of Leadbetter Point, which juts into the ocean to protect and create the shallow estuary, is one of the popular rest stops along the Pacific Flyway. Thousands of shorebirds fill the shores in spring and fall—Dunlin, Sanderling, Western and Least Sandpiper, and others—as the birds feed and build up their energy along their migratory routes. Meanwhile, waterfowl fill the bay, especially in winter, when Brant, loons, and huge rafts of Canada Geese descend on the area.

The Willapa National Wildlife Refuge (NWR) is one of the least-developed refuges in the state. As such, it takes a little exploring to reach the best bird habitat. But for those willing to take a walk along the salt marsh at Leadbetter Point or to paddle to Long Island to explore its old-growth forest habitat, this is one of the best bird-watching spots on the Washington coast.

You can start exploring Willapa Bay and the refuge by making a stop at the headquarters on U.S. Highway 101 north of Ilwaco. This location offers a boat ramp with easy access to Long Island as well as interpretive information in a kiosk outside the headquarters, which offers maps and details about the 11,000-acre refuge. The headquarters itself is open only on weekdays. If you stop at the headquarters in summer, you can find swallows, Killdeer, and songbirds flitting in the bushes and trees that surround the site.

Better bird-watching opportunities are available just south of the headquarters off US 101, where a blue goose sign alongside a small road signals access to the Lewis Unit. Drive to the end of the road and park, then get out and wander along the roads that top dikes in this section of the bay to see Marsh Wren, Song Sparrows, Pied-billed Grebes diving in the shallow water. Trumpeter Swans have been seen in this area in past years, and the marsh could also be good habitat for vagrant Great Egret. Many of the roads in the Lewis Unit are open for walkers, but they are not accessible by car.

To reach the rest of the Willapa NWR you have to hop in the car and drive to the Long Beach Peninsula, a 28-mile sandy land mass that forms the outer edge of the Willapa Bay estuary—the second-largest estuary on the Pacific Coast. The far northern tip of the peninsula is Leadbetter Point.

Leadbetter Point is under joint management with the state park system running the forested portion of the point in Leadbetter Point State Park and the Willapa NWR running the sand dune and salicornia marsh area at the tip of the peninsula. Hiking trails wind through the forest and to the beach and inner bay at Leadbetter Point. Three trails leave from the parking lot at the end of Stackpole Road, including a 1.1-mile interpretive trail and a pair of trails to the ocean beach, one 1.8 miles and the other 1.3 miles. Yet another trail goes to the edge of Willapa Bay and offers a rugged route to the tip of the point. This trail and all access to the sand dune habitat at the tip of Leadbetter Point are closed each year from March to September to protect nesting Snowy Plovers. This is one of the most reliable nesting locations for the endangered species.

Spring and fall are the best times to visit Leadbetter Point for bird-watching. When the ocean side of the point opens to hikers, it offers the chance to see migrating shorebirds and seabirds, including some pelagic species. In the spring more than 100,000 shorebirds flock to Willapa Bay. During the winter the walk along the Willapa Bay side of the point offers views of throngs of waterfowl, including Dusky and Aleutian subspecies of Canada Geese, Brant, American Wigeon, and many other species. Winter birders also have seen vagrant Snowy Owl and other hard-to-find species in remote sections of the refuge. Be aware, however, that the hike along the bay side of Leadbetter Point is flooded during much of the winter.

As a testament to the importance of the habitat in Willapa Bay and at Leadbetter Point, Audubon Washington identifies four sites in the area as Important Bird Areas—Leadbetter Point, Sand and Gunpowder Islands (off the northern tip of Leadbetter Point), Shoalwater Bay at the south end of the Willapa NWR (including the Lewis Unit), and the Willapa River estuary near Raymond and South Bend. As you visit the bay and its surrounding critical habitats, be mindful to protect this wet corner of the state. Stay on the trail, pack out everything you pack in on your birding journey, and consider supporting local habitat restoration and protection efforts through such organizations as the Friends of Willapa National Wildlife Refuge.

THE ENDANGERED SNOWY PLOVER

Snowy Plover are small, largely white shorebirds with black legs and black bills. The diminutive birds are listed as an endangered species in Washington and have threatened status on the federal list. The sandy tip of Leadbetter Point along with a section of Midway Beach and Damon Point near Ocean Shores are the three Snowy Plover nesting areas known in Washington, and efforts are taken to protect the nesting habitat in each location. There are approximately forty Snow Plovers in Washington at the time this book is going to press.

The Snowy Plover nest on sandy beaches above the high-tide line, and they can often be seen feeding with other shorebirds along the surf throughout the year. Bird-watchers are advised to tread carefully when in known Snowy Plover habitat because the birds' nests are so well camouflaged that they can easily be trod on, and it is very easy to scare the nesting plover away from its nest. This is the reason that the Pacific Ocean side and the northern tip of Leadbetter Point are closed each year during the Snowy Plover breeding and nesting season.

Other key birds: Red-throated and Pacific Loons; Horned, Pied-billed, Red-necked, and Western Grebes; Sooty Shearwater; American Bittern; Green Heron; Wood Duck; Green-winged Teal; American and Eurasian Wigeons; Northern Pintail; Northern Shoveler; Canvasback; Ring-necked Duck; Lesser Scaup; Black, White-winged, and Surf Scoters; Common Goldeneye; Bufflehead; Common, Red-breasted, and Hooded Mergansers; Turkey Vulture; Osprey; Merlin; Virginia Rail; Semipalmated Plover; Greater and Lesser Yellowlegs; Spotted Sandpiper; Whimbrel; Sanderling; Dunlin; Western and Least Sandpipers; Long-billed Dowitcher; Wilson's Snipe; Pomarine and Parasitic Jaegers; Ring-billed, California, and Herring Gulls; Caspian Tern; Western Screech- and Northern Saw-whet Owls; Downy and Hairy Woodpeckers; Olive-sided and Willow Flycatchers; Northern Shrike; Warbling Vireo; Chestnut-backed Chickadee; Bushtit; Brown Creeper; Winter, Bewick's, and Marsh Wrens; Swainson's and Varied Thrushes; American Pipit; Orange-crowned, Black-throated Gray, Yellow, and Wilson's Warblers; Common Yellowthroat; Western Tanager; Fox, Savannah, Lincoln's, and Golden-crowned Sparrows; Black-headed Grosbeak; Purple Finch; Red Crossbill.

Nearby opportunities: Tideflats and other habitat around Bay Center offer some of the best birding on Willapa Bay, and not many bird-watchers make the side trip to the area. Hard-to-find species such as Northern Mock-ingbird and Tropical Kingbird have been seen around Bay Center in past years.

Directions: The headquarters for the Willapa National Wildlife Refuge is located northwest of Ilwaco on US 101, and it can be reached by taking US 101 north from Ilwaco or by taking State Route 4 north near Naselle and turning left onto US 101 southbound. To reach Leadbetter Point State Park, take US 101 to Seaview and turn right onto State Route 103. Stay on SR 103 until you pass through Oysterville, then turn left and follow the signs to the park, eventually taking Stackpole Road to its conclusion in the park parking lot.

DeLorme map grid: Page 58, D3.

Elevation: 20 feet.

Access: Some wheelchair-accessible trails, and wheelchair-accessible bathrooms at Leadbetter Point State Park.

Bathrooms: Yes.

Hazards: High tide or stormy surf conditions.

Nearest food, gas, and lodging: Long Beach and Ilwaco.

Nearest camping: Fort Canby State Park.

For more information: A series of Web sites offer information about the Willapa National Wildlife Refuge and Leadbetter Point. Check the Willapa NWR page at willapa.fws.gov or the page for the Friends of Willapa Bay National Wildlife Refuge at www.willapabay .org/~fwnwr. The headquarters for the Willapa NWR is open Monday through Friday from 8:00 A.M. to 4:30 P.M.

30 Cape Disappointment

Habitats: Saltwater marsh, freshwater marsh, sandy beach, mixed forest, cliffs.

Specialty birds: Common Loon; Brown Pelican; Pelagic and Brandt's Cormorants; Brant; Greater Scaup; Bald Eagle; Peregrine Falcon; Black-bellied Plover; Ruddy and Black Turnstones; Surfbird; Rock, Baird's, and Pectoral Sandpipers; Heerman's, Bonaparte's, Mew, Thayer's, and Western Gulls; Common Murre; Pigeon Guillemot; Band-tailed Pigeon; Short-eared Owl; Vaux's Swift; Rufous Hummingbird; Pileated Woodpecker; Red-breasted Sapsucker; Pacific-slope Flycatcher; Hutton's Vireo.

Best times to bird: Year-round.

Brown Pelicans glide effortlessly overhead along the jetty at the mouth of the Columbia River. The pelicans can be seen in the summer months and into early fall from Cape Disappointment north along the Washington coast.

About the site:

When the Lewis and Clark Expedition reached Cape Disappointment in November 1805, they made little mention of birdlife at the mouth of the Columbia River, except for a gathering of California Condor feeding on a dead whale, and that members of the expedition shot a Brant on the Oregon side of the river. They reveled in reaching the Pacific Ocean, but they were more concerned about the endless winter rains and finding shelter than bird-watching.

Today's explorers will find that Cape Disappointment and Fort Canby State Park are full of birds. The condor are gone, but the remaining birds range from seasonal migrants that stop after crossing the river in the spring to Brandt's Cormorant nesting along the bluffs and Brown Pelicans flying effortless patrols along the north jetty in the summer and early fall. The entire cape is included in the 1,882-acre state park, which includes 27 miles of shoreline as well as old-growth forest, freshwater and saltwater marshes, and both rocky and sandy beaches.

Start exploring Cape Disappointment with a visit to the Lewis and Clark Interpretive Center on its perch atop a 200-foot bluff with views of the river and the Pacific Ocean. The mixed-forest habitat around the interpretive center holds Brown Creeper, woodpeckers, nuthatches, and songbirds. You can extend your birding in the high grounds of the cape by walking the trail to the Cape Disappointment Lighthouse. There you can take in an even more sweeping view of the mouth of the Columbia River and the view across the dangerous Columbia River bar, which has helped this stretch of the coast earn its nickname as Graveyard of the Pacific.

Walking back to the parking area at the base of the hill, pay close attention to the underlying brush for warblers and other songbirds, especially during the spring migration. Since the park is a stopover for birds making their way north after crossing the river, Cape Disappointment can be a migrant trap where species not usually seen in Washington or not seen in such large numbers can suddenly appear in the mixed habitats within the park. If you have been birding for a few years and know the songs of common birds in the area, careful listening for unfamiliar birdsong could be the key to locating a great bird.

After driving down from the parking area near the bluff, turn left into the picnic area of the park and find a parking spot on the sandy beach and reed grass area beyond the park pay gates. From here you can venture down to the ocean shore, scan for birds in the low-lying brush and grasses along the beach to the north, or scramble up onto the north jetty for more close-up views of the river's mouth. Standing atop the jetty, you can watch cormorant, Common Murre, and Brown Pelicans feeding in the intermingling river and ocean waters. Pay close attention to the surf conditions though, because large waves can crest the jetty. Also watch for rock birds—Wandering Tattler, Surfbird, Black and Ruddy Turnstone, and Rock Sandpiper. You can also set up a spotting scope or use binoculars and watch the horizon for passing Sooty Shearwater in the late summer and fall.

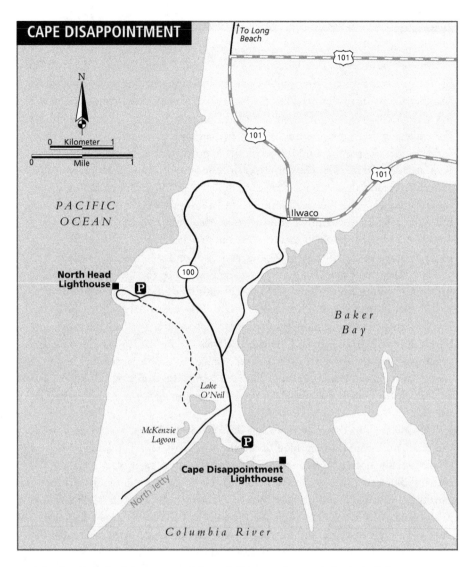

CAPE DISAPPOINTMENT

To Long Beach

101

101

Ilwaco

101

PACIFIC OCEAN

North Head Lighthouse

100

Baker Bay

Lake O'Neil

McKenzie Lagoon

Cape Disappointment Lighthouse

North Jetty

Columbia River

After leaving the jetty, turn north, or left, onto the road that winds between McKenzie Lagoon and Lake O'Neil on its way to the campgrounds within the park. The freshwater lake and lagoon can hold grebes, ducks, and occasionally swans during the winter months.

You can extend your birding around Cape Disappointment by taking the road off State Route Loop 100 toward North Head Lighthouse. This can be another location to look out over the ocean for gatherings of murres, scoters, and diving ducks, as well as to watch flocks of shearwaters passing over the ocean. Also nearby a short road leads to a parking lot for Beard's Hollow, a site featuring a series of ponds and wetlands with habitat for songbirds as well as a trail leading to the ocean shore.

Other key birds: Red-throated and Pacific Loons; Horned, Pied-billed, Red-necked, and Western Grebes; Sooty Shearwater; American Bittern; Green Heron; Wood Duck; Green-winged Teal; American and Eurasian Wigeons; Northern Pintail; Northern Shoveler; Canvasback; Ring-necked Duck; Lesser Scaup; Black, White-winged, and Surf Scoters; Common Goldeneye; Bufflehead; Common, Red-breasted, and Hooded Mergansers; Turkey Vulture; Osprey; Merlin; Sanderling; Dunlin; Western and Least Sandpipers; Wilson's Snipe; Ring-billed and California Gulls; Caspian Tern; Downy and Hairy Woodpeckers; Warbling Vireo; Chestnut-backed Chickadee; Brown Creeper; Winter, Bewick's, and Marsh Wrens; Swainson's, Hermit, and Varied Thrushes; Orange-crowned, Black-throated Gray, Yellow, MacGillivray's, and Wilson's Warblers; Common Yellowthroat; Western Tanager; Fox, Savannah, Lincoln's, and Golden-crowned Sparrows; Black-headed Grosbeak; Red Crossbill.

Nearby opportunities: Chinook County Park in Chinook offers views of the Columbia River and sand islands at the head of Baker Bay. By crossing the bridge to Astoria, Oregon, you will find that the southern edges of the mouth of the Columbia River offer more birding opportunities.

Directions: From Ilwaco, take SR Loop 100 from the only stoplight in town and follow the signs toward Fort Canby State Park.

DeLorme map grid: Page 58, B1.

Elevation: 15 feet.

Access: The Lewis and Clark Interpretive Center offers wheelchair access and the park offers three ADA-approved barbecue stations.

Bathrooms: In the interpretive center, which is open year-round from 10:00 A.M. to 5:00 P.M.

Hazards: Cliffs are fenced, but beware along the edges, and be wary of surf conditions along the edges of Fort Canby State Park and the north jetty.

Nearest food, gas, and lodging: Ilwaco.

Nearest camping: Fort Canby State Park.

For more information: Fort Canby State Park's Web site offers camping information as well as more background about the park at www.parks.wa.gov/parkpage.asp?selected park=Fort%20Canby&pageno=1

BROWN PELICANS BOUNCING BACK FROM DDT

In the 1960s and 1970s, Brown Pelicans were nearly wiped out in the United States, with major populations found only along the coasts of Florida. The cause—the chemical compound DDT, which caused the pelicans' egg shells to grow thinner over time, leading to severe declines in successful hatching of their young. The ban of DDT in the United States in 1973 and the listing of Brown Pelicans as an endangered species under the Endangered Species Act, coupled with the passage of time, have allowed the regal pelicans to bounce back.

Brown Pelicans are a common sight along the mouth of the Columbia River and to the north along the Pacific Ocean shores to Neah Bay. The pelicans can be seen between June and October, when nonbreeding birds and recently fledged birds disperse from their nesting grounds. Cape Disappointment is an opportune place to see the large, gliding birds with their 6.5-foot wingspans, since they can be seen from above on the bluffs near the Lewis and Clark Interpretive Center and from below along the north jetty in Fort Canby State Park.

As you watch the Brown Pelicans, note how they soar single file over the water, often nearly skimming the surface as they search for the fish that make up their diet. Brown Pelicans dive from up to 60 feet in the air for their fish dinners and scoop the fish and seawater into the pouch on the lower section of their bills. Then they filter the water out of the pouch by tilting their bills forward while the fish slosh around in an attempt to escape. Once the water is filtered out, the pelicans throw their heads back to swallow their fish.

Scientists believe that Brown Pelican populations are still growing on the West Coast, but the success or failure of the species is tied to the continued ban of DDT. DDT continues to be used in many other countries around the world.

Julia Butler Hansen Refuge for the Columbian White-tailed Deer

Habitats: Open fields, freshwater and tidal wetlands, riparian.

Specialty birds: Tundra Swan, Greater White-fronted Goose; Greater Scaup; White-tailed Kite; Bald Eagle; Peregrine Falcon; Black-bellied Plover; Bonaparte's and Mew Gulls; Band-tailed Pigeon; Short-eared Owl; Vaux's Swift; Rufous Hummingbird; Pileated Wood-pecker; Red-breasted Sapsucker; Pacific-slope Flycatcher; Hutton's Vireo; Purple Martin.

Best times to bird: Fall and winter.

White-tailed Kites and a wide range of year-round birds are not the only highlights at the Julia Butler Hansen Refuge for the Columbian White-tailed Deer. Watch the open fields for the deer that give the refuge its name.

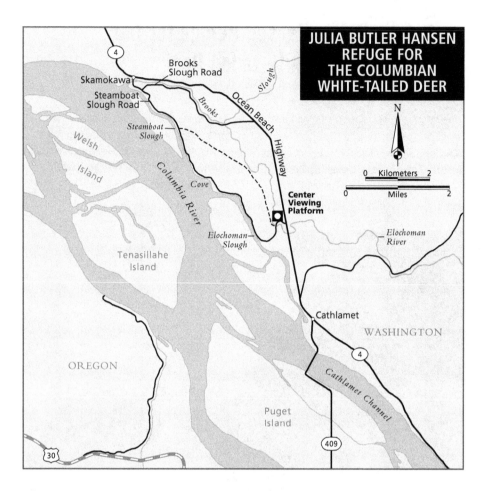

About the site:

Julia Butler Hansen Refuge for the Columbian White-tailed Deer consists of 56,000 acres of tidal and freshwater wetlands, open fields, riparian zones, sloughs, and marshes. The varied habitat makes interesting birding. Stop at the refuge head-quarters to take a close view of the sparrows and warblers that inhabit the shrubs along the edges of the slough. In recent years a Black Phoebe, a rare Washington visitor, has taken up winter residence near the center. Unless you walk the Center Road Trail, which is closed to automobiles and runs from the refuge center to the river, this is the closest you'll get to a pond. You also may see nutria and possibly otter, mink, and a handful of Columbian white-tailed deer from the viewing plat-form. Make sure you scan all of the fence posts and check the field to the west of the slough for raptors. We've seen Northern Harriers feasting in these fields as well as Merlin and quite a few American Kestrels hunting from fence posts.

From the headquarters, take the road that leads around the perimeter of the mainland unit. On the way out to the edge of the Columbia River, the road is sandwiched between alternating fields and wooded copses on the west side and the Elochoman River sloughs on the east. Check the sloughs for waterfowl, Great Blue and Green Herons, and Belted Kingfisher. We have yet to visit this refuge without seeing several raptors hunting in the fields, especially the tippling Northern Harrier, which find plenty of prey skulking through the long grasses. Songbirds forage and rear young in the shrubs and trees that skirt the fields. One day we stopped to watch an American Kestrel searching the fields from the top of a maple tree, and across the road we heard some songbirds peeping and rustling in the underbrush. When I pished them out we discovered Fox Sparrows, a pair of Spotted Towhees, Black-capped Chickadees, juncoes, a small flock of Yellow-rumped Warblers, and Golden-crowned Kinglets. Above them all, we saw a Downy Woodpecker foraging on the narrow trunk of a young Sitka spruce.

Before the dikes were built, these fields, as well as the intrachannel islands in the Columbia River that are also part of the refuge, flooded as the tide rose. Now the channeled waterways, dikes, and pumps control the water level in the fields. As a result, the water in the fields never gets too deep to attract wintering ducks, geese, swans, and shorebirds. About 4 miles around the loop, the road passes by some fields that flood in winter. If you bring a scope, this is the place to get it out and take a closer look. On dim days, sandpipers and dowitchers blend into the background and are impossible to see with the naked eye. If you're lucky, you'll see the peeps take wing while Peregrine Falcons and other raptors dive into the ball of birds to make a kill. In these fields as well as in the fields next to the Columbia River, White-tailed Kites provide ample entertainment as they hover, dive, and pounce on prey.

Just before the road meets the river, you'll see an outbuilding on the right side. Park here and walk to the outer edge of the road to overlook a tidal marsh. What you find here depends on the tide. When the tide is in, you'll see waterfowl, grebes, and possibly a few loons and cormorants. When the tide is out, shorebirds and herons muck about picking gooey morsels out of the mud. Take time at the riverside to scan the wide expanse for loons, rafts of grebes, and ducks. From the river's edge, turn right onto Brooks Road to head back to State Route 4. This road passes through a short, dense copse of mixed, broadleaf trees—mostly alder— before emerging between another slough to the west and open fields to the east. We always see Canada Geese—including cackling, dusky, and Aleutian sub-species—in these fields, and in winter, Tundra Swans and a variety of ducks join the geese. American Kestrels favor the power lines that parallel the road, and in winter Rough-legged Hawks perch on the poles. Stop at the viewing platform on SR 4 for a chance to see deer, elk, and more raptors stationed on the fence posts.

From June to September you can also walk Center Road, which leads from the refuge headquarters to the edge of the river. To see more of the refuge, we recommend hopping in a kayak or canoe to explore the sloughs and island channels; both can be rented at Skamokawa. Be careful when you are on the river since the wakes from passing ships can overturn smaller boats. Exploring the refuge by boat, however, will let you get closer to the birds, otters, and mink that make the refuge their home. The islands that are part of the refuge are accessible only by boat, although once on Tenasillahe Island (on the Oregon side of the river), you can walk on the dike road. The sloughs inside the mainland and island units are closed to fishing; the Elochoman and Columbia Rivers and Steamboat and Brooks Sloughs are open to fishing. Waterfowl can be hunted in season on Hunting and Wallace Islands.

Other key birds: Horned, Pied-billed, and Western Grebes; American Bittern; Green Heron; Wood Duck; Gadwall; Green-winged, Blue-winged, and Cinnamon Teals; American and Eurasian Wigeons; Northern Pintail; Northern Shoveler; Canvasback; Ring-necked Duck; Lesser Scaup; Common Goldeneye; Bufflehead; Common, Red-breasted, and Hooded Mergansers; Turkey Vulture; Osprey; Rough-legged Hawk; Merlin; Ruffed Grouse; Virginia Rail; Sora; Greater Yellowlegs; Spotted Sandpiper; Dunlin; Western and Least Sandpipers; Wilson's Snipe; Ring-billed and California Gulls; Caspian Tern; Western Screech- and Northern Saw-whet Owls; Downy and Hairy Woodpeckers; Olive-sided Flycatcher; Western Wood-Pewee; Willow Flycatcher; Northern Shrike; Warbling Vireo; Western Scrub-jay; Chestnut-backed Chickadee; Bushtit; Brown Creeper; Winter, Bewick's, and Marsh Wrens; Swainson's, Hermit, and Varied Thrushes; American Pipit; Orange-crowned, Black-throated Gray, Townsend's, Yellow, MacGillivray's, and Wilson's Warblers; Common Yellowthroat; Western Tanager; Fox, Savannah, Lincoln's, and Golden-crowned Sparrows;

Black-headed Grosbeak; Bullock's Oriole; Purple Finch, Red Crossbill; Evening Grosbeak.

Nearby opportunities: Puget Island, Willapa National Wildlife Refuge.

Directions: From Longview, take SR 4 west. The entrance to the refuge, Steamboat Slough Road, is about 2 miles from Cathlamet, just west of the Elochoman River bridge.

DeLorme map grid: Page 31, C5.

Elevation: 10 feet.

Access: Restrooms and viewing platforms are wheelchair accessible. Center Road Trail is not.

Bathrooms: At refuge headquarters.

Hazards: Storms and ship wakes if exploring the refuge by kayak or canoe.

Nearest food, gas, and lodging: Food and gas can be found at Clatskanie and Skamakowa. Lodging can be found on Puget Island.

Nearest camping: Skamakowa Vista Campground just outside of Skamakowa.

For more information: Call the refuge headquarters at (360) 795–3915 or visit refuges.fws.gov.

TOUCHED BY LEWIS AND CLARK

Lewis and Clark traded with the Chinook Indians on the Elochoman River. In their journals they talked about the abundance of the Columbian White-tailed deer. When white settlers came to the area, they destroyed deer habitat and hunted them to near extinction. In 1972, this refuge, then named Columbian White-tailed Deer National Wildlife Refuge, was created to help preserve the few remaining deer on the lower Columbia. Approximately 300 deer live on the refuge. In addition to the mainland unit, the refuge also includes four islands in the Columbia River and two more units in Oregon near Westport. In order to preserve habitat for the white-tailed deer, the refuge occasionally airlifts and relocates Roosevelt elk. Coyotes, the deer's main predator, are also relocated. Keep your eyes open for painted turtles, red-legged frogs, otter, mink, muskrats, and the invasive and nonnative nutria.

32 Ridgefield National Wildlife Refuge

Habitats: Wetland, riparian, meadow, lakes.

Specialty birds: Great Egret; Tundra Swan; Greater White-fronted Goose; Brant; Greater Scaup; White-tailed Kite; Bald Eagle; Peregrine Falcon; Sandhill Crane; Black-bellied Plover; Black-necked Stilt; Pectoral Sandpiper; Bonaparte's, Mew, Thayer's, and Western Gulls; Band-tailed Pigeon; Short-eared and Northern Pygmy-Owls; Vaux's Swift; Anna's and Rufous Hummingbirds; Pileated Woodpecker; Red-breasted Sapsucker; Hammond's and Pacific-slope Flycatchers; Hutton's and Cassin's Vireos; Purple Martin.

Best times to bird: Year-round, most variety during fall and spring migration.

Time your visit to the River "S" Unit at the Ridgefield National Wildlife Refuge in the late afternoon and evening for chances to see birds silhouetted against amazing sunsets.

About the site:

In a recurring dream I am walking along an urban trail and everywhere I turn I see birds—songbirds flitting in the branches of the trees or rustling in the leaves beneath, herons fishing in wetlands, cranes foraging in fields, and hawks and eagles landing on fence posts. The nearest I have come to living that dream was during a fall trip along the River "S" Unit auto tour at the Ridgefield National Wildlife Refuge (NWR). Birds were everywhere. Large, mixed flocks of wigeon, Northern Shoveler, Canvasback, and other ducks floated on the first ponds we came to. Hundreds of cranes came in to land near a damp, soggy field that was already covered with thousands of Canada Geese, more ducks, and a handful of swans. When we got out at the photo blind, we saw sparrows and heard wrens in the trees and on the duff and watched American Coots bobbing on the pond. Along the back side of the loop we saw Red-tailed Hawks perched in the leafless tops of trees surrounded by crows, and more songbirds flitted beneath; Dunlin and other shorebirds fed along the edges of the ponds and wetlands. And then we came to the homestretch and saw dozens of hawks hunting and eating in the dry, grassy fields: Northern Harrier, Rough-legged, and more Red-tailed Hawks, and an immature Bald Eagle. As the sun set and chased us out of the refuge, I knew that this trip had turned into one of those unforgettable events every bird-watcher hopes for.

Ridgefield NWR is easily one of the most popular bird-watching destinations in the state. The refuge offers a variety of habitats in three separate units, totaling more than 5,100 acres. Much of the lower Columbia River used to look like Ridgefield NWR. Today, few spots remain of what was once a stupendously large range of wetlands that hosted birds throughout the year, but most especially during spring and fall migration. The site remains important to the state's bird population, as evidenced by its designation as an Important Bird Area by Audubon Washington.

Tour the Carty Unit by walking the 2-mile Oaks to Wetlands Trail. After crossing the steep, arched bridge that crosses the railroad, you can go one of two ways. Veer left for the short walk to the Carty Lake observation deck to see waterfowl and the ubiquitous Red-winged Blackbirds. If you go right you'll pass through an oak grove, walk by Duck Lake, through a riparian zone of mixed-broadleaf forest, and on to the edge of a large wetland populated with ghostly, dead trees. The northern most loop of the trail is on private land, and while it is open from March 1 to September 30, it is closed to the public during the rest of the year. The trail branches at several locations, and all branches are not clearly marked. We have run into quite a few visitors who got separated from their parties and turned around. While the trail is not strenuous or extensive, we do suggest you pick up a map at the trailhead to prevent getting lost. We like to walk the longer loop trail and end our hike at the Carty Lake overlook.

This trail is an example of the edge habitat that offers so many options for bird-watching that it can almost be overwhelming, especially during spring and fall

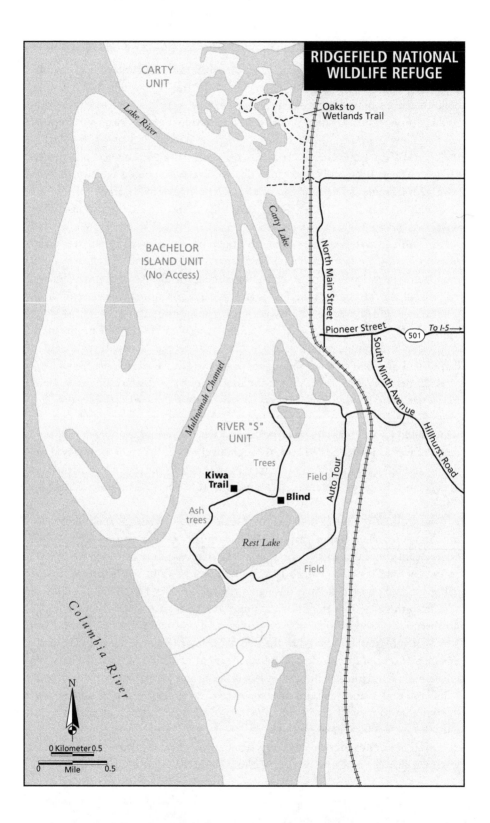

RIDGEFIELD NATIONAL
WILDLIFE REFUGE

CARTY
UNIT

Lake River

Oaks to
Wetlands Trail

Carty Lake

BACHELOR
ISLAND UNIT
(No Access)

North Main Street

Pioneer Street   501   To I-5→

South Ninth Avenue

Multnomah Channel

Hillhurst Road

RIVER "S"
UNIT

Trees

Field

Auto Tour

**Kiwa
Trail** ■

■ **Blind**

Ash
trees

Rest Lake

Field

Columbia River

N

0 Kilometer 0.5

0   Mile   0.5

migration. It's easy to get sidetracked here. When the warblers are flitting about in the Garry oak trees near the beginning of the trail, time can pass quite quickly while you stare into the high canopy to count the different species crowded into a single tree. Some of the few remaining west-side White-breasted Nuthatches can be found in this area. You might see turtles sunning themselves in Duck Lake next to mergansers, ducks, and herons. Check the wooded areas for Brown Creepers, thrushes, towhees, and other woodland songsters. When you reach the ghost trees, you'll be treated to the aerobatic displays of numerous swallows that nest in cavities carved into the dead trees. Purple Martins sometimes join the show, and Vaux's Swifts fly within sight on cloudy days. Where there are dead trees, you'll also find such other cavity nesters as Northern Flickers, and Pileated, Downy, and Hairy Woodpeckers. The trail is not open at night, but if you are hiking near dusk, you may be treated to owls calling.

The River "S" Unit features a 4.2-mile auto tour, a wheelchair-accessible blind, and a 1.5-mile foot trail. Visitors must stay in their cars, which make excellent blinds, between October 1 and April 30, but they may hike the autoroute during the rest of the year. Although you may be eager to cross the railroad tracks on your way to the main part of the refuge, take time on the hill to listen and look in the mixed woods for songbirds such as kinglets and vireos near the top, and Western Tanagers, Black-headed Grosbeak, warblers, and an occasional Red-breasted Sapsucker at various lower points on the hill.

As soon as you pass the restroom at the beginning of the loop, you will reach the wetlands and lakes, and most likely you will see your first ducks and geese paddling around and foraging in these ponds, including Ruddy Duck, American and Eurasian Wigeon, Northern Pintail, and Canada Geese—lots of Canada Geese. More-advanced birders will notice that several subspecies of Canada Geese abound at the refuge during migration, including Cackling, Aleutian, and Dusky. In fact, Ridgefield NWR was created specifically for the benefit of the Dusky subspecies. During the 1964 Alaska earthquake, their nesting grounds were lifted 6 feet. This alteration meant that the land was no longer part of the riparian/wetland habitat needed for safe nests. Providing the geese with a safe haven in winter would at least ensure that more geese returned to Alaska to find new places to breed.

Look along the edges of the ponds, and along the dikes that separate them, for skulking Wilson's Snipe, Virginia Rails, and Green Herons. The cattails are often topped by singing Red-winged Blackbirds; occasionally Yellow-headed Blackbirds, which nest on the refuge, move through and join the chorus. Where the road turns south at the end of Quigley Lake, it enters a stretch of alder, maple, and cottonwood trees edged by narrow, grassy fields. Western Scrub Jays and Steller's call loudly from these trees. In recent years bird-watchers have seen Red-shouldered Hawks on the refuge. These trees are one of the places to look. Look also for sparrows, including Chipping Sparrows, in the fields next to the trees. While Chipping Sparrows are common on the east side of the state, they are a treat to see on the west side.

Nearly 2 miles around the loop, a photo blind provides birders with a place to watch the many ducks floating on Rest Lake, the largest lake on the loop. If you love ducks, this is the place to spend some extra time. Bring a scope along for a closer look. The reeds and shrubs along the edge of the lake often hide Sora, more rails, and American Bittern. During one spring trip, we were fortunate enough to witness the mating behavior of a bittern as it gug-a-lumped like a frog. With each guttural iteration of its mating call, the bittern contracted its neck and then shot it upward, beak pointing to the sky at the end of the "song." On your way to and from the blind, check the trees and their many cavities for wrens and Spotted Towhees, as well as Tree Swallows, and Downy and Hairy Woodpeckers. If your timing is right, the White-breasted Nuthatches that are seen on the refuge might be foraging in the area.

On the road again, just beyond the blind, the trees give way to a small, sometimes grassy, sometimes wet field, depending on the weather. During migration, this field can be filled with a mixed flock consisting of thousands of geese, ducks, swans, and a handful of Sandhill Cranes. Check such flocks carefully for Snow Geese, Greater White-fronted Geese, and Trumpeter Swans as well as rarities that may be mixed in. It's yet another special Ridgefield experience that birders savor. Across from this field the wheelchair-accessible Kiwa Trail begins. Visitors can hike the 1.5-mile trail between May 1 and September 30. The trail winds through an oak woodland and wetlands, and between four small lakes. A boardwalk spans the sometimes-flooded expanses of the wetlands. Bird-watchers like the trail for its plentiful passerines, including Lincoln's and Fox Sparrows. Birders have also logged a handful of sightings of Black Phoebe and Red-shouldered Hawk near the trailhead.

Beyond the trail, the loop enters a sparsely wooded low ridge that divides Canvasback and South Lakes. Look to the west in South Lake for coots and Pied-billed Grebes. Hawks sometimes use these trees as hunting perches, and Yellow-rumped Warblers flit through the canopy while White-crowned Sparrows and their ground-loving friends explore the shrubs and roadside. Look east in Canvasback, Rest, and Swartz Lakes for more waterfowl, including Cinnamon, Green-winged, and Blue-winged Teals; Bufflehead; Common Goldeneye; and more geese and swans. Check also for Black Terns, which visit the refuge on their way to and from their northern breeding grounds. Look along the grassy and muddy edges of these lakes and in the damp fields along the route for shorebirds, such as Greater and Lesser Yellowlegs, Western and Least Sandpipers, and Long-billed Dowitchers. Check the flocks of dowitchers carefully for some of the Short-billed Dowitchers that are reported each year. Ridgefield is also one of the only places on the west side of the state where Black-necked Stilts are seen on rare occasions.

The last part of the route takes a straight line through grassy fields. It is in these fields that we saw the most amazing raptor scene we have ever witnessed. Northern Harriers, Bald Eagles, Red-tailed Hawks, and Rough-Legged Hawks all hunting and feasting simultaneously on the rodents and reptiles that live here and on the shorebirds that pass through during migration. You may also see White-tailed Kites in the trees edging the fields and Peregrine Falcons making flybys or scaring up the peeps.

Other key birds: Horned, Pied-billed, and Western Grebes; American Bittern; Black-crowned Night- and Green Herons; Snow Goose; Wood Duck; Gadwall; Green-winged, Blue-winged, and Cinnamon Teals; American and Eurasian Wigeons; Northern Pintail; Northern Shoveler; Canvasback; Redhead; Ring-necked Duck; Lesser Scaup; Common Goldeneye; Bufflehead; Common and Hooded Mergansers; Ruddy Duck; Turkey Vulture; Osprey; Red-shouldered and Rough-legged Hawks; Merlin; Ruffed Grouse; Virginia Rail; Sora; Semipalmated Plover; Greater and Lesser Yellowlegs; Spotted Sandpiper; Dunlin; Western and Least Sandpipers; Long-billed Dowitcher; Wilson's Snipe; Ring-billed, California, and Herring Gulls; Caspian Tern; Western Screech-Owl; Downy and Hairy Woodpeckers; Western Wood-Pewee; Willow Flycatcher; Northern Shrike; Red-eyed and Warbling Vireos; Western Scrub-Jay; Chestnut-backed Chickadee; Bushtit; White-breasted Nuthatch; Brown Creeper; House, Winter, Bewick's, and Marsh Wrens; Swainson's, Hermit, and Varied Thrushes; American Pipit; Orange-crowned, Black-throated Gray, Townsend's, Yellow, and Wilson's Warblers; Common Yellowthroat; Western Tanager; Chipping, Fox, Savannah, Lincoln's, White-throated, and Golden-crowned Sparrows; Black-headed Grosbeak; Yellow-headed Blackbird; Bullock's Oriole; Purple Finch; Red Crossbill; Evening Grosbeak.

Directions: From I-5, take exit 14 for State Route 501, also known as Pioneer Street, toward Ridgefield. To get to the River "S" Unit, follow the sign at the edge of town directing you to turn left onto South Ninth Avenue, also known as South Hillhurst Road. After about 0.6 mile, turn right into the refuge entrance. Note the gate closing time, which changes seasonally. To get to the Oaks to Woodlands Trail, remain on SR 501/Pioneer Street and turn right onto Main Street. Stay on Main Street until you reach the entrance to the Carty Unit.

Nearby opportunities: Shorebirds, neotropical passerines, and winter resident ducks visit Sauvie Island, located in the middle of the Columbia River on the Oregon side. To see more ducks, migrating Sandhill Cranes, hawks, and a few pairs of White-tailed Kites, head to Shillapoo Wildlife Area and Vancouver Lake, just a short distance north of Ridgefield and with easy access from I-5, the Woodland Dike Access road cuts through agricultural lands that flood seasonally and along the Columbia River to offer habitat for shorebirds, gulls, waterfowl, grebes, cranes, and other migrants and winter residents.

DeLorme map grid: Page 22, B2.

Elevation: 20 feet.

Access: Restrooms are wheelchair accessible, and most of site can be seen by car; Oaks to Wetland Trail is not wheelchair accessible.

Bathrooms: On-site at trail heads.

Hazards: Note the gate closing time when you enter the "S" Unit—more than one bird-watcher has been locked inside. A portion of the "S" Unit is open to hunters during the season.

Nearest food, gas, and lodging: Vancouver.

Nearest camping: Battleground State Park.

For more information: For more details and a history lesson, visit the refuge Web site at pacific.fws.gov/ridgefield/Ridge.htm.

Central

Washington's Central Region extends from the state's highest peaks in the Cascade Mountains in the west to the Columbia River as it cuts a path through the flood basalts of eastern Washington. With the Canadian border as the region's northern edge and the Columbia River as the border in the south, this region offers the best mountain birding in the state. As such, if you are looking for a hard-to-find White-tailed Ptarmigan or Gray-crowned Rosy-Finches in their breeding plumage, this is the region for you.

But you'll find more than mountains in the Central Region. It also includes some of the state's best shrub-steppe habitat in the Quilomene Wildlife Area near Vantage, some of the least-birded areas in the state such as the Sinlahekin Wildlife Area near the Canadian border and the Swakane Wildlife Area north of Wenatchee, and popular birding locations that combine a variety of habitats such as in the Wenas Creek valley near Yakima. The region also has its share of national wildlife refuges, with Conboy Lake in the south and Toppenish near Yakima.

Birds that highlight the region include the westernmost population of Bobolinks in the United States at the Toppenish National Wildlife Refuge, Gray Catbirds, Ferruginous and Swainson's Hawks, Golden Eagles, and a full host of fly-catcher species, including Least Flycatchers.

Much of the Central Region is hard to reach during the winter months, so plan to visit the area in the spring, summer, or fall.

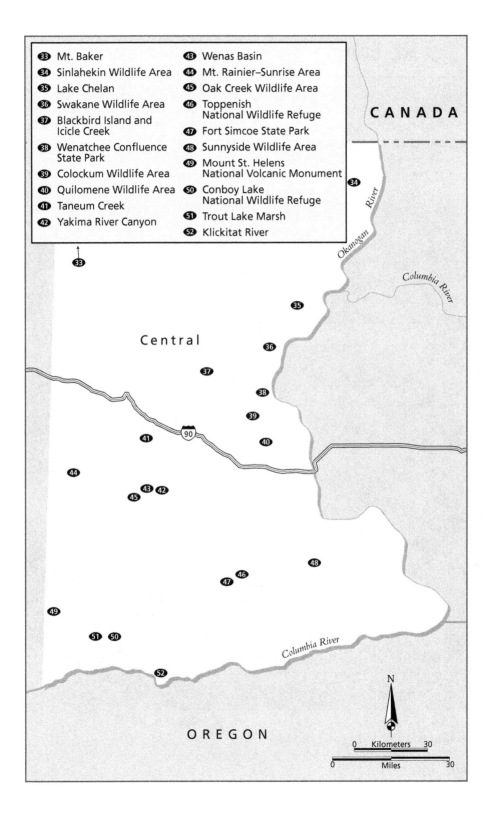

33	Mt. Baker	**43**	Wenas Basin
34	Sinlahekin Wildlife Area	**44**	Mt. Rainier–Sunrise Area
35	Lake Chelan	**45**	Oak Creek Wildlife Area
36	Swakane Wildlife Area	**46**	Toppenish National Wildlife Refuge
37	Blackbird Island and Icicle Creek	**47**	Fort Simcoe State Park
38	Wenatchee Confluence State Park	**48**	Sunnyside Wildlife Area
39	Colockum Wildlife Area	**49**	Mount St. Helens National Volcanic Monument
40	Quilomene Wildlife Area	**50**	Conboy Lake National Wildlife Refuge
41	Taneum Creek	**51**	Trout Lake Marsh
42	Yakima River Canyon	**52**	Klickitat River

CANADA

Okanogan River

Columbia River

Central

90

Columbia River

N

OREGON

0   Kilometers   30

0   Miles   30

33 Mt. Baker

Habitats: Mountain riparian, mixed forest, old-growth forest, subalpine, alpine meadow.

Specialty birds: Bald Eagle; Northern Goshawk; Blue Grouse; White-tailed Ptarmigan; Northern Pygmy-Owl; Black and Vaux's Swifts; Rufous Hummingbird; Pileated Woodpecker; Red-breasted Sapsucker; Hammond's and Pacific-slope Flycatchers; Gray Jay; Gray-crowned Rosy-Finch; Pine Grosbeak.

Best times to bird: Summer and fall.

Stunning scenery, such as this view of Mt. Shuksan, and high-mountain bird-watching are the attractions at Artist's Point near Mt. Baker.

About the site:

With an elevation topping 5,000-feet, Artist's Point and the Heather Meadows at Mt. Baker offer glimpses of birds that can't be seen in the lowlands of western and eastern Washington. Gray-crowned Rosy-Finch and White-tailed Ptarmigan are among the bird species found only on the state's higher peaks, and with its location in the northern tier of the state, Mt. Baker also offers good chances to see birds more typically associated with the deep woods of the north, such as Northern Goshawk.

As with many other bird-watching locations, timing is critical when you make the long, scenic trip up State Route 542 to Mt. Baker. Given its high elevation, the road to Artist's Point and Heather Meadows at the end of the highway is open for a limited time each year, normally starting around mid-July and continuing into the early fall. To save yourself from making a wasted trip toward Mt. Baker, be sure to check the Web site for Mt. Baker–Snoqualmie National Forest or read the newspapers for reports of when access to the upper reaches of SR 542 opens.

State Route 542 leaves the lowlands of western Washington in Bellingham and climbs and winds uphill along the course of the Nooksack River as it passes through farmlands, second-growth, and then old-growth forests on the way to Mt. Baker. The entire route from Bellingham to Mt. Baker offers bird-watching opportunities, including Bald Eagles that feed on salmon runs in the Nooksack River, Osprey that nest in the area, and warblers and flycatchers that frequent the wetlands and marshes along the river's course. Make stops at area campgrounds and even at wide pullouts along the road to look and listen for birds, especially paying attention to edge habitats where coniferous and deciduous forests come together, or along the edges of pastures.

As the road climbs away from the river valley, it enters a section of highway listed as a national scenic byway. Watch for Common Ravens flying along the highway, where they look for roadkill and other food, and you may spy a Pileated Woodpecker or Red-breasted Sapsucker flying in the mixed forests along this section of the road. Take advantage of pullouts on the way up the mountain to look across talus slopes where pika and small squirrels can be seen and heard as they sun themselves on the loose rocks.

Shortly after the highway passes the Mt. Baker Ski Area, it comes to the first of the visitor areas near the mountain at the Heather Meadows Visitor Center. Paved trails wind along the rocky landscape here, offering picnic areas as well as views of lakes and streams that flow down from the mountains. We didn't find any waterfowl on these high mountain lakes during one summer visit, but be sure to scan the lake surface and to look along the edges of the lake, where Spotted Sandpiper may be seen bobbing along the shore in search of food.

The next stop along the way to Artist's Point and the Austin Pass picnic area is the Lake Ann trailhead, which is the starting point for a 4-mile hike down to Lake Ann. Be sure to put on mosquito repellent before setting off on this hike, since the

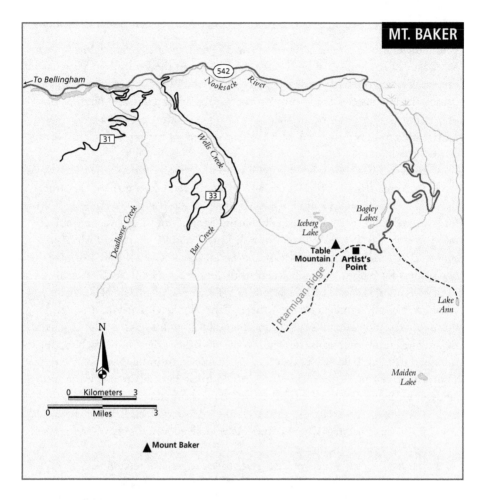

To Bellingham

542

Nooksack River

31

Wells Creek

33

Deadhorse Creek

Bar Creek

Iceberg Lake

Bagley Lakes

Table Mountain

Artist's Point

Ptarmigan Ridge

Lake Ann

N

Maiden Lake

0   Kilometers   3

0   Miles   3

▲ Mount Baker

bugs can be a problem in this area, with its standing water and damp summer habitat that is so conducive to the insects. If you are up for the hike, this trail offers more bird-watching opportunities. We watched a flock of ten to fifteen Gray-crowned Rosy-Finches fly past us while we walked the upper portion of the trail, and the lakeshore is sure to offer more glimpses of Spotted Sandpiper and waterfowl. Also listen for the sounds of juncoes, chickadees, and Gray Jays that might follow you on your walk.

The highway ends at Artist's Point, where snow clings to the hillsides and even surrounds the parking area late into the summer. Trails lead off higher into the mountains surrounding Mt. Baker from the parking lot, and if you venture up to the area ahead of the main tourist traffic there may be the chance of seeing White-tailed Ptarmigan and their young along the trail to Ptarmigan Ridge. Even if you show up later in the day with tourists who venture to Mt. Baker, by walking a little beyond the crowd and listening for the clear sounds of birds in the high mountain habitat, you are sure to enjoy the visit to Mt. Baker.

Snow remains on the trails near Mt. Baker late into the summer.

COMMON RAVEN

When you arrive at Artist's Point and Heather Meadows at the end of the road near Mt. Baker, the first prominent bird you are likely to see is a Common Raven. The Common Raven is seen throughout Washington, except in urban areas. They are regularly seen on the Olympic Peninsula and in the Cascade Mountains, but they are even more likely to be seen in eastern Washington. In these high elevations, Common Ravens prey on small birds, small wildlife, and carrion. They also patrol the parking lots looking for handouts and food left unattended by visitors. Ravens hold a special place in the mythology of the native peoples of the Pacific Northwest, and their distinct calls ring out loudly over the mountain landscape around Mt. Baker. Take the time to note the differences between the American Crows that are so widespread in urban areas and the Common Raven. The ravens are up to four times larger than crows, they have much larger beaks, and in flight a Common Raven has a wedge-shaped tail when compared to the squared-off tail of an American Crow.

Other key birds: Turkey Vulture; Osprey; Merlin; Ruffed Grouse; Spotted Sandpiper; Barred, Western Screech-, and Northern Saw-whet Owls; Downy and Hairy Woodpeckers; Olive-sided Flycatcher; Western Wood-Pewee; Red-eyed and Warbling Vireos; Clark's Nutcracker; Mountain and Chestnut-backed Chickadees; Brown Creeper; Winter, Bewick's, and Marsh Wrens; Swainson's, Hermit, and Varied Thrushes; American Pipit; Orange-crowned, Black-throated Gray, Townsend's, Yellow, MacGillivray's, and Wilson's Warblers; Common Yellowthroat; Western Tanager; Fox, Lincoln's, and Golden-crowned Sparrows; Black-headed Grosbeak; Bullock's Oriole; Purple Finch; Red Crossbill; Evening Grosbeak.

Nearby opportunities: Lake Whatcom.

Directions: From Bellingham, take SR 542 east until it reaches its end at Mt. Baker.

DeLorme map grid: Page 110, B3.

Elevation: 5,100 feet.

Access: None.

Bathrooms: None.

Hazards: Snow.

Nearest food, gas, and lodging: Bellingham.

Nearest camping: Silver Fir, Nooksack, and Douglas Fir campgrounds along SR 542.

For more information: Check the Web page for the Mt. Baker–Snoqualmie National Forest at www.fs.fed.us/r6/mbs. There is a parking fee required for visiting Artist's Point and Heather Meadows.

Sinlahekin Wildlife Area

Habitats: Mixed forest, cliffs, prairie, riparian, lakes.

Specialty birds: Common Loon; Tundra Swan; Greater Scaup; Barrow's Goldeneye; Golden and Bald Eagles; Northern Goshawk; Swainson's Hawk; Gyrfalcon; Chukar; Sandhill Crane; Long-billed Curlew; Short-eared and Northern Pygmy-Owls; Vaux's Swift; Black-chinned, Calliope, and Rufous Hummingbirds; Lewis's and Pileated Woodpeckers; Williamson's and Red-naped Sapsuckers; Hammond's, Dusky, and Pacific-slope Flycatchers; Cassin's Vireo; Pygmy Nuthatch; Western Bluebird; Bohemian Waxwing; Common Redpoll.

Best times to bird: Spring, summer, and fall.

The oldest wildlife area in Washington, the Sinlahekin area in the far northern reaches of central Washington is not widely used by the state's bird-watchers. This is one example of an accessible wildlife area where out-of-place birds could be discovered.

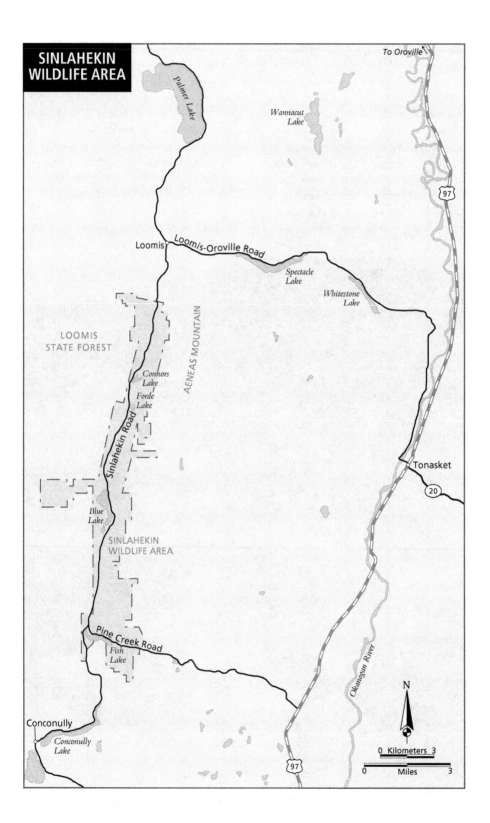

About the site:

You have to work to get to the Sinlahekin River Valley, but the variety of habitats and tranquil, panoramic views of quaking aspen, water birch, and ponderosa pine against craggy ancient cliffs will reward you for your efforts. The narrow valley may be one of the best-kept birding secrets in the state, since it is an under-birded site for all that it has to offer. Several lakes, some bounded by wetlands and emergent vegetation and some with rocky shores and deep centers, host nesting and migrating waterfowl; the forested habitat along the creek and the thickets along the shores of the lakes attract passerines; and the grasslands separating the other habitats draw hawks, Golden Eagles, and falcons. Ample stocks of game birds bring hunters to the area each fall.

Start your valley sojourn in Conconully by taking Sinlahekin Road out of town and driving along the side of Conconully Lake, which fills a narrow canyon. Look in the shrubby edges on the opposite shore for Gray Catbirds and warblers. About 5 miles outside of Conconully, the road passes through a dense Douglas fir forest. Pull off the road to look for Winter Wren, Mountain Chickadees, thrushes, and Hammond's Flycatchers. Drive on until you reach the entrance of the Sinlahekin Wildlife Area just south of Fish Lake, which has woods on either side and low shrubs along the edges. Check the shrubs for vireos, sparrows, and Common Yellowthroats. A series of roads circle the lake, which is popular with anglers. Sinlahekin Road continues through more forest until the landscape opens into the narrow, glacier-carved canyon. To get the most out of the valley, stop at each lake and anywhere you see thickets of water birch, alder, and willow or stands of cottonwood or quaking aspen, which turn brilliantly gold in the fall.

Look along the cliff ledges for nesting hawks and Golden Eagles like the one we saw stooping like a raven when we visited one fall. The eagle climbed high over the pines on the east side of the valley before it swooped down in a deep dive before climbing again. Simultaneously, on the other side of the road, a pair of Northern Harriers tippled low over the ground as they looked for rodents in the grass. Check the rocky, sometimes wooded cliff slopes for Chukar and Wild Turkey, and the grassy fields for California Quail and Ring-necked Pheasant. The trees on these slopes, mostly accessible on the west side of the road, also can host Dusky Flycatcher, Lewis's Woodpecker, Red Crossbill, and Western Tanager.

Blue Lake, the largest lake in the valley, is deep enough to host such diving ducks as Common and Barrow's Goldeneyes and Bufflehead, as well as Common Loon and Canada Geese. Just beyond Blue Lake, Sinlahekin Creek enters the valley and several beaver dams create marshy impoundments surrounded by shrubs that host more passerines. Between Forde and Conners Lakes, check aspen groves, willow thickets, and wetlands for Willow and Pacific-slope Flycatchers, Red-naped Sapsucker, Black-chinned and Calliope Hummingbirds, and Yellow-breasted Chat. Conners Lake is edged by marsh and low shrubs. The lake hosts a multitude of nesting waterfowl and grebes. Take your time here and wander into the campsites to find views of the lake, where you may see Wood and Ruddy Ducks, Lesser Scaup, Red-necked Grebes, and teals. If you like to hike, get out of the car and walk Spillway Trail, which passes between the granite hills and the east side of the creek. After Conners Lake, the forest takes over, with periodic openings, until the road reaches the edge of the wildlife area, just short of the town of Loomis.

The Sinlahekin Wildlife Area is the oldest wildlife area in the state. It was initially designated to protect mule deer. The area has grown to encompass 13,814 acres and in addition to birds and mule deer, the valley hosts white-tailed deer, moose, bighorn sheep, fourteen bat species and many rodents, beaver, porcupine, black bear, bobcat, and mountain lion. While the wildlife draws hunters and anglers, the impressive landscape and birds that call the valley home are well worth a long drive for birders.

Other key birds: Pied-billed and Red-necked Grebes; American Bittern; Wood Duck; Gadwall; Green-winged, Blue-winged, and Cinnamon Teals; American and Eurasian Wigeons; Northern Pintail; Northern Shoveler; Canvasback; Redhead; Ring-necked Duck; Lesser Scaup; Common Goldeneye; Bufflehead; Common and Hooded Mergansers; Ruddy Duck; Turkey Vulture; Osprey; Virginia Rail; Sora; Greater and Lesser Yellowlegs; Spotted Sandpiper; Wilson's Snipe; Ring-billed and California Gulls; Black Tern; Long-eared, Barred, Western Screech-, and Northern Saw-whet Owls; Common Nighthawk; Common Poorwill; White-throated Swift; Downy and Hairy Woodpeckers; Olive-sided Flycatcher; Western Wood-Pewee; Willow Flycatcher; Say's Phoebe; Western and Eastern Kingbirds; Northern Shrike; Warbling Vireo; Clark's Nutcracker; Bank Swallow; Mountain Chickadee; White-breasted Nuthatch; Brown Creeper; House, Winter, Rock, and Marsh Wrens; American Dipper; Mountain Bluebird; Townsend's Solitaire; Veery; Swainson's, Hermit, and Varied Thrushes; Gray Catbird; American Pipit; Orange-crowned, Nashville, Townsend's, Yellow, and Wilson's Warblers; Common Yellowthroat; Yellow-breasted Chat; Western Tanager; Chipping, Brewer's, Lark, Fox, Savannah, Lincoln's, and Vesper Sparrows; Black-headed Grosbeak; Lazuli Bunting; Yellow-headed Blackbird; Bullock's Oriole; Cassin's Finch; Red Crossbill; Evening Grosbeak.

Nearby opportunities: See loons, grebes, ducks, and big horn sheep at Palmer Lake, north of Loomis, or head south to Loup Loup for Williamson's Sapsucker.

Directions: From U.S. Highway 97 north of Omak, exit west onto Riverside Drive. Turn right onto Cherry Avenue, which becomes Kermel Road, and then turn right onto Conconully Road. Drive through the small town of Conconully, perhaps taking a detour to visit the state park and Conconully Reservoir, and then turn right onto Sinlahekin Road.

DeLorme map grid: Page 114, 3B.

Elevation: Ranges from 2,300 feet at Conconully to 4,000 feet at Loomis; the valley averages about 1,500 feet.

Access: None.

Bathrooms: Pit toilets at some camping spots.

Hazards: Rough roads.

Nearest food, gas, and lodging: Tonasket or Omak.

Nearest camping: Twenty primitive campsites are in the wildlife area. For more amenities, visit Conconully State Park or Spectacle Lake.

For more information: Visit the area's Web site at www.wdfw.wa.gov/lands/r2snlhkn.htm for more information on campsites and species lists.

 **Lake Chelan**

Habitats: Riparian, wetland, mixed forest.

Specialty birds: Common Loon; Greater Scaup; Barrow's Goldeneye; Bald Eagle; Northern Goshawk; Chukar; Northern Pygmy-Owl; Black and Vaux's Swifts; Black-chinned, Calliope, and Rufous Hummingbirds; White-headed, Lewis's, Black-backed, and Pileated Woodpeckers; Red-naped Sapsucker; Hammond's, Dusky, and Pacific-slope Flycatchers; Cassin's Vireo; Western Bluebird; Bohemian Waxwing.

Best times to bird: Spring, summer, and fall.

About the site:

Although it is better known as a tourist destination, Lake Chelan and its surrounding areas have a lot to offer bird-watchers. From Bald Eagles fishing off the lakeshore to Red-naped Sapsucker and mountain waterfowl species that can be seen on the south end of the 55-mile-long lake, this is an interesting place to explore in the late spring, summer, and early fall months.

Bird-watching can start anywhere around the town of Chelan. Wetlands along the south shore and the area just above the dam in town are full of waterfowl in the fall, as grebes and mergansers share the shallow feeding areas with ever-present Mallards. Bird diversity gets more interesting west of town along South Lakeshore Road. Bald Eagles are commonly seen in the Douglas fir and ponderosa pine that rise along the lakeshore and, depending on the season, you may also see and hear Clark's Nutcracker in the treetops along the road. A few wide spots in the road offer the chance to look for more birds on the lake, but the best birding opportunity is when you reach 127-acre Lake Chelan State Park.

Lake Chelan State Park is a popular destination in the summer months, when hot temperatures lure people to the sandy shores and the campground is packed every weekend. In order to find more birds than people in the park, plan to visit in the late spring before schools are out, or in the fall when temperatures start to drop. In the spring the cottonwood, locust, and ash trees along the lake are teeming with migrating songbirds, and the undergrowth of Oregon grape, snowberry, Nootka rose, and elderberry is active as well. Be sure to check the treetops for flycatchers. Trails wind through portions of the park and alongside a small stream that empties into the lake near a boat ramp, and this riparian area offers the best opportunities to see woodpeckers, sapsuckers, and other species that prefer mixed-forest habitat.

If you make your visit to Lake Chelan between April 1 and October 13, you have the option to explore the lakeshores farther to the northwest at 235-acre Twenty-Five Mile Creek State Park. Just as with Lake Chelan State Park, this larger park got its start long before the arrival of settlers. Both sites were used by Native Americans as base camps for fishing and hunting in the rugged mountains and valleys along the lake. Twenty-Five Mile Creek is a more-rugged park and not quite

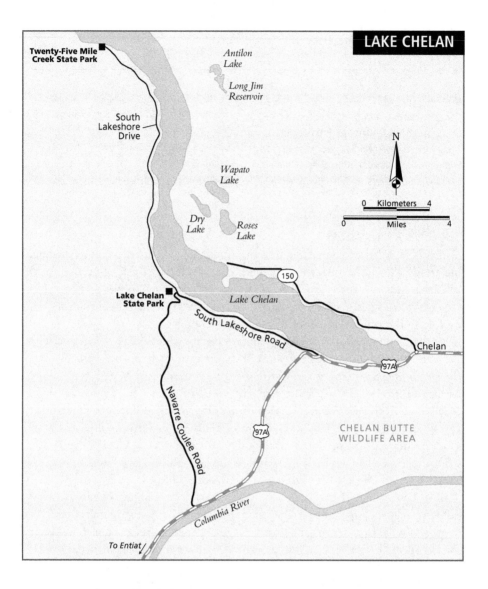

as easy to reach as Lake Chelan State Park, so it can be a better birding option in the summer months. It is also a jumping-off point for hiking opportunities that lead deep into the mature forests on the south side of the lake.

As you explore within and between these two parks, be sure to watch and listen around mature ponderosa-pine stands, since hard-to-find White-headed Woodpeckers are known to frequent the area. Also, if you start exploring in an area where a fire burned through in recent years, be sure to watch for Black-backed Woodpeckers as well, since they move into areas previously ravaged by fire.

If your birding route takes you south from Lake Chelan State Park, be sure to drive State Route 971 south through Navarre Coulee. This road is not as heavily traveled as many other highways, and it offers ample opportunities to pull to the road side and check the trees and rugged outcrops for birds. This dry, rugged land is prime habitat for Golden Eagles, and a lucky bird-watcher may even catch a glimpse of a migrating Northern Goshawk flying along the mountaintops.

THE FORMATION OF LAKE CHELAN

Thank the hard work of dueling glaciers for carving the deep basin that holds Lake Chelan. The Chelan Glacier reached down from the center of the northern Cascade Mountains while the continental ice sheet that reached down from Canada across much of central Washington helped carve out the wide expanses along the lower part of the lake. The result of this tug-of-war of ice and rock is a 55-mile-long lake that is 1,486 feet deep, including the deepest portion that actually dips 395 feet below sea level. A dam at the eastern edge of the lake controls its water level and generates hydroelectric power.

Other key birds: Horned, Eared, Pied-billed, Red-necked, and Western Grebes; Wood Duck; Gadwall; Green-winged and Cinnamon Teals; American and Eurasian Wigeons; Northern Pintail; Northern Shoveler; Canvasback; Red-head; Ring-necked Duck; Lesser Scaup; Common Goldeneye; Bufflehead; Common and Hooded Mergansers; Ruddy Duck; Turkey Vulture; Osprey; Merlin; Ruffed Grouse; Spotted Sandpiper; Wilson's Snipe; Ring-billed and California Gulls; Northern Saw-whet Owl; Common Nighthawk; Common Poorwill; White-throated Swift; Downy and Hairy Woodpeckers; Olive-sided Flycatcher; Western Wood-Pewee; Willow Flycatcher; Say's Phoebe; Western and Eastern Kingbirds; Northern Shrike; Warbling Vireo; Clark's Nutcracker; Bank Swallow; Mountain Chickadee; Brown Creeper; House and Winter Wrens; American Dipper; Mountain Bluebird; Townsend's Solitaire; Veery; Swainson's, Hermit, and Varied Thrushes; American Pipit; Orange-crowned, Nashville, Townsend's, Yellow, MacGillivray's, and Wilson's Warblers; Western Tanager; Chipping, Fox, Savannah, Lincoln's, Vesper, and Golden-crowned Sparrows; Black-headed Grosbeak; Lazuli Bunting; Bullock's Oriole; Cassin's Finch; Red Crossbill; Evening Grosbeak.

Nearby opportunities: Twenty-five Mile Creek State Park.

Directions: From Wenatchee, take U.S. Highway 97A north on the west side of the Columbia River and follow the signs toward Chelan. U.S. Highway 97A goes through a tunnel and follows Knapp Coulee to the lake. Turn left onto South Lakeshore Road, also known as SR 971, to begin exploring along the edges of the lake.

DeLorme map grid: Page 83, A7.

Elevation: 1,130 feet.

Access: None.

Bathrooms: Wheelchair accessible.

Hazards: None.

Nearest food, gas, and lodging: Chelan.

Nearest camping: Lake Chelan State Park.

For more information: Check the Web page for the park at www.parks.wa.gov/parks.

36 Swakane Wildlife Area

Habitats: Mountain riparian, prairie, mixed coniferous forest, cliffs.

Specialty birds: Golden Eagle; Northern Goshawk; Chukar; Blue Grouse; Northern Pygmy-Owl; Black and Vaux's Swifts; Black-chinned, Calliope, and Rufous Hummingbirds; White-headed, Lewis's, and Pileated Wood-peckers; Williamson's and Red-naped Sap-suckers; Hammond's, Dusky, and Pacific-slope Flycatchers; Cassin's Vireo; Western Bluebird; Bohemian Waxwing.

Best times to bird: Spring, summer, and fall.

Swakane Canyon opens into a wide meadow, foraging ground for elk in the winter and full of birdsong in the spring and summer.

About the site:

The Swakane Wildlife Area is one of those places you cannot judge from its entrance. It may not look like much from the gravel road heading west into the narrow canyon near the Rocky Reach Dam north of Wenatchee, but once you drive up the hill and see the mixed habitat with open views of ponderosa pine and grassy hillsides, the birding value of the site becomes apparent.

As the road sets off on its climb past an apple orchard on the right, be sure to stop and survey the treetops and edges of rock outcroppings. Hawks commonly sit in the trees here, but you also may see a Golden Eagle as we did on a spring visit when it was hassled so much by a pair of Red-tailed Hawks that it was forced to land and sit out the onslaught for a few minutes before moving on to other hunting grounds. Also check the telephone wires for kingbirds and bluebirds. The first mile or two of the road into the wildlife area skirts a riparian area along Swakane Creek, so pay attention to the edges of the habitat for songbirds. Vast growth of nettles means that butterfly-watching should be good in this area as well, especially for Red Admirable and Lorquin's Admiral butterflies that use nettles as their host plant.

After starting out at about 700 feet elevation at the bottom on the gravel road, the route steadily climbs until it takes a right-hand turn at the foot of a wide valley that serves as feeding habitat for elk and deer in the winter time. The road gets rougher from here on out as it climbs alongside this open field, but the birding opportunities pick up with Rock Wrens singing in season along the steep canyon walls and Western Meadowlark calling in the shrubby habitat between the road and the valley floor.

The farther the road climbs into the backcountry, the more trees dot the hillside. These are survivors and newcomers to the area since a huge forest fire swept through the canyon and across the hills to the north toward Entiat in 1988. That fire drastically changed the habitat in Swakane Canyon, burning off the underbrush and opening the terrain to hold more of a grassy understory while more fire-resistant trees, such as the ponderosa pine, took over as the dominant tree species.

Birders with standard passenger cars will most likely want to turn around at the 4-mile mark in the road, where the road surface gets markedly rougher and starts to climb steeply into the mountain forest areas deep in Swakane Canyon. When we researched this area we sat out a rain squall at a turnaround point near the 4-mile mark, and when we emerged from the car to do some birding, we found a male-female pair of White-headed Woodpeckers feeding in the ponderosa pine on the uphill side of the road.

As you make your way back down and out of Swakane Canyon, be sure to stop and bird the side canyons that follow the path of runoff as it makes its way to the

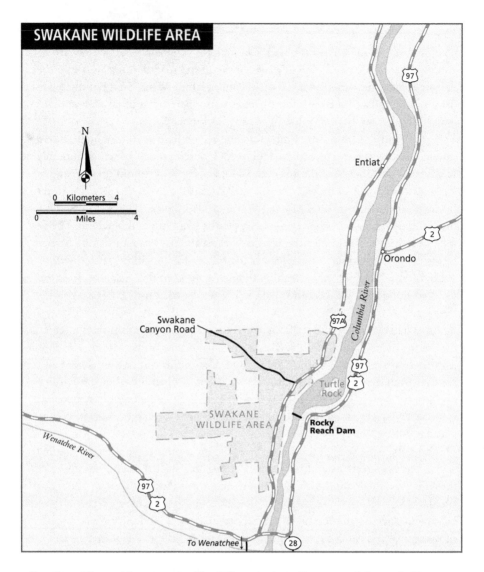

SWAKANE WILDLIFE AREA

N

0 Kilometers 4
0 Miles 4

Entiat

97

2

Orondo

Columbia River

Swakane
Canyon Road

97A

97

2

Turtle
Rock

SWAKANE
WILDLIFE AREA

Rocky
Reach Dam

Wenatchee River

97

2

To Wenatchee

28

valley floor. These side canyons offer different microclimates and denser habitat where you might see warblers and other songbirds.

Swakane is one of the most underbirded sites in central Washington, and one reason just might be the rugged road leading into the site. The first 4 miles of the single-lane gravel and dirt road described in this chapter had us swerving to avoid puddles and driving slowly to avoid banging the bottom of the car on the roadway. You can get more out of this site, including better access to higher-elevation birding farther up the road, with a four-wheel-drive or an all-wheel-drive car with high clearance. But those with standard vehicles can bird this area effectively, especially if they are willing to get out of the car and walk up some of the side roads for more birding opportunities and different niche habitats.

Side canyons and rocky outcroppings mark the sides of Swakane Canyon. Each small canyon houses plant communities in the niches in the canyon walls.

Other key birds: Turkey Vulture; Merlin; Wild Turkey; Ruffed Grouse; Barred, Western Screech-, and Northern Saw-whet Owls; Common Nighthawk; Common Poorwill; White-throated Swift; Downy and Hairy Woodpeckers; Olive-sided Flycatcher; Western Wood-Pewee; Willow Flycatcher; Say's Phoebe; Western and Eastern Kingbirds; Northern Shrike; Warbling Vireo; Clark's Nutcracker; Mountain Chickadee; White-breasted Nuthatch; Brown Creeper; House, Winter, Rock, and Canyon Wrens; Mountain Bluebird; Townsend's Solitaire; Veery; Swainson's and Hermit Thrushes; Orange-crowned, Nashville, Townsend's, Yellow, MacGillivray's, and Wilson's Warblers; Western Tanager; Chipping, Fox, Lincoln's, Vesper, and Golden-crowned Sparrows; Black-headed Grosbeak; Lazuli Bunting; Bullock's Oriole; Cassin's Finch; Red Crossbill; Evening Grosbeak.

Nearby opportunities: Entiat River Valley.

Directions: From Wenatchee, take U.S. Highway 97A north along the west side of the Columbia River north to the Rocky Reach Dam. Just past the dam, turn left off the highway onto the gravel road marked with signs as the Swakane Wildlife Area.

DeLorme map grid: Page 83, D6.

Elevation: Route described ranges from 700 feet to 1,700 feet.

Access: None.

Bathrooms: None.

Hazards: Rough gravel road may not be suitable for all passenger cars.

Nearest food, gas, and lodging: Wenatchee.

Nearest camping: Wenatchee Confluence State Park or a number of campsites to the north along the Entiat River.

For more information: Visit www.wdfw.wa.gov/wdfw/lands/r2chelan.htm on the Web.

37 Blackbird Island and Icicle Creek

Habitats: Riparian.

Specialty birds: Harlequin Duck; Bald Eagle; Northern Pygmy-Owl; Black and Vaux's Swifts; Black-chinned, Calliope, and Rufous Hummingbirds; Lewis's, Black-backed, and Pileated Woodpeckers; Red-breasted and Red-naped Sapsuckers; Hammond's and Pacific-slope Flycatchers; Cassin's Vireo; Gray Jay; Pygmy Nuthatch; Pine Grosbeak.

Best times to bird: Spring through fall.

A Gray Catbird calls alongside the Wenatchee River on Blackbird Island in Leavenworth. Catbirds nest in riparian habitats in eastern Washington, where they can be seen in the spring and summer.

About the site:

Most people know Leavenworth for its Bavarian-themed lodging, shopping, and seasonal festivals. Fewer know of the gem that sits at the heart of the city on what once was a mill pond; Blackbird Island is small, but birders find it irresistible. Three miles of trail connect Riverfront Park, Blackbird Island, and Enchantment Park.

Primarily covered with mature cottonwood trees, the island also contains ponderosa pine, willow, cherry, black elderberry, and plenty of Nootka Rose. Take your time walking the three trails. The trail on the city side of the island has less canopy cover than the other two trails. Northern Flickers show off on cottonwood stumps and snags, and sparrows rustle in the shrubs flanking the water's edge. The center trail passes through a stand of tall cottonwoods, a great place to look for flashy Yellow-rumped, Wilson's, and other warblers. Check all of the snags for Pacific-slope Flycatchers, chickadees, and woodpeckers. The trail on the river side of the island features a number of places where you can watch the river for waterfowl, including Common Mergansers.

At the Enchantment Park end of the trail, swallows swoop and dive in hot pursuit of insects that fly low over the water. Sometimes the young fledglings, worn out from the chase, perch on the snags in the water off the tip of the island. During one short session near the large log at the beginning of the riverside trail, we saw twenty birds, including California Quail, Spotted Towhee, Song and Fox Sparrows, Yellow-rumped, Orange-crowned, and Yellow Warblers, Cedar Waxwing, an immature Bullock's Oriole, and a secretive Veery. Also on this end of the island, Rufous Hummingbirds frequently nest in the shrubs near the bridge, zooming out to buzz anyone who dares to come too close to the tiny, hidden nests. The thick shrubs attract Gray Catbirds. During another visit to the island, a catbird cried out over and over again until we found him by walking part-way onto the bridge. He then sat and preened, as if putting on a show just for us. We welcomed the opportunity to closely examine this gregarious bird.

At the opposite end of the island, the Waterfront Park side, look for Say's Phoebes perched near the trail and Brown-headed Cowbirds near the bridge. While you walk the water-side trails on the island and through the parks, keep your ears open for the sounds of shrublovers, including grosbeaks, vireos, Common Yellowthroats, and Lazuli Buntings. You'll also see kingfishers diving into the water, and if you look up, especially during migration, you might see Turkey Vultures kettling overhead.

After you've warmed up with Blackbird Island, head south on State Route 2 and turn left onto Icicle Creek Road. Icicle Creek—also called Icicle River— offers miles of hiking trails and acres of wilderness, a great place to combine two passions. A 2001 fire burned through parts of the wilderness around the creek. Stands of burnt snags alternate with open spaces to provide prime habitat for the much-sought-after White-headed and Black-backed Woodpeckers. The creek is most impressive in the spring and early summer, when it rages with white-water

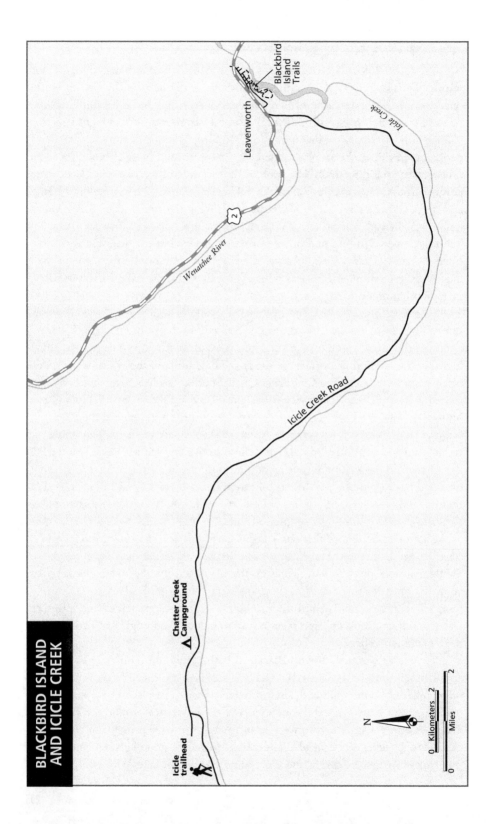

BLACKBIRD ISLAND AND ICICLE CREEK

Blackbird Island Trails

Leavenworth

Wenatchee River

Icicle Creek

Icicle Creek Road

Chatter Creek Campground

Icicle trailhead

N

0 Kilometers 2

0 Miles 2

rapids, butterflies puddle along the road, and migrating birds flit in abundance in the pines and firs and among the many shrubs that edge the road, including Oregon grape, soapberry, mountain boxwood, snowbrush, and oceanspray. Farther along the road, and higher up, western larch starts to take over the landscape. On your way up the road, you may want to stop at the Icicle Creek Nature Trail, a 1-mile interpretive trail at the Leavenworth National Fish Hatchery where you may be able to see Common Mergansers and American Dippers. White-headed Woodpeckers work over the pines. Stop to look over the creek at the Icicle Ridge trailhead, just a short way up the road, and then drive or walk through the campgrounds as you continue along the road. Drive 1 mile past the Chatter Creek campground—our favorite place to camp—to the 3.5-mile Icicle Gorge Loop Trail, an easy loop that takes you along both sides of the creek and into the forest. Look here, and at other spots that let you access the stream, for Spotted Sandpipers bobbing on the shore, Harlequin Ducks, and American Dippers.

If you like to camp, pitch your tent at the Chatter Creek campground. Owls will serenade you throughout the night, and morning brings a symphony of calls and songs from the Clark's Nutcrackers, Red Crossbills, flycatchers, and Red-breasted, White-breasted, and Pygmy Nuthatches that forage in the cedar, hemlock, pines, and maples in the campground. Although birders fully expect to see Red-naped Sapsuckers and Pileated Woodpeckers in this campground, you may also be surprised to see Red-breasted Sapsucker, a bird more commonly found on the west side of the Cascades. Before you pack up and head down the road, walk through the campground and look for Calliope Hummingbirds, Brown-headed Cowbirds, Black-Headed Grosbeaks, Townsend's Warblers, and Hermit Thrushes.

The combination of these two habitats, the subalpine and high-elevation riparian zones along with the riparian habitat at Blackbird island, makes Leavenworth worthy of more than shopping.

Other key birds: Wood Duck; Common and Hooded Mergansers; Turkey Vulture; Osprey; Merlin; Ruffed Grouse; Spotted Sandpiper; Barred, Western Screech-, and Northern Saw-whet Owls; Common Nighthawk; Downy and Hairy Woodpeckers; Olive-sided Flycatcher; Western Wood-Pewee; Willow Flycatcher; Say's Phoebe; Western and Eastern Kingbirds; Warbling Vireo; Clark's Nutcracker; Mountain and Chestnut-backed Chickadees; White-breasted Nuthatch; Brown Creeper; House and Winter Wrens; American Dipper; Mountain Bluebird; Townsend's Solitaire; Veery; Swainson's, Hermit, and Varied Thrushes; Gray Catbird; Orange-crowned, Nashville, Townsend's, Yellow; MacGillivray's, and Wilson's Warblers; Common Yellowthroat; Yellow-breasted Chat; Western Tanager; Chipping, Fox, Lincoln's, and Golden-crowned Sparrows; Black-headed Grosbeak; Lazuli Bunting; Bullock's Oriole; Purple and Cassin's Finches; Red Crossbill; Evening Grosbeak.

Nearby opportunities: Head to Wenatchee Lake and Tumwater Canyon for more of the birds found in this typical riparian and ponderosa-pine zone.

Directions: Take SR 2 to the center of Leavenworth. Turn southeast onto Ninth Street and then turn right onto Commercial Street. Park at the end of Commercial Street. You can also park anywhere downtown and walk to the park.

DeLorme map grid: Page 82, D3.

Elevation: 1,180 feet.

Access: Not wheelchair accessible.

Bathrooms: Restrooms in the park, but they are not always open.

Hazards: Rattlesnakes on some trails up Icicle Creek.

Nearest food, gas, and lodging: Leavenworth.

Nearest camping: Several campgrounds are available along Icicle Creek. Our favorite is at Chatter Creek.

For more information: Call the Leavenworth Chamber of Commerce at (509) 548-5807 or visit their Web site at www.leavenworth.org.

BIRD LOVERS INVADE LEAVENWORTH

Tourists have long headed to Leavenworth for its yuletide tree-lighting ceremonies, summer art festivals, and Oktoberfests. Many of these tourists do not know about the ample recreational activities offered in the region: rafting, kayaking, rock climbing, hiking, cross-country skiing, snowshoeing, and camping. However, the city has begun to pay more attention to the active-recreation fans that come to the area, including birders. The environment friendly Sleeping Lady Mountain Retreat recognizes the importance of birds in our lives and culture with its Wren Recital Hall and Kingfisher Outdoor Stage—it even serves shade-grown coffee in order to help protect migratory birds. Local businesses such as Sleeping Lady joined together with the North Central Washington Audubon Society and other agencies in 2003 to add the first annual Leavenworth Spring Bird Fest to the city's extensive event calendar. The festival will coincide each year with the International Migratory Bird Day, the second Saturday in May. Festival events include concerts, field trips, and workshops on everything from birding by ear to nature painting and photography. A new Audubon center graces the shores of the Wenatchee River near Blackbird Island.

Wenatchee Confluence State Park

Habitats: Lowland riparian, wetland, parkland.

Specialty birds: Common Loon; Greater White-fronted Goose; Greater Scaup; Barrow's Goldeneye; Golden and Bald Eagles; Black and Vaux's Swifts; Calliope and Rufous Hum-mingbirds; Lewis's and Pileated Woodpeckers; Red-naped Sapsucker; Hammond's Flycatcher; Cassin's Vireo; Western Bluebird.

Best times to bird: Year-round.

About the site:

Confluence State Park may be the easiest site in central Washington to access and to study continuously. The confluence of the Wenatchee and Columbia Rivers gives the park its name and provides birds with the perfect aquatic canvas on which to arrange themselves. The 197-acre site is divided by a footbridge into a recreation section on the north side and the Horan Natural Area on the south side.

Other than gulls, geese, and perhaps a few foraging shorebirds in the wet grass, you won't find much on the green lawns of the north side. However, if you walk across the grass to the water's edge in winter or during migration, you may be treated to an impressive site with large flocks of ducks and grebes bobbing on the water. In addition, you also may be able to see a few out-of-place gulls that stop along the river during their migrations. Those seen in the last few years include Herring and Little Gulls as well as Pomarine Jaegers. Where the rivers merge here, they create a wide expanse of swirling, food-rich water that attracts the passing migrants and winter residents. When you see large flocks of Canada Geese flying by or touching down, check them carefully for vagrant Snow Geese and flocks of Greater White-fronted Geese. Sandpipers and yellowlegs sometimes take breaks here as well. To see them, check the edges of the river, especially the sandbars and grassy fields.

When you've had your fill of the waterfowl on the river, make your way to the footbridge that connects the two parts of the park. Look over the edge of the bridge at the intrachannel islands for more shorebirds, mergansers and other ducks and, depending on the season, check the Osprey nest on top of the railroad bridge. If you've ever wanted a close encounter with Cliff Swallows, plan on spending some time here—they nest under the bridge and give watchers incredible displays of their flying abilities. This is also a good vantage to look for Bald Eagles hunting, and at either end of the bridge, check the trees and shrubs for passerines.

The 2-mile loop trail that circles through the ninety-seven-acre Horan Natural Area begins directly after the bridge. Turn left to walk along the river. Several observation platforms around the trail provide more advantageous points to over-look the river, ponds, and wetlands. The cottonwood trees shelter passerines such as Yellow-rumped, Orange-crowned, and MacGillivray's Warblers. Where the trees

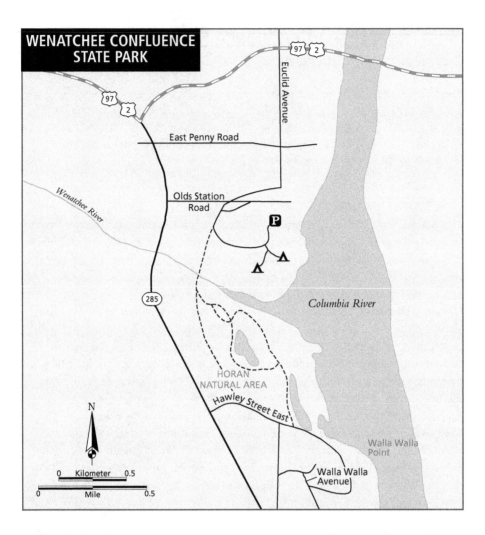

WENATCHEE CONFLUENCE STATE PARK

Euclid Avenue

East Penny Road

Wenatchee River

Olds Station Road

HORAN NATURAL AREA

Hawley Street East

Columbia River

Walla Walla Point

Walla Walla Avenue

N

0   Kilometer   0.5
0   Mile   0.5

grow more closely and the understory is shrubbier, check for Brown Creepers on the sides of the trees and thrushes and wrens below. You're also likely to find and hear Western Wood-Pewee and Olive-sided flycatchers near canopy openings and trail edges. Where the trail turns, check the trees for Black-headed and Evening Grosbeaks as well as Bullock's Orioles.

If you choose to walk the out-and-back trail from here to the radio towers, which parallels a small tributary and passes through grassy fields, look for Savannah and Vesper Sparrows and shrikes in the dry grass. The south side of the loop trail overlooks more fields and marshy wetlands, and Marsh Wrens skulk in the reeds. Northern Harriers also hover over these fields. The south side of the trail passes closer to the ponds and offers good looks at the Pied-billed Grebes and dabbling ducks, including Wood Ducks, Mallards, and teals on the ponds and blackbirds in the reeds. You also might see the sun glinting off a turtle's shell as it climbs out of the water. If you continue south on the trail, you will eventually reach Walla Walla Point Park, which offers more access to the Columbia River.

The tribes from this area used to gather at the confluence to meet and fish. They understood the richness of animal diversity offered in such areas. Today, the park is sure to provide birders with something exceptional due to its habitats. Repeated visits will give you a better chance of seeing the rarities that are attracted to the area and will help you observe the changing seasons based on the progression of bird life.

Other key birds: Horned, Pied-billed, and Western Grebes; Black-crowned Night-Heron; Wood Duck; Gadwall; Green-winged Teal; American Wigeon; Canvasback; Redhead; Ring-necked Duck; Lesser Scaup; Common Goldeneye; Bufflehead; Common and Hooded Mergansers; Ruddy Duck; Turkey Vulture; Osprey; Merlin; Virginia Rail; Sora; Greater Yellowlegs; Wilson's Snipe; Ring-billed and California Gulls; Caspian Tern; Northern Saw-whet Owl; Common Nighthawk; Downy and Hairy Woodpeckers; Olive-sided Flycatcher; Western Wood-Pewee; Willow Flycatcher; Say's Phoebe; Western and Eastern Kingbirds; Northern Shrike; Warbling Vireo; Bank Swallow; Brown Creeper; House and Winter Wrens; Veery; Swainson's, Hermit, and Varied Thrushes; American Pipit; Orange-crowned, Nashville, Townsend's, Yellow, and Wilson's Warblers; Common Yellowthroat; Yellow-breasted Chat; Western Tanager; Chipping, Brewer's Fox, Savannah, Lincoln's, Vesper, and Golden-crowned Sparrows; Black-headed Grosbeak; Lazuli Bunting; Bullock's Oriole; Purple and Cassin's Finches; Red Crossbill; Evening Grosbeak.

Nearby opportunities: Walla Walla Point Park in Wenatchee, which is connected to the Horan Natural Area by a footpath, offers chances to see more gulls and waterfowl. Also head west toward Cashmere to Mission Creek Road and Sand Creek Road for a variety of neotropical migrants and ponderosa pine-loving birds.

Directions: Drive through Wenatchee on State Road 2 and turn south onto Euclid Avenue, which becomes Olds Station Road where the road turns to the west. Turn right onto the park road and park near the bathrooms to visit the confluence or go straight and park near the footbridge to visit the nature area.

DeLorme map grid: Page 67, A6.

Elevation: 800 feet.

Access: Wheelchair-accessible trails.

Bathrooms: Wheelchair-accessible restrooms on-site.

Hazards: None.

Nearest food, gas, and lodging: Wenatchee.

Nearest camping: Inside the park.

For more information: Check the Web page for the park at www.parks.wa.gov.

Colockum Wildlife Area

Habitats: Shrub-steppe, lowland riparian, mountain riparian, freshwater marsh, mixed forest, cliffs.

Specialty birds: Golden and Bald Eagles; Northern Goshawk; Swainson's Hawk; Peregrine Falcon; Chukar; Blue Grouse; Flammulated and Northern Pygmy-Owls; Vaux's Swift; Black-chinned, Calliope, and Rufous Hummingbirds; White-headed, Lewis's, Black-backed, and Pileated Woodpeckers; Williamson's and Red-naped Sapsuckers; Hammond's, Gray, Dusky, and Pacific-slope Flycatchers; Cassin's Vireo; Gray Jay; Pygmy Nuthatch; Western Bluebird; Sage Thrasher; Gray-crowned Rosy-Finch; Pine Grosbeak.

Best times to bird: Spring and early summer.

The northern foothills of the Colockum Mountains beckon bird-watchers looking for such birds as Williamson's Sapsucker. The Colockum Wildlife Area covers the land from Wenatchee south toward Kittitas.

About the site:

As one of the least-explored and least-accessible wildlife areas in central Washington, the Colockum Wildlife Area and the road up and over Colockum Pass offer some of the best bird-watching secrets in the state. The trouble is determining the best way to view the area without the need for a rugged four-wheel-drive vehicle. The road up to Colockum Pass is not recommended for passenger cars.

Although the route described here won't get you to the top of 5,373-foot Colockum Pass, it does allow you to explore the northern edges of the wildlife area without a four-wheel-drive by venturing into the shrub-steppe habitat from the north along Colockum Creek. Just south of Wenatchee, Colockum Creek meanders down from Naneum Ridge to flow alongside Colockum Road and down to the Columbia River. By driving south of Wenatchee on Malaga-Alcoa Highway and following Colockum Road up into the lower reaches of the mountains, you can bird-watch along the creek's lowland riparian areas that are full of warblers and other songbirds in the spring. Flycatchers, vireos, and hummingbirds also frequent the low-lying trees and shrubs on this edge of the wildlife area.

The road starts to climb toward higher elevations as the number of houses drops off farther up the valley, with the creek running through a riparian zone to the left of the road and grass and sage habitat starting to show on the dry right side of the road. Colockum Road is paved most of the way up toward the county line, but before crossing the creek and starting to drive farther up the road, go straight when the main road veers left. Continue up a rugged gravel road that climbs past a few more homes and then past a trio of beaver dams that hold excellent habitat and the last major water before the road rises into a grassy zone and then into dispersed ponderosa-pine habitat along the south fork of Colockum Creek. We were able to drive our passenger car up to about the 2,500-foot level before we found a wide area to turn around and make our way slowly back down the single-lane gravel road.

After returning to Colockum Road, you can continue driving up the hill past a sign that warns there are no turnarounds on the road ahead. If your vehicle isn't up to the rough roads ahead, this is a good spot to turn around and start birding back down the creek. If your vehicle can handle the rugged roads, continue up toward Colockum Pass for some real bird treats as the higher elevation and the remoteness of the area open up a whole new world of bird-watching. As Colockum Road climbs, the habitat changes to modified shrub-steppe (modified by cattle grazing) that can hold Sage, Lark, Vesper, and Grasshopper Sparrow, Sage Thrasher, and other species associated with more mature shrub-steppe habitat. As the elevation rises the road passes through pine forest and mixed forest that can hold Williamson's Sapsucker, White-headed Woodpecker, Three-toed Woodpecker, and other species more associated with mountainous forests. Given its high elevation, Colockum Pass isn't normally snow-free until late May or well into June,

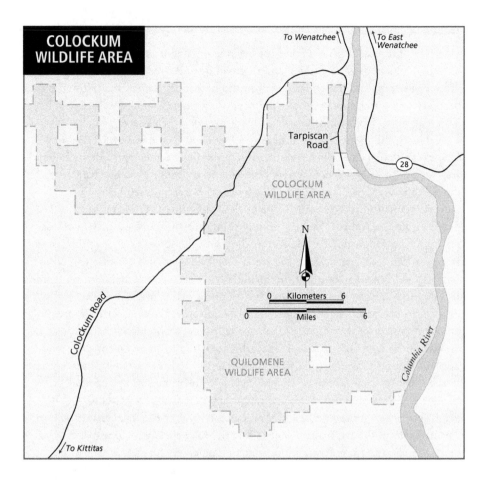

COLOCKUM
WILDLIFE AREA

To Wenatchee

To East
Wenatchee

Tarpiscan
Road

28

COLOCKUM
WILDLIFE AREA

N

0   Kilometers   6

0   Miles   6

Colockum Road

QUILOMENE
WILDLIFE AREA

Columbia River

To Kittitas

depending on the winter snowfall, so be prepared to turn back if snow impedes driving. The best advice is to come prepared for the conditions.

If you drive all of the way up and over Colockum Pass, the rugged road makes its way into the area around Ellensburg.

If you don't have a four-wheel-drive vehicle and you aren't taking on the upper reaches of Colockum Road, drive back down alongside the creek to the point where the road makes a Y, and this time turn right onto Tarpiscan Road to drive toward the headquarters building for the Colockum Wildlife Area. This gravel road follows the Columbia River south for a few miles before reaching the wildlife area entrance, with more grazing-modified shrub-steppe habitat and dry, rocky, and grassy grounds leading up into a small riparian zone along Tarpiscan Creek. This wildlife area is popular in the fall with hunters, but in the spring and summer it can offer more room to explore in your car or on foot. Roads marked with green dots on the roadside poles are open for vehicles. The wildlife area is also open to bikes, so this could be a good location to do some birding by bicycle.

Throughout the rest of the Colockum Wildlife Area, which along with the Quilomene Wildlife Area to the south is listed by Audubon Washington as one of the state's Important Bird Areas (IBA), a series of creeks provides riparian habitat with nesting areas for Lewis's Woodpecker, wrens, Bullock's Oriole, and American Kestrel. This is interspersed with grass and shrub-steppe habitat, with mixed forest in the higher elevations. There is room for exploration in the rest of the wildlife area, but it is far from accessible, which is good for the nesting birds in the area. Since this is an IBA site, be sure to tread lightly to help protect the valuable bird-watching habitat so that it can remain a resource for the bird and animal life of the rugged area.

Other key birds: Turkey Vulture; Osprey; Rough-legged Hawk; Merlin; Prairie Falcon; Gray Partridge; Ruffed Grouse; Virginia Rail; Sora; Wilson's Snipe; Ring-billed Gull; Western Screech- and Northern Saw-whet Owls; Common Nighthawk; Common Poorwill; White-throated Swift; Downy, Hairy, and Three-toed Woodpeckers; Olive-sided Flycatcher; Western Wood-Pewee; Willow Flycatcher; Say's Phoebe; Western and Eastern Kingbirds; Loggerhead and Northern Shrikes; Warbling Vireo; Clark's Nutcracker; Bank Swallow; Mountain Chickadee; White-breasted Nuthatch; House, Winter, Rock, and Canyon Wrens; Mountain Bluebird; Townsend's Solitaire; Veery; Swainson's, Hermit, and Varied Thrushes; Gray Catbird; Orange-crowned, Townsend's, Yellow, MacGillivray's, and Wilson's Warblers; Yellow-breasted Chat; Western Tanager; Chipping, Brewer's, Lark, Fox, Savannah, Lincoln's, Vesper, and Golden-crowned Sparrows; Black-headed Grosbeak; Lazuli Bunting; Yellow-headed Blackbird; Bullock's Oriole; Cassin's Finch, Red Crossbill; Evening Grosbeak.

Nearby opportunities: Side canyons branching off Colockum Road, such as along Kingsbury Road. Beware of rough road conditions.

Directions: From Wenatchee, take State Route 2 south through town to Mission Street and continue south on Mission. When Mission Street turns left and crosses a bridge over the Columbia River, continue going straight for 1 block, then turn left before turning right onto the Malaga-Alcoa Highway. Stay on this road through Malaga and past the Alcoa plant. Turn right at a Y in the road onto Colockum Road. To reach the Colockum Wildlife Area headquarters, turn left at the Y onto Tarpiscan Road and continue driving south.

DeLorme map grid: Page 67, C7.

Elevation: 650 feet at the bottom of Colockum Road.

Access: None.

Bathrooms: None.

Hazards: Bad road conditions, snows in the higher elevations.

Nearest food, gas, and lodging: Wenatchee.

Nearest camping: Wenatchee Confluence State Park.

For more information: Check the Web page for the Colockum Wildlife Area at www.wdfw.wa.gov/lands/r3colock.htm. A Vehicle Use Permit is required for parking in the wildlife area.

Quilomene Wildlife Area

Habitats: Shrub-steppe, lowland riparian, mountain riparian, cliffs.

Specialty birds: Golden and Bald Eagles; Swainson's Hawk; Peregrine Falcon; Vaux's Swift; Black-chinned, Calliope, and Rufous Hummingbirds; Lewis's and Pileated Woodpeckers; Red-naped Sapsucker; Hammond's, Gray, Dusky, and Pacific Slope Flycatchers; Cassin's Vireo; Western Bluebird; Sage Thrasher; Sage Sparrow.

Best times to bird: Year-round, but late spring and summer for specific shrub-steppe species.

Thunderclouds loom over the Columbia River in the distance while sunshine highlights the mature sagebrush in the Quilomene Wildlife Area, at the entrance to the area just off the Old Vantage highway.

About the site:

The Quilomene Wildlife Area may be the easiest place in the state to see Sage Sparrows, Sage Thrashers, and other birds associated with the dwindling shrub-steppe habitat that makes up much of this rugged wildlife area. If you are lucky and you time things right, many of these birds can be seen right alongside the Vantage Highway at the entrance to the wildlife area. But if you really want to see the natural diversity of the area, which in combination with the Colockum Wildlife Area to the north covers a wide swath of mountain land between Vantage and Wenatchee, you have to explore the rugged backroads of the Quilomene.

What is called the Quilomene Wildlife Area on the roadside signs along the Vantage Highway is actually two wildlife areas combined. The Whiskey Dick Wildlife Area is just north of the highway, and it covers nearly 29,000 acres of sagebrush, bitterbrush, and bunchgrass habitat, with diverse plant and animal life in the higher elevations around 3,878-foot Whiskey Dick Mountain. A little farther to the north, the Quilomene Wildlife Area covers nearly 18,000 acres in the southeastern foothills of the Colockum Mountains, and it offers a series of steep slopes alongside narrow riparian areas that border streams that run east to empty into Wanapum Lake, otherwise known as the Columbia River.

With more than 46,000 acres in the areas commonly referred to as the Quilomene Wildlife Area, there is a lot of room for exploration and birding. Just as with the Colockum Wildlife Area to the north, only those with four-wheel-drive vehicles or sturdy hiking boots can venture into the backcountry in Quilomene. The wildlife area is marked with roads denoted by green dots on the roadside to let drivers know which areas are open to vehicles and which are off-limits. For our purposes, we have done most of our birding in this wildlife area from near the Vantage Highway. Parking at the entrance point for the wildlife area and walking into the site offers ample birding opportunities, even though you can't experience the full breadth of what lies in the Quilomene.

Just birding from the parking area has been rewarding for us. Show up in the morning hours in late spring and early summer for chances to see Sage, Brewer's, Vesper, and Grasshopper Sparrow in the tall sagebrush to the north and west of the parking area. Just watch and listen for movement and you may be rewarded with some close views of these shrub-steppe species, along with Sage Thrasher, Rock Wren, and others. Also keep an eye out for raptors in the area. We commonly see Prairie Falcon hunting at the site, and on one visit we watched two of the speedy falcons fly right past us as they chased each other.

If you venture farther into the wildlife area, you will find that the terrain is rugged and dramatically marked by runoff and by a series of small coulees that carve their way to the east toward the Columbia River. Rocky Coulee is the first you encounter heading to the north, and then a series of steep riparian areas along Whiskey Dick Creek, Skookumchuck Creek, and Quilomene Creek offer an oasis

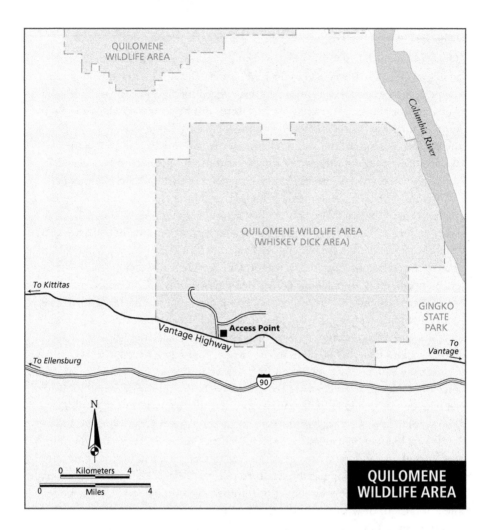

of water-side habitat for woodpeckers, flycatchers, and songbirds. Lewis's Wood-pecker are known to frequent the hard-to-access riparian areas and, close to the mouths of these creeks where the water cascades down to the river, riverside bluffs are used as nesting habitat for Peregrine Falcons.

Besides the birding opportunities at this site, it also can be an excellent area for seeing wildflowers associated with the shrub-steppe habitat, as well as butterfly species that rely on the arid lands and associated plants. The area also hosts the Colockum elk herd, and the Department of Fish and Wildlife has been working to establish bighorn sheep in the area since they historically roamed in the Colockum Mountains.

Although some of the rugged roads of the Quilomene Wildlife Area are open to vehicles, another reason to stick to exploring the edges of the area rather than tackling its core is that it has been named by Audubon Washington as one of the

Important Bird Areas in the state. As such, if you do go deep into the sagebrush country, take every step to minimize your impact on the habitat, and only enter the area in very early spring or late summer to avoid disturbing nesting birds.

You can round out your birding in this section of Kittitas County by watching for birds along Vantage Highway between the town of Kittitas on the west side of the highway and Vantage on the east end of the highway. Both Eastern and Western Kingbirds are common in the spring and summer along the highway, and Western and Mountain Bluebirds are common as well. Wilson's Snipe are regularly seen along damp farm fields close to Kittitas. On the eastern end of the highway at Ginko Petrified Forest State Park, the oasis of trees and grass around the park residence has been known to be a migrant trap that can hold a wide range of eastern Washington bird species. Be ready for windy conditions when you bird in this area though, since afternoon winds can really whip up Schnebly Coulee, which the highway follows on its route down to Vantage and the Columbia River.

THE DISAPPEARING SHRUB-STEPPE HABITAT

Shrub-steppe habitat used to cover the entire Columbia basin with bunchgrass, sagebrush, rabbitbrush, and bitterbrush. That was before dams blocked the Columbia River and the resulting increase in irrigation and farming converted huge tracts of shrub-steppe land into endless fields of wheat and potatoes. And it was before development and golf courses displaced even more of the habitat that was widely viewed as barren wasteland by those whose only encounters with the habitat was whisking past it at 70 miles per hour on I-90.

Less than 40 percent of Washington's native shrub-steppe habitat remains, according to the Washington Department of Fish and Wildlife, and much of what remains has been compromised by cattle grazing, fire, and other human-caused alterations. This is bad news for the birds, plants, and animals that rely on the shrub-steppe as their niche in the Pacific Northwest environment. Greater Sage Grouse depend on mature sagebrush habitats that are not overrun by cattle or the cheatgrass that cattle grazing leaves in its wake even years after the end of active grazing. The same can be said for Sharp-tailed Grouse and Burrowing Owls, and the shrinking shrub-steppe habitat is the main reason that the pygmy rabbit is an endangered species in Washington.

Wildlife agencies are working with conservation groups to help protect some of the remaining shrub-steppe habitat in Washington, and areas such as the Quilomene Wildlife Area and the Colockum Wildlife Area are key figures in preserving mature sagebrush communities and the species that depend upon this habitat for their survival.

Other key birds: Turkey Vulture; Osprey; Rough-legged Hawk; Prairie Falcon; Gray Partridge; Ruffed Grouse; Ring-billed Gull; Caspian Tern; Common Nighthawk; Common Poorwill; White-throated Swift; Say's Phoebe; Western and Eastern Kingbirds; Loggerhead and Northern Shrikes; Warbling Vireo; Bank Swallow; Mountain Chickadee; White-breasted Nuthatch; House, Winter, Rock, and Canyon Wrens; Mountain Bluebird; Townsend's Solitaire; Veery; Swainson's, Hermit, and Varied Thrushes; Gray Catbird; Orange-crowned, Yellow, MacGillivray's, and Wilson's Warblers; Western Tanager; Chipping, Brewer's, Lark, Grasshopper, Fox, Savannah, Lincoln's, Vesper, and Golden-crowned Sparrows; Black-headed Grosbeak; Lazuli Bunting; Bullock's Oriole; Cassin's Finch; Red Crossbill; Evening Grosbeak.

Nearby opportunities: Ginko Petrified Forest State Park.

Directions: From Interstate 90, exit at Vantage and drive north through the town and up the hill along Vantage Highway past the Ginko Petrified Forest State Park. The entrance to the Quilomene Wildlife Area is farther up the hill and west of the state park. Watch for a sign denoting the entrance to the wildlife area and cross a cattle grate to enter a parking area at the start of the wildlife area.

DeLorme map grid: Page 51, A7.

Elevation: 1,200 feet.

Access: None.

Bathrooms: None.

Hazards: Rough roads recommended only for four-wheel-drive vehicles.

Nearest food, gas, and lodging: Vantage.

Nearest camping: Wanapum State Park.

For more information: Check the Web page for the Quilomene Wildlife Area at www.wa.gov/wdfw/lands/r3quilmn.htm.

41 Taneum Creek

Habitats: Lowland riparian, prairie, mountain riparian, mixed forest, cliffs.

Specialty birds: Golden and Bald Eagles; Northern Goshawk; Flammulated and Northern Pygmy-Owls; Black and Vaux's Swifts; Black-chinned, Calliope, and Rufous Hummingbirds; White-headed and Pileated Woodpeckers; Williamson's, Red-breasted, and Red-naped Sapsuckers; Hammond's, Dusky, and Pacific-slope Flycatchers; Cassin's Vireo; Gray Jay; Western Bluebird; Gray-crowned Rosy-Finch; Pine Grosbeak.

Best times to bird: Spring, summer, and fall.

Taneum Creek flows east out of the Cascade Mountains, providing a riparian corridor through the L. T. Murray Wildlife Area.

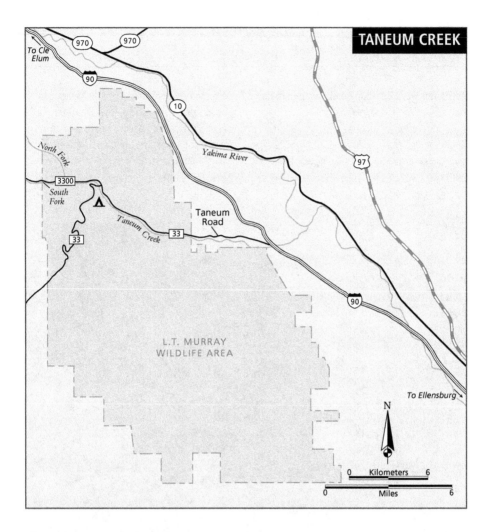

About the site:

There are few quicker routes in the state to go from a major highway to rugged wilderness than the drive into Taneum Creek Canyon. The canyon cuts a path between South Cle Elum Ridge and Manastash Ridge while bordering and going through the L. T. Murray Wildlife Area en route to the heart of the Cascade Mountains on Taneum Ridge. Along the way the roads traverse habitats ranging from lowland riparian areas and prairie at the start of Taneum Creek Road to steep canyons with cliffs and rock outcroppings and into mixed forest as the road climbs toward the ridge.

Get ready for variety when birding Taneum Creek. Sparrows, Black-headed Grosbeaks, and Lazuli Bunting can be seen and heard at the outset of the route heading west along Taneum Creek Road, where it pays to watch the edges of the fields and tree-lined borders for the best opportunities. Also check the tops of fence posts for bluebirds. The fields along this stretch of the road can hold elk and deer in the early spring and late fall, so be ready to watch mammals as well as winged wildlife during those times of year.

Just a short distance up the road, the route passes by and under a huge outcrop of rock that marks the beginning of habitat for Rock Wren and Canyon Wren as well as Cliff Swallows. The steep hillside is marked with ponderosa pine in this area, offering a preview of the mixed-pine forest found higher in the hills, while the creek side offers birch, cottonwood, willow, flowering spirea, ocean spray, and other riparian plants. The brushy creek side and a small wetland area full of reeds a little farther up the road offer habitat for warblers and blackbirds.

The road switches to gravel and is labeled as Forest Road 33 as it continues west along the creek en-route to another good birding stop, picnic site, and bathrooms at the Taneum Campground. During one summer visit to this campground, I was watching both birds and butterflies. While I was trying to get a photo of a butterfly as it fluttered overhead, a bird swooped down from the tree canopy above and snatched the butterfly in midair. The entire route along Taneum Creek offers prime butterfly habitat, so this kind of wildlife interaction can be common here. Whether you see it or not depends on luck and timing.

Continuing west past the campground, stick with FR 33 until the road comes to an intersection by a small campground along Taneum Creek, which is often full of mountain bikers and other active sports enthusiasts during weekends. Here you can continue up to higher elevations along Taneum Ridge by taking Forest Road 3300 up a steep climb that breaks away from the creek. The birding changes completely as the road climbs into heavily wooded hills. Common Raven and large raptors such as Golden Eagle and even the occasional Northern Goshawk may be seen by looking across the canyons and at the rock walls on the opposite side as the road climbs. Explore any of the side roads at these higher elevations in search of forest birds such as White-headed and Pileated Woodpeckers and Williamson's Sapsucker. Heavy pine forest areas could also hold Pine Grosbeak. Just linger and listen for unique bird calls to cue your explorations. If you bird the area early in the morning or late in the evening, be alert for owls that prowl the forests through the night hours.

To end your trip along Taneum Creek and Taneum Ridge, retrace the route back to the lower reaches of Taneum Creek Road. You can rejoin I–90 either by going back along Elk Heights Road or by taking Thorp Cemetery Road east alongside I–90 to the next on-ramp.

Other key birds: Turkey Vulture; Merlin; Ruffed Grouse; Spotted Sandpiper; Wilson's Snipe; Western Screech- and Northern Saw-whet Owls; Common Nighthawk; White-throated Swift; Downy and Hairy Woodpeckers; Olive-sided Flycatcher; Western Wood-Pewee; Willow Flycatcher; Say's Phoebe; Western and Eastern Kingbirds; Northern Shrike; Warbling Vireo; Clark's Nutcracker; Mountain and Chestnut-backed Chickadees; White-breasted Nuthatch; Brown Creeper; House, Winter, Rock, Canyon, and Marsh Wrens; American Dipper; Mountain

Bluebird; Townsend's Solitaire; Veery; Swainson's, Hermit, and Varied Thrushes; Orange-crowned, Nashville, Townsend's, MacGillivray's, and Wilson's Warblers; Western Tanager; Chipping, Fox, Lincoln's, and Golden-crowned Sparrows; Black-headed Grosbeak; Lazuli Bunting; Bullock's Oriole; Cassin's Finch; Red Crossbill; Evening Grosbeak.

Nearby opportunities: John Wayne Pioneer Trail access in Thorp.

Directions: From I-90 eastbound, take exit 93 for Elk Heights Road. Turn left at the end of the off-ramp, cross over I-90, and turn right onto Elk Heights Road heading east in parallel with I-90. Stay on Elk Heights Road for 4 miles and then turn right onto Taneum Road, again crossing over I-90 before making a right turn onto Taneum Creek Road.

DeLorme map grid: Page 66, D2.

Elevation: 1,700 feet

Access: None.

Bathrooms: Taneum Creek Campground.

Hazards: Mountain bikers use the area extensively and may be on some trails, especially on weekends. Beware birding this area in high winds to avoid falling limbs and trees.

Nearest food, gas, and lodging: Cle Elum or Ellensburg.

Nearest camping: Taneum Creek Campground.

For more information: Visit www.wdfw.wa .gov/lands/r3murray.htm on the Internet.

42 Yakima River Canyon

Habitats: Lowland riparian, mixed forest, shrub-steppe.

Specialty birds: Golden and Bald Eagles; Northern Goshawk; Swainson's Hawk; Chukar; Vaux's Swift; Black-chinned, Calliope, and Rufous Hummingbirds; Lewis's Woodpecker; Dusky Flycatcher; Western Bluebird; Sage Thrasher; Gray-crowned Rosy-Finch; Pine Grosbeak.

Best times to bird: Spring, summer, and fall.

Yellow-breasted Chat can be found around wetlands and riparian areas in eastern Washington during the late spring and summer. This chat sings alongside the Yakima River at the Umtanum Recreation Area.

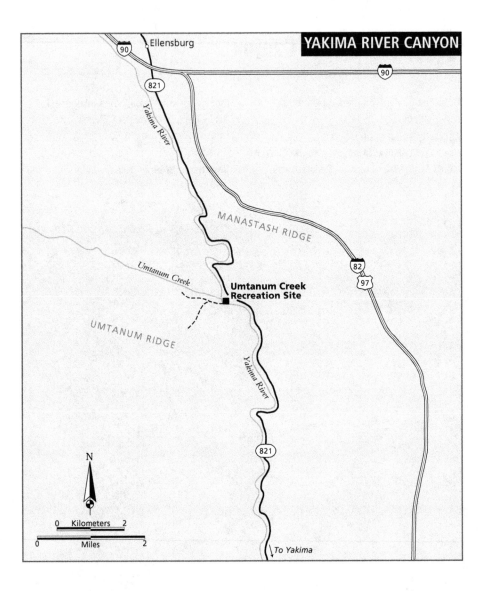

About the site:

Late spring is the time to make the scenic drive along the meandering Yakima River as it slices through the Yakima River Canyon between Ellensburg and Selah. The canyon cuts a deep gash through the anticline ridges that march in a line to the south from Ellensburg—Manastash Ridge and Umtanum Ridge—and the river offers a great corridor for the passage of birds and butterflies. Visit the site in May and you are likely to find Yellow-breasted Chat and Lazuli Bunting along Umtanum Creek while small blue butterflies feed on wildflower blooms and Osprey pick their nest sites in the pine trees along the riverside.

The arrival of spring in the Yakima River Canyon starts a cascade of natural events that culminates in late spring, when birds begin to nest and wildflowers reach their peak bloom along the hillsides and basalt cliffs. As soon as the snow and ice melts in spring, nature starts its work, and bird-watchers can benefit from the changing seasons as migrant species make their way through the canyon. Warblers, tanagers, and Black-headed Grosbeaks arrive in the canyon with the sunshine, and by late May, when temperatures can rise and get balmy enough to invite throngs of rafters to float down the Yakima River, many of these spring arrivals are building nests and laying their eggs.

To bird the Yakima Canyon from its northern end, take Canyon Road south from Ellensburg and follow the winding road as it hugs the eastern banks of the river. Cottonwood and ponderosa-pine trees dot the riverside, with elderberry, currant, and serviceberry bushes mixed in along the banks. Passerines feed in the habitat along the riverbank, while raptors such as Swainson's Hawk can be seen in the small clusters of pine trees on the hillsides opposite of the road. Be sure to look along the sides of the hills on the east side of the road. During winter you may find small flocks of Gray-crowned Rosy-Finch along the hillsides, and during one spring visit we watched and took photos of marmots chasing each other and feeding on grass seed on the talus slopes. All of this can be seen from various wide

The Yakima River Canyon twists and bends on its course through the mountains between Ellensburg and Yakima. The canyon hosts a wide range of bird species, including Yellow-breasted Chat and many raptors.

areas along Canyon Road. Be sure to pull well off the road and be careful of impeding traffic. Weekday visits to the canyon would be less hectic than on sunny weekends, when fishers, hikers, and rafters rush to the area.

After winding through the steepest sections of the canyon, pull into the Umtanum Creek Recreation Area in the middle of the canyon, where Umtanum Creek meets the Yakima River and a series of trails offer access to the sagebrush-dotted habitat accessible on the west side of the river after you walk across a suspension bridge. Warblers, including Yellow-breasted Chat, and other songbirds such as Lazuli Bunting are common highlights along Umtanum Creek during the spring. Walk the trails through the sagebrush along the creek and watch overhead for Prairie Falcon, Golden Eagle, and other raptors. More than twenty-one species of raptors have been found in the canyon, including Bald Eagles in the winter.

The Yakima River Canyon ends near the town of Selah, where the river flows into shrub-steppe habitat on its way south through Yakima and its eventual merge with the Columbia River in the Tri-Cities. The canyon is designated by Audubon Washington as one of the state's Important Bird Areas, largely due to its importance to birds that rely on shrub-steppe habitat and also for the raptors and other species that nest along basalt cliffs in the canyon.

Other key birds: Common and Hooded Mergansers; Turkey Vulture; Osprey; Prairie Falcon; Gray Partridge; Spotted Sandpiper; Ring-billed and California Gulls; Common Nighthawk; Common Poorwill; White-throated Swift; Say's Phoebe; Western and Eastern Kingbirds; Loggerhead and Northern Shrikes; Warbling Vireo; House, Rock, and Canyon Wrens; Mountain Bluebird; Veery; Hermit Thrush; Orange-crowned, Nashville, Yellow, and Wilson's Warblers; Yellow-breasted Chat; Western Tanager; Chipping, Brewer's, Lark, Fox, Lincoln's, Vesper, and Golden-crowned Sparrows; Black-headed Grosbeak; Lazuli Bunting; Bullock's Oriole; Cassin's Finch; Red Crossbill; Evening Grosbeak.

Nearby opportunities: The Wenas Basin follows Wenas Creek into the foothills west from the southern end of the Yakima River Canyon. Farther to the south, the Ahtanum Ridge area offers more birding due west of Union Gap on Ahtanum Road.

Directions: From the north, take the Canyon Road exit off I-90 at Ellensburg and drive south on Canyon Road, also known as State Route 821. From the south, take U.S. Highway 82/State Route 97 north from Yakima and take the exit for Firing Center Road and State Road 182 north of Selah. Follow SR 182 into the Yakima River Canyon.

DeLorme map grid: Page 51, B5.

Elevation: 1,300 feet.

Access: None.

Bathrooms: At the Umtanum Recreation Area.

Hazards: None.

Nearest food, gas, and lodging: Ellensburg in the north and Yakima in the south.

Nearest camping: At the Umtanum Creek Recreation Area.

For more information: Check the Web page for the Wenas Wildlife Area at www.wdfw.wa.gov/lands/r3wenas.htm or the L.T. Murray Wildlife Area at www.wdfw.wa.gov/lands/r3murray.htm.

43 Wenas Basin

Habitats: Mountain riparian, mixed forest, shrub-steppe.

Specialty birds: Golden and Bald Eagles; Northern Goshawk; Swainson's Hawk; Chukar; Blue Grouse; American Avocet; Baird's and Pectoral Sandpipers; Flammulated and Northern Pygmy-Owls; Vaux's Swift; Black-chinned, Calliope, and Rufous Hummingbirds; White-headed, Lewis's, and Pileated Woodpeckers; Williamson's and Red-naped Sapsuckers; Least, Hammond's, Gray, Dusky, and Pacific-slope Flycatchers; Cassin's Vireo; Pygmy Nuthatch; Western Bluebird; Sage Thrasher.

Best times to bird: Spring, summer, and fall.

A group of bird-watchers scope out a rare Blue-gray Gnatcatcher in Hardy Canyon as shadows pass over the Wenas Valley.

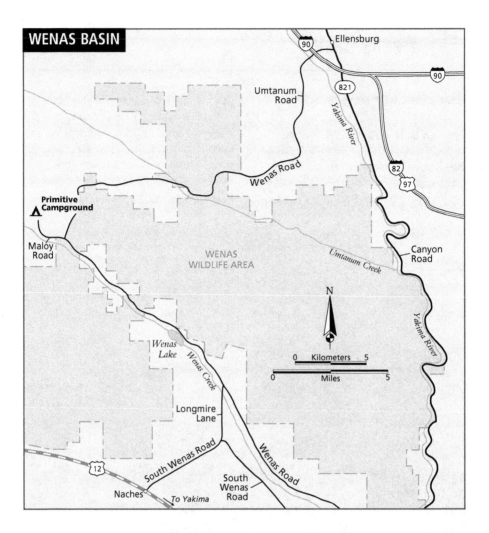

WENAS BASIN

Ellensburg

Umtanum Road

Yakima River

Wenas Road

Primitive Campground

Maloy Road

WENAS WILDLIFE AREA

Umtanum Creek

Canyon Road

Yakima River

N

Wenas Lake

Wenas Creek

0   Kilometers   5

0   Miles   5

Longmire Lane

South Wenas Road

Wenas Road

Naches

To Yakima

South Wenas Road

About the site:

It's hard to beat the bird-watching diversity in the Wenas Basin. From the shores of Wenas Lake, which offer some of the best shorebird-watching in eastern Washington, to the canyons that reach down into the basin from atop Cleman Mountain and Umtanum Ridge and the riparian habitats along Wenas Creek, the area has a lot to offer.

There are two ways to reach the Wenas Basin—driving up from Naches and exploring the area from Wenas Lake up toward the mountains or driving south from Ellensburg and exploring the high country on Umtanum Ridge before dropping down to the Wenas Valley. The first route into Wenas Basin from State Route 12 is the easiest for quick access, and it offers instant gratification with shorebirds along Wenas Lake during the migration season. But the second route heading south from I–90 has the most to offer in terms of variety of bird habitat.

To get to the Wenas Basin from Ellensburg, take Umtanum Road out of town. The road gradually climbs and shifts to a gravel surface as it rises toward the summit of Umtanum Ridge, a nearly 4,000-foot ridge that can hold snow late into the spring. As the road climbs through a riparian area in Shushuskin Canyon, watch for Lazuli Bunting, Black-headed Grosbeak, and other songbirds in the brush during the spring.

Once the road switches to gravel, the surrounding habitats change as well, making a transition from lowland riparian to modified shrub-steppe and steppe habitat on the hills overlooking the Kittitas Valley. Although the sagebrush areas are not as impressive as they once were thanks to cattle grazing, the remaining sage, bitterbrush, rabbitbrush, and native bunchgrass caters to birds such as Sage Thrasher, Brewer's and Vesper Sparrow, and other birds that depend on the shrub-steppe. The area on top of this first ridge can also be frequented by raptors such as Prairie Falcon and Golden Eagle.

Umtanum Road climbs a little more before dropping down to another riparian area along Umtanum Creek. The creekside habitat draws songbirds and flycatchers in the spring and summer months, and the cottonwood snags and pine trees on the ridges along the creek are favorite habitat for Lewis's Woodpeckers, which can often be seen sullying out for insects from their nest trees. One particular section of the gravel road in this area can offer a wealth of butterfly-viewing as well, as fritillaries, sulphurs, and white butterflies gather on the side of the damp road in a behavior known as puddling. The butterflies come to the damp area for water but also to get minerals from the soil.

A Calliope Hummingbird sits on its nest alongside the trail into Hardy Canyon in the Wenas Valley.

Although the name of the road changes in this creekside area, switching from Umtanum Road to Wenas Road, don't worry. Just stick to the main road and it will lead you up and over another ridge at Ellensburg Pass and then wind down into the Wenas Valley on the other side. At the point where Wenas Road returns to a paved surface, take a sharp right onto Wenas Road North. This road is rugged and not recommended for passenger vehicles with low ground clearance, but if you take it slow and easy you should be able to drive up this road past a series of rock outcroppings to the Wenas Creek Campground.

In addition to offering an option for overnight camping, the campground, which is the site of an annual state Audubon Society campout, appropriately offers great bird-watching. Red-naped Sapsucker and Veery are right in the campground, and mountain bird species such as White-headed Woodpecker, White-breasted and Pygmy Nuthatch, Mountain Chickadee, and more are in the area west of the campground. The walkable roads that lead farther into the hills from the Wenas Creek Campground are also known to offer bird-watchers the chance to watch, and more likely to hear, species such as Common Poorwill and many owls.

After exploring the area around the campground and the North Fork of Wenas Creek, return to Wenas Road to make your way back onto the pavement and to head east toward Wenas Lake. Notice how a large number of side canyons reach down into the basin from Cleman Mountain on your right and Umtanum Ridge on your left. Some of these side canyons offer additional birding opportunities with access points and small parking areas along Wenas Road. One such area is Hardy Canyon, which was well visited by the state's birders in 2002 and 2003 when a rare Blue-gray Gnatcatcher was seen in the area each summer during those years. A trail up into Hardy Canyon also offers a chance to see hummingbirds and warblers along the lower reaches of the trail, including Yellow-breasted Chat just on the other side of Wenas Creek.

Wenas Lake is a man-made reservoir just down the hill from Hardy Canyon. Many of the state's hot-shot birders visit the lake regularly in August and September each year to check the water levels and see what kinds of shorebirds are hanging out along the muddy shore. Western, Least, Semipalmated, Spotted, and Baird's Sandpiper can be seen here, along with Wilson's Snipe, numerous Killdeer, Greater and Lesser Yellowlegs, and other shorebirds. The lake also draws waterfowl.

To get to SR 12 from Wenas Lake, take Longmire Lane and follow it down a steep and winding canyon into the town of Naches, or continue down Wenas Road into the town of Selah.

Other key birds: Horned, Eared, and Pied-billed Grebes; Wood Duck; Gadwall; Green-winged and Cinnamon Teals; American Wigeon; Northern Pintail; Northern Shoveler; Canvasback; Redhead; Ring-necked Duck; Lesser Scaup; Common Goldeneye; Buffle-head; Common and Hooded Mergansers; Ruddy Duck; Turkey Vulture; Osprey; Merlin; Prairie Falcon; Ruffed Grouse; Virginia Rail; Sora; Greater and Lesser Yellowlegs; Spotted Sandpiper; Semipalmated, Western, and Least Sandpipers; Wilson's Snipe; Ring-billed and

Califonia Gulls; Long-eared, Western Screech-, and Northern Saw-whet Owls; Common Nighthawk; Common Poorwill; Downy and Hairy Woodpeckers; Olive-sided Flycatcher; Western Wood-Pewee; Willow Flycatcher; Say's Phoebe; Western and Eastern Kingbirds; Loggerhead and Northern Shrikes; Warbling Vireo; Clark's Nutcracker; Bank Swallow; Mountain and Chestnut-backed Chickadees; White-breasted Nuthatch; Brown Creeper; House, Winter, Bewick's, Rock, Canyon, and Marsh Wrens; American Dipper; Mountain Bluebird; Townsend's Solitaire; Veery; Swainson's, Hermit, and Varied Thrushes; Gray Catbird; Orange-crowned, Nashville, Townsend's, Yellow, MacGillivray's, and Wilson's Warblers; Common Yellowthroat; Yellow-breasted Chat; Western Tanager; Chipping, Brewer's, Fox, Savannah, Lincoln's, and Vesper Sparrows; Black-headed Grosbeak; Lazuli Bunting; Bullock's Oriole; Cassin's Finch; Red Crossbill; Evening Grosbeak.

Nearby opportunities: Oak Creek Wildlife Area.

Directions: From Naches, take South Naches Road to East 2nd Street and turn right. The road name changes to Old Naches Highway. Turn left at Allen Road and then right onto Naches-Wenas Road. Turn left onto Longmire Lane and then left onto Wenas Road to climb up to Wenas Lake and the rest of the basin. From Ellensburg, take the Canyon Road exit from I-90 and go north before taking a left onto Damman Road. Damman Road goes back under I-90 before crossing a creek. Go straight after crossing the street and you are on Umtanum Road. Just follow the route described above from that point.

DeLorme map grid: Page 50, B3.

Elevation: Ranges from 1,000 feet at the Yakima River to more than 3,800 feet on Umtanum Ridge.

Access: None.

Bathrooms: None.

Hazards: Rough roads.

Nearest food, gas, and lodging: Naches and Selah.

Nearest camping: Wenas Creek Campground.

For more information: Check the Web page for the Wenas Wildlife Area at www.wdfw .wa.gov/lands/r3wenas.htm.

Habitats: Mountain riparian, mixed forest, old-growth forest, subalpine, alpine meadow.

Specialty birds: Bald Eagle; Northern Goshawk; Blue Grouse; White-tailed Ptarmigan; Spotted and Northern Pygmy-Owls; Vaux's Swift; Calliope and Rufous Hummingbirds; Pileated Woodpecker; Red-breasted Sapsucker; Pacific-slope Flycatcher; Gray Jay; Gray-crowned Rosy-Finch; Pine Grosbeak.

Best times to bird: Summer and fall.

Mt. Rainier looms over the Sunrise area on the northeastern corner of the national park. With an elevation of 6,400 feet, Sunrise is a destination for high-mountain bird-watching.

About the site:

High-elevation bird-watching can be a tenuous pastime. Sunrise on the northeastern flanks of Mt. Rainier is one example. Although the site and its hiking trails can offer passage to views of hard-to-find, high-elevation birds such as White-tailed Ptarmigan and Gray-crowned Rosy-Finch, the area is open only for a few months each year, and when it opens it is so popular with tourists that you have to hike a while to get away from the crowds and into the best bird habitat. If you are willing to take a walk or to explore some of the easy but less popular trails, you will be rewarded.

The Sunrise area on Mt. Rainier, at an elevation of 6,400 feet, is one of the last locations in the national park to open each summer, and after a couple of months of summer wildflower blooms and birdsong, the area closes around Labor Day weekend. So there is a narrow window of time when bird-watchers can drive up the mountain. August and September are the best months to visit.

You can start birding anywhere along the approach to Mt. Rainier National Park. Pull off on some of the side roads and explore.

Once you arrive in the Sunrise parking lot and jockey around for a parking spot, start your bird-watching by looking along the treetops around the parking lot. Raptors sit in the treetops in late August and September when large numbers of Merlin, American Kestrel, Red-tailed Hawks, and Prairie Falcons pass through the Sunrise area during their migration. When the raptors aren't present, Clark's Nutcracker are sure to be chattering from the treetops.

After checking the trees around the parking area and the smaller trees in the meadows with your binoculars or a spotting scope, it can pay off to stop by the ranger station and ask the on-duty ranger if there have been any interesting birds sighted recently. The rangers may be able to clue you in to the locations where White-tailed Ptarmigan have been seen.

The premier trail that bird-watchers take to get early morning and evening views of ptarmigan and Gray-crowned Rosy-Finch is the Burroughs Mountain Trail, which climbs more than 900 feet in 4.8 miles en route to First Burroughs Mountain and more than 1,200 feet in 6 miles to Second Burroughs Mountain. These are strenuous hikes, but they offer the best chances to see hard-to-find mountain bird species. Beware though, since sections of the trail remain snow- and ice-covered late into the summer.

Other trails that can offer good bird-watching include the Sourdough Ridge Trail that climbs more than 500 feet in 3 miles, or even the 1.5-mile Sunrise Nature Trail that climbs just 300 feet after departing from the upper end of the picnic area. Other high-elevation birds to keep an eye out for include Red and White-winged Crossbills, Mountain Bluebirds, and Pine Grosbeak. If you are willing to take the time to get away from the crowds and listen closely for birdsong, just about any trail at Sunrise can offer rewarding birding. Just be sure to stop, look, and listen often while you drink in the scenery on the edge of the active

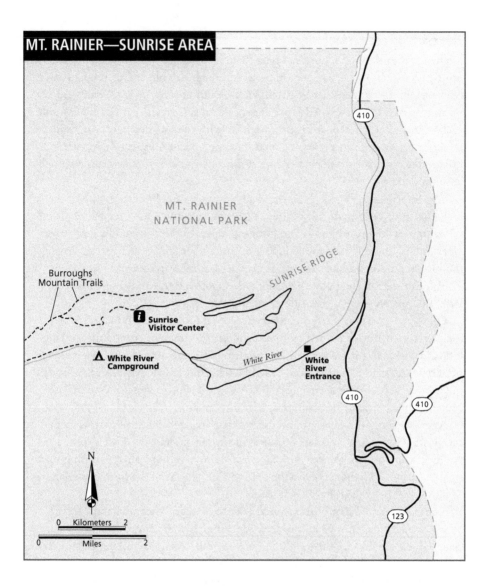

MT. RAINIER
NATIONAL PARK

SUNRISE RIDGE

Burroughs
Mountain Trails

i **Sunrise
Visitor Center**

▲ **White River
Campground**

White River

■ **White
River
Entrance**

410

410

410

123

N

0   Kilometers   2

0   Miles   2

volcano. Whatever you do, stay on the trail when walking at Sunrise and other high-elevation sites in the state. Alpine and subalpine habitat is slow to recover from the trampling of hundreds of bird-watchers' feet, so even if it means missing a better view of that ptarmigan or other hard-to-find bird, stay on the trail.

Bird-watching is just one of the attractions at Sunrise. Wildflower photography and viewing, as well as butterfly-watching are two other great ways to maximize a visit to Sunrise. The ranger station offers handouts with the names of wildflowers that can be seen at both Sunrise and Paradise, the two main high-elevation visitor centers in the national park. Bring along a guide to wildflowers to help you identify some of the flora in the area during the times when birds are not very active.

Other key birds: Rough-legged Hawk; Merlin; Prairie Falcon; Ruffed Grouse; Spotted Sandpiper; Western Screech-, Northern Saw-whet, and Boreal Owls; Downy and Hairy Woodpeckers; Warbling Vireo; Clark's Nutcracker; Mountain and Chestnut-backed Chickadees; Brown Creeper; Winter and Bewick's Wrens; Swainson's, Hermit, and Varied Thrushes; American Pipit; Orange-crowned, Townsend's, Yellow, MacGillivray's, and Wilson's Warblers; Western Tanager; Fox, Savannah, Lincoln's, and Golden-crowned Sparrows; Purple Finch; Red Crossbill.

Nearby opportunities: Try walking trails that leave from the White River Campground area within the national park. Other locations with good birding trails include Paradise and the Carbon River entrance to the park.

Directions: From I-5, take State Route 167, also known as Puyallup River Road, east and follow the signs to take State Route 410 eastbound. Stay on SR 410 eastbound until you enter Mt. Rainier National Park, then turn right to go into the White River entrance to the park. Pay your entrance fee and follow the signs up the steep and winding road from the White River Valley to Sunrise.

DeLorme map grid: Page 48, A3.

Elevation: 6,400 feet.

Access: Wheelchair-accessible restrooms and selected interpretive trails.

Bathrooms: On-site.

Hazards: Sudden weather changes.

Nearest food, gas, and lodging: Greenwater.

Nearest camping: White River Campground.

For more information: Check the Mt. Rainier National Park Web site at www.nps.gov/mora/index.htm. You can also call (360) 569-2211.

Oak Creek Wildlife Area

Habitats: Oak woodlands, pine and fir woodlands.

Specialty birds: Golden and Bald Eagles; Northern Goshawk; Flammulated and Northern Pygmy-Owls; Vaux's Swift; Black-chinned, Calliope, and Rufous Hummingbirds; White-headed, Lewis's, and Pileated Woodpeckers; Williamson's and Red-naped Sapsuckers; Hammond's and Pacific-slope Flycatchers; Western Bluebird.

Best times to bird: Spring, summer, and fall.

A fire swept through the lower reaches of the Oak Creek Wildlife Area in Oak Creek Canyon in 2002, and in the aftermath woodpeckers flocked to the recovering Oregon white oak trees in 2003.

About the site:

Sometimes habitats change slowly, other times they change quickly, as Oak Creek Canyon did during the writing of this book when a fire zipped through the oak woodland in the lower portion of the canyon. Although some of the oaks, though singed, survived, the shrubby undergrowth and many of the oaks and other trees now stand as ghosts. While it saddens us to see so many of the sentinel oaks destroyed, we look forward to this opportunity to see what birds arrive with the change in habitat: Birds that prefer more open and burned habitats such as Black-backed Woodpeckers and Nighthawks may begin nesting in the area.

Oak Creek Canyon is an underbirded area, but it will provide diligent birders with ample opportunity for discovery with its different habitats, which include cliffs, burned oak woodland, beaver ponds, pocket canyons, mixed-pine and -fir forests giving way to mixed fir and mixed larch above, and open fields surrounding the elk feeding station and visitor center. Located on the eastern slope of the Cascades, Oak Creek is a prime spot for seeing species that occasionally cross over from the west, and it is one of the westernmost spots for reliably seeing certain east-side birds, such as Calliope Hummingbird and Cassin's Finch.

Although the birding highlight of Oak Creek is the creek canyon, we suggest you start with a quick check of the elk feeding station and visitor center. The open fields and deciduous trees attract different birds than the canyon, such as Brewer's Blackbird, California Quail, finches, sparrows, and Say's Phoebe. As you drive from the center to the canyon entrance, check the cliff faces across the river for raptors—we've seen Turkey Vultures, Red-tailed Hawks, Bald and Golden Eagles. Also check the river itself for Harlequin Ducks, and check the oak trees for Lewis's Woodpeckers, which you might see flying over the freeway as you drive to the site. The area around Oak Creek is almost guaranteed to give birders a good look at the gregarious and striking woodpeckers. The dead oaks left by the burn will ensure that they remain at Oak Creek, since they use snags to nest, and they forage among live oaks as well as ponderosa pine.

The lower portion of the canyon is filled with Garry Oak. At this point many of them are burnt to a crisp, but we saw tons of acorns littering the ground in the spring after the burn. The eastern wall of the canyon alternates between steep, hills dotted with sage and bunchgrass, and basalt cliffs. Take time to stop and check the cliffs for Rock and Canyon Wren and Cliff Swallow. The lower canyon also seems to be a favored hunting spot for kestrels. Once you reach the first campsite, also the site where the fire started, the landscape begins to change as the oaks give way to fir and pine with heavier undergrowth. The edges of the creek still sport decid-uous trees and riparian shrubs.

As you drive through the pine and fir forest, stop occasionally to check for other woodpeckers, thrushes, Townsend's Solitaire, and Red Crossbill. Where the undergrowth is not so dense, check for wild turkey and grouse—and be aware that during hunting season, many of the people you see here will be hunting these

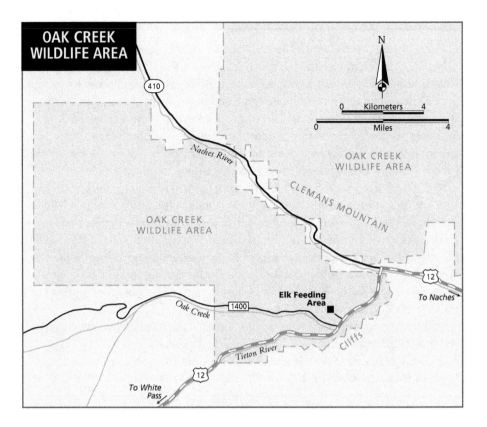

birds. Approximately 3 miles from the entrance to the canyon, a horse camp offers yet another change in habitat with open field surrounded by more deciduous trees: Look here for sparrows, Western Tanager, and Western Wood-Pewee. And look up through the opening to see if you spot any swifts flying overhead. A short way up the road a beaver has dammed the creek to create a pond on the left side of the road. The pond is surrounded by willows, alder, and other deciduous trees— prime warbler and flycatcher habitat. Some of the pocket canyons that are tucked into the hill on the east side of the road contain similar habitat. In fact, on one of our trips up the canyon, we were greeted at NPK Canyon by a Yellow-rumped Warbler singing from the canyon's entrance sign. We normally turn around at the 3.6-mile mark where the road enters private land before rejoining the wildlife area, but if your vehicle is worthy of bumpy, sometimes rutted roads, you may elect to drive the entire 12-mile route to Bear Lake, a popular destination for anglers and hunters.

Although the area encompassed by the canyon is narrow, the transitional habitats make this area a prime spot for bird-watching and, as a nice bonus, in the spring the understory is abloom with wildflowers.

A WINTER ELK HAVEN

More than 100,000 people visit the Oak Creek elk feeding station each year for a chance to get close to these giant beasts. Every winter since 1945, the Department of Fish and Wildlife has doled out hay and feed for the overwintering Roosevelt Elk that live in the 42,000-acre Oak Creek Wildlife Area. In addition to Oak Creek Canyon, another site included in this book, Wenas Valley, is also encompassed by the wildlife area. However, at certain times of the year in the Wenas Valley, you are more likely to see herds of grazing cattle than you are the impressive elk.

Other key birds: Turkey Voulture, Osprey; Merlin; Ruffed Grouse; Western Screech- and Northern Saw-whet Owls; Common Nighthawk; White-throated Swift; Downy and Hairy Woodpeckers; Olive-sided Flycatcher; Say's Phoebe; Western Kingbird; Northern Shrike; Warbling Vireo; Clark's Nutcracker; Mountain Chickadee; White-breasted Nuthatch; House, Winter, Bewick's, Rock, and Canyon Wrens; Mountain Bluebird; Townsend's Solitaire; Swainson's Hermit, and Varied Thrushes; Orange-crowned, Nashville, Townsend's, Yellow, MacGillivray's, and Wilson's Warblers; Western Tanager; Chipping, Fox, and Lincoln's Sparrows; Black-headed Grosbeak; Lazuli Bunting; Cassin's Finch; Red Crossbill; Evening Grosbeak.

Nearby opportunities: Wild Rose Campground and Clear Lake.

Directions: The entrance to the canyon is on State Route 12 just 0.2 mile west of the Oak Creek Wildlife Area headquarters and elk feeding station.

DeLorme map grid: Page 50, C2.

Elevation: 2,000 to 2,700 feet.

Access: Wheelchair-accessible pit toilets at the headquarters; most of site can be explored by car.

Bathrooms: Pit toilets at headquarters and some campsites.

Hazards: Rattlesnakes.

Nearest food, gas, and lodging: Find all three in Naches or stop for diner-style food and a few more birds that you'll find at the feeders at Trout Lodge in Rimrock.

Nearest camping: On-site camping.

For more information: Go to www.wdfw.wa .gov/lands/r3oakcrk.htm on the Internet.

Habitats: Freshwater marsh, wetland, lowland riparian, shrub-steppe.

Specialty birds: Tundra Swan; Barrow's Goldeneye; Golden Eagle; Swainson's and Ferruginous Hawks; Peregrine Falcon; Chukar; Short-eared Owl; Vaux's Swift; Black-chinned, Calliope, and Rufous Hummingbirds; Lewis's Woodpecker; Cassin's Vireo; Western Bluebird; Sage Thrasher.

Best times to bird: Spring, summer, and fall.

The fields and wetlands at the Toppenish National Wildlife Refuge offer a green summer contrast to the dry hills of Toppenish Ridge to the south of the refuge.

About the site:

The 1,700-acre Toppenish National Wildlife Refuge (NWR) is one of the reasons the Yakima River Valley is so well-known to Washington birders. The refuge spans the drainages of two creeks, Toppenish and Snake Creeks, and through habitat management and steps taken to manipulate water levels in the low-lying fields at the site, the refuge transforms each fall from a series of riparian zones along the creeks to a vast wetland and pond complex that hosts more than 30,000 migrating waterfowl. In the times between the flooding and draining of the fields, warblers, flycatchers, and other songbirds flood into the refuge for the summer breeding season.

Up to 250 bird species have been seen at the wildlife refuge, including some of the westernmost occurrences of Bobolink in the spring and early summer in fields south of Yost Road. As with many of the other migratory bird stopovers in the area, the real birding highlights take place in fall and early winter when thousands of waterfowl descend on the area. But Toppenish is a great place to bird year-round.

Since the refuge is widely spread across the valley, where it covers nearly 27 miles from end-to-end, much of the best birding can be done by pulling off roads that dissect the site. A great place to start is at the viewing platform near the refuge office, just off U.S. Highway 97 on Pumphouse Road. Views from the platform cover a riparian area along Toppenish Creek where you can see waterfowl, swallows, warblers, and even Black-crowned Night Heron in the Russian olive and willow trees in the distance. There is also a mowed walking path that diverges from the paved pathway to the viewing platform, but we would advise against taking the path through the field since we had close encounters with ticks in the grass here, as have others since our summer visit in 2002. The best bet to avoid exposure to hungry ticks is to walk along the gravel road toward the refuge office.

Even if you arrive at the refuge too late to visit the office while it is open, consider walking to the office for views of quail and to scan the trees that surround the office for songbirds. During one summer visit we observed a Great Horned Owl and its offspring sitting in plain sight on the lower branches of trees around the refuge office.

Once you finish exploring the area around the refuge office, the next-best bet is to bird from the roads that crisscross the refuge. Head west along Pumphouse Road to get started, then cut up either Old Goldendale Road or Lateral C to bird the north side of the refuge from Marion Drain Road and Yost Road. To make the most of your explorations, keep an eye out for edges where habitats come together—low-lying shrubs reaching the edge of open water, creek edges, and fence lines that divide brushy areas from agricultural fields. In a refuge such as this, where there is no one place that serves as the best birding habitat at the site, it pays to use the knowledge you have of birding habitats and to think like a kid exploring new territory. Use the freedom to simply explore, and you never know what kinds of birds will show themselves.

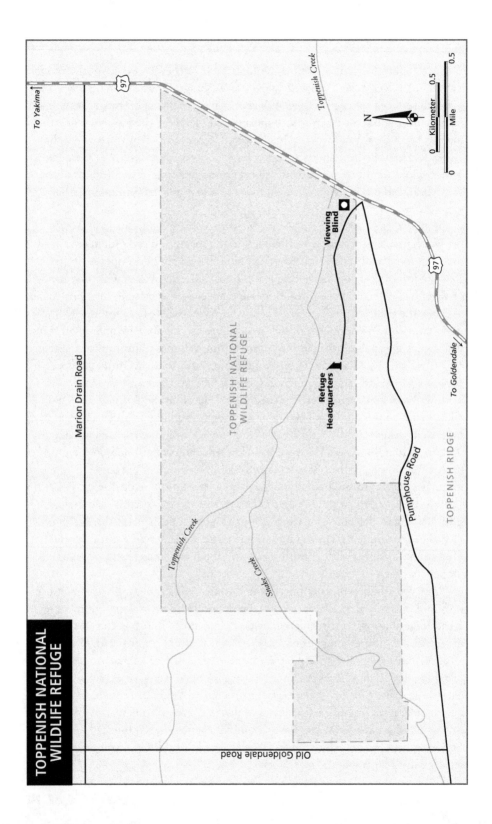

TOPPENISH NATIONAL
WILDLIFE REFUGE

To Yakima

Marion Drain Road

97

Toppenish Creek

TOPPENISH NATIONAL
WILDLIFE REFUGE

Toppenish Creek

Snake Creek

Viewing
Blind

Refuge
Headquarters

97

To Goldendale

Pumphouse Road

TOPPENISH RIDGE

Old Goldendale Road

N

0   Kilometer   0.5

0   Mile   0.5

BOBOLINK AND THE MOVE WESTWARD

Bobolink are long-distance migratory birds that winter in the southern reaches of South America and arrive in Washington in late spring. While they are more associated with northeastern Washington, where they reliably are found in fields at the foot of the Aeneas Valley along State Route 20 east of Tonasket, they also can be found in the westernmost reaches of the Toppenish National Wildlife Refuge. The small breeding colony of Bobolink at the Toppenish refuge may be the westernmost colony in the United States.

Finding Bobolink is a simple process. Look over the tall grass hay fields in the Toppenish NWR for birds slightly smaller than blackbirds with bright white rumps and yellow patches on the back of their heads. The female Bobolink is harder to distinguish, with a dark cap on its head, a dark supercilium line back from its eye, and a generally yellowish tinge overall. They rely on tall grass fields for breeding sites, and they can be found in migration in marshy areas.

Other key birds: Pied-billed Grebe; American Bittern; Black-crowned Night-Heron; Wood Duck; Gadwall; Green-winged and Cinnamon Teals; American Wigeon; Northern Pintail; Northern Shoveler; Canvasback; Redhead; Ring-necked Duck; Lesser Scaup; Common Goldeneye; Bufflehead; Common and Hooded Mergansers; Turkey Vulture; Prairie Falcon; Virginia Rail; Sora; Wilson's Snipe; Ring-billed Gull; Long-eared Owl; Common Nighthawk; Common Poorwill; Say's Phoebe; Western and Eastern Kingbirds; Loggerhead and Northern Shrikes; Bank Swallow; House, Rock, and Marsh Wrens; Mountain Bluebird; Orange-crowned, Yellow, and Wilson's Warblers; Common Yellowthroat; Yellow-breasted Chat; Chipping, Brewer's, Lark, Savannah, and Vesper Sparrows; Black-headed Grosbeak; Lazuli Bunting; Bobolink; Yellow-headed Blackbird; Bullock's Oriole; Cassin's Finch; Red Crossbill; Evening Grosbeak.

Nearby opportunities: Fort Simcoe State Park.

Directions: From Yakima, take State Route 12 south to the intersection with US 97. Take US 97 south to Toppenish and continue south toward Toppenish Ridge. The refuge sign is on the right. Turn right onto Pumphouse Road to access to refuge.

DeLorme map grid: Page 37, B6.

Elevation: 800 feet.

Access: Wheelchair-accessible trail to an observation deck at the main refuge entrance.

Bathrooms: In the visitor center.

Hazards: Watch out for ticks in open grassy fields.

Nearest food, gas, and lodging: Toppenish.

Nearest camping: Yakima Sportsman State Park in Yakima.

For more information: For a bird list and more information, check midcolumbianriver.fws.gov/toppenpage.htm or call (509) 865-2405. The refuge office is located at 21 Pumphouse Road, Toppenish, WA 98948. It is open weekdays from 8:00 A.M. to 4:00 P.M.

Fort Simcoe State Park

Habitats: Lowland riparian, shrub-steppe.

Specialty birds: Golden Eagle; Swainson's and Ferruginous Hawks; Chukar; Vaux's Swift; Rufous Hummingbird; Lewis's and Pileated Woodpeckers; Cassin's Vireo; Sage Thrasher.

Best times to bird: Spring, summer, and fall.

About the site:

Just try to visit Fort Simcoe State Park without feeling you are in an oasis in the middle of sagebrush-strewn country at the northern base of Toppenish Ridge. The 200-acre park that includes the grounds of an 1850s-era military installation offers riparian habitat along springs that bubble from the ground at the park's edge as well as a small stand of Garry oak trees that offers another type of bird habitat. But venture just west or south of the park and the nature of this slice of the Yakama Indian Reservation is obviously shrub-steppe.

This intersection between the watered grounds of the park and the arid lands surrounding it creates a number of edge habitats that make the day-use park and interpretive site a fun stop for anyone birding the lower Yakima River Valley. To get started, park in the large lot near the park entrance and scan the trees within and at the edges of the park for Lewis's Woodpecker, a featured bird that is one reason the park is well-known to birders. The woodpeckers can be seen in any of the trees within the park, but pay attention to the middle and upper branches of the canopy for flicker-size birds that fly out from their perch and grab insects in midair before returning to perch. Lewis's Woodpecker stand out among woodpeckers for this summer feeding behavior.

Another area to watch carefully is the riparian zone of short willow trees and brush at the northern edge of the park. Walk through the carefully tended grassy park grounds toward the interpretive center, paying close attention for movement of warblers and other songbird species in the dense brush that grows over and around the springs that bubble to the surface. This riparian area is where you are most likely to see and hear a Yellow-breasted Chat or to hear a Lazuli Bunting calling from the top of a Russian olive tree.

After taking a few minutes to tour the interpretive center, walk south toward the officers' buildings and scan the treetops for woodpeckers and any other birds you can find. If you wander to the back edges of the park, where the irrigated parkland meets the edge of the shrub-steppe habitat outside the park, you have the best chance to see species more associated with the arid landscape, such as Sage Thrasher, Sage and Lark Sparrow, and Prairie Falcon hunting over the shrub-steppe.

Wrap up your birding at the park by completing a loop around the grounds and scanning both the inner park and the outer edges of the park. Since Fort Simcoe is a green oasis in the middle of arid lands, it can serve as what is known as a migrant

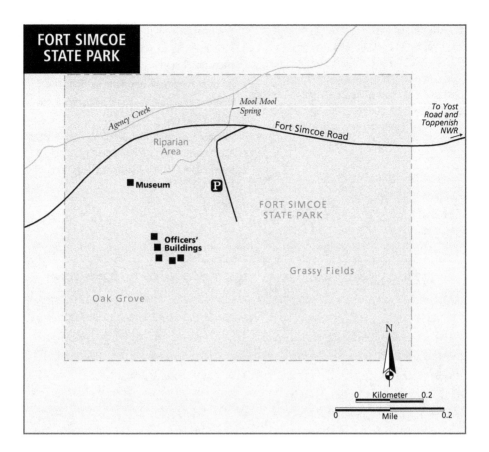

FORT SIMCOE STATE PARK

Agency Creek

Mool Mool Spring

To Yost Road and Toppenish NWR

Fort Simcoe Road

Riparian Area

■ Museum

🅿

FORT SIMCOE STATE PARK

■ Officers'
■ Buildings
■ ■■

Grassy Fields

Oak Grove

N

| 0 | Kilometer | 0.2 |
| 0 | Mile | 0.2 |

trap—an area where out-of-place birds may land during their migrations to somewhere else.

To make the most of a visit to Fort Simcoe, be sure to spend some time exploring the interpretive center on the park grounds. It is open between April 1 and October 1 Wednesday through Sunday from 9:30 A.M. to 4:30 P.M., and it documents the history of the site that served as an outpost of the U.S. Army for three years before it was turned over to the Yakama Indian Agency. Prior to its time as a fort, the area served as a meeting place for prehistoric tribes from across Washington State. It is at the junction of a number of Native American trails that go west toward Mt. Adams and east toward the Yakima River Valley and points beyond.

Other key birds: Turkey Vulture; Prairie Falcon; Virginia Rail; Sora; Wilson's Snipe; Long-eared Owl; Common Nighthawk; Common Poorwill; Ash-throated Flycatcher; Say's Phoebe; Western and Eastern Kingbirds; Northern Shrike; Warbling Vireo; House and Rock Wrens; Mountain Bluebird; Orange-crowned, Yellow, and Wilson's Warblers; Common Yellowthroat; Yellow-breasted Chat; Western Tanager; Chipping and Savannah Sparrows; Black-headed Grosbeak; Lazuli Bunting; Bullock's Oriole; Red Crossbilll; Evening Grosbeak.

Nearby opportunities: Toppenish National Wildlife Refuge.

Directions: From Yakima, take State Route 12 south to the intersection with U.S. Highway 97. Take US 97 south to Toppenish and turn right onto Fort Road. Drive about 20 miles west to the town of White Swan and follow the signs to the park entrance, taking a left onto Signal Peak Road and then a right onto Fort Simcoe Road. The park is 7 miles southwest of White Swan.

DeLorme map grid: Page 36, B2.

Elevation: 980 feet.

Access: The park offers a few paved trails and roads.

Bathrooms: Both in the park and at the interpretive center.

Hazards: None.

Nearest food, gas, and lodging: Toppenish.

Nearest camping: Yakima Sportsman State Park in Yakima.

For more information: Check the park's Web site at www.parks.wa.gov/parkpage.asp?selectedpark=Fort%20Simcoe&pageno=1 or call (509) 874-2372.

THE DISAPPEARING LEWIS'S WOODPECKER

Fort Simcoe is one of the most reliable places in Washington to see this red-faced woodpecker that was first discovered during the Lewis and Clark expedition in 1804–1806. At one time the Lewis's Woodpecker could be found in burned-over areas in western Washington, but they have been pushed out of the area with the arrival of European Starling, which outcompete them for nesting cavities. At Fort Simcoe the woodpeckers are common in spring and summer, and they breed and nest in the oak trees near the fort's old buildings, where they can fly out from the treetops and snatch insects, and where they harvest acorns and stash them in hollowed-out trees or small holes in the sides of trees for storage to be eaten in the fall and winter.

Lewis's Woodpecker also can be found in other areas in central Washington, especially where stands of oak trees are found. The Oak Creek Wildlife Area is another reliable location, and the bird also can be found nesting in lone trees in areas such as the Wenas Creek area. One summer we even found a Lewis's Woodpecker flycatching from a power pole north of Moses Lake in the Gloyd Seeps Wildlife Area. So stay on the lookout for the striking, dark green–backed woodpecker with its pink belly and red face.

Sunnyside Wildlife Area

Habitats: Lowland riparian, freshwater marsh, wetland.

Specialty birds: Golden and Bald Eagles; Swainson's and Ferruginous Hawks; Peregrine Falcon; Vaux's Swift; Rufous Hummingbird.

Best times to bird: Late fall through spring.

The riparian habitat at the Sunnyside Wildlife Area is full of songbirds in the spring, while the Yakima River waters and nearby ponds serve as nesting habitat for waterfowl.

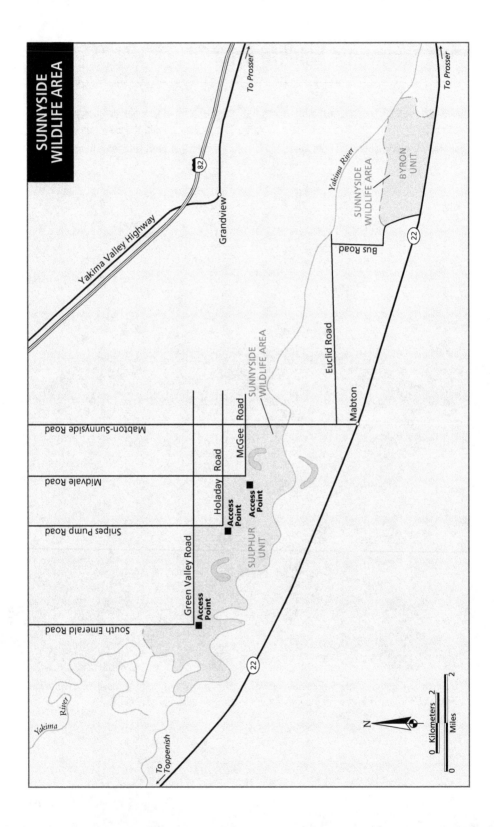

SUNNYSIDE
WILDLIFE AREA

About the site:

As one of the largest gathering places for migrating waterfowl in the Yakima River Valley, the 2,800-acre Sunnyside Wildlife Area earns the designation as one of the state's Important Bird Areas from Audubon Washington. That designation alone isn't enough to make the area a great birding stop. The key to great birding in Sunnyside is timing. Arrive in the summer and birds will be hard to find, but show up in the fall and the area will be hopping with waterfowl.

The Sunnyside Wildlife Area is a scattered assembly of wetlands, shrubby uplands, and riparian areas along the Yakima River between the towns of Mabton and Sunnyside, where the river meanders through a series of oxbows before straightening out toward its confluence with the Columbia River in nearby Richland. It is an oasis of habitat nestled in between the arid lands to the north and south of the wildlife area.

There are two main routes to start exploring this wildlife area—one heading north from State Route 22 in Mabton on Sunnyside-Mabton Road and the other heading south from Sunnyside on the same road. Heading north from Mabton, where the road crosses a bridge over the Yakima River, look for McGee Road on the left, which leads north between Morgan Lake and Bridgeman Pond to the first of a series of parking areas where you can set out walking or just step out of the car for birding. Keep the timing of your visit in mind since the roads and trails that crisscross the wildlife area are closed from February 1 through August 1 each year to protect nesting birds. But even in the summer months, you can find good

A Ring-necked Pheasant runs across a gravel road at the Sunnyside Wildlife Area.

birding in the area. During a summer visit we watched young Pied-billed Grebes scrambling over lily pads in Morgan Lake, and raptors were plentiful in the area, with a Prairie Falcon diving after prey in one area and a number of Northern Harrier being hassled over a farm field by a Swainson's Hawk that figured prominently in our birding.

The western portion of the wildlife area, known as the Sulphur Unit, offers more birding from nearby Haladay Road, Green Valley Road, and Wendell Phillips Road, and in the fall the gravel access roads beyond the gate at the end of McGee Road offer views of waterfowl for those willing to walk in for the viewing. The boundary between small farms and fields that hold cattle, hay, and hops just outside the wildlife area contrast with the wild plants in the wildlife area to offer a great edge habitat, where birds move from one habitat to another. Check the boundary between the irrigated farmlands and the modified shrub-steppe within the uplands of the wildlife area, and then check the riparian and freshwater wetlands for waterfowl and songbirds.

The Byron Unit of the wildlife area is east of Mabton-Sunnyside Road and less accessible by car than the Sulphur Unit. To get a good overview of the Byron Unit, explore along the roads leading east out of Mabton, such as Euclid Road, which goes through town and borders the Yakima River. Stay on the south side of the river and explore along these gravel roads to find parking areas and trails leading off of Euclid Road, Bus Road, and SR 22. You'll find parking areas with trail access along each of these roads.

Other key birds: Pied-billed Grebe; American Bittern; Black-crowned Night-Heron; Gadwall; Green-winged and Cinnamon Teals; American Wigeon; Northern Pintail; Northern Shoveler; Canvasback; Redhead; Ring-necked Duck; Lesser Scaup; Common Goldeneye; Bufflehead; Common and Hooded Mergansers; Turkey Vulture; Rough-legged Hawk; Prairie Falcon; Virginia Rail; Sora; Wilson's Snipe; Ring-billed Gull; Long-eared Owl; Common Nighthawk; Common Poorwill; Say's Phoebe; Western and Eastern Kingbirds; Loggerhead and Northern Shrikes; Warbling Vireo; Bank Swallow; House, Rock, and Marsh Wrens; Orange-crowned, Yellow, and Wilson's Warblers; Common Yellowthroat; Yellow-breasted Chat; Western Tanager; Chipping and Savannah Sparrows; Black-headed Grosbeak; Lazuli Bunting; Yellow-headed Blackbird; Bullock's Oriole; Evening Grosbeak.

Nearby opportunities: Toppenish National Wildlife Area.

Directions: From Yakima, drive south on State Route 12 and turn onto U.S. Highway 97. Stay on US 97 until reaching SR 22 and then follow SR 22 south through Satus to Mabton. Turn left in Mabton onto State Route 241, also known as Mabton-Sunnyside Road. Access to the Sunnyside Wildlife Area is offered from side streets to the east and west once you cross the bridge over the Yakima River. Alternatively, you can turn right onto Euclid Road East in Mabton to reach the eastern portions of the wildlife area in the Byron Unit.

DeLorme map grid: Page 37, B8.

Elevation: 708 feet.

Access: None.

Bathrooms: None.

Hazards: None.

Nearest food, gas, and lodging: Sunnyside for food and gas, Yakima for lodging.

Nearest camping: Hood Park near the mouth of the Snake River.

For more information: Visit www.wdfw .wa.gov/lands/r3sunny.htm or call (509) 837-7644.

BE SURE TO PAY YOUR WAY

The Sunnyside Wildlife Area was set aside by the U.S. Army Corps of Engineers as part of the Lower Snake River Fish and Wildlife Compensation program, a way to mitigate for the natural habitat changed by dams and the immense walls of water behind them on the Snake River. The wildlife area is a cooperative effort of the Washington State Department of Fish and Wildlife (WDFW) and the Corps of Engineers, and users of the site need to obtain a vehicle-use permit from WDFW to park in any parking lots. The $10 annual permits are available at many stores where fishing and hunting gear is sold or online from the WDFW Web site (www.wdfw.wa.gov).

Mount St. Helens National Volcanic Monument

Habitats: Mountain riparian, freshwater marsh, wetland.

Specialty birds: Barrow's Goldeneye; Bald Eagle; Northern Goshawk; Blue Grouse; Vaux's Swift; Rufous Hummingbird; Hutton's and Cassin's Vireo.

Best times to bird: Spring, summer, and fall.

Large sections of the Birth of a Lake Trail are wheelchair accessible and offer great views of one of Washington's newest lakes.

Mount St. Helens looms over the Hummocks Trail, where walkers can see how plant and bird life is returning to the site of the May 18, 1980, eruption.

About the site:

When it comes to birding new habitat, no other place in Washington offers the degree of new opportunities found along the Birth of a Lake Trail and the rugged Hummocks Trail in the blast zone of the Mount St. Helens National Volcanic Monument. Each trail offers dramatic evidence of the volcanic eruption that changed the area from deep forest to barren wasteland in a matter of moments back in 1980. But more importantly the trails offer a look at which birds are returning to the mountain terrain as trees and shrubs create more cover and wetland plants fill the borders of lakes and streams.

Birth of a Lake Trail offers a quarter-mile, wheelchair-accessible out-and-back trail along Coldwater Lake. The lake was created by the 1980 eruption when huge chunks of earth blocked a canyon, trapping the creek's waters to form the lake. Although it is not as large as Spirit Lake, Coldwater Lake offers a stopping place and feeding area for waterfowl. Scan the lake's waters for summer residents such as Bufflehead and Common Goldeneye, and be sure to check the edges of the water for the bobbing behavior of Spotted Sandpiper. Cattails and other wetland plants offer habitat for wrens and songbirds, and even in the late fall you can see flocks of Dark-eyed Junco and other mountain bird species before they flee in anticipation of winter snows.

In contrast to the short Birth of a Lake Trail, the Hummocks Trail offers a vigorous workout and great birding habitat as well as some of the most amazing

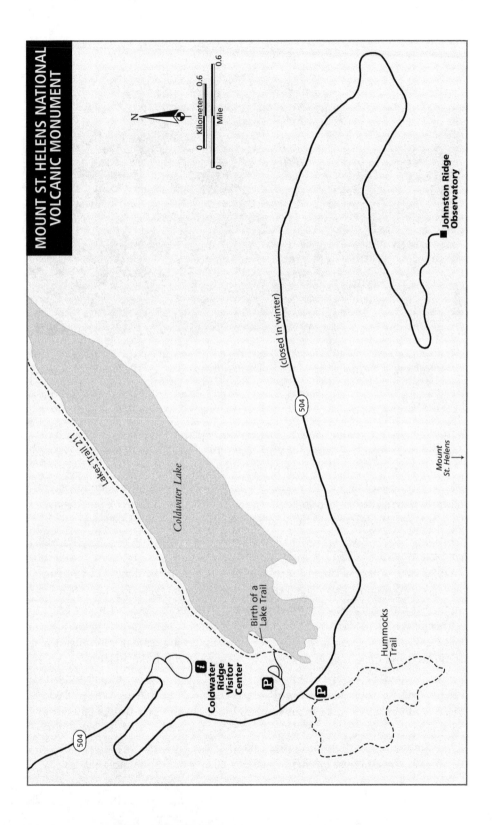

MOUNT ST. HELENS NATIONAL
VOLCANIC MONUMENT

N

0   Kilometer   0.6

0   Mile   0.6

504

(closed in winter)

■ Johnston Ridge
  Observatory

Coldwater Lake

Lakes Trail 211

Birth of a
Lake Trail

504

Coldwater
Ridge
Visitor Center

i

P

P

Hummocks
Trail

Mount
St. Helens →

terrain you will find at the base of the still-steaming volcano. Birch, alder, and willow trees share the hilly terrain between the hummocks, which are large chunks of rock and mud that landed here during the peak of the eruption. The trail winds between the hummocks and drops down into the Toutle River Valley along a route that can be steep at times. Bring good shoes and a walking stick, and watch the tops of the trees for flycatchers and warblers in summer and small raptors looking for a quick meal. Also be sure to look up toward the tops of nearby Coldwater and Johnston Ridges for larger raptors circling as they ride thermals.

Besides the birding opportunities along these two short trails, other areas of the volcanic monument offer interesting birding along with views of the changing landscape around Mount St. Helens. The Windy Ridge area south of Randle, on the other side of the blast zone from Coldwater Lake and the Toutle River Valley, offers more edge habitat where the blast zone meets the start of the forested zone. In this area many dead tree snags stand as testament to the power of the eruption, and they serve as great homes to nesting birds that rely on snags for their homes— chickadees, bluebirds, flickers, sapsuckers, and woodpeckers. But beware that there is no easy way to get to the Windy Ridge side of the monument from the Coldwater area. Instead, plan a separate trip to access the northern portion of the monument by driving south from State Route 12 at Randle and following Forest Road 25 and then Forest Road 26 toward Windy Ridge.

RECOVERING FROM DISASTER

In the years since Mount St. Helens exploded on May 18, 1980, bird, plant, and animal life have rejuvenated the blast zone. Red and black alder, noble and Douglas fir, willow, and cattails dot the landscape in the wetlands along the Hummocks Trail and the Birth of a Lake Trail. Pearly everlasting, daisy, salal, and Oregon grape fill the spaces in between the young trees that are slowly building a new succession forest where dense forests once stood. Birds returned to the blast zone soon after the eruption, and although the list of species that can be seen in the volcanic monument today is much different from a pre-eruption bird list, the numbers of bird species will continue to expand and change as forests return to Mount St. Helens in the coming decades. Of course, all of this depends on whether the smoldering volcano roars back to life or remains restlessly steaming in the background.

Other key birds: Horned and Pied-billed Grebes; Common Goldeneye; Bufflehead; Common and Hooded Mergansers; Turkey Vulture; Spotted Sandpiper; Willow Flycatcher; Red-eyed and Warbling Vireos; Clark's Nutcracker; Winter, Bewick's, and Marsh Wrens; Mountain Bluebird; Swainson's, Hermit, and Varied Thrushes; Orange-crowned, Yellow, and

Wilson's Warblers; Common Yellowthroat; Western Tanager; Fox, Lincoln's, and Golden-crowned Sparrows; Bullock's Oriole.

Nearby opportunities: Silver Lake.

Directions: From I-5, take the exit for the Spirit Lake Highway, State Route 504, following the signs to go eastbound to the Mount St. Helens National Volcanic Monument. Follow the highway to its conclusion at Coldwater Ridge, and follow the signs to Coldwater Lake. Parking for Coldwater Lake is on the left side of the road, and a short distance down the road is parking for the Hummocks Trail.

DeLorme map grid: Page 33, B6.

Elevation: 2,490 feet.

Access: Paved walking trail at Coldwater Lake, none at the Hummocks Trail.

Bathrooms: Seasonal, wheelchair-accessible bathrooms along Coldwater Lake.

Hazards: Winter weather in early spring and late fall.

Nearest food, gas, and lodging: Castle Rock.

Nearest camping: Seaquest State Park.

For more information: Check the Mount St. Helens National Volcanic Monument Web site at www.fs.fed.us/gpnf/mshnvm or call (360) 449-7800. Also keep in mind that visitors need to purchase a Monument Pass for either a daily or multiday rate to visit the volcanic monument.

Conboy Lake National Wildlife Refuge

Habitats: Wetland, mixed forest.

Specialty birds: Tundra Swan; Greater Scaup; Barrow's Goldeneye; Golden and Bald Eagles; Swainson's Hawk; Sandhill Crane; Short-eared and Northern Pygmy-Owls; Calliope and Rufous Hummingbirds; Lewis's and Pileated Woodpeckers; Red-naped Sapsucker; Hammond's, Gray, Dusky, and Pacific-slope Flycatchers; Cassin's Vireo; Pygmy Nuthatch; Western Bluebird.

Best times to bird: Spring, summer, and fall.

Mt. Adams looms over fields and marshes, part of the Conboy Lake National Wildlife Refuge near Glenwood.

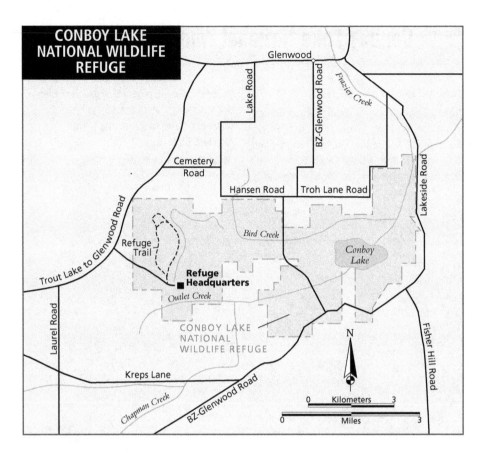

CONBOY LAKE
NATIONAL WILDLIFE
REFUGE

Glenwood

Lake Road

BZ-Glenwood Road

Frazier Creek

Cemetery
Road

Hansen Road   Troh Lane Road

Lakeside Road

Bird Creek

Refuge
Trail

Conboy
Lake

Trout Lake to Glenwood Road

**Refuge
Headquarters**

Outlet Creek

Laurel Road

CONBOY LAKE
NATIONAL
WILDLIFE REFUGE

N

Fisher Hill Road

Kreps Lane

Chapman Creek

BZ-Glenwood Road

0   Kilometers   3

0   Miles   3

About the site:

The Conboy Lake National Wildlife Refuge (NWR) can be a confusing place. If you go to the area looking for a lake, as we did one summer, you will be surprised to find a number of wetland areas along the roads that ring the refuge but nothing that you could call a lake. Visit the site in spring or fall, though, and the seasonal lake is more apparent.

Whether there is a year-round lake or not isn't an issue for the birds that call the Conboy Lake NWR home. In fact, the mixed-wetland and forest habitat is perfect for a small nesting colony of Sandhill Crane, the only nesting colony for this majestic bird in Washington. In all, 165 bird species can be seen throughout the year at Conboy Lake, with the most species in the area during spring and fall.

Conboy Lake is an easy place to track the progress of the seasons, from the cold winter when the site can be hard to reach due to its high elevation and snow, to spring, when the lake is most apparent and Sandhill Cranes start to arrive along with songbirds and waterfowl that are making the migration to the north. Summer is a slow season for birds, but the refuge offers a diverse selection of butterflies that feed on summer blooms. During one summer visit we saw five butterfly species in one small area of pearly everlasting blooms, and while we watched and photographed the butterflies we could hear the calls of Sandhill Cranes ringing out from the ponderosa- and lodgepole-pine forest that covers some upland sections of the refuge. When summer gives way to fall, the flocks of migrating waterfowl make their way through the refuge, taking advantage of the streams and wetlands as a stopover on their flight to the south.

Two major parking areas and a self-guided walking trail offer the best access to wildlife at the Conboy Lake NWR. If you visit the area on a weekday between 7:30 A.M. and 4:00 P.M. you can stop at the refuge office, just off Trout Lake to Glenwood Road on Wildlife Refuge Road. The road to the office also offers access to the Willard Spring Trail, a 2-mile walk along open marshland that serves as the best overview of the entire refuge. Walk this trail in May to see a wealth of warblers, flycatchers, and other spring songbirds as they mix with year-round residents at the refuge. Sandhill Cranes may be seen from the trail in the early spring, before they start nesting and become harder to see. A secondary access point for the refuge is along BZ-Glenwood Road near the shores of Bird Creek.

Besides birding, another attraction at Conboy Lake NWR is a rebuilt replica of a pioneer cabin, the Whitcomb-Cole Hewn Log House. The house is listed on the

A replica of the Whitcomb-Cole Hewn Log House sits on the refuge grounds near the refuge headquarters.

National Register of Historic Places and is open for viewing. The house harks back to the early 1900s when the area was known to early settlers as Camas Prairie. Prior to the arrival of European settlers, the prairie was a seasonal gathering place for Native Americans, including the Klickitat and Yakima peoples who would come to the area to gather camas root each spring.

A CRANE COMEBACK

The story of Sandhill Cranes at Conboy Lake NWR is an exciting comeback tale. This crane species, which is the widest-spread species of crane in the world, is actually an endangered species in Washington. Until the first documented return of nesting cranes at Conboy Lake in 1975, it appeared that breeding populations that had used the areas before farmers altered the habitat by draining wetlands were gone for good. After many years when only a single pair of Sandhill Cranes nested at Conboy Lake NWR, since the mid-1990s there have been between two and nine breeding pairs of birds nesting at the refuge each year. The cranes arrive in March and leave to migrate south in late September and October.

Besides the breeding Sandhill Cranes seen at Conboy Lake NWR, there have been records of another small breeding colony on the Yakama Indian Reservation. Thousands of Sandhill Cranes migrate through Washington each year, with the greatest numbers seen in the spring in the Columbia River Basin in eastern Washington and lesser numbers in places on the west side of the state, such as around the Ridgefield National Wildlife Refuge.

Other key birds: Horned and Pied-billed Grebes; American Bittern; Gadwall; Green-winged and Cinnamon Teals; American Wigeon; Northern Pintail; Northern Shoveler; Canvasback; Redhead; Ring-necked Duck; Lesser Scaup; Common Goldeneye; Bufflehead; Common and Hooded Mergansers; Turkey Vulture; Ruffed Grouse; Virginia Rail; Sora; Spotted Sandpiper; Wilson's Snipe; Western Screech- and Northern Saw-whet Owls; Common Nighthawk; Olive-sided Flycatcher; Western Wood-Pewee; Willow Flycatcher; Western Kingbird; Northern Shrike; Warbling Vireo; Bank Swallow; Mountain and Chestnut-backed Chickadees; House, Winter, Bewick's, and Marsh Wrens; Mountain Bluebird; Townsend's Solitaire; Swainson's, Hermit, and Varied Thrushes; Orange-crowned, Nashville, Black-throated Gray, Townsend's, Yellow, MacGillivray's, and Wilson's Warblers; Common Yellowthroat; Yellow-breasted Chat; Western Tanager; Chipping, Fox, Savannah, and Vesper Sparrows; Black-headed Grosbeak; Lazuli Bunting; Yellow-headed Blackbirds; Bullock's Oriole; Cassin's Finch; Red Crossbill; Evening Grosbeak.

Nearby opportunities: Trout Lake Marsh is about 10 miles away to the west, and mountain birding can be found by taking any of the forest roads out of Glenwood toward Mt. Adams.

Directions: From State Route 14 along the Columbia Gorge, turn onto State Route 141 and drive to the intersection with BZ-Glenwood

Road. Turn right onto BZ-Glenwood Road and follow the road to the northeast as it cuts through forested sections of the refuge.

DeLorme map grid: Page 25, A6.

Elevation: 1,900 feet.

Access: None.

Bathrooms: At the refuge office, open weekdays from 7:30 A.M. to 4:00 P.M.

Hazards: Snow in winter.

Nearest food, gas, and lodging: Trout Lake or Glenwood.

Nearest camping: Guler County Park in Trout Lake.

For more information: On the Internet, check pacific.fws.gov/ridgefield/Conboy.htm or refuges.fws.gov/profiles/index.cfm?id=13522. On the site, stop by the refuge office on Wildlife Refuge Road. You can also call (509) 364–3410 or send mail to Conboy Lake National Wildlife Refuge, 100 Wildlife Refuge Road, Glenwood, WA 98619.

51 Trout Lake Marsh

Habitats: Wetland, freshwater marsh, riparian, mixed forest.

Specialty birds: Greater Scaup; Barrow's Goldeneye; Golden and Bald Eagles; Short-eared and Northern Pygmy-Owls; Calliope and Rufous Hummingbirds; Lewis's and Pileated Woodpeckers; Red-naped Sapsucker; Hammond's, Gray, Dusky, and Pacific-slope Flycatchers; Cassin's Vireo; Western Bluebird.

Best times to bird: Spring, summer, and fall.

Mt. Adams reflected in the waters of Trout Lake Marsh. This wetland, with its vast amount of emergent vegetation, is a great resource for central Washington birds.

Trout Lake Marsh is known to host up to 150 bird species each year, including 50 nesting species. The 918-acre marsh is one of the largest in the state.

About the site:

Nestled near the base of Mt. Adams and just outside the small town of Trout Lake, the 918-acre Trout Lake Marsh is one of the most scenic birding locations in the state. The 12,276-foot volcano reflects in the reed-filled waters near a small parking area while songbirds sing in the Douglas fir and other trees that border the wetland on one shore and in the willow and riparian plants along the east side of the marsh. More than 150 bird species can be seen in and around the marsh, including 50 nesting species.

The key to getting the most out of birding at Trout Lake Marsh is to pay attention to the mix of habitats in the area. The wetland birds such as Marsh Wren and Wilson's Snipe can be seen along the edges of the reeds and cattails that border open water flowing through the marsh, while the ten warbler species known to nest at the site—Orange-crowned, Nashville, Yellow, Yellow-rumped, Black-throated Gray, Townsend's, MacGillivray's, Wilson's, and Hermit, as well as Common Yellowthroat—will be seen in the willows and along the shrubs and trees at the upland edges of the marsh. As is usually the case, if you pay attention to the edge habitats you are likely to see more birds at this site.

This area, located in the center of the Cascade Mountain range that serves as a dividing line between bird species of Eastern and Western Washington, offers a few interesting bird combinations within the same habitat. Trout Lake is one of the westernmost locations to see Gray Catbird and Veery and, with its elevation around 1,900 feet, it can also offer mountain species such as White-headed Woodpecker on rare occasions.

While Trout Lake Marsh holds so many bird species and so many habitats that it is among the sites listed by Audubon Washington as an Important Bird Area, it

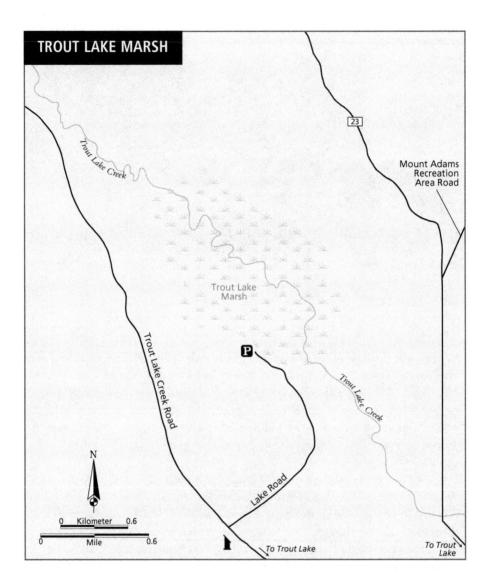

TROUT LAKE MARSH

Trout Lake Creek

23

Mount Adams
Recreation
Area Road

Trout Lake
Marsh

Trout Lake Creek Road

Trout Lake Creek

P

Lake Road

N

| 0 | Kilometer | 0.6 |
| 0 | Mile | 0.6 |

To Trout Lake

To Trout
Lake

can be a difficult site to access. You can view the site from a small two-car parking area at the end of Lake Road or by pulling off Forest Road 23 as it passes the eastern edge of the marsh just north of the town of Trout Lake. Try visiting both access points and spending time using binoculars or a spotting scope to locate birds in the dense marsh foliage. But be careful and tread lightly on the habitat in the area. Another way to increase the birding opportunities along the marsh is to walk portions of the abandoned roadway just up a short hill from the parking area at the end of Lake Road.

As with many Washington birding spots, species at Trout Lake Marsh will change drastically from week to week, especially during the spring and fall migration periods. Warblers will be commonplace in late spring, while waterfowl will flow through the area in greater numbers with the fall migration. But don't plan to bird the area in winter unless you are ready to deal with snowy and cold conditions. Much of the marsh can freeze over and birding is limited.

Other key birds: Horned and Pied-billed Grebes; American Bittern; Gadwall; Blue-winged and Cinnamon Teals; American Wigeon; Northern Pintail; Northern Shoveler; Canvasback; Redhead; Ring-necked Duck; Lesser Scaup; Common Goldeneye; Bufflehead; Common and Hooded Mergansers; Turkey Vulture; Rough-legged Hawk; Merlin; Ruffed Grouse; Virginia Rail; Sora; Spotted Sandpiper; Wilson's Snipe; Western Screech- and Northern Saw-whet Owls; Common Nighthawk; Downy and Hairy Woodpeckers; Olive-sided Flycatcher; Western Wood-Pewee; Willow Flycatcher; Western Kingbird; Northern Shrike; Warbling Vireo; Mountain and Chest-nut-backed Chickadees; House, Winter, Bewick's, and Marsh Wrens; Mountain Bluebird; Townsend's Solitaire; Swainson's, Hermit, and Varied Thrushes; Orange-crowned, Nashville, Black-throated Gray, Townsend's, Yellow, MacGillivray's, and Wilson's Warblers; Common Yellowthroat; Yellow-breasted Chat; Western Tanager; Chipping, Fox, Savannah, and Lincoln's Sparrows; Black-headed Grosbeak; Lazuli Bunting; Yellow-headed Blackbird; Bullock's Oriole; Cassin's Finch; Red Crossbill; Evening Grosbeak.

Nearby opportunities: Conboy Lake National Wildlife Refuge is just a few miles from here near Glenwood, offering more lowland birding opportunities and looks at waterfowl during the spring and fall migrations. Those birding in the summer may want to take FR 23 north into the Gifford Pinchot National Forest for mountain birding.

Directions: From State Route 14 along the Columbia Gorge, turn onto State Route 141 and drive to the small town of Trout Lake. In town, follow Trout Lake Creek Road past the Mt. Adams ranger station and then turn right onto Lake Road. Drive to the end of this gravel road and park in the small parking area for views of the marsh and Mt. Adams in the distance. Parking at the site is very limited. Portions of the site also can be birded along FR 23 directly north of Trout Lake.

DeLorme map grid: Page 34, D4.

Elevation: 1,900 feet.

Access: None.

Bathrooms: None.

Hazards: None.

Nearest food, gas, and lodging: Trout Lake.

Nearest camping: Guler County Park in Trout Lake.

For more information: The Mt. Adams ranger station in Trout Lake, near the turnoff to the site, sells a bird list compiled by local birders and may offer more information about the site.

52 Klickitat River

Habitats: Lowland riparian, wetland, freshwater marsh, prairie, mixed forest.

Specialty birds: Greater Scaup; Golden and Bald Eagles; Northern Goshawk; Swainson's Hawk; Peregrine Falcon; Chukar; Northern Pygmy-Owl; Calliope and Rufous Humming-birds; Acorn, Lewis's, and Pileated Woodpeckers; Red-naped Sapsucker; Hammond's, Dusky, and Pacific-slope Flycatchers; Cassin's Vireo; Western Bluebird.

Best times to bird: Year-round.

Near the bottom of the Klickitat River, the waters flow through a wide canyon lined with Oregon white oak. Watch for Bank Swallows over the river and raptors soaring on thermals over the mountains on each side of the river.

About the site:

As one of the most bird-rich and least-birded portions of Washington, the corridor along the banks of the Klickitat River is a natural attraction for adventurous bird-watchers. Up to 290 species of birds and 176 species of breeding birds can be seen in Klickitat County, and many of them, including the hard-to-find Acorn Woodpecker, Ash-throated Flycatcher, and Lesser Goldfinch, can be seen around the Klickitat River.

There are a number of routes that can be used to bird-watch in Klickitat County, but one of the easiest and most diverse routes is to follow the Klickitat River as it winds northeast out of the town of Lyle. The Klickitat River is popular with anglers and hunters, and it is a destination for white-water rafting when water conditions are right. It is one of the longest free-flowing rivers in Washington at more than 100 miles long, and it follows a wide canyon dotted with riparian habitat as well as small pockets of Oregon white oak trees—also called Garry Oak trees—that are favorites of Lewis's and Acorn Woodpeckers, as well as Ash-throated Flycatchers.

State Route 142, the road that runs alongside the Klickitat River before it rises onto a plateau en route to Goldendale, starts in Lyle and quickly climbs up a hill with views of the river below. The slice carved into the mountains by the river is wide here, offering views to the south toward the Columbia River Gorge and to the hills above the river where raptors can be seen riding thermals. Look at the sandy banks along the highway for areas pockmarked by Bank Swallow holes. The diminutive swallows are seen flying along the river in summer.

The highway slowly climbs and crosses the river as it passes through a series of small towns—Pitt, Klickitat, and Wahkiacus. As you drive up the river, pull over in wide spots along the road to look and listen for bird life in the oak trees and riparian areas. Also watch for butterflies, as the number of individuals and species can be impressive in Klickitat County in summer. Some of the wide areas alongside the road are commonly used by people who park and walk to the river's edge to fish. If there is room, get out and wander around, checking the trees for woodpeckers and watching the river's edge for warblers.

If you have time for only an out-and-back birding route along the Klickitat River, a good place to turn around and spend some more time birding is at a hairpin turn where the highway crosses Canyon Creek. The narrow road climbs dramatically past Canyon Creek, with views from pullouts along the road above that look down on the Little Klickitat River where it meets the larger Klickitat River. If you have the time to make a circular route and try bird-watching on the upper plateau, the highway winds through farmland before reaching Goldendale. You can turn right onto U.S. Highway 97 and drive across and down the Columbia Hills to State Route 14 and then turn right and return to the Lyle area and the Columbia River Gorge.

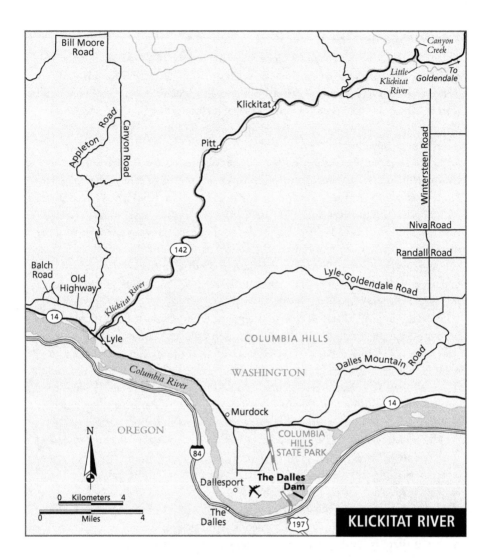

Besides the birding opportunities along the Klickitat River, another bird-watching area is along Old Highway and Balch Road, just on the other side of the river from Lyle. Old Highway climbs away from SR 14 and veers left, offering panoramic views of Mt. Hood in the distance on clear days. Oak trees line the north side of the road as you approach Balch Road. Turn right onto Balch Road and drive slowly and watch for birds along the edges of the road as well as in the oak trees. This area can be teeming with woodpeckers, including Acorn, Lewis's, Pileated, Hairy, and Downy Woodpeckers. Western Scrub-Jay are common here, and you may be able to catch a glimpse of a Lesser Goldfinch in the open fields along the road. Also watch for waterfowl on the small lakes alongside the road.

THE COLUMBIA HILLS IMPORTANT BIRD AREA

Just east and up the ridge from the Klickitat River are the Columbia Hills, an area that stretches to the east toward Rock Creek, east of U.S. Highway 97. The Columbia Hills have been designated by Audubon Washington as an Important Bird Area for the critical habitat offered to the hundreds of raptors, including up to thirteen different species, that spend their winter in the area. According to data edited by Audubon's Tim Cullinan in Important Bird Areas of Washington, the area supports five Prairie Falcon aeries, three Golden Eagle aeries, Swainson's Hawk nests, nesting and wintering Lewis's Woodpeckers, and even Long-billed Curlew that can be seen in spring in farm fields and in native grassland areas.

Other key birds: Pied-billed Grebe; Gadwall; Green-winged and Cinnamon Teals; American Wigeon; Northern Pintail; Northern Shoveler; Canvasback; Redhead; Ring-necked Duck; Lesser Scaup; Common Goldeneye; Bufflehead; Common and Hooded Mergansers; Turkey Vulture; Osprey; Rough-legged Hawk; Merlin; Prairie Falcon; Gray Partridge; Wild Turkey; Ruffed Grouse; Virginia Rail; Sora; Wilson's Snipe; Ring-billed Gull; Common Nighthawk; Downy and Hairy Woodpeckers; Olive-sided and Ash-throated Flycatchers; Say's Phoebe; Western Kingbird; Northern Shrike; Warbling Vireo; Bank Swallow; Chestnut-backed Chickadee; House, Winter, Bewick's, Rock, Canyon, and Marsh Wrens; Mountain Bluebird; Townsend's Solitaire; Swainson's, Hermit, and Varied Thrushes; Orange-crowned, Nashville, Black-throated Gray, Townsend's, Yellow, MacGillivray's, and Wilson's Warblers; Common Yellowthroat; Yellow-breasted Chat; Western Tanager; Chipping, Fox, Savannah, Lincoln's, Vesper, and Golden-crowned Sparrows; Black-headed Grosbeak; Lazuli Bunting; Yellow-headed Blackbird; Bullock's Oriole; Cassin's Finch, Red Crossbill; Lesser Goldfinch; Evening Grosbeak.

Nearby opportunities: Rowland Lake, west of Lyle along SR 14, offers some rare county sightings for waterfowl from time to time, and the Columbia River also can hold some interesting birds throughout the year.

Directions: From SR 14 eastbound through the Columbia River Gorge, take a left onto State Route 142 at Lyle. SR 142 winds to the north-northeast along the banks of the Klickitat River. From Goldendale on US 97, turn right onto SR 142 and drive west to the Klickitat River. The river and our route begins once you descend along the steep and narrow highway to the hairpin turn at Canyon Creek.

DeLorme map grid: Page 25, C6.

Elevation: Ranges from 140 feet at Lyle to 550 feet at Wahkiacus and more than 1,600 feet at Goldendale.

Access: None.

Bathrooms: None.

Hazards: None.

Nearest food, gas, and lodging: Goldendale and Lyle.

Nearest camping: Columbia Hills State Park, formerly known as Horsethief Lake State Park.

For more information: Check the Birding Klickitat County Web page at community.gorge.net/birding. It offers information about birding sites as well as bird-count information dating from 1996.

Northeast

The Northeast Region of Washington features some of the best winter birding opportunities in the state. The Okanogan Highlands are popular with winter birders seeking glimpses of such uncommon birds as Bohemian Waxwings and Common Redpolls; the Waterville Plateau is a destination for bird-watchers looking for Snowy Owls and other winter raptors.

Washington's northeastern corner is bound by the Okanogan and Columbia Rivers in the west, the Canadian border in the north, the Idaho border in the east, and Interstate 90 in the south. It includes the state's third-largest city, Spokane, as well as some of the least populated areas in the state such as the Colville Indian Reservation and the Selkirk Mountains. The northern tier of the region includes some of the more mountainous areas in the state, including easily accessible birding along State Route 20 on Sherman Pass and the highest elevation refuge in the national wildlife refuge system in the Little Pend Oreille National Wildlife Refuge.

Given its close border with Canada, the Northeast Region offers chances to see some birds normally associated with the boreal forests of the north, such as Boreal Owls and Boreal Chickadees. It is also home to Spruce Grouse, Northern Waterthrush, and American Redstarts.

Residents of the Spokane don't have to venture too far afield to reach prime bird habitat. The Spokane River corridor offers readily accessible trails for bird-watchers, and the Little Spokane River Natural Area is within easy reach of the northern end of Spokane.

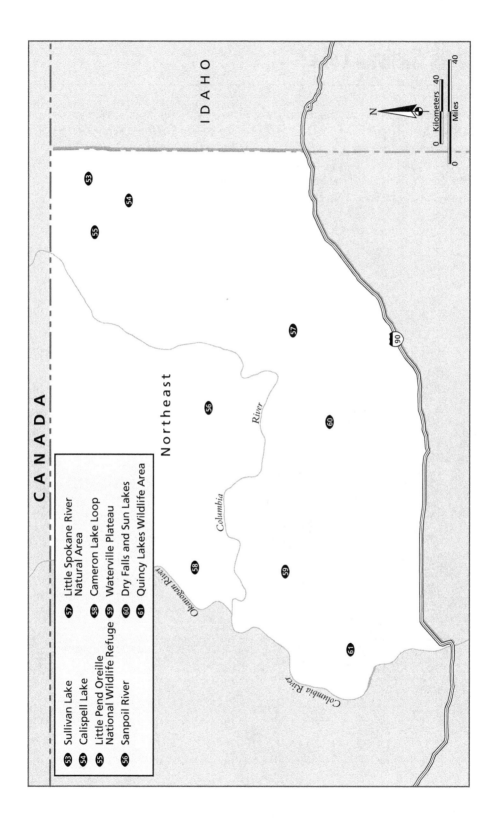

CANADA

IDAHO

Northeast

53 Sullivan Lake
54 Calispell Lake
55 Little Pend Oreille
National Wildlife Refuge
56 Sanpoil River

57 Little Spokane River
Natural Area
58 Cameron Lake Loop
59 Waterville Plateau
60 Dry Falls and Sun Lakes
61 Quincy Lakes Wildlife Area

Columbia River

Okanogan River

Columbia River

River

90

N

0   Kilometers   40
0   Miles   40

53 Sullivan Lake

Habitats: Mountain riparian, mixed forest, wetland, freshwater marsh.

Specialty birds: Common Loon; Barrow's Goldeneye; Bald Eagle; Northern Goshawk; Blue Grouse; Flammulated and Northern Pygmy-Owls; Vaux's Swift; Black-chinned, Cal- liope, and Rufous Hummingbirds; Pileated Woodpecker; Red-naped Sapsucker; Hammond's Flycatcher; Cassin's Vireo; Gray Jay; Northern Waterthrush; American Redstart.

Best times to bird: Summer and fall.

Sullivan Lake is one of the few places in Washington where Common Loons nest.

About the site:

Tucked into the far northeastern corner of the state, Sullivan Lake is a hidden gem for bird-watchers looking for scenery and solitude. The lake covers nearly 1,400 acres and is surrounded by towering mountains that host bighorn sheep and mountain goats, as well as a diverse number of bird species. Best of all, nearly all of the lake shoreline is accessible by either road or hiking/biking trails.

As with so many other bird-watching sites around the state, paying close attention to the habitats is the key to finding good birds at Sullivan Lake. Mixed forests surround the lake, with more coniferous forests on the mountains above the lake and more deciduous trees mixed into the areas along the lakeshore. The best places to access this edge habitat along the lakeshore are at the Noisy Creek campground, the Sullivan Lake campground, and the Mill Pond campground downstream from the main lake.

On one visit to Sullivan Lake, we started our birding at first light in the Noisy Creek campground after spending the night being serenaded by Great Horned Owls. The campground offers lakeshore access, a small boat launch, and a few walking trails that wind through the mixed habitat with its aspen, birch, alder, and towering cottonwood trees along the creek. The mountainsides above are dotted with larch, grand and Douglas fir, and pine trees. As the sun rose and cleared the mountains to the east of the camp, the tree canopy teemed with bird life. Red-breasted Nuthatches called from the coniferous trees, while kinglets, juncoes, and Yellow and Yellow-rumped Warblers fed in the deciduous trees overhead. Meanwhile, from the lakeshore it was easy to pick out a Red-necked Grebe far out on the lake and a pair of Common Merganser closer to the shore.

After exploring in the Noisy Creek area, the next logical place to find birds is in the Sullivan Lake campground, at the other end of the 3.6-mile-long lake. The road to the campground clings to the western shore of the lake, offering more chances to see waterfowl on the lake's surface. A couple of pullouts, including one with an interpretive historical sign with details about the lake, offer viewing points along the way to the campground.

The Sullivan Lake campground offers more mixed forests and lake shoreline, as well as an open field just beyond the trees that serves as an airfield. We found Red-naped Sapsucker in the trees near the lake, more mergansers on the lake, and songbirds more commonly found around open fields along the edges of the airfield. If you have access to a canoe, the campground offers a good place to start paddling around on the lake to watch the water's edges. The campground also offers access to a 4-mile trail along the east side of the lake that winds along the shoreline back to the Noisy Creek campground. Just a couple of miles farther north of Sullivan Lake is the backwater behind a dam at the Mill Pond campground. While Sullivan Lake offers wide-open water, the millpond features more marshy and wetland habitat that caters to other bird species. This is where you are more likely to see

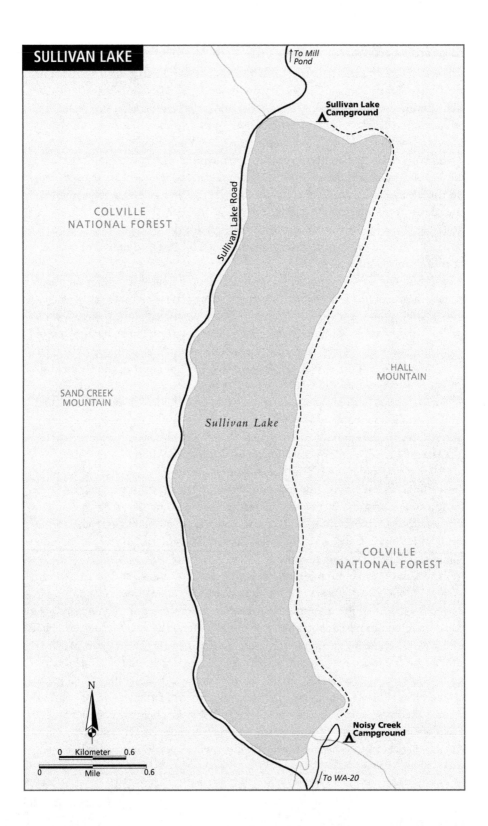

SULLIVAN LAKE

To Mill
Pond

Sullivan Lake
Campground

COLVILLE
NATIONAL FOREST

Sullivan Lake Road

HALL
MOUNTAIN

SAND CREEK
MOUNTAIN

Sullivan Lake

COLVILLE
NATIONAL FOREST

N

Noisy Creek
Campground

0   Kilometer   0.6

0   Mile   0.6

To WA-20

Pied-billed Grebe, dabbling ducks, and flycatchers sallying out for insects from perches along the wetland shores. Be sure to walk the interpretive trail, which provides notes about the historic uses of the millpond, as it will offer more chances to see passerines in the trees that line the pond. The habitat along the old mill-pond is where you could find hummingbirds feeding on flowering bushes in the spring and summer, and where you are likely to find an American Redstart flitting among the foliage.

Although it is unlikely you would run into any of them in the campgrounds mentioned here, it would be wise to keep in mind some of the other wildlife that visit and live in this remote section of Washington. The Sullivan Lake Ranger District notes that along with the possibility of encountering moose and elk on nearby trails in the Salmo-Priest Wilderness, the area has been host to gray wolf, woodland caribou, and very rare visits from grizzly bear. In short, be ready to make noise while walking in the woods in order to avoid startling big wildlife.

COMMON LOONS ARE NOT THAT COMMON

Despite their name, Common Loons are not that common as nesting birds in Washington. Sullivan Lake is one of the only locations in the state where the birds, whose calls are so associated with the deep woods, actually nest every year. Most Common Loons nest on large lakes that offer plenty of room for takeoffs and landings, a plentiful supply of small fish to feed on, and some kind of seclusion where they can create their nests in reeds near the shore. According to the Birdweb.org Web site, during the last decade there have been roughly twenty confirmed nesting sites for Common Loons in Washington. Common Loon are most frequently seen in the winter and early spring, when they frequently show up on Puget Sound, along the Washington coast, and occasionally on freshwater lakes.

Other key birds: Pied-billed and Red-necked Grebes; American Bittern; Gadwall; Green-winged, Blue-winged, and Cinnamon Teals; American Wigeon; Northern Pintail; Northern Shoveler; Redhead; Ring-necked Duck; Lesser Scaup; Common Goldeneye; Bufflehead; Common and Hooded Mergansers; Turkey Vulture; Osprey; Wild Turkey; Ruffed Grouse; Sora; Spotted Sandpiper; Wilson's Snipe; Barred and Boreal Owls; Common Nighthawk; Western Wood-Pewee; Willow Flycatcher; Eastern Kingbird; Red-eyed and Warbling Vireos; Clark's Nutcracker; Mountain and Chestnut-backed Chickadees; Brown Creeper; House, Winter, and Marsh Wrens; American Dipper; Townsend's Solitaire; Swainson's, Hermit, and Varied Thrushes; Gray Catbird; Orange-crowned, Townsend's, Yellow, MacGillivray's, and Wilson's Warblers; Common Yellowthroat; Western Tanager; Chipping, Fox, Savannah, and Lincoln's Sparrows; Black-headed Grosbeak; Lazuli Bunting; Cassin's Finch; Red Crossbill; Evening Grosbeak.

Nearby opportunities: Boreal Chickadees and Boreal Owls can be found on Salmo Mountain, northeast of Sullivan Lake.

Directions: Take State Route 20 to Tiger and turn north onto State Route 31. Before reaching the town of Ione, turn right onto Sullivan Lake Road and follow this road to the lake.

DeLorme map grid: Page 119, B6.

Elevation: 2,588 feet.

Access: None.

Bathrooms: In the campgrounds.

Hazards: None.

Nearest food, gas, and lodging: Metaline Falls.

Nearest camping: Noisy Creek, Sullivan Lake, or Millpond campgrounds.

For more information: Check the Web page for the Sullivan Lake Ranger District at www.povn.com/byway/towns/Sullivan.html.

54 Calispell Lake

Habitats: Wetland, freshwater marsh, mixed forest.

Specialty birds: Tundra and Trumpeter Swans; Barrow's Goldeneye; Bald Eagle; Northern Goshawk; Blue Grouse; Sandhill Crane; Wilson's Phalarope; Northern Pygmy-Owl; Vaux's Swift; Black-chinned, Calliope, and Rufous Hummingbirds; Pileated Woodpecker; Red-naped Sapsucker; Hammond's and Dusky Flycatchers; Cassin's Vireo.

Best times to bird: Spring and fall.

A small section of open water in the center of Calispell Lake as seen from the roadside. The lake rises and falls throughout the year, bottoming out in late summer due to irrigation uses of its waters.

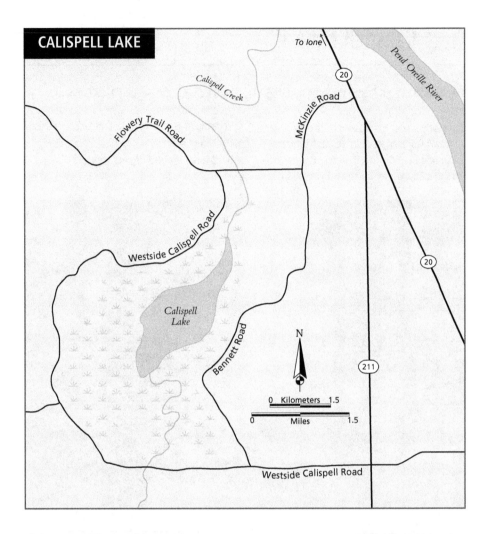

CALISPELL LAKE

To Ione

Calispell Creek

Pend Oreille River

20

McKinzie Road

Flowery Trail Road

Westside Calispell Road

Calispell
Lake

Bennett Road

N

20

211

0 Kilometers 1.5

0 Miles 1.5

Westside Calispell Road

About the site:

Maps depict Calispell Lake as a vast marsh surrounding a relatively small lake, but to migrating waterfowl and shorebirds, the lake and the emergent vegetation around it must look like a huge bull's-eye and the perfect place to stop during spring and fall migrations. Sandhill Cranes and Tundra and Trumpeter Swans are among the birds that settle on the privately owned land around Calispell Lake, and the fields that surround the wetlands are also known to host Bobolink. The trick is finding a good vantage point to see the birds around the lake.

Approaching Calispell Lake from the south along State Route 211, turn left onto Westside Calispell Road and drive west to skirt along the southern edge of the wetland and lake. Pull to the side of the road once you see the open fields and the lake in the distance to the north. Use binoculars or a spotting scope to look across the fields, where we watched a number of American Kestrel, Brewer's and

Red-winged Blackbirds, Brown-headed Cowbirds, and dozens of Chipping Sparrows during one fall visit. It will be hard to pick out waterfowl on the lake from this vantage point so, after checking the field, continue driving down Westside Calispell Road heading west as the road passes over Calispell Creek before veering to the right to follow the edge of the marsh and lake. Osprey nests sit on top of power poles on the ridge above the road on the southwest corner of the marsh. Although the concentrations of Osprey along the lake are not overwhelming, Calispell Lake is fairly close to the Pend Oreille River, which has the highest concentration of nesting Osprey in Washington. Keep an eye on the tops of fir and pine trees for Bald Eagles.

As the road veers north and winds along open fields on the left side of the road and the marsh on the other, watch along fence posts for kestrels and hawks and out over the open water for waterfowl. There are wide spots in the road, and the road is not very busy, so you should be able to pull over and safely bird without impeding traffic. Also, watch the pine trees for signs of Pileated, Downy, and Hairy Woodpecker feeding in the area.

Westside Calispell Road ends at an intersection with Flowery Trail Road. Turn right to cross the wetland at the northern end of Calispell Lake. If you turn left you can drive into the mountains that drain into the lake on your way to the 49

As much a wetland as it is a lake, Calispell Lake provides critical habitat for migrating waterfowl, Sandhill Cranes, and shorebirds.

Degrees North Ski Area, and the road goes through to the town of Chewelah on State Route 395. Turn right to continue exploring the lake and wetlands.

Flowery Trail Road crosses the wetland and offers the closest views of the lake in this section of the site. If traffic is cooperative, pull to the side of the road and scan the wetland and listen closely for the sounds of Wilson's Snipe, Virginia Rail, and American Bittern. Once you are across the wetland, Flowery Trail Road meets McKinzie Road. You can either take McKinzie Road to connect with State Route 20 along the Pend Oreille River or turn right onto Bennett Road and drive south to complete the loop around Calispell Lake by driving through a mixed-forest area.

Calispell Lake and its surrounding marsh are noted by Audubon Washington as one of the state's Important Bird Areas. The area receives this distinction due to its importance as a staging ground for migrating waterfowl, shorebirds, and Sandhill Cranes. To maximize your chances of seeing some of these birds, plan to visit Calispell Lake during the fall. Shorebirds show up at the site in late July and August, while swans commonly arrive in late September and October. Sandhill Cranes can be seen in spring and fall as they migrate north to the Yukon and back to southern Oregon, California, and Texas in the fall.

Calispell Lake doesn't offer one distinct stop for the best bird-viewing, but its unique habitat nestled between the Pend Oreille River and the mountains to the west make it a worthwhile destination. There is also an opportunity for discovery in the area, since it is not visited by many bird-watchers.

Other key birds: Pied-billed and Red-necked Grebes; American Bittern; Gadwall; Green-winged, Blue-winged, and Cinnamon Teals; Northern Pintail; Northern Shoveler; Redhead; Ring-necked Duck; Lesser Scaup; Common Goldeneye; Bufflehead; Common and Hooded Mergansers; Turkey Vulture; Osprey; Rough-legged Hawk; Wild Turkey; Ruffed Grouse; Sora; Wilson's Snipe; Black Tern; Barred Owl; Common Nighthawk; Western Wood-Pewee; Willow Flycatcher; Eastern Kingbird; Red-eyed and Warbling Vireos; Brown Creeper; House, Winter, and Marsh Wrens; Mountain Bluebird; Gray Catbird; Orange-crowned, Townsend's, Yellow, MacGillivray's and Wilson's Warblers; Common Yellowthroat; American Redstart; Western Tanager; Chipping, Fox, Savannah, and Lincoln's Sparrows; Black-headed Grosbeak; Lazuli Bunting; Bobolink; Yellow-headed Blackbird; Cassin's Finch; Red Crossbill; Evening Grosbeak.

Nearby opportunities: Pend Oreille River along SR 20.

Directions: Take State Route 2 north from Spokane toward Newport. Take a left onto SR 211 and drive north to the intersection with Westside Calispell Road. Turn left onto Westside Calispell Road.

DeLorme map grid: Page 105, B6.

Elevation: 2,029 feet.

Access: None.

Bathrooms: None.

Hazards: None.

Nearest food, gas, and lodging: Newport.

Nearest camping: Skookum Creek campground on east side of the Pend Oreille River.

Little Pend Oreille National Wildlife Refuge

Habitats: Mountain riparian, mixed-conifer forest; forest, mixed wetland, freshwater marsh.

Specialty birds: Common Loon; Greater Scaup; Barrow's Goldeneye; Golden and Bald Eagles; Northern Goshawk; Blue Grouse; Wilson's Phalarope; Short-eared, Flammulated, and Northern Pygmy-Owl; Vaux's Swift; Black-chinned, Calliope, and Rufous Hummingbirds; White-headed, Lewis's, Black-backed, and Pileated Woodpeckers; Red-naped Sapsucker; Hammond's and Pacific-slope Flycatchers; Cassin's Vireo; Gray Jay; Pygmy Nuthatch; Western Bluebird; Bohemian Waxwing; Northern Waterthrush; Gray-crowned Rosy-Finch; White-winged Crossbill; Pine Grosbeak.

Best times to bird: Summer and fall.

The Little Pend Oreille River winds through the wildlife refuge, offering habitat for American Dipper and other birds.

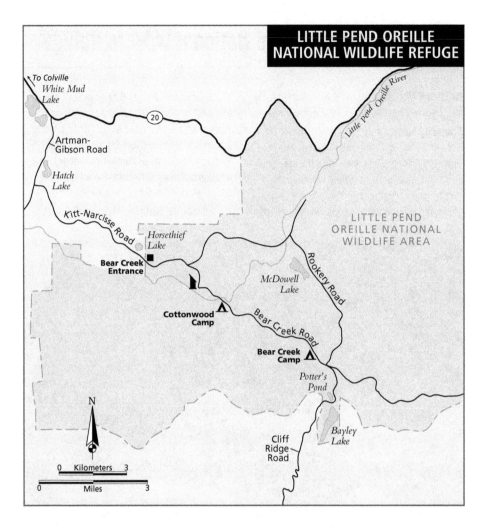

About the site:

Many things make the Little Pend Oreille National Wildlife Refuge (NWR) stand out as a bird-watching destination. It is the only mountainous, mixed-conifer forest refuge in the contiguous United States, it ranges in elevation from 1,800 feet along its western edges to 5,600 feet along its eastern border, and it is one of the least-visited refuges in Washington due to it location in the remote northeast corner of the state. All of these facts make Little Pend Oreille a playground for bird-watchers.

More than 185 species of birds are on the list of possible species for the 40,000-acre refuge, with peak bird diversity occurring in the late spring and early summer migration and nesting seasons. Some birds on the list are more likely to be seen in the winter months, such as Bohemian Waxwing, White-winged Crossbill, and Gyrfalcon. It can be hard to reach portions of the refuge in the winter months, however, due to its elevation and winter weather.

The Pines Natural Area is a section of the refuge managed specifically to monitor the development of native ponderosa-pine forest and associated plants and animals.

There are nine main entrances to the refuge, some of which are open only in the summer months once snow melts in the mountains. The best way to get an overview of the refuge is to take a loop route starting on Bear Creek Road, veering east onto Rookery Road, and then going left after passing McDowell Lake onto Starvation Flat Road to rejoin Bear Creek Road.

You can start exploring Little Pend Oreille NWR before you even reach the refuge office and kiosk where you'll find information about the site along Bear Creek Road. After veering to the right onto Bear Creek Road from Kitt-Narcisse Road, refuge land surrounds the road on both sides in an area of mixed-coniferous forest dominated by second- and third-growth pine trees. The western portions of the refuge offer the most altered habitats, with farm fields and old homestead sites along the roadside in an area that was once dotted with logging camps, homesteads, and farms. There are bluebird boxes on some of the fence posts, and the pine trees along the road were filled with nuthatches, crossbills, and chickadees while Chipping Sparrows moved through the undergrowth and Downy Woodpeckers hunted for insects in the trees during our visit to the refuge.

The Little Pend Oreille River crosses Bear Creek Road just past the open farm fields near the first of four campgrounds on the refuge. The river can offer glimpses of American Dipper and passerines that use the riverside mountain riparian habitat with its quaking aspen, cottonwood, willow, and brushy plants that offer cover from raptors and the weather. The deciduous trees and shrubs along streams and the river offer the best viewing opportunities for warblers.

Continuing on Bear Creek Road, the habitat changes back to mixed-coniferous forest, with its hosts of woodpeckers, sapsuckers, chickadees, and nuthatches. Near Bear Creek Camp the road passes The Pines Natural Area—habitat maintained to offer a more natural ponderosa-pine area in the midst of the areas that were formerly logged. Prescribed burns and other management methods help maintain this stand of huge pine trees, and this is one of the best places to see birds that associate with mature pine forest, such as White-headed Woodpecker.

Just past the Bear Creek Camp, look for Rookery Road on the left. Turn onto this road to drive the loop up around McDowell Lake. If you miss the turn, as we did during our visit to the site, you will climb high into the mountains on the southern edge of the refuge. Rookery Road climbs as well, moving through more mixed-conifer forest enroute to McDowell Lake. Once you reach the lake, which is one of the largest bodies of open water in the refuge, be sure to view its edges for nesting waterfowl and check the treetops for Osprey. Goldeneye, Bufflehead, mergansers, and other waterfowl can be on the lakes in the refuge.

Not far past the lake, take a left onto Starvation Flat Road to complete the loop drive when it intersects with Bear Creek Road at the northern end of the refuge. Throughout the forested areas, keep an eye out for Pygmy Nuthatches, woodpeckers, and grosbeaks.

There are a number of other routes you could use to explore Little Pend

Oreille NWR. The Bear Creek, Narcisse Creek, and Buffalo-Wilson entrances to the refuge are open year-round, while the Starvation Lake entrance opens April 14. Most roads in the refuge are closed from January 1 through April 14, but visitors can hike, bike, or even ski into the refuge on marked roads.

Other key birds: Horned, Pied-billed, Red-necked, and Western Grebes; Gadwall; Green-winged, Blue-winged, and Cinnamon Teals; American Wigeon; Northern Pintail; Northern Shoveler; Redhead; Ring-necked Duck; Lesser Scaup; Common Goldeneye, Bufflehead; Common and Hooded Mergansers; Ruddy Duck; Turkey Vulture; Osprey; Wild Turkey; Ruffed Grouse; Spruce Grouse; Virginia Rail; Sora; Spotted Sandpiper; Wilson's Snipe; Barred and Northern Saw-whet Owls; Common Nighthawk; Common Poorwill; Downy and Hairy Woodpeckers; Olive-sided Flycatcher; Western Wood-Pewee; Willow Flycatcher; Say's Phoebe; Western and Eastern Kingbirds; Northern Shrike; Red-eyed and Warbling Vireos; Clark's Nutcracker; Bank Swallow; Mountain and Boreal Chickadees; White-breasted Nuthatch; Brown Creeper; House, Winter, Rock, and Marsh Wrens; Mountain Bluebird; Townsend's Solitaire; Veery; Swainson's, Hermit, and Varied Thrushes; Gray Catbird; Orange-crowned, Nashville, Townsend's, Yellow, MacGillivray's, and Wilson's Warblers; Common Yellowthroat; American Redstart; Western Tanager; Chipping, Savannah, and Lincoln's Sparrows; Black-headed Grosbeak; Lazuli Bunting; Yellow-headed Blackbird; Bullock's Oriole; Cassin's Finch; Red Crossbill; Evening Grosbeak.

Nearby opportunities: Little Pend Oreille Lakes along State Route 20, east of the refuge.

Directions: From SR 20, turn south onto Artman-Gibson Road near White Mud Lake and Keogh Lakes. When the road comes to a T, turn left onto Kitt-Narcisse Road and follow the signs to the refuge, turning right onto Bear Creek Road.

DeLorme map grid: Page 103, A3.

Elevation: 1,300 feet.

Access: The fishing dock at Potter's Pond and a restroom at the site are wheelchair accessible.

Bathrooms: At Potter's Pond.

Hazards: Rugged roads.

Nearest food, gas, and lodging: Colville.

Nearest camping: Camping is available in the refuge at Cottonwood Camp, Bear Creek Camp, LPO River Camp, and Horse Camp.

For more information: Check the Web page for the refuge at littlependoreille.fws.gov or give the refuge a call at (800) 344-WILD or (509) 684-8384.

56 Sanpoil River

Habitats: Mountain riparian, mixed forest, wetland, freshwater marsh.

Specialty birds: Common Loon; Barrow's Goldeneye; Golden and Bald Eagles; Northern Pygmy-Owl; Black-chinned, Calliope, and Rufous Hummingbirds; Lewis's and Pileated Woodpeckers; Red-naped Sapsucker; Hammond's, Dusky, and Pacific-slope Flycatchers; Cassin's Vireo; Pygmy Nuthatch; Western Bluebird; Northern Waterthrush.

Best times to bird: Summer and fall.

About the site:

Bird-watching along the banks of the Sanpoil River in Ferry County offers up close views of some of northeastern Washington's best birds. The riparian habitats mixed with pine forest and interspersed with steep and rocky slopes dotted with native wildflowers can hold a wide range of passerines, and hard-to-find birds such as Northern Waterthrush and American Redstart can be seen along the route. The trick is getting off the main road through the area—State Route 21—and driving along the rugged eastern shore of the river.

Approaching the Sanpoil River from the south, the best way to access the area is from Wilbur along SR 2. After making the winding drive north on SR 21 and down a canyon to the edges of the Columbia River at Keller Ferry, a quick and free ferry ride across Roosevelt Lake offers you the chance to see waterfowl and to try to imagine what this region would be like if the river's waters were not bunched up behind the Grand Coulee Dam, many miles downriver from the ferry landing. If you have time while waiting for the Keller ferry, check out the trees in the campground near the ferry landing for songbirds such as Bullock's Oriole and Cedar Waxwings.

On the north side of the river, follow SR 21 toward the town of Keller. Watch for Osprey nests in trees along the highway and for shrikes, kingbirds, and passerines in the grasslands and mixed forest on the roadside. Keller Park makes a good wayside to check for birds near the mouth of the Sanpoil River, and it offers restrooms during the spring, summer, and early fall months.

You will find the bulk of birds along the Sanpoil River on East Sanpoil Road, which follows the river's east side from Keller in the south to a couple of bridge crossings at Bridge Creek Road and Thirtymile Road in the north. Starting in the south, the road winds through a young mixed-coniferous forest composed mainly of ponderosa pine. Wildflowers and low-lying brush offer nectar sources for hummingbirds, and this can be a great site for seeing both Black-chinned and Calliope Hummingbirds. During sunny summer days the sides of this rugged, single-lane road also can host a number of butterfly species. Beware of trying to take this road in soggy conditions, it could become impassable due to mud.

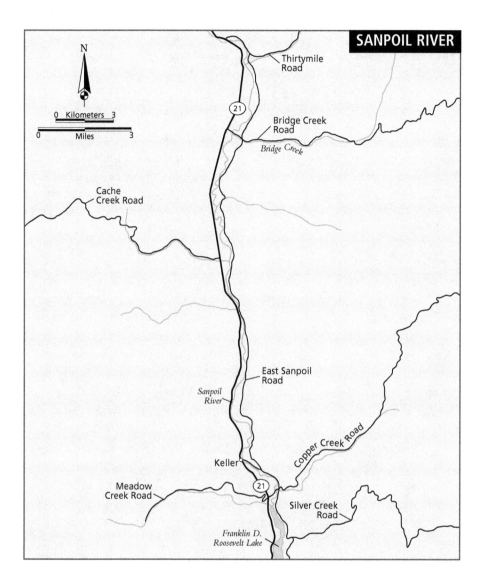

N

0   Kilometers   3

0   Miles   3

Thirtymile
Road

21

Bridge Creek
Road

Bridge Creek

Cache
Creek Road

East Sanpoil
Road

*Sanpoil
River*

Copper Creek Road

Keller

Meadow
Creek Road

21

Silver Creek
Road

*Franklin D.
Roosevelt Lake*

Continuing north, the road moves closer to the river, offering peekaboo views from bluffs above the river in some cases and skirting right alongside the riparian zone in other areas. One section along the lower reaches of the river hugs the bank, offering views of both riverbanks. We viewed and listened to a Yellow-breasted Chat in this area during one June visit.

The road pulls away from the river and offers birding along mixed-forest habitat and then alongside some farm fields before reaching the intersection with Bridge Creek Road. Just north of Bridge Creek Road, East Sanpoil Road offers views over a meandering section of the river, where the water slows and wetlands and freshwater marsh habitat offer views of Gray Catbird, warblers, and if you are lucky, an occasional American Redstart. East Sanpoil Road continues north to Thirtymile Creek Road, but you can turn around after exploring the meandering wetlands and take a right onto Bridge Creek Road to return to SR 21. If you return to SR 21, you might catch a glimpse of a Northern Waterthrush in the stagnant ponds along the highway. Check the ponds north and south of Bridge Creek Road for these quiet birds.

There is more to the Sanpoil River and this part of Ferry County for bird-watchers who are willing to explore. Go north on SR 21 toward Republic to hook up with State Route 20 and loop into the Okanogan highlands, or go back south on SR 21 to take the Keller ferry back toward Wilbur. Either way, be sure to bird along the route. You never know what you may find in this underbirded part of the state.

MIXING BUTTERFLY-WATCHING WITH BIRDING

If you find yourself out in the wild and the temperatures are climbing too high or it is simply the wrong time of the day for good bird-watching, take the opportunity to look for some of the other wild creatures in your surroundings. Especially in eastern Washington and along riparian corridors such as the Sanpoil River, where butterflies linger during sunny days to nectar on wildflowers and flowering bushes, butterfly-watching can add more variety to the midday explorations during the time that bird activity is at its low point.

Along the Sanpoil River, watch for butterflies such as the Lorquin's Admiral, Western Tiger and Pale Swallowtail, Two-tailed Swallowtail, Mourning Cloak, and the small blue butterflies that often escape the view of those looking for big showy butterflies. Also watch for large congregations of butterflies along the muddy edges of the river or even along small streams or puddles in the road. Butterflies gather along these damp places, exhibiting a behavior known as puddling. The butterflies drink from the damp ground and also gather salts and other minerals from the soil. Butterfly-watching is becoming more popular as inquisitive bird-watchers branch into other areas of nature study. If you are interested in watching butterflies or dragonflies, keep in mind that some binoculars can be used for close viewing and allow amazing glimpses of the detailed patterns on the wings of butterflies and dragonflies.

Other key birds: Horned, Pied-billed, Red-necked, and Western Grebes; Gadwall; Green-winged and Cinnamon Teals; American Wigeon; Northern Pintail; Northern Shoveler; Redhead; Ring-necked Duck; Lesser Scaup; Common Goldeneye; Bufflehead; Common and Hooded Mergansers; Ruddy Duck; Turkey Vulture; Osprey; Merlin; Wild Turkey; Ruffed Grouse; Virginia Rail; Sora; Spotted Sandpiper; Wilson's Snipe; Ring-billed, California, and Herring Gulls; Barred and Northern Saw-whet Owls; Common Nighthawk; Common Poorwill; Olive-sided Flycatcher; Western Wood-Pewee; Willow Flycatcher; Say's Phoebe; Western and Eastern Kingbirds; Red-eyed and Warbling Vireos; Clark's Nutcracker; Bank Swallow; Mountain Chickadee; White-breasted Nuthatch; Brown Creeper; House, Winter, and Marsh Wrens; American Dipper; Mountain Bluebird; Townsend's Solitaire; Veery; Swainson's, Hermit, and Varied Thrushes; Gray Catbird; Orange-crowned, Nashville, Townsend's, Yellow, MacGillivray's, and Wilson's Warblers; Common Yellowthroat; Yellow-breasted Chat; American Redstart; Western Tanager; Chipping, Fox, Savannah, and Vesper Sparrows; Black-headed Grosbeak; Lazuli Bunting; Bullcok's Oriole; Red Crossbill; Evening Grosbeak.

Nearby opportunities: West Fork Sanpoil Road and Gold Creek.

Directions: From the south, take SR 21 north from State Route 2 near Wilbur to the free Keller ferry across Franklin D. Roosevelt Lake, otherwise known as the Columbia River. Continue north on SR 21 to Keller and then turn right onto Silver Creek Road. After crossing the Sanpoil River, turn left onto East Sanpoil Road.

DeLorme map grid: Page 102, D3.

Elevation: 1,300 feet.

Access: None.

Bathrooms: Seasonal restrooms at Keller Park.

Hazards: Rugged roads.

Nearest food, gas, and lodging: Wilbur in the south and Republic in the north.

Nearest camping: Keller Park.

For more information: The Republic Chamber of Commerce site offers information about the area at www.televar.com/chambers/republic/chamber.html.

57 Little Spokane River Natural Area

Habitats: Riparian, mixed forest, cliffs.

Specialty birds: Bald Eagle; Northern Pygmy-Owl; Black-chinned, Calliope, and Rufous Hummingbirds; Pileated Woodpecker; Red-naped Sapsucker; Hammond's and Pacific-slope Flycatchers; Cassin's Vireo; Pygmy Nuthatch; Western Bluebird; Bohemian Waxwing.

Best times to bird: Spring through fall.

Osprey and Bald Eagles fish in the meandering Little Spokane River as it winds through the Natural Area en route to join the Spokane River.

About the site:

If we lived near Spokane, we would spend a large portion of our free time birding the Little Spokane River. It's easy to get to and near a large population center, but the trail is calm and quiet. Visitors also can explore the area by canoe, something we strongly suggest if you are so inclined. For those who prefer exploring on terra firma, the 3.6-mile out-and-back (7.2-mile total) interpretive trail that we bird travels a narrow passage between a steep hill, often faced with craggy rocks, and the twisting river below. The trail travels past a variety of habitats, including rocky cliffs, pine forest, wetland, meadow, and riparian. You can start hiking at either end of the trail, but you'll find more parking available at the east end by the Indian Painted Rocks area. Look in the open field near the Painted Rocks parking lot for Western Bluebirds and sparrows that may be using the bluebird boxes that have been placed there.

Mature cottonwood trees claim both ends of the trail—great places to look for warblers and Western Tanagers, and on the edges, look for Red-naped Sapsuckers. Be sure to stop and listen for woodpeckers knocking on the trees. We watched a pair of raucous Pileated Woodpeckers working over some of these trees while warblers flitted just out of the way of the falling debris. Near the Painted Rocks end of the trail, check rocky walls to the side for Rock and Canyon Wrens. Starting from the Painted Rocks, trail and river meet at several spots through the first third of the route. In summer, the river's edge is overgrown with green: willows, water birch, more cottonwood, grasses, and reeds. Plant lovers especially will be pleased to see wapato growing out of the shallow muck in the oxbow lake near the beginning of the trail. Gray Catbirds sit in the trees and meow loudly, often offering nice, long looks for dedicated bird-watchers. Yellow-breasted Chats, Willow Flycatchers, and Lazuli Buntings also frequent these shrubs. A short side trail marked by a Wood Duck box leads to the edge of the river at one point near the beginning of the trail. The protected oxbow fills with migrating waterfowl, including Hooded Mergansers and Green-winged Teal. The open views of the river farther along the trail also make good places to look for dabblers and Wood Ducks.

As the trail climbs away from the river, deciduous trees give way to pine forest. Listen for Downy and Hairy Woodpeckers, Red-breasted and Pygmy Nuthatches, and Mountain Chickadees. Near the east end of the trail (the Painted Rocks end), a large granite slab blocks the trail, offering a perfect perch to sit on while watching the shrubs below for Bullock's Oriole, Black-headed Grosbeak, and vireos. While it may be nice for sitting on, the slab makes footing in this section a bit treacherous; take a walking stick to ensure firmer footing. If you don't want to skirt this obstacle but still want to walk most of the trail, we recommend walking to the slab and back from both ends.

Nearer the west end of the trail where the trees overlook a meadow, you often can see Bald Eagle and Osprey roosting or feasting on their catches in these tall ponderosa pines. Check near the base of the trees for Bewick's Wrens and the tops

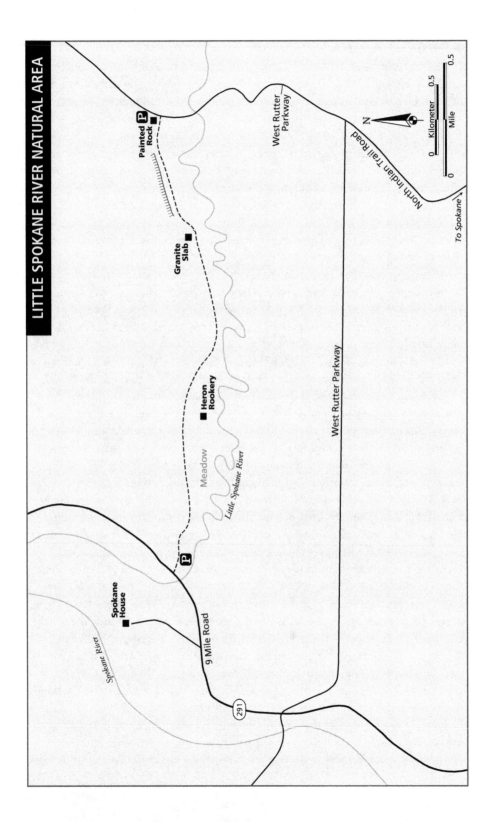

LITTLE SPOKANE RIVER NATURAL AREA

Spokane River

Spokane House

9 Mile Road

291

West Rutter Parkway

Meadow

Little Spokane River

Heron Rookery

Granite Slab

Painted Rock

West Rutter Parkway

North Indian Trail Road

To Spokane

N

0   0.5   Kilometer
0   0.5   Mile

of snags for Pacific-slope Flycatchers. Cassin's Finches, Chipping Sparrows, and Say's Phoebes may be rustling in the grasses, flowers, and shrubs in the meadow. Hummingbirds also swoop in display flights along the shrubby edges near the trail-head, and Clark's Nutcrackers chatter from tree to tree, making sure you know they are there.

At the midpoint, especially during summer, you may begin to hear the guttural *groks* of nesting Great Blue Herons. Please be careful to stay on the trail here. As tempting as it may be to see the heron rookery up close, we'd hate to think that anybody would risk endangering the young birds for that purpose.

The site is open from 6:30 A.M. until dusk, and you will need to pay a $5.00 fee for parking at the Indian Painted Rocks lot. Because the wetlands and oxbow lake host mosquitoes, you'll need to apply insect repellent before hitting the trail. To add more birds to your visit, head next to Spokane House, established in 1810 by Northwest Company fur traders, and the confluence with the Spokane River, where you will see more waterfowl.

A trail cuts through the natural area from the Indian Painted Rocks on the east side to the mouth of the river on the west side.

Other key birds: Pied-billed Grebe; American Wigeon; Common and Hooded Mergansers; Turkey Vulture; Osprey; Merlin; Gray Partridge; Ruffed Grouse; Virginia Rail; Sora; Western Screech-Owl; Common Nighthawk; Downy and Hairy Woodpeckers; Olive-sided Flycatcher; Western Wood-Pewee; Willow Flycatcher; Say's Phoebe; Western and Eastern Kingbirds; Northern Shrike; Red-eyed and Warbling Vireos; Clark's Nutcracker; Mountain and Chestnut-backed Chickadees; White-breasted Nuthatch; Brown Creeper; House, Winter, Rock, Canyon, and Marsh Wrens; Mountain Bluebird; Townsend's Solitaire; Swainson's, Hermit, and Varied Thrushes; Gray Catbird; Orange-crowned, Nashville, Townsend's, Yellow, MacGillivray's, and Wilson's Warblers; Common Yellowthroat; Yellow-breasted Chat; American Redstart; Western Tanager; Chipping, Fox, Savannah, and Lincoln's Sparrows; Black-headed Grosbeak; Lazuli Bunting; Yellow-headed Blackbird; Bullock's Oriole; Cassin's Finch; Red Crossbill; Evening Grosbeak.

Nearby opportunities: Riverside State Park provides stunning views of the Spokane River, complete with topside views of swooping Cliff Swallows.

Directions: In Spokane, go north on Division Street and turn left onto Francis Road. Continue on Francis Road until you reach Indian Trail Road, which is in a residential area. Turn right onto Indian Trail Road and continue until you see the parking lot for Indian Painted Rocks. To get to the west end of the trail, turn right onto Rutter Road, which connects with State Route 291. Turn right and then take the next right into a small single-car parking area. Do not continue up the hill, which leads to a residential development.

DeLorme map grid: Page 88, B4.

Elevation: 1,600 feet.

Access: Not wheelchair accessible.

Bathrooms: None.

Hazards: Rattlesnakes.

Nearest food, gas, and lodging: Spokane.

Nearest camping: Riverside State Park.

For more information: Since the Little Spokane River Natural Area falls under the control of Riverside State Park, visit the park site at www.riversidestatepark.org/little_spokane.htm

58 Cameron Lake Loop

Habitats: Shrub-steppe, prairie, mixed-coniferous forest, cliffs, wetland, freshwater marsh.

Specialty birds: Greater Scaup; Barrow's Goldeneye; Golden and Bald Eagles; Northern Goshawk; Swainson's Hawk; Gyrfalcon; Sandhill Crane; American Avocet; Solitary Sandpiper; Long-billed Curlew; Baird's Sandpiper; Wilson's and Red-necked Phalaropes; Vaux's Swift; Black-chinned, Calliope, and Rufous Hummingbirds; Lewis's and Pileated Woodpeckers; Red-naped Sapsucker; Hammond's, Gray, Dusky, and Pacific-slope Flycatchers; Cassin's Vireo; Pygmy Nuthatch; Western Bluebird; Sage Thasher; Bohemian Waxwing; Common Redpoll.

Best times to bird: Year-round.

A bird-watcher scans a sandbar in Duley Lake for shorebirds. Duley Lake is one of the dozens of lakes that can be seen on the Cameron Lake loop.

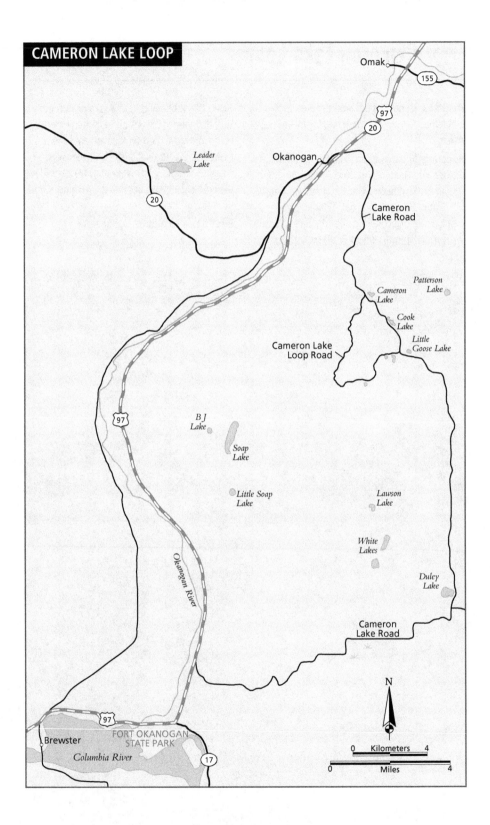

About the site:

A high plateau pockmarked with small lakes and seasonal wetlands is what greets bird-watchers who explore the natural world along Cameron Lake Road, on the border between the central and northeastern regions of the state. Spring and fall migrants make the Cameron Lake loop popular for viewing shorebirds and Sandhill Cranes during migration, and the high-elevation and snow-covered plateau make the area popular for winter birding, with the chance to see raptors that feast on roving flocks of Horned Lark, Snow Bunting, and Lapland Longspur that feed here. Throw in the nesting waterfowl and the chance to see Gray and Dusky Flycatchers along the route during the summer and it is easy to see why the area is a gem for birders.

Cameron Lake Road covers roughly 30 miles as it winds between lakes and rural homes on the highlands east of State Route 97. The road stretches from the city of Okanogan in the north nearly to the confluence of the Okanogan and Columbia Rivers in the south, and it crosses dryland farming areas as well as open grazing land. On one of our visits to the area, we had to pull to the side of the road and watch from inside our car as hundreds of cattle passed by during a cattle drive that completely blocked the road. Although this is a rare occurrence, it is worth keeping in mind as you drive along the dusty gravel road.

Starting in the north near Okanogan, Cameron Lake Road climbs to the east and into the hills, quickly rising from the heavily modified shrub-steppe habitat at an elevation of 1,100 feet to mixed-coniferous forest dominated by pine trees in the mountains. About 4 miles up the road, the route passes through an area scarred by an old forest fire that has left ghost trees mixed in with the living pines in an area that caters to flycatchers during the summer. Western Wood-Pewee and Dusky, Gray, and Hammond's Flycatchers can be seen here, along with the occasional Pacific-slope Flycatcher. Also watch in the trees for woodpeckers, as Downy and Hairy Woodpeckers are commonly sighted along the forested portions of the road, and there is the possibility of seeing a Black-backed Woodpecker working on the ghost trees in the burned sections of the forest.

The road continues to climb as you drive south, and in another mile it passes the first of the ponds and wetlands that make the loop so productive. American Coot and other waterfowl can be seen in this lake, as well as occasional shorebirds such as Spotted Sandpiper. During one early summer visit, we watched an American Coot on this pond with its young climbing onto its back for a quick ride.

Just a short distance down the road, take a right onto Cameron Lake Loop Road. This road climbs to the highest elevations on the route, topping out around 2,700 feet, and its steepness and elevation may make it a rough option in winter. During the summer months it offers access to an area hit by wildfire in recent years. Woodpeckers and flycatchers are easy to pick out against the stark, charred backdrop of burned pine trees. As the habitat recovers from the fire, it is filling in with thistles, fireweed, and other opportunistic plants that draw American

Goldfinch and other songbirds that feed on the supply of seeds. Cameron Lake Loop Road winds through the burned area and past a series of small wetlands and ponds that can hold phalaropes, gulls, and waterfowl. The road then meets with Cameron Lake Road. Turn right to continue exploring.

Heading south again on Cameron Lake Road, the habitat changes from pine-speckled mountains to a rocky prairie with occasional outcrops that jut above the grasslands. In the late spring and summer, this section of the drive can offer glimpses of shrikes, American Kestrel, and Red-tailed and Swainson's Hawks hunting over the prairie. In the winter it is a good area to watch for northern-dwelling raptors that spend their winters in Washington—Rough-legged Hawks, Northern Goshawk, Gyrfalcon, and possibly even Snowy Owl during irruptive years. The high prairie and farmlands along the plateau also offer views of winter flocks of Horned Lark that can include smaller numbers of Snow Bunting and longspurs.

One of the biggest highlights of the Cameron Lake Loop is the birding along Duley Lake, a large lake situated alongside the road and a tall rock outcropping toward the end of the route. The lake has emergent plant life that caters to blackbirds, rails, and coots, but it also holds sections of shallow water and gradual, sandy beaches that offer habitat for migrating shorebirds. The grasslands along the edges of Duley Lake also are popular in the spring for migrating Sandhill Cranes. Another summer highlight of birding along Duley Lake is watching hundreds of Cliff Swallows that build their mud nests on the cliff right alongside the road. The cliff side can also host Rock and Canyon Wren.

The Cameron Lake Loop finishes by continuing south and then dropping back down to US 97 just north of the confluence of the Okanogan and Columbia Rivers. The road passes one more seasonal wetland on the upper plateau, which can hold Virginia Rail and other wetland species, before it drops down to the highway. Keep an eye on the telephone and power poles along the road for more raptors on this last section of the drive. Golden and Bald Eagles can be seen here as well as Osprey. If you visit the loop in winter, take a few minutes to look over the snow-covered fields with rocks protruding above the snow along this last section of the plateau. The rocks were dropped during the last ice age, when glaciers covered the area.

Other key birds: Horned, Eared, Pied-billed, Red-necked, and Western Grebes; American Bittern; Gadwall; Green-winged, Blue-winged, and Cinnamon Teals; American Wigeon; Northern Pintail; Northern Shoveler; Canvasback; Redhead; Ring-necked Duck; Lesser Scaup; Common Goldeneye; Bufflehead; Common and Hooded Mergansers; Ruddy Duck; Turkey Vulture; Osprey; Rough-legged Hawk; Virginia Rail; Sora; Greater and Lesser Yellowlegs; Spotted, Western, and Least Sandpipers; Long-billed Dowitcher; Wilson's Snipe; Ring-billed and California Gulls; Caspian and Black Terns; Long-eared, Western Screech-, and Northern Saw-whet Owls; Common Nighthawk; Common Poorwill; White-throated Swift; Olive-sided Flycatcher; Western Wood-Pewee; Say's Phoebe; Western and Eastern Kingbirds; Northern Shrike; Warbling Vireo; Bank Swallow; Mountain Chickadee; White-breasted Nuthatch;

Brown Creeper; House, Winter, Rock, Canyon, and Marsh Wrens; Mountain Bluebird; Veery; Swainson's, Hermit, and Varied Thrushes; Orange-crowned, Nashville, Townsend's, Yellow, MacGillivray's, and Wilson's Warblers; Common Yellowthroat; Western Tanager; Chipping, Brewer's, Lark, Fox, Savannah, Lincoln's, and Vesper Sparrows; Lapland Longspur; Snow Bunting; Black-headed Grosbeak; Lazuli Bunting; Yellow-headed Blackbird; Bullock's Oriole; Red Crossbill; Evening Grosbeak.

Nearby opportunities: Fort Okanogan State Park and Chief Joseph State Park. Look in orchards near Bridgeport and Fort Okangogan State Park in winter for Bohemian Waxwings.

Directions: Cameron Lake Road departs from US 97 to the east of Monse in the south and east of Okanagon in the north. The road can be driven in any order you like, but the route described in this chapter starts in the north near Okanogan.

DeLorme map grid: Page 100, B4.

Elevation: Ranges from 1,045 to 2,700 feet.

Access: None.

Bathrooms: None.

Hazards: Rugged roads, snow and weather during the winter.

Nearest food, gas, and lodging: Omak and Okanogan in the north and Brewster in the south.

Nearest camping: Bridgeport State Park.

Waterville Plateau

Habitats: Prairie, shrub steppe.

Specialty birds: Golden and Bald Eagles; Northern Goshawk; Swainson's Hawk; Peregrine Falcon; Gyrfalcon; Chukar; Sharp-tailed Grouse; Sandhill Crane; Short-eared Owl; Vaux's Swift; Cassin's Vireo; Pygmy Nuthatch; Western Bluebird; Sage Thrasher; Bohemian Waxwing; Sage Sparrow; Gray-Crowned Rosy-Finch; Common Redpoll.

Best times to bird: Winter, but any time of the year would work.

The bright yellow eye of a Red-tailed Hawk stares down at its unwary prey.

About the site:

The rocky outcrops and rolling, snow-covered hills of the Waterville Plateau offer the perfect mix for overwintering raptors and roving flocks of passerines. At an elevation of nearly 2,000 feet, this plateau, bound by the Columbia River in the north and west and mountains to the south, is covered in snow for much of the winter. Exposed to the winter winds and snows, the plateau offers rugged habitat for roving flocks of winter bird species such as Snow Bunting, Horned Lark, Lapland Longspur, and possibly an elusive Gray-crowned Rosy-Finch. These small birds also draw predators to the area—Rough-legged Hawks, Goshawk, Gyrfalcon, and Golden Eagles among them—to feed on the winter bounty that comes each year to graze on the grain and seeds left over from the previous summer.

There is more than one way to bird the Waterville Plateau, but what we have found most useful is to start in the town of Waterville and drive north along North Road until you reach Lamoine Road, then turn right onto Lamoine Road and continue east through the small town of Lamoine until reaching State Route 172 near Withrow. Along this route, check the snow-covered fields for flocks of birds and try to avoid hitting the Horned Larks that often fly just in front of your car or alongside the road as you drive. Key places to watch for birds in this section of the plateau include farms, along the edges of tree-covered areas, and along power lines and power poles where raptors are likely to sit and watch for their prey.

To continue on the plateau loop, turn right onto SR 172 and drive south into the tiny town of Withrow. Check the areas around this town for finches, including such species as Common Redpoll. Although not an every year occurrence, redpolls have been known to show up in the Waterville Plateau during irruptive years when an overpopulation of immature birds head farther south than normal for winter feeding.

Outside of Withrow there are a number of options for where to bird next. Take a right onto Slusser Road just south of town to check out birding along a farm that sits on the bank of Lamoine Creek just a short distance down the road. The water running through Lamoine Creek draws birds to the area, such as an American Tree Sparrow we saw in the trees along the bank one winter. This site also held a Northern Shrike on another winter visit. To explore other birding options around Withrow, head south to meet up with State Route 2 for a return trip to Waterville or points to the east such as Moses Coulee, Banks Lake, or Dry Falls. Another option is to drive north from Withrow following SR 172 through more rocky terrain and into the town of Mansfield. No matter what route you choose, continue to keep an eye out for raptors and large flocks of smaller birds along the road.

To add more birding to this slice of eastern Washington, drive north from SR 172 just a mile or two west of Mansfield, turning left onto Mathieson Road where signs direct drivers toward Bridgeport. A short distance down this route,

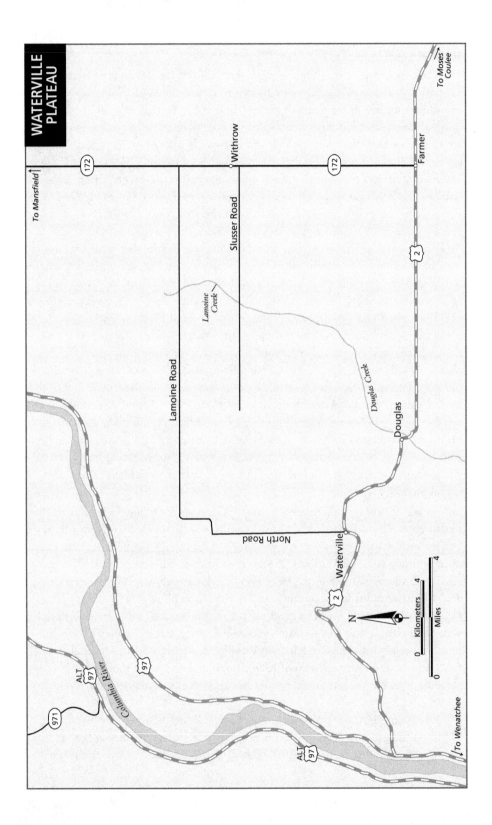

WATERVILLE PLATEAU

Mathieson Road becomes Bridgeport Hill Road and follows Foster Creek through the Foster Creek Wildlife Area. Especially in the morning hours right around dawn, you can check the water birch trees along Foster Creek for glimpses of Sharp-tailed Grouse.

INTERESTING GEOLOGY

The Waterville Plateau lies at the southern reach of the last ice age, meaning that glaciers once covered everything north of the plateau. As a result of being located at the southern terminus of the old glaciers, the plateau holds interesting geological features such as Mima Mounds, similar to those found south of Olympia in western Washington, and large rocks scattered randomly across the prairie where they were dropped when the glaciers retreated. Geologists refer to this area as the Withrow Moraine, and it, along with the features of the Moses Coulee and Grand Coulee directly east of the plateau, make this part of eastern Washington a great playground for amateur geologists.

Other key birds: Turkey Vulture; Rough-legged Hawk; Merlin; Prairie Falcon; Gray Partridge; Wilson's Snipe; Common Nighthawk; Common Poorwill; White-throated Swift; Downy and Hairy Woodpeckers; Loggerhead and Northern Shrikes; Red-eyed and Warbling Vireos; Bank Swallow; House, Rock, Canyon, and Marsh Wrens; Mountain Bluebird; Orange-crowned, Yellow, and Wilson's Warblers; Yellow-breasted Chat; Western Tanager; American Tree, Chipping, Brewer's, Lark, Grasshopper, Savannah, and Vesper Sparrows; Lapland Longspur; Snow Bunting; Black-headed Grosbeak; Lazuli Bunting; Yellow-headed Blackbird; Bullock's Oriole; Cassin's Finch; Red Crossbill; Evening Grosbeak.

Nearby opportunities: Bridgeport Bar and the area around the Fort Okanogan State Park offer more birding.

Directions: Follow SR 2 east from Wenatchee to the town of Waterville.

DeLorme map grid: Page 83, C8.

Elevation: 1,900 feet.

Access: None.

Bathrooms: None.

Hazards: Winter weather.

Nearest food, gas, and lodging: Bridgeport.

Nearest camping: Bridgeport State Park or Fort Okanogan State Park.

For more information: Contact the Waterville Chamber of Commerce at (509) 745-8871.

60 Dry Falls and Sun Lakes

Habitats: Cliffs, shrub-steppe, wetland, freshwater marsh.

Specialty birds: Common Loon; Greater Scaup; Barrow's Goldeneye; Golden and Bald Eagles; Swainson's Hawk; Peregrine Falcon; Gyrfalcon; American Avocet; Black-necked Stilt; Long-billed Curlew; Baird's and Pectoral Sandpipers; Wilson's and Red-necked Phalaropes; Short-eared Owl; Calliope and Rufous Hummingbirds; Lewis's Woodpecker; Gray, Dusky, and Pacific-slope Flycatchers; Cassin's Vireo; Western Bluebird; Sage Thrasher; Sage Sparrow; Gray-crowned Rosy-Finch.

Best times to bird: Summer and fall.

The gaping crater formed by ice age floods at Dry Falls is one of the most dramatic geological landmarks in the state, but the site also offers great birding. Listen for Canyon Wrens along the rim of the ancient falls and watch diving ducks swim underwater in the ponds below.

About the site:

Dramatic geology and a wealth of waterfowl await bird-watchers who visit Dry Falls and Sun Lakes State Park. Located in the middle of the state, the site draws birds from around the region, since it is the only water source for miles around the parched portion of eastern Washington. Meanwhile, the cliffs and opportunities to view eagles, swallows, and White-throated Swifts from above at the Dry Falls Interpretive Center make this a unique stop.

The first place to explore at Dry Falls is the viewing area at the Dry Falls Interpretive Center. Although the center is open only from mid-May to the end of September, the viewing areas along the parking lot are open year-round. Take the time to read the interpretive signs that offer details about the formation of Dry Falls, then walk to the edge of the precipice and look down on the cliff edges and the ponds and wetlands below. If you listen carefully, you may hear Canyon Wren calling from the edges of the cliff, and both Golden and Bald Eagles can be seen here as well.

During one late winter visit, we looked down on a Common Raven flying just below the cliff's edge, weaving in and out of the thermal drafts rising from the rocky ground below. If you are lucky, you may also get a view from above of White-throated Swifts or even of an eagle passing below the cliff edge, offering the kind of view that would be hard to find anywhere else. We also have enjoyed watching waterfowl from the cliff's edge, where you can see them dive and "fly" through the clear water in the ponds. Use good binoculars or a spotting scope to watch the diving birds from the cliff.

Next, head south on State Route 17 to the entrance to Sun Lakes State Park, about 2 miles south of the interpretive center. This park, which encompasses Dry Falls, covers more than 4,000 acres of ponds, wetlands, and rocky shrub-steppe habitat. The edges of some of the lakes in Sun Lakes offer emergent vegetation that caters to Red-winged and Yellow-headed Blackbirds, as well as wrens and sparrows. And if you are lucky, you could find a Virginia Rail or Sora feeding in the shallow edges among the reeds.

While exploring the park, be sure to venture to the far eastern portion, past the main camping and picnic grounds, to look along the roads that lead north from the main park and into the shrub-steppe habitat and along the edges of some of the smaller ponds. One road leads to a parking lot for the pond that is just below the Dry Falls Interpretive Center, but bring a rugged vehicle for the road into that parking lot. Ruts and large rocks in the road kept us from driving to the area in our passenger car during one summer visit. As you explore the sagebrush country north of the main park, keep an eye out for birds such as Sage Thrasher, Sage Sparrow, Say's Phoebe, and other species that frequent shrub-steppe habitats. Both Western and Eastern Kingbirds can be seen in this area as well.

Dry Falls and Sun Lakes State Park are just two of a number of birding sites along the corridor that once flowed with the ice age floods that created the falls. Banks Lake Wildlife Area stretches to the north of the dam on State Route 2

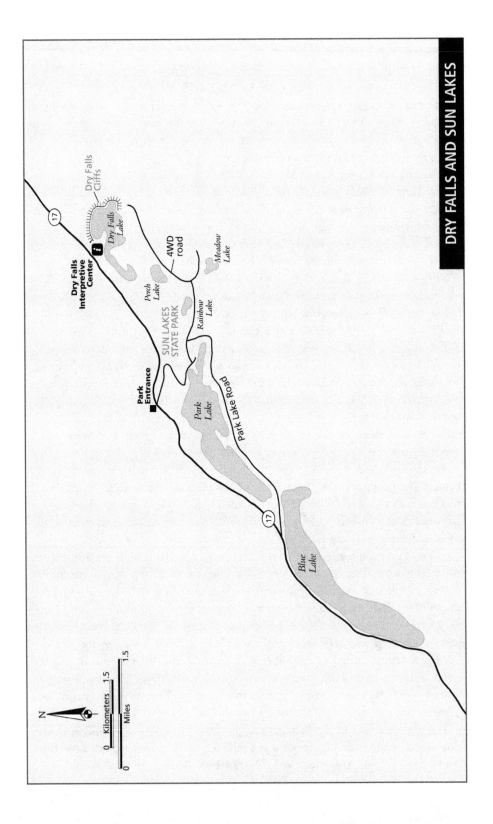

toward Grand Coulee, with Steamboat Rock State Park marking another good bird-watching site. To the south of Dry Falls toward Soap Lake, a series of small lakes dot the landscape, and they host waterfowl during the spring and fall migrations, as well as a few hardy waterfowl that hang around through the winter months. Some of these lakes to the south also have gradual shorelines that can hold shorebirds, mostly during the fall migration season.

Other key birds: Horned, Eared, Pied-billed, and Western Grebes; Gadwall; Green-winged, Blue-winged, and Cinnamon Teals; American Wigeon; Northern Pintail; Northern Shoveler; Canvasback; Redhead; Ring-necked Duck; Lesser Scaup; Common Goldeneye; Bufflehead; Common and Hooded Mergansers; Ruddy Duck; Turkey Vulture; Osprey; Rough-legged Hawk; Prairie Falcon; Gray Partridge; Virginia Rail; Sora; Greater and Lesser Yellowlegs; Spotted, Western, and Least Sandpipers; Long-billed Dowitcher; Wilson's Snipe; Black Tern; Common Nighthawk; White-throated Swift; Willow Flycatcher; Say's Phoebe; Western and Eastern Kingbirds; Loggerhead and Northern Shrikes; Warbling Vireo; Bank Swallow; House, Winter, Rock, Canyon, and Marsh Wrens; Mountain Bluebird; American Pipit; Orange-crowned, Yellow, MacGillivray's, and Wilson's Warblers; Common Yellowthroat; Yellow-breasted Chat; Western Tanager; Chipping, Brewer's, Lark, Grasshopper, Savannah, Lincoln's, and Vesper Sparrows; Black-headed Grosbeak; Lazuli Bunting; Yellow-headed Blackbird; Bullock's Oriole; Cassin's Finch; Red Crossbill.

Nearby opportunities: Banks Lake Wildlife Area and Steamboat Rock State Park, north of the area along SR 155, and Moses Coulee, which is west of the area along SR 2.

Directions: From I-90, go north toward Ephrata on State Route 283. Continue going north through Ephrata and follow State Route 28 to Soap Lake. Take SR 17 north from Soap Lake to start exploring the lower lakes before reaching Dry Falls near the intersection with SR 2.

DeLorme map grid: Page 85, D5.

Elevation: 1,300 feet.

Access: None.

Bathrooms: At Sun Lakes State Park.

Hazards: Rugged roads, heat.

Nearest food, gas, and lodging: Soap Lake.

Nearest camping: Sun Lakes State Park.

For more information: Check the Web page for Sun Lakes State Park at www.parks.wa.gov/parkpage.asp?selectedpark=Sun%20Lakes&pageno=1.

DRY FALLS

It is hard to comprehend what Dry Falls would have looked like when the ice age floods that created it swept over the 400-foot precipice and formed a waterfall more than ten times the size of Niagra Falls, nearly 3.5 miles wide. A visit to the Dry Falls Interpretive Center offers details about the geological history of Dry Falls and how the lakes from Soap Lake all the way up to the current lakes that are below the cliffs of Dry Falls today were formed—as erosion undercut the cliffs again and again, the location of the waterfall migrated upstream. The impact of the falls today is seen in the diversity of wildlife that flourishes along each of the lakes.

61 Quincy Lakes Wildlife Area

Habitats: Shrub-steppe, lowland riparian, wetland.

Specialty birds: American White Pelican; Great Egret; Tundra Swan; Greater Scaup; Barrow's Goldeneye; Golden and Bald Eagles; Swainson's Hawk; Peregrine Falcon; Chukar; Sandhill Crane; American Avocet; Black-necked Stilt; Solitary Sandpiper; Long-billed Curlew; Baird's and Pectoral Sandpipers; Wilson's and Red-necked Phalaropes; Bonaparte's Gull; Forster's Tern; Short-eared and Burrowing Owls; Dusky Flycatcher; Cassin's Vireo; Sage Thrasher; Sage Sparrow.

Best times to bird: Year-round.

A Great Egret stands along the shore of Quincy Lake in the Quincy Lakes Wildlife Area. Egrets join American White Pelicans and other birds at the site during the summer months.

About the site:

Rugged geology and a series of lakes and wetlands filled by seepage from nearby irrigation channels make the Quincy Lakes Wildlife Area an interesting stop for bird-watchers. Waterfowl, pelicans, and Great Egret spend their summer months at the wildlife area. In the fall and winter, thousands of waterfowl use the lakes and wetlands—interspersed with basalt outcroppings and pillars—as a stopover on their migration route.

Quincy Lakes is located just east of the Columbia River and southwest of the town of Quincy, in the heart of farm country. The wildlife area covers more than 15,000 acres, and its geology is marked by the clear signs of ancient lava flows that are exposed from the Missoula Floods that swept down the Columbia River during the last ice age. The result is a terrain pockmarked by varied habitats—steep basalt cliffs, ponds, mesas, wetlands, and areas of mature shrub-steppe. Some of the most accessible parts of the wildlife area center around the wetlands and lakes near Quincy, but the area also includes lands closer to the Columbia River and a natural area in Frenchman Coulee, just north of I–90 near Silica Road.

The best place to start exploring Quincy Lakes Wildlife Area is from its northern end off 5 NW Road. Drive the gravel road south and the habitat shifts from farm fields to sagebrush and tall grasses. The road descends first to the shores of Stan Coffin Lake. Look for Great Egret, American White Pelican, Forster's Tern, and phalaropes in the lake, and American Coot, Pied-billed Grebe, and other birds are commonly found along the edges of the lake. The lake has a boat ramp, and visitors are allowed to camp in the wildlife area, so your visit to Stan Coffin Lake and other lakes in this highly accessible portion of the wildlife area could vary depending on the number of people camping and boating.

A gravel road leads south from Stan Coffin Lake along the edge of a wetland that can offer very close viewing opportunities for egrets and other birds. The only drawback is that motorists are not allowed to stop driving along this stretch of the road, so any close views of birds will be fleeting as you drive past. After passing the wetland, a pullout on the left side of the road offers great views of Quincy Lake. This lake was full of waterfowl, with terns hunting overhead and Great Egrets feeding along the edges of the lake, when we made a summer visit. This lake has extensive cattail- and reed-filled wetlands along its edges, where we saw sparrows and heard coots mingling in the dense vegetation. Just beyond the wetlands, rocky outcroppings offer perfect habitat for Rock Wrens.

The gravel access road continues past Quincy Lake to Burke Lake, and then to Evergreen Lake—the largest of the lakes in the wildlife area. Each of these lakes is packed with waterfowl in the migration season, and each serves as nesting grounds for a number of species as well.

Another access point for the wildlife area is west of SR 281 on 3 NW Road. This route offers views of Burke and Evergreen lakes along with more shrub-steppe habitat that is full of Western Meadowlark, Horned Lark, Brewer's and

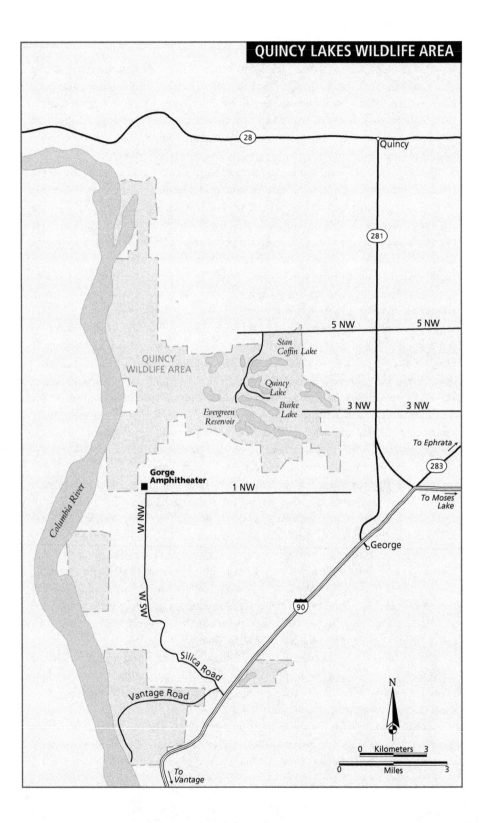

QUINCY LAKES WILDLIFE AREA

A basalt mesa stands in the background at Quincy Lake, offering habitat for Rock Wrens. Cattails and emergent vegetation along open ponds host Marsh Wrens.

Vesper Sparrows, and other species that prefer sagebrush, rabbitbrush, and bitter-brush.

For a glimpse of even more mature sagebrush and native shrub-steppe habitat, head south to I–90 and go west toward the Columbia River. Exit at Silica Road and then turn left off Silica Road onto Vantage Street SW. This road winds down through the rugged country toward the Columbia River through Frenchman Coulee. Portions of the Quincy Lakes Wildlife Area are found here, including a community of rare native shrub-steppe plants. The big sagebrush and other shrub-steppe plants signal possibilities of seeing Sage and Lark Sparrow, Sage Thrasher, and other sagebrush-dependent species.

Other key birds: Horned, Eared, Pied-billed, and Western Grebes; American Bittern; Black-crowned Night Heron; Gadwall; Green-winged, Blue-winged, and Cinnamon Teals; American Wigeon; Northern Pintail; Northern Shoveler; Canvasback; Redhead; Ring-necked Duck; Lesser Scaup; Common Goldeneye; Buffle-head; Common and Hooded Mergansers; Ruddy Duck; Turkey Vulture; Osprey; Rough-legged Hawk; Prairie Falcon; Gray Partridge; Virginia Rail; Sora; Greater and Lesser Yel-lowlegs; Spotted, Western, and Least Sand-pipers; Long-billed Dowitcher; Wilson's Snipe; Ring-billed, California, and Herring Gulls;

Caspian and Black Terns; Long-eared Owl; Common Nighthawk; Common Poorwill; White-throated Swift; Say's Phoebe; Western and Eastern Kingbirds; Loggerhead and Northern Shrikes; Warbling Vireo; Bank Swallow; House, Rock, Canyon, and Marsh Wrens; American Pipit; Orange-crowned, Yellow, MacGillivray's, and Wilson's Warblers; Common Yellowthroat; Yellow-breasted Chat; Western Tanager; Chipping, Brewer's, Lark, Grasshopper, Savannah, Lincoln's, and Vesper Sparrows.

Nearby opportunities: Winchester Wasteway Wildlife Area is east of Quincy Lakes and can be reached by taking 5 NW Road.

Directions: From I-90, take the exit for SR 281 at George. Drive north on SR 281 toward Quincy. Turn left onto 5 NW Road and drive past the local golf course before reaching the entrance to the wildlife area on a gravel road on the left marked with signs for public fishing.

DeLorme map grid: Page 68, C1.

Elevation: 1,200 feet.

Access: None.

Bathrooms: Pit toilets at Stan Coffin Lake.

Hazards: None.

Nearest food, gas, and lodging: Quincy.

Nearest camping: Inside the wildlife area.

For more information: Check the Web page for the Quincy Lakes Wildlife Area at www.wdfw.wa.gov/lands/r2quincy.htm.

Southeast

I t may be easy to pass off Washington's Southeast Region as the driest and hottest area in the state, but bird-watchers know that there is much more to this region, which encompasses varied habitats such as the Columbia Basin, the Palouse, and the Blue Mountains. Among the rolling hills and the ragged basalt ruins—reminders of glacial floods that swept through the region during the last ice age—are pockets of habitat that support a wide range of birds, from the state's largest colony of nesting American White Pelicans to rare gulls and out-of-place shorebirds that visit the mouth of the Walla Walla River in the fall.

The Southeast Region is bounded by Interstate 90 in the north, the Idaho border in the east, the Oregon border in the south, and the Columbia River in the west. It includes some of the state's prime agricultural land interspersed with areas of modified shrub-steppe habitat, as well as Crab Creek, which holds the claim as the longest creek in the United States.

Among the birds that define this region are the thousands of Sandhill Cranes that descend on the Columbia National Wildlife Refuge near Othello each spring during their migration, Grasshopper Sparrows and Ferruginous Hawks in the Hanford Reach National Monument, Loggerhead Shrike along Crab Creek, and nesting Long-billed Curlews in the Seep Lakes Wildlife Area.

The Blue Mountains—and the island of damp mountain bird habitat they create in the far southeastern corner of the region—add the chance to see Green-tailed Towhees and the Cordilleran type of Pacific-slope Flycatchers, which are a hot topic among ornithologists and bird-watchers in the area.

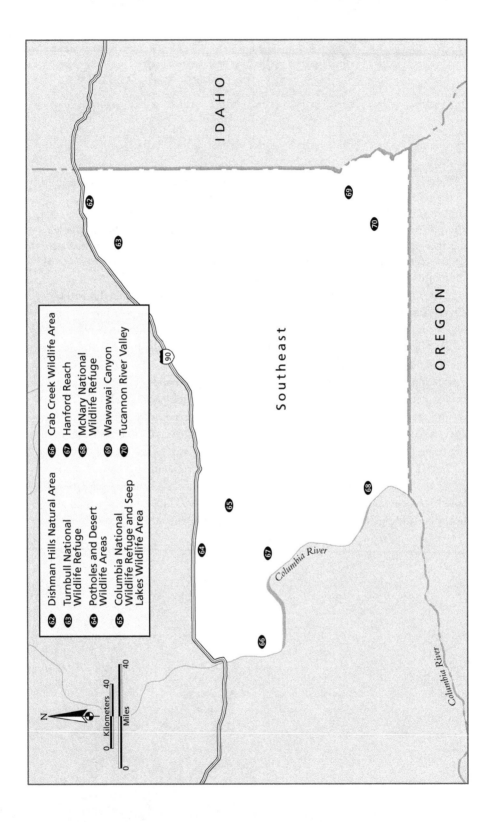

62 Dishman Hills Natural Area

Habitats: Mixed forest, wetlands.

Specialty birds: Northern Goshawk; Northern Pygmy-Owl; Black-chinned, Calliope, and Rufous Hummingbirds; Pileated Woodpecker; Red-naped Sapsucker; Hammond's, Dusky, and Pacific-slope Flycatchers; Cassin's Vireo; Pygmy Nuthatch; Western Bluebird; Bohemian Waxwing.

Best times to bird: Spring through fall.

A series of trails provide access to the upland, mixed forest, and wetland habitats at the Dishman Hills Natural Area in Spokane.

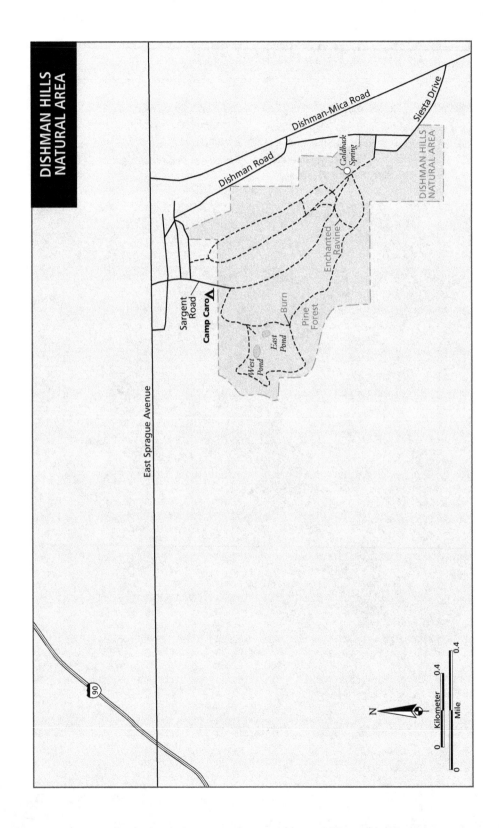

DISHMAN HILLS
NATURAL AREA

East Sprague Avenue

90

Dishman Road

Dishman-Mica Road

Siesta Drive

Sargent
Road

Camp Caro

West
Pond

East
Pond

Burn

Pine
Forest

Enchanted
Ravine

Goldback
Spring

DISHMAN HILLS
NATURAL AREA

N

0   Kilometer   0.4

0   Mile   0.4

About the site:

Who would imagine that barely outside of Spokane, surrounded by car dealers, pavement, and subdivisions, a little plot of bird nirvana is tucked into the landscape? Set aside in order to preserve a "pre-pioneer ecosystem," Dishman Hills offers a much-needed rest stop for spring and fall migrants as well as a breeding spot for summer residents among the mixed ponderosa-pine and fir forests and the small ponds surrounded by cottonwood and quaking aspen. Several trails crisscross the 518-acre site. The trail system is circuitous and complicated, so to avoid getting lost, take the map with you, and even with the map, note landmarks and trail markings to ensure you can easily find your way out when you want to. Those who are less sure on their feet may also want to take a sturdy walking stick. Any trail you choose to take will be a good choice, but if you can take the time to hike to one of the ponds, you will have a better chance of seeing more birds due to the changes in vegetation.

Our suggested route starts out at Camp Caro. Before you head to the trail though, take some time to scan the perimeter of the camp along the treetops for warblers, grosbeaks, sparrows, and Cedar Waxwings. Walk through the passageway by the restrooms to get to the trailhead. Along this lower stretch of the trail, watch and listen for the aerial displays of flirting hummingbirds. We were lucky enough to watch a male Calliope Hummingbird showing off for his mate with a series of aerobatic Js, with the valley of each J marked with a flashy buzz.

A short way up the trail, stairs climb to a log-benched ampitheater used for educational programs that are well-utilized by area schools. This is also the first of the interesting rock formations you will see. These formations are the sculptural creations of the Lake Missoula Floods that contributed to so much of the landscape in Eastern Washington and the Columbia Basin. Though much of the trail is carpeted with wildflowers and small shrubs such as lupine, starflower, wild Solomon's seal, phlox, and the brilliant yellow arrow balsam root, occasional balds dot the area. In spring and early summer, these balds sport bitterroot as well as an interesting tapestry of mosses and lichens. Check the areas around the balds for thrushes and wrens that also scratch in the fallen leaves under the shrubby thickets that flank the trail in the valleys later along the trail. Stay on the main trail until you reach a V. Just before the V, you will pass an outcrop that looks over a swampy ravine. Take some time to look over the canopy here for Western Tanager, Townsend's Solitaire, warblers, and flycatchers. Since you will be standing above the canopy, you will have a rare chance to see these birds from above as they fly between the cottonwoods and maples below you.

At the V, take a right to begin the descent into the Enchanted Ravine. The trail on the left heads to Goldback Spring, a worthy out-and-back detour from our route. As you descend into the ravine, the habitat quickly changes from pine and fir forest to a riparian-based habitat with shrubby undergrowth, in part consisting of Pacific ninebark, oceanspray, Oregon grape, Wood's rose, and red osier dogwood.

A male Calliope Hummingbird perches on a twig after making a territorial display along the trail at Dishman Hills.

The shrubs arch overhead to create a tunnel of green in the spring. Stay on the main path by staying on the right when the trail Vs. Eventually you will begin climbing into mixed-pine and -fir forest before entering a small burn from a 1998 fire that singed the area. Listen here for the tapping of Pileated Woodpeckers and Red-naped Sapsuckers. In the midst of the burned area, the trail again branches to the left. Whether you go straight or go left depends on whether you want to extend or shorten your walk. The trail to the left winds through more mixed forest, a good place to look for Brown Creepers and Western Wood-Pewees, before passing by both West and East Pond. If you go straight, the shorter route, take a left at the next V to go by the ponds. From the ponds, if you take the shorter route, you will want to backtrack and continue on the trail to head out of the woods at the edge of Camp Caro and the parking lot.

Dishman Hills is one of those pleasant surprises tucked into corners of our urban landscapes. These areas seem to be overlooked often by many bird-watchers, due in part to the fact that they are popular local haunts but not known as bird-watching destinations like some of the other spots included in this book. Nevertheless, these areas are worth taking extra time to visit whenever you happen to be in the area. And if you are lucky enough to live nearby, they make great places to visit often in order to track the changing bird population with a yearlong, targeted bird list.

ONE IS ALL IT TAKES

Several of the areas featured in this book exist as natural areas or reserves due to the actions of one person or one small group of people, including Nisqually and Protection Island National Wildlife Refuges and Dishman Hills. In the mid-1960s, Tom Rogers, a biology teacher who used the area for class field trips, gathered a group of like-minded conservationists in order to protect the area from encroaching developers. In 1987, due in part to the efforts of the group he helped create, Dishman Hills Natural Areas Association, the state's Department of National Resources (DNR) created a new category of properties called Natural Resource Conservation Areas (NRCAs). NRCAs are areas that are set aside specifically for conservation and preservation when they contain "critical wildlife habitat, prime natural features, examples of native ecological communities, and environmentally significant sites threatened with conversion to other uses," according to DNR. Dishman Hills was one of the first four sites designated as an NRCA. The 518 acres that are collectively known as Dishman Hills are separately held by three different organizations: DNR, Dishman Hills Natural Areas Association, and Spokane County.

Other key birds: Ruffed Grouse; Western Screech-Owl; Common Nighthawk; Downy and Hairy Woodpeckers; Olive-sided Flycatcher; Western Wood-Pewee; Wilson's Flycatcher; Say's Phoebe; Western and Eastern Kingbirds; Northern Shrike; Red-eyed and Warbling Vireos; White-breasted Nuthatch; Brown Creeper; House, Winter, Rock, and Marsh Wrens; Mountain Bluebird; Townsend's Solitaire; Swainson's, Hermit, and Varied Thrushes; Gray Catbird; Orange-crowned, Nashville, Townsend's, Yellow, MacGillivray's, and Wilson's Warblers; Western Tanager; Chipping, Fox, Savannah, and Lincoln's Sparrows; Black-headed Grosbeak; Lazuli Bunting; Bullock's Oriole; Red Crossbill; Evening Grosbeak.

Nearby opportunities: Riverfront State Park.

Directions: Take the Sprague exit off of I-90 and head east until the road becomes Apple Way Boulevard (also called E. Sprague). Turn right onto Sargent Road and drive to the end of the road, where you will find a small parking lot for the Ina Hughes Natural Area.

DeLorme map grid: Page 89, C6.

Elevation: 1,980 to 2,200 feet.

Access: Bathrooms at Camp Caro are wheelchair accessible, but the trails are not.

Bathrooms: Camp Caro.

Hazards: Poison ivy.

Nearest food, gas, and lodging: Spokane.

Nearest camping: Riverfront State Park.

For more information: Visit www.dnr .wa.gov/nap/nrcadesc.html on the Internet. Or, for an interesting look from the viewpoint of elementary-school students who study the site, visit the Web site www.sd81.k 12.wa.us/regal/DishmanHills/56Dhill.htm.

Turnbull National Wildlife Refuge

Habitats: Wetland, mixed forest, prairie, ponds and lakes, shrub-steppe.

Specialty birds: Tundra Swan; Greater White-fronted Goose; Barrow's Goldeneye; Bald Eagle; Northern Goshawk; American Avocet; Wilson's and Red-necked Phalaropes; Short-eared and Northern Pygmy-Owls; Black-chinned, Calliope, and Rufous Hummingbirds; Pileated Woodpecker; Red-naped Sapsucker; Hammond's, Dusky, and Pacific-slope Fly-catchers; Cassin's Vireo; Gray Jay; Pygmy Nuthatch; Western Bluebird; Bohemian Waxwing; Common Redpoll.

Best times to bird: Spring through fall.

A female Calliope Hummingbird perches on a bush, while a male performs its mating dance nearby.

About the site:

Turnbull National Wildlife Refuge (NWR) is like a crazy quilt. Wildflowers and native grasses edge up to exposed basalt balds, also known as scabrock. The balds surround ponds, lakes, and marshy wetlands that interrupt stands of pine and aspen. Just as Ridgefield NWR and Columbia NWR are migratory hotspots, the diversity of habitats found at Turnbull likewise attracts more than 200 bird species, 100 of which have nested on the site, including most of the species of ducks found in the state. Reports of nesting birds also include Northern Goshawk, Long-eared and Short-eared Owls, Trumpeter Swan, and American Redstart. As a result, Audubon Washington has designated Turnbull NWR as an Important Bird Area.

Before white settlers drained the wetlands, ponds, and lakes, logged the trees, planted grain crops, and let their cattle loose to graze on the land, area tribes gathered here to hunt and harvest the fruits and roots of the many plants that you can still see, including bitterroot and camas. The explosion of spring flowers on the prairie and in the woods is one of the extra treats that birders enjoy on the refuge. In order to provide secure and undisturbed habitat for the birds and mammals that live here, the water levels in the ponds and lakes are managed to provide habitat for both dabblers and diving ducks, and most of the 16,000 acres is off-limits to visitors; but, 2,200 acres are accessible in the public-use area.

When you stop at the pay station, check the nearby pines for Red Crossbills and nuthatches, including White-breasted and Pygmy Nuthatches. Western Meadowlark, Western and Mountain Bluebirds, magpies, and blackbirds call and flock in the surrounding fields. From the parking area near the Pine Lake Loop Trail, you can hear the nesting birds calling below. In the reeds at the lake's edge, you will see bright and loud Yellow-headed and Red-winged Blackbirds and sparrows. Coots scoot around the lake with their young perched on their backs or swimming close beside them. As with most of the lakes on the refuge, this small lake contains a few islands made from dredging spoils. Some birds nest on them, including some of the ducks that abound on the refuge such as Canvasbacks and Redheads. Look south over Cheever Lake in the summer to see Black Terns flocking and diving into the water. In recent years, a small flock of American White Pelicans has been seen on some of the lakes east of the refuge and have begun visiting some of the larger refuge lakes, including Cheever Lake.

You can also start hiking part of Headquarters Trail here, which extends from the south end of Cheever Lake to the refuge headquarters, where it becomes Bluebird Trail. The three trails combine to offer more than 7 miles of out-and-back, bird-worthy hiking. Near the edges of the shrub-steppe and ponderosa-pine forests, listen carefully for Gray and Dusky Flycatchers, especially during migration.

The 5.5-mile Pine Creek Auto Tour offers several spaces to pull off the road for observation as well as six additional, short observation trails, including two boardwalks (wheelchair-accessible), and several vault toilets. The longest trail on the

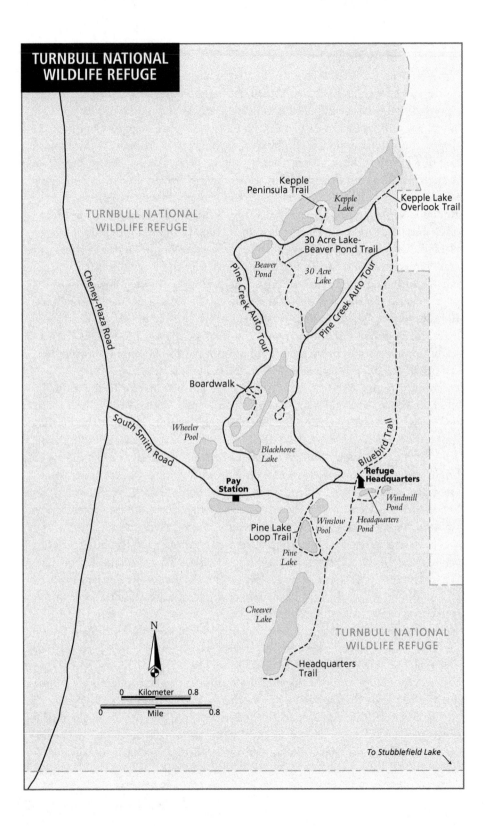

TURNBULL NATIONAL WILDLIFE REFUGE

TURNBULL NATIONAL
WILDLIFE REFUGE

Cheney-Plaza Road

Pine Creek Auto Tour

Kepple
Peninsula Trail

*Kepple
Lake*

Kepple Lake
Overlook Trail

30 Acre Lake-
Beaver Pond Trail

*Beaver
Pond*

*30 Acre
Lake*

Pine Creek Auto Tour

Boardwalk

South Smith Road

*Wheeler
Pool*

*Blackhorse
Lake*

Bluebird Trail

**Refuge
Headquarters**

*Windmill
Pond*

**Pay
Station**

*Headquarters
Pond*

Pine Lake
Loop Trail

*Winslow
Pool*

*Pine
Lake*

*Cheever
Lake*

TURNBULL NATIONAL
WILDLIFE REFUGE

N

| 0 | Kilometer | 0.8 |
| 0 | Mile | 0.8 |

Headquarters
Trail

To Stubblefield Lake

route extends from the south end of 30 Acre Lake to the south end of Kepple Lake and the edge of a beaver pond. Near Kepple Lake, the road makes a hairpin turn in an aspen grove. Look into the opening at the snags to find an Osprey nest. At the Kepple Lake overlook, you may be able to see an Osprey hunting while ducks flock on the water. As you continue your tour, stop to check the aspen groves for possible American Redstarts, Gray Catbirds, and Red-naped Sapsuckers. Ruffed Grouse can be heard thrumming in the dense shade. Least Flycatchers, which prefer aspen groves, have been seen on the refuge, so take some time to listen and keep an eye out for the small yellow-gray bird. In the winter you'll want to check these areas for Bohemian Waxwings.

When you get to Blackhorse Lake near the end of the tour, walk the interpretive boardwalk to the edge of the lake. Look for Northern Harriers flying on the opposite shore and Gadwalls, Canada Geese, teals, and Ring-necked Ducks on the water. Walk to nearby Swan Pond to find Wood Ducks and the breeding, blue-billed Ruddy Ducks. Wilson's Snipes also can be heard winnowing in the spring as they erupt into display flights. Black-chinned, Calliope, and Rufous Humming-birds all nest on the refuge, and their springtime flirting often takes place near the edges of the pine stands and wetlands. Turnbull hosts one of the largest nesting populations of Black-chinned Hummingbirds in the state, so if the diminutive hummer has eluded you elsewhere, you're likely to see it here. In the winter, look in these edge habitats with willows and alder for the much-sought Common Redpolls.

The auto route exits onto Smith Road. If you have allotted enough time, we suggest you circle back to the refuge headquarters and walk at least part of the Bluebird or Headquarters Trail to see more of the grasslands that aren't part of the auto tour.

Although Stubblefield Lake is not accessible except by previously obtained, written permission, its muddy shores attract shorebirds during migration, including Semipalmated Plover, yellowlegs, Baird's and Pectoral Sandpipers, Long-billed Dowitcher, Red-necked Phalaropes, and American Avocets. Wilson's Phalaropes also nest beside the lake. Occasionally, the shorebirds explore some of the shallow wetlands in the public-use area. While summer is a fun time to visit since the refuge features so many nesting ducks and passerines, bird numbers peak in October during the fall migration, when you also can see Horned Grebe, Snow and Greater White-fronted Geese, and passerines such as Western Tanager, Black-headed Grosbeak, and Lincoln's Sparrow. In addition to the many birds on the site, you also may be lucky enough to see badger, river otter, beaver, or moose moving through the area.

The refuge headquarters is located just beyond the entrance to the Pine Creek Auto trail. Although closed on the weekends, the headquarters offers educational materials and displays during weekdays. Refuge brochures are usually available here or at the pay station on weekends. A wheelchair-accessible restroom and picnic tables are provided at the headquarters. The refuge is open year-round. Access from November 1 to April 30 is free, and there is a small per-car fee from May 1 to October 31. A 4.75-mile section of the Columbia Plateau Trail, a converted railtrail, passes through the refuge, but hikers must remain on the trail since it crosses the "off-limits" part of the refuge. Access the trail at Cheney-Sprague Road or Amber Lake.

Other key birds: Horned, Eared, Pied-billed, and Western Grebes; American Bittern; Gadwall; Green-winged, Blue-winged, and Cinnamon Teals; American Wigeon; Northern Pintail; Northern Shoveler; Canvasback; Redhead; Ring-necked Duck; Lesser Scaup; Common Goldeneye; Bufflehead; Common and Hooded Mergansers; Ruddy Duck; Turkey Vulture; Osprey; Merlin; Gray Partridge; Wild Turkey; Ruffed Grouse; Virginia Rail; Sora; Greater and Lesser Yellowlegs; Spotted, Western, and Least Sandpipers; Wilson's Snipe; Black Tern; Western Screech-Owl; Common Nighthawk; Common Poorwill; Downy and Hairy Woodpeckers; Olive-sided Flycatcher; Western Wood-Pewee; Willow Flycatcher; Say's Phoebe; Western and Eastern Kingbirds; Northern Shrike; Red-eyed and Warbling Vireos; Bank Swallow; Mountain Chickadee; White-breasted Nuthatch; Brown Creeper; House, Winter, Rock, and Marsh Wrens; Mountain Bluebird; Townsend's Solitaire; Veery; Swainson's, Hermit, and Varied Thrushes; Gray Catbird; Orange-crowned, Nashville, Townsend's, Yellow, MacGillivray's, and Wilson's Warblers; Common Yellowthroat; Yellow-breasted Chat; American Redstart; Western Tanager; Chipping, Lark, Fox, Savannah, Lincoln's, and Vesper Sparrows; Black-headed Grosbeak; Lazuli Bunting; Yellow-headed Blackbird; Bullock's Oriole; Cassin's Finch; Red Crossbill; Evening Grosbeak.

Nearby opportunities: Steptoe Butte near Colfax acts as a migrant trap. The Reardon Ponds north of I-90 can offer good birding.

Directions: Take I-90 to Cheney and exit onto State Route 904 through Cheney. Look for the "Blue Goose" National Wildlife Refuge markers on your way through town. Turn left onto Cheney-Plaza Road at the TURNBULL NWR sign and drive 4.5 miles to the entrance of the refuge. A wood sign at the entrance will help guide you.

DeLorme map grid: Page 72, A4.

Elevation: 2,200 feet.

Access: Wheelchair-accessible pit toilets and a boardwalk at Blackhorse Lake. Accessible sidewalks are planned for all of the educational sites on the auto tour.

Bathrooms: At the refuge headquarters, and several pit toilets are offered at educational sites on the auto tour.

Hazards: Ticks.

Nearest food, gas, and lodging: Cheney.

Nearest camping: Riverside State Park in Spokane.

For more information: To talk with refuge personnel, call (509) 235-4734. Visit the NWR Web site at turnbull.fws.gov, or visit the Friends of Turnbull NWR site at www.tincan.org/ftnwr. Both sites offer more general information, and the Friends site contains some wonderful photos of refuge flora and fauna.

Potholes and Desert Wildlife Areas

Habitats: Shrub-steppe, wetland, lakes, ponds.

Specialty birds: Common Loon; American White Pelican; Great Egret; Tundra Swan; Greater Scaup; Barrow's Goldeneye; Golden and Bald Eagles; Swainson's and Ferruginous Hawks; Sandhill Crane; American Avocet; Black-necked Stilt; Long-billed Curlew; Baird's and Pectoral Sandpipers; Wilson's and Red-necked Phalaropes; Bonaparte's Gull; Forster's Tern; Short-eared and Burrowing Owls; Cassin's Vireo; Sage Thrasher; Sage Sparrow.

Best times to bird: Spring and late summer.

A male Burrowing Owl stares into the camera lens in the evening light along Dodson Road in the Desert Wildlife Area.

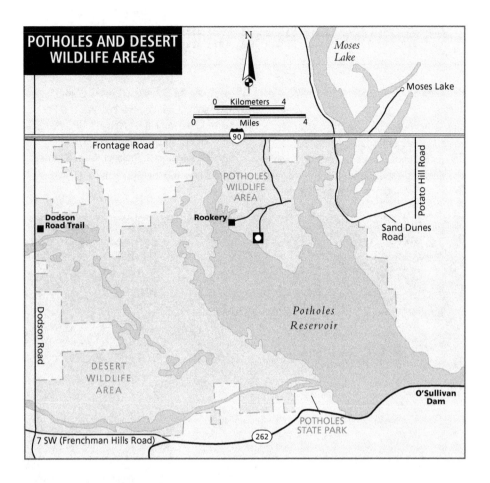

POTHOLES AND DESERT
WILDLIFE AREAS

N

0   Kilometers   4

0   Miles   4

90

Frontage Road

POTHOLES
WILDLIFE
AREA

Dodson
Road Trail

Rookery

Dodson Road

DESERT
WILDLIFE
AREA

7 SW (Frenchman Hills Road)

262

POTHOLES
STATE PARK

Potholes
Reservoir

Moses
Lake

Moses Lake

Potato Hill Road

Sand Dunes
Road

O'Sullivan
Dam

About the site:

This site is proof yet again that all it takes is water to draw migrating birds from the sky. The Potholes Wildlife Area sits at the northwest end of the Potholes Reservoir. From the site's entrance, you would never guess that down a dirt road you can find lush, tree-edged ponds thick with sandpipers, herons, and songbirds. Perhaps that is why we find this site so hard to bypass whenever we are headed east on Interstate 90. Right next to the Potholes site, as if to illustrate the drastic differences between the water-filled reservoir and the native steppe, the Desert Wildlife Area provides a complimentary site, complete with Burrowing Owls and an interpretive trail that will help you learn more about the high-desert habitat.

We won't guarantee that you will build a phenomenal list each time you visit these two sites, but when you hit these sites on a good day, you will understand why so many birders have added this to their lists of favorite places. The upper portions of the Potholes Wildlife Area looks like an overused and abused stretch of compromised shrub-steppe. Nonnative desert shrubs, such as tumbleweed, and grasses, such as cheat grass, break up clumps of rabbitbrush, and giant and tri-tip sage and native grasses such as needle-and-thread grass and Idaho fescue. Grazing and off-road driving and biking have contributed to the worn-out look of the landscape. Nevertheless, you will find Sage Thrashers, Horned Lark, and Lark and Brewer's Sparrows. Look on the power poles for Osprey, eagles, and hawks who may be tearing into a fish or recently caught shorebird. At a V in the road, you can either veer left to head up to look out over the main reservoir, a great place to see winter-resident and migrating geese and ducks, or you can head to the right. The road to the left takes you to a peninsula that looks over the main reservoir, and a trail leads to the edge of the reservoir and some of the smaller dune ponds and lakes, often filled with migrant ducks, geese, gulls, and terns at the right times of year.

The road to the right takes you to the hidden Shangri-la of the site, an offshoot from the main reservoir. As you take the road down to the dike, look to your left to find more dry-land passerines like the ever-calling Western Meadowlark. You may also see Loggerhead Shrike hunting from the sage. Sparrows, including Sage and Vesper Sparrows, forage and nest at the base of the shrubs. Below you on the right side of the road, a few seasonal ponds host waterfowl and a handful of shorebirds, including American Avocets and Black-necked Stilts, which have both nested here. In the late spring and summer, you will hear grating calls as you get closer to the dike. Step out of the car about 1 mile from the V and pull out your scope to look at the masses of nests in the trees along the shore of the lake. This special heron rookery houses Great Blue Herons, Great Egrets, elegant Black-crowned Night Herons, and Double-crested Cormorants. Other waterbirds also nest on the lagoon near the rookery. During migration, you also may see Sandhill Cranes on the site, and nonbreeding White Pelicans also gather in the area during the summer and in the fall before heading off on the next leg of their migratory journey.

Continue heading down the road until it curves to the right. At this corner, you may be able to get closer looks at the tall birds fishing in this shallow pond. Remember that your car will make a good blind and will keep you from scaring the birds away. Continue on to the dike that separates the rookery pond from the main reservoir. Park anywhere on the dike and walk along it looking for shorebirds during migration, including Baird's, Pectoral, and Least Sandpipers. Ring-billed, California, and Bonaparte's Gulls fish here, and you may see Red-necked and Wilson's Phalaropes foraging in the water as well. One summer day, we saw three tern species all hunting in the same area: Caspian Terns flew above the Forster's, which flew above the small Black Terns. All were diving and catching small fingerlings. Dozens of Killdeer also nest here, as do Ring-billed and California Gulls and Forster's and Caspian Terns. Black Terns nest among some of the reed-covered islands in the Potholes as well. And during migration, more ducks touch down on both sides of the dike, including Wood Duck and Cinnamon and Blue-winged Teals. If you limit your observations to the water, you will miss seeing some of the other migrants and summer residents that live and nest in the trees and shrubs that soften the lake edges, including Common Yellowthroat, Black-headed Grosbeak, and Yellow and Orange-Crowned Warblers. In part, due to the presence of the rookery, Audubon Washington has listed this area as one of the state's Important Bird Areas.

Once you have had your fill of the rookery, head back to Frontage Road and turn left. Remain on Frontage Road until you reach Dodson Road, perhaps one of the most frequently birded roads in the state. Turn left onto Dodson Road, which parallels the Desert Wildlife Area, including the Winchester Wasteway, to the east. Although it doesn't look much like a desert now, it was all desert and sand dunes before the O'Sullivan Dam raised the water table and flooded the sand dunes to create all of these small ponds and lakes. Winchester Wasteway is a canal that carries overflow and unused water back to the reservoir from the agricultural fields. The reed- and willow-edged waterways all along this road can hold more Great Egrets and Black-crowned and Great Blue Herons, as well as ducks, geese, and, during migration, swans. Look on power lines for Western and Eastern Kingbirds and American Kestrels. Northern Harriers fly low over the fields hunting for rodents, and Loggerhead Shrikes perch on treetops and fence posts to sally out for lizards, large insects, and small rodents.

To walk into the habitat, stop at the Audubon Dodson Road Trail, which offers a wheelchair-accessible interpretive trail and two viewing blinds, where you can sit close to the water and watch the ducks that fill the ponds, including Ruddy Ducks, Gadwalls, all three teals, Redheads, and Goldeneyes. Brewer's, Red-winged, and Yellow-headed Blackbirds sing from the tops of the cattails. Say's Phoebes, kingbirds, and five species of swallow also are seen flying and fly catching in the area. The drier shrub-steppe and dunes beyond host Long-billed Curlew, and while they may be too far away to see, you might see or hear them flying over the wetlands. Wetland-loving birds like American Bittern, Sora, Wilson's Snipe, and coots also inhabit the reeds around the edges all along Dodson Road. Unfortunately, much of this wetland is in danger from invasive, nonnative plants such as purple loosestrife and reed canary grass.

Near the corner of Dodson Road and Frenchman Hills Road (referred to as 7 SW on maps) is one of the many reasons that birders stop here—to look for the Burrowing Owls that nest in man-made burrows placed in the area for them. Often these owls sit on the fence posts right along the road just north of the Russian olive trees that start at Frenchman Hills Road. Although they are easy to see and seem rather tame, please do not approach too closely, especially early in the season and when you see young around. From here, if you turn west onto Frenchman Hills Road and go about .5 mile, you can do more birding at Birder's Corner, where you will find more of the above-mentioned water-loving birds.

The one caveat we offer for these sites is that you avoid visiting the Potholes Wildlife Area during those spring and summer three-day weekends that bring out all the campers. We made the mistake of visiting the rookery during Memorial Day weekend and were disappointed to see how many people camped along the dike; we were further disappointed to see how poorly they treated the land. Several access points allow deeper exploration of the wildlife areas off of State Route 262 and Frenchman Hills Road, including access to the dunes at Road C SE, just before the entrance to Potholes State Park. While the birding is best around the Potholes and Desert Wildlife Areas in the spring and late summer during migration, we find raptors in winter, including Bald Eagles and Prairie Falcons, and nesting residents during the heat of the summer.

Other key birds: Horned, Eared, Pied-billed, Clark's, and Western Grebes; American Bittern; Black-crowned Night Heron; Gadwall; Green-winged, Blue-winged, and Cinnamon Teals; American Wigeon; Northern Pintail; Northern Shoveler; Canvasback; Redhead; Ring-necked Duck; Lesser Scaup; Common Goldeneye; Bufflehead; Common and Hooded Mergansers; Ruddy Duck; Rough-legged Hawk; Merlin; Prairie Falcon; Virginia Rail; Sora; Greater and Lesser Yellowlegs; Spotted, Western, and Least Sandpipers; Long-billed Dowitcher; Wilson's Snipe; Ring-billed, California, and Herring Gulls; Caspian and Black Terns; Long-eared Owl; Common Nighthawk; Common Poorwill; Say's Phoebe; Western and Eastern Kingbirds; Loggerhead and Northern Shrikes; Warbling Vireo; Bank Swallow; Rock and Marsh Wrens; Orange-crowned, Yellow, and Wilson's Warblers; Common Yellowthroat; American Tree, Chipping, Brewer's, Lark, Grasshopper, Savannah, Lincoln's, and Vesper Sparrows; Black-headed Grosbeak; Lazuli Bunting; Yellow-headed Blackbird; Bullock's Oriole.

Nearby opportunities: For more waterfowl, grebes, and terns, head to Moses Lake State Park.

Directions: On I-90, east of George and west of Moses Lake, take exit 169 onto South Frontage Road. Head east approximately 2 miles to the Potholes Wildlife Area entrance. Once you have finished at Potholes, return to Frontage Road and turn left. Remain on Frontage until you come to Dodson Road. Turn left onto Dodson Road. The Desert Wildlife Area flanks Dodson Road all the way to 7 SW, also known as Frenchman Hills Road.

DeLorme map grid: Pages 68 and 69, D4 and D5.

Elevation: 1,050 feet.

Access: Potholes is not wheelchair accessible, but part of the Audubon trail on Dodson Road is wheelchair accessible.

Bathrooms: Pit toilet at Audubon site in Desert Wildlife Area.

Hazards: Rattlesnakes.

Nearest food, gas, and lodging: Moses Lake.

Nearest camping: Potholes State Park—you must make reservations during the summer months.

For more information: To get more information about individual access sites, visit the Fish and Wildlife site at www.wdfw .wa.gov/lands/r2pothls.htm.

65 Columbia National Wildlife Refuge and Seep Lakes Wildlife Area

Habitats: Shrub-steppe, cliff, riparian, lakes, grassland, wetland, ponds.

Specialty birds: Common Loon; American White Pelican; Great Egret; Greater Scaup; Barrow's Goldeneye; Golden and Bald Eagles; Swainson's and Ferruginous Hawks; Sandhill Crane; American Avocet; Black-necked Stilt; Solitary Sandpiper; Long-billed Curlew; Baird's and Pectoral Sandpipers; Wilson's and Red-necked Phalaropes; Bonaparte's Gull; Forster's Tern; Short-eared and Burrowing Owls; Calliope and Rufous Hummingbirds; Cassin's Vireo; Sage Thrasher; Sage Sparrow.

Best times to bird: Spring and fall.

A Long-billed Curlew watches from the prairie habitat at the Seep Lakes Wildlife Area, where these endangered birds nest in the spring.

About the site:

The 23,000 acres of the Columbia National Wildlife Refuge are scattered around several units, including the Marsh units abutting the Seep Lakes Wildlife Area. This site makes it easy to imagine what it was like before the dams were built for agricultural irrigation. In fact, the refuge overlaps part of the Drumheller Channels National Monument. Look at the dry shrub-steppe and imagine that all the lakes and ponds are empty potholes. Before the dams were built in the 1950s, this area was a string of mesas, dry potholes, and narrow canyons, all carved by the glacial Lake Missoula Floods. As the water table rose, the potholes filled and became the seep lakes that host migrating waterfowl, cranes, and songbirds. This varied habitat, located at a strategic spot on the Pacific Flyway, is well-suited to attract a wide diversity of bird life, including more than 100,000 ducks that overwinter here. The refuge is so important to migrating and overwintering birds that Audubon Washington has designated it as an Important Bird Area.

Although right next door, the Seep Lakes landscape has been continually compromised by fire and grazing, and the landscape is primarily composed of cheatgrass and Sandburg bluegrass. In addition to 2,800 acres of wetlands, the refuge has larger areas of shrub-steppe habitat composed of native grasses such as needle-and-thread grass and bluebunch wheatgrass mixed with sages and rabbitbrush. Before segmentation and environmental degradation, the two areas combined to host large flocks of sage obligates such as Sage and Sharp-tailed Grouse. A few extant stands of giant sage still exist, which attract passerines such as Brewer's and Sage Sparrows, especially after the young fledge and disperse to the lowland shrub-steppe.

While Long-billed Curlew nest on both sites, we have had better luck seeing them in the more compromised landscape of Seep Lakes. In the spring you can sometimes see the males in display flights of alternating fluttering and gliding combined with their high, repeated *whits.* They build shallow nests on the ground next to clumps of grass, small bushes, or rocks. If you are fortunate to see them fleeing from one of the many raptors that hunt these grasslands, you will hear the loud, plaintive *cur-lee,* from which this striking bird gets its name. The steep, rocky shores of the lakes in the wildlife area feature less of the wetland habitat that is found on the refuge. As a result, you'll find fewer shorebirds at the wildlife area, but waterfowl flock to all of the lakes during migration, including both Green-winged and Blue-winged Teal, Ruddy Duck, Gadwall, and Redhead.

To see what these two sites offer, we suggest a loop starting at Seep Lakes Road off of O'Sullivan Dam Road. The road bisects the natural area, and several side roads lead to some of the larger lakes, including Warden, Long, and Windmill Lakes. The road also passes through a small section of the wildlife refuge near North and South Teal Lakes. A side road here leads deeper into the refuge and Lower Hampton Lake. Check the stands of sage and rabbitbrush in the upland areas for Sage Thrasher, Loggerhead Shrike, and Sage Sparrow.

Take time to leave your car and walk a short way off the road to listen for

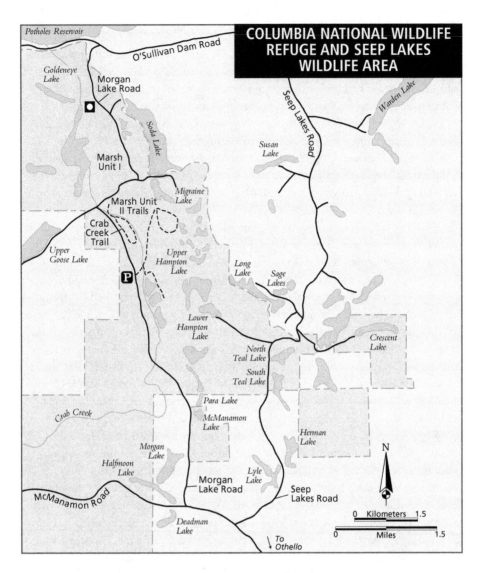

COLUMBIA NATIONAL WILDLIFE
REFUGE AND SEEP LAKES
WILDLIFE AREA

Potholes Reservoir

O'Sullivan Dam Road

Goldeneye
Lake

Morgan
Lake Road

Soda Lake

Warden Lake

Seep Lakes Road

Susan
Lake

Marsh
Unit I

Migraine
Lake

Marsh Unit
II Trails

Crab
Creek
Trail

Upper
Goose Lake

Upper
Hampton
Lake

Long
Lake

Sage
Lakes

Lower
Hampton
Lake

Crescent
Lake

North
Teal Lake

South
Teal Lake

Crab Creek

Para Lake

McManamon
Lake

Herman
Lake

Morgan
Lake

Halfmoon
Lake

Lyle
Lake

Morgan
Lake Road

Seep
Lakes Road

McManamon Road

N

Deadman
Lake

To
Othello

0   Kilometers   1.5

0   Miles   1.5

birdsong. In the wildlife area, you can do this anytime, but on the refuge, you can hike only on marked trails during hunting and fishing seasons. One of our favorite places to do this is at a mesa located approximately 4.5 miles from the McManamon Road entrance at Seep Lakes where a deep wash tracks to the east. One day we stopped and after fifteen minutes of waiting, watching, and listening between wind gusts, we had seen Common Raven, Rock and Canyon Wrens, Say's Phoebe, Western Kingbird, Horned Lark, and a passing Red-tailed Hawk and a coyote, who stopped to stare at us before trotting down the wash. Just as we were getting back into the car, a half-dozen Long-billed Curlews flew over, calling in alarm as yet another hawk flew past their nesting grounds.

Where Seep Lakes Road exits the wildlife area at McManamon Road, turn right and then take the next right onto Morgan Lake Road, which passes through the refuge. The area at the beginning of this road is private property, and the road is paved. However, Morgan Lake and a small patch of refuge land surrounding McManamon Lake provide good places to pull off and look for passerines more commonly associated with agricultural lands. Check here also for American Tree Sparrows, Bullock's Orioles, American Goldfinches, and Chipping Sparrows. Look along the edges of the lakes for American Bitterns, rails, and blackbirds.

The road turns to gravel where it enters the main refuge unit at the cattle grate until it ends at O'Sullivan Dam Road. The open landscape near the grate provides a vantage point from which to spy raptors, ravens, and waterfowl flying to the refuge. The road then enters a stretch of dry, open grassy fields in between and opposite the first basalt-columned plateaus until it crosses Crab Creek. Look for Vesper and Savannah Sparrows in the grass and tippling Northern Harriers or diving Prairie Falcons hunting over the fields. At the cliffs, Canyon Wrens emit their telltale downward spirals, and Rock Wrens sing from their ledges as Golden Eagles and hawks hunt from the upper terraces while their young huddle below.

Across from one of these plateaus, about 3.5 miles from McManamon Road, two trails provide access to the riparian wetlands of Marsh Unit II, including Frog Lake and a marshy section of Crab Creek. Farther up the road, a third trail—the Crab Creek Trail—passes through slightly drier riparian habitat near another section of the creek. Parts of these trails are closed in winter. The lower trails to the lakes and around the wetlands are well-marked and well-used. The upper trail is not as well-marked, and in many places it looks like a deer trail, so use caution and try to remain on the trail. Walk the lower trails to see marsh lovers and shorebirds, including Black-necked Stilts, Black-crowned Night Herons, American Avocets, and Wilson's Phalaropes. In late summer during fall migration, look for yellowlegs, plovers, and sandpipers. Look in the shrubs and along the upper trail for Lazuli Bunting, Yellow-breasted Chat, Eastern Kingbirds, Song Sparrows and other sparrows, vireos, and warblers. Bank, Violet-green, Barn, Cliff, and Northern Rough-winged Swallows skim the tops of the lakes and grassy margins in twisting, swooping displays of their flying abilities.

Before reaching the upper trail, Morgan Lake Road comes to a T. Turn right to walk the third trail. Alternately, turn left to pass between two mesas, beyond the borders of the refuge and onto Department of Fish and Wildlife land at Upper Goose Lake. Park near the boat ramp and check the lake for waterfowl and the shrubby base of the mesa for White-crowned and Golden-Crowned Sparrows and kingbirds. A game trail hugs the ledge here, and if you don't see any deer, you might see some entertaining marmots munching on the arrow balsam root and other green delicacies offered on the shady side of the cliff. This lake, as well as the other deep lakes on the refuge, host Hooded Mergansers, Common Goldeneye, Bufflehead, Common Loons, and grebes, among other diving ducks.

After stopping at the lake and Crab Creek Trail, continue on to stop next at the

Marsh Unit I overlook and hike to the edge of the wetland when the trail is open. Although access to this unit is closed during migration, a scope will help you see much of what the unit offers. This is one of the best places on the refuge to see migrating Sandhill Cranes, Canada and White-fronted Geese, swans, and herons. Next stop at Soda Lake Dam, where you can look over Soda and Migraine Lakes. Migraine Lake is closed for part of the year and its marshy, saline waters host more shorebirds and dabblers—as do the other shallow lakes on the refuge—while the freshwater Soda Lake hosts diving ducks and sometimes White Pelicans as well as resident and migrating gulls. A spotting scope is also useful here to look over the lakes, especially when Migraine Lake is closed. When the road is open in the summer, you can drive farther to Pillar and Wigeon Lakes to check for more passerines and dabblers, including teals, Gadwall, Northern Shovelers, and American and possibly Eurasian Wigeon in the spring.

Because the refuge and seep lakes act as migrant traps and host so many nesting summer and winter residents, frequent visits will pay off when you learn which areas are more likely to harbor rarities and vagrants such as White-faced Ibis and Tri-colored Blackbirds. In winter, visit to see Bald Eagles roosting and waterfowl such as Bufflehead, Common Goldeneye, and Mallards. In addition, frequent visits during migration will ensure that you catch most of the shorebirds and waterfowl that touch down on their long flights to and from their breeding grounds.

Other key birds: Horned, Eared, Pied-billed, Clark's, and Western Grebes; American Bittern; Black-crowned Night Heron; Gadwall; Green-winged, Blue-winged, and Cinnamon Teals; American Wigeon; Northern Pintail; Northern Shoveler; Canvasback; Redhead; Ring-necked Duck; Lesser Scaup; Common Goldeneye; Bufflehead; Common and Hooded Mergansers; Ruddy Duck; Turkey Vulture; Rough-legged Hawk; Prairie Falcon; Virginia Rail; Sora; Greater and Lesser Yellowlegs; Spotted, Western, and Least Sandpipers; Long-billed Dowitcher; Wilson's Snipe; Ring-billed, California, and Herring Gulls; Caspian and Black Terns; Long-eared Owl; Common Nighthawk; Common Poorwill; Say's Phoebe; Western and Eastern Kingbirds; Loggerhead and Northern Shrikes; Warbling Vireo; Bank Swallow.

Nearby opportunities: Back at O'Sullivan Dam Road, make sure you check Lind Coulee, near the Seep Lakes entrance, for flotillas of ducks and a variety of shorebirds. The Royal Lake overlook, also part of the refuge at the south end of Byers Road, is one of the best places to see every kind of duck, goose, and swan known to the area during migration.

Directions: From State Route 262 turn south at the Seeps Lake Wildlife Area sign, 3 miles east of O'Sullivan Dam.

DeLorme map grid: Page 53, B6.

Elevation: 1,000 feet.

Access: Not wheelchair accessible, but much may be explored from a car.

Bathrooms: On-site pit toilets.

Hazards: Rattlesnakes and ticks.

Nearest food, gas, and lodging: Othello.

Nearest camping: On-site camping at several of the lakes in the Seep Lakes Wildlife Area.

For more information: Check the Washington Department of Fish and Wildlife's site for the Potholes area at www.wdfw.wa.gov/lands/r2pothls.htm.

66 Crab Creek Wildlife Area

Habitats: Lowland riparian, freshwater marsh, wetland, prairie, modified shrub-steppe, cliffs.

Specialty birds: American White Pelican; Great Egret; Golden and Bald Eagles; Swainson's and Ferruginous Hawks; Chukar; Sandhill Crane; Short-eared, Snowy, and Burrowing Owls; Cassin's Vireo; Sage Thrasher; Sage Sparrow.

Best times to bird: Anytime of the year.

About the site:

It is no wonder that the riparian areas along Crab Creek are such a draw for birds. As the only source of water for miles around, the creek offers an oasis for birds and other wildlife that extends from the shore of the Columbia River near Beverly to the far-away source of the creek a few miles west of Spokane. All of this water filtered through the sunshine of eastern Washington gathers in the Crab Creek Wildlife Area, where shrub-steppe habitat modified by years of grazing meets the wetlands under the shadow of the Saddle Mountains.

Birding along Lower Crab Creek starts in the town of Beverly. Lower Crab Creek Road leads east from its intersection with State Route 243 and cuts a path between wetlands, fishing holes, and short stands of Russian olive trees. Along the way it passes an area of sand dunes that is heavily used by off-road-vehicle enthusiasts on weekends and a series of fishing areas that offer views of waterbird species as well as initial glimpses of the modified shrub-steppe habitat surrounding these watering holes.

Pull off the road at the Washington Department of Fisheries and Widllife site on the north side of the road to reach Nunnally Lake, a popular fishing area that also can offer glimpses of rails, waterfowl, and raptors. The pullout for Nunnally Lake is also near an area of Russian olive that burned in 2000, and in the evenings it is possible to find Long-eared Owls sitting in the remains of the brush.

Heading east the road crosses Crab Creek and gradually fades away from the waterway, giving better close-up views of both the sagebrush habitat and the looming cliffs and talus slopes of the Saddle Mountains. It is in this section of the road between the creek crossing and the small farming settlement of Smyrna that shrikes can be seen in the spring as they perch on top of sage and other short brush before making dashes toward the ground to hunt. Just to the north of the road in this area is a leaning and soon to collapse shack that can hold perching Barn Owls, and Tree Sparrows can be seen in the winter and early spring in the stretch of habitat north of the road toward Smyrna. The sagebrush habitat here also offers the best opportunities to see Sage Thrasher, Sage Sparrow, and Lark Sparrow. Also be sure to watch the lower edges of the talus slopes along the base of the Saddle Mountains for Chukar, and look up to the tops of the ridges to see Golden Eagle and other raptors riding the thermals.

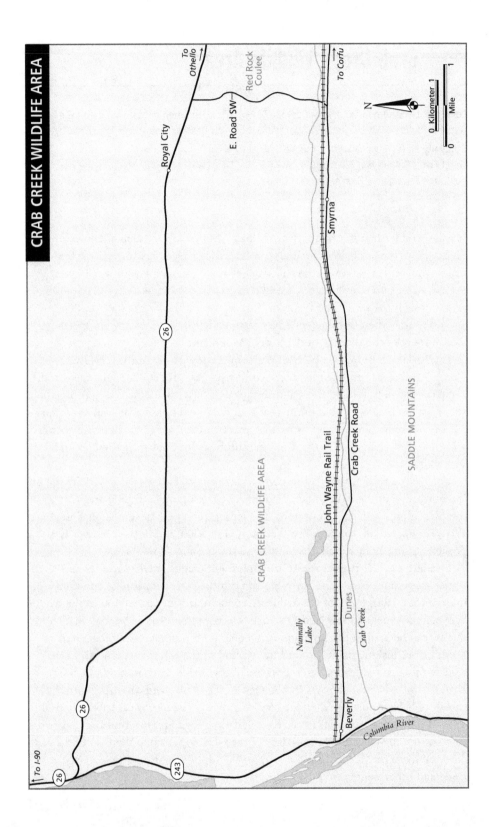

CRAB CREEK WILDLIFE AREA

Lower Crab Creek Road returns to being a paved road near Smyrna, and it continues through the farming area, where Sandhill Cranes often can be seen in the fields during their March migration, before giving you the choice to turn left and drive toward State Route 26 through Red Rock Coulee, to turn back toward Beverly, or to take a rugged gravel road that continues east alongside lands that are part of the Columbia National Wildlife Refuge. Unless you have a four-wheel-drive vehicle, opt for the turn-around or for continuing to SR 26.

A CREEK RUNS THROUGH IT

Widely cited as the longest creek in the United States, Crab Creek starts its journey to the Columbia River just a few miles west of Spokane and then meanders across the northern edges of the Columbia Basin, first flowing into Moses Lake and then into the Potholes Reservoir before trickling out through a series of creeks and wasteways, including the main stream of Crab Creek that emerges from behind the O'Sullivan Dam and flows through the Columbia National Wildlife Refuge near Othello. Along its route the 200-plus-mile creek drains a huge expanse of eastern Washington, providing an oasis of bird habitat along the only riparian zone within miles in any direction.

Other key birds: Pied-billed Grebe; American Bittern; Gadwall; Green-winged, Blue-winged, and Cinnamon Teals; American Wigeon; Northern Pintail; Northern Shoveler; Canvasback; Redhead; Ring-necked Duck; Lesser Scaup; Common Goldeneye; Bufflehead; Common and Hooded Mergansers; Turkey Vulture; Prairie Falcon; Virginia Rail; Sora; Ring-billed, California, and Herring Gulls; Long-eared Owl; Common Nighthawk; Common Poorwill; White-throated Swift; Say's Phoebe; Western and Eastern Kingbirds; Loggerhead and Northern Shrikes; Warbling Vireo; Bank Swallow; Rock, Canyon, and Marsh Wrens; Orange-crowned, Yellow, and Wilson's Warblers; Common Yellowthroat; American Tree, Chipping, Brewer's, Lark, Savannah, Lincoln's, and Vesper Sparrows; Black-headed Grosbeak; Lazuli Bunting; Yellow-headed Blackbirds; Bullock's Oriole; Evening Grosbeak.

Nearby opportunities: Just south of Crab Creek is the Priest Rapids Wildlife Area and north of Crab Creek you can stop at the Wanapum Dam Visitor Center to view the Columbia River, where loons often are found in the winter months feeding in the outflow from the dam.

Directions: From Interstate 90, follow SR 26 south along the east side of the Columbia River. Turn right onto SR 243 and continue south past the Wanapum Dam and under the abandoned Vernita Bridge to Beverly, then turn left onto Lower Crab Creek Road.

DeLorme map grid: Page 52, B1.

Elevation: 550 feet.

Access: The entire site can be birded from a car.

Bathrooms: Seasonal pit toilets, some wheelchair-accessible.

Hazards: None.

Nearest food, gas, and lodging: Beverly for food and gas, Vantage or Othello for lodging.

Nearest camping: Primitive camping can be done in sections of the wildlife area, but campsites are available near Vantage at Wanapum State Park.

For more information: Visit www.wdfw.wa.gov/lands/r2crabcr.htm or call (509) 765-6641.

Habitats: Lowland riparian, shrub-steppe, cliffs.

Specialty birds: American White Pelican; Barrow's Goldeneye; Golden and Bald Eagles; Swainson's and Ferruginous Hawks; Chukar; Bonaparte's Gull; Burrowing Owl; Sage Thrasher; Sage Sparrow.

Best times to bird: Spring, summer, and fall.

The White Bluffs boat launch provides the best access to the Columbia River in the Hanford Reach National Monument.

About the site:

If you are looking for shrub-steppe birding at its finest, its hard to beat the Hanford Reach National Monument. Along with the last free-flowing stretch of the Columbia River, the monument offers the best of eastern Washington birding rolled up into its component parts—the Saddle Mountain National Wildlife Refuge, the Wahluke Slope Wildlife Area, and the Fitzner/Eberhardt Arid Lands Ecology Reserve. The trick is knowing how to see as much of the birding habitat as possible with limited access to most areas in the monument.

Both the Saddle Mountain National Wildlife Refuge and the Fitzner/Eberhardt Arid Lands Ecology Reserve are closed to the general public. They can be explored in a limited way by birding from the wide shoulders of State Route 24, but to get a close-up look at what the monument has to offer, you have to venture into the Wahluke Slope unit that is open year-round for day use. Within its 57,000 acres are some of the best habitats in the monument, including the upland area with amazing views atop the Saddle Mountains and the riverside views and habitat at the White Bluffs boat ramp.

The upland areas of Wahluke Slope north of SR 24 offer prime examples of shrub-steppe habitat, with accompanying bird species—Horned Lark, Sage Thrasher, and Brewer's, Sage, and Grasshopper Sparrow. The best way to explore the area is to take SR 24 east to a narrow, paved road near milepost 60. The road heads north and toward the Saddle Mountains, with fairly mature sagebrush, rabbitbrush, and other shrub-steppe plants on both sides of the road. Make frequent stops along the initial paved section of the road to look for bird activity in the brush. Also keep looking overhead for Swainson's and Ferruginous Hawks as well as Prairie Falcons that often hunt in the area.

As the road starts to climb toward the crest of the Saddle Mountains, it crosses an irrigation canal and switches to gravel. We were able to drive the rest of the way in our passenger car, but the road is rugged and could be tough to drive depending on the season, so take it slowly. From the viewpoint at the top of the Saddle Mountains, you'll find expansive panoramas of the Potholes area north of the hills and the national monument south of the hills. Be sure to scan the horizon for views of Golden Eagles and other raptors riding thermals as they hunt, and scan the creases and folds in the hillsides to find sparrows, Sage Thrashers, and other songbirds moving in the brush.

After making your way back down to SR 24, turn left to drive a couple of miles to a gravel road that cuts south toward the White Bluffs boat ramp—the main public access point for boaters who want to ply the waters on the longest free-flowing section of the Columbia River. This road crosses more mature shrub-steppe habitat that offers glimpses of species that rely on the sagebrush and native plants. The dusty road covers about 8 miles before coming to a T. Turn left to explore the area around Wahluke Lake or right to drop down to the White Bluffs boat ramp. Both areas offer views of waterfowl, but if you have to choose just one

Seasonal runoff carves dramatic folds in the terrain along the northern side of Wahluke Slope in the Hanford Reach National Monument.

site, opt for the boat ramp and the picturesque views of the river and the bluffs. Besides waterfowl, you may see the occasional migrating shorebird on the sandy shores of the river, songbirds in the willow, and Russian olive and locust trees near the boat ramp. This area also can be good for seeing porcupine.

Besides its importance as a nuclear research and testing site, the area around the White Bluffs boat launch also holds historical significance dating from prehistory as a place where aboriginal peoples gathered to hunt and fish. Artifacts from previous peoples have been found along the bluffs and in the sandy soils along the river's shore, and the Saddle Mountains area was a major hunting ground for Native American tribes. When European explorers arrived in eastern Washington, the White Bluffs area became a major crossroads for settlers crossing the river and making their way east or west.

Other key birds: Eared, Pied-billed, and Western Grebes; American Bittern; Black-crowned Night Heron; Gadwall; Green-winged, Blue-winged, and Cinnamon Teals; American Wigeon; Northern Pintail; Northern Shoveler; Canvasback; Redhead; Ring-necked Duck; Lesser Scaup; Common Goldeneye; Bufflehead; Common and Hooded Mergansers; Turkey Vulture; Osprey; Rough-legged Hawk; Prairie Falcon; Virginia Rail; Sora; Spotted Sandpiper; Wilson's Snipe; Ring-billed, California, and Herring Gulls; Long-eared Owl; Common Nighthawk; Common Poorwill; White-throated Swift; Say's Phoebe; Western and Eastern Kingbirds; Loggerhead and Northern Shrikes; Bank Swallow; Rock and Marsh Wrens; Orange-crowned, Yellow, and Wilson's Warblers; Chipping, Brewer's, Lark, Grasshopper, Lincoln's, and Vesper Sparrows; Black-headed Grosbeak; Lazuli Bunting; Yellow-headed Blackbird; Evening Grosbeak.

Nearby opportunities: Go east on SR 24, east on State Road 26, and then south on State Road 17 to explore waterfowl on Scooteney Reservoir (DeLorme Map Grid: Page 53, C8).

Directions: From I-90, take SR 26 south along the east side of the Columbia River and

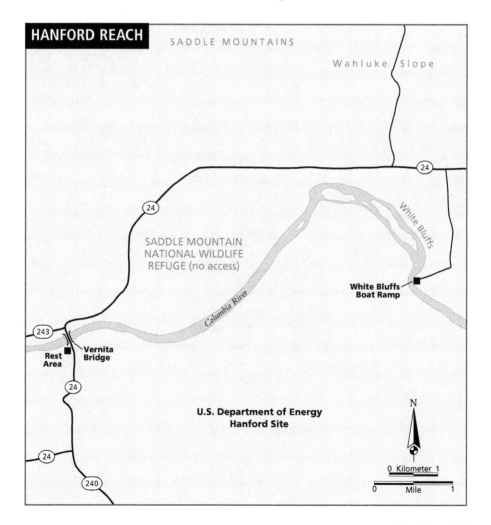

then continue south along the river on State Road 243 until it intersects with SR 24. Stay on the east side of the river for views from the highway overlooking the Saddle Mountain National Wildlife Refuge. Access to the upland section of the Wahluke Wildlife Area is offered north of SR 24 along a signed road near milepost 60, and access to the lower section of the reach is offered to the south of SR 24 by taking a gravel road near milepost 63.

DeLorme map grid: Page 53, C5.

Elevation: 480 feet.

Access: None.

Bathrooms: A rest area on the west side of the Vernita Bridge offers restrooms, and portable toilets are offered at the White Bluffs boat ramp from June through October.

Hazards: Rattlesnakes and heat.

Nearest food, gas, and lodging: Othello.

Nearest camping: Desert Aire Campground northwest of the Vernita Bridge along SR 24.

For more information: The Hanford Reach National Monument site offers more information at hanfordreach.fws.gov. You also can reach the monument administration by calling (509) 371-1801.

AN ACCIDENTAL REFUGE

The Hanford Reach National Monument and the refuge lands within it are a leftover benefit of the nuclear research and development related to World War II and the Cold War that took place across the river at the Hanford Nuclear Reservation. Lands around the reservation were vacated during the time that nuclear testing and research was under way at the reactors, and it is because these lands were closed to the public that some of the largest remnants of steppe and shrub-steppe habitat in eastern Washington were protected from conversion to farming and irrigated land, much to the benefit of the plants and animals that rely on sagebrush country for their survival. The monument is known to support 43 species of fish, 40 mammal species, 246 bird species, 4 amphibian species, 11 reptile species, and more than 1,500 invertebrate species. Add in the thirty rare plant taxa growing in various locations across the site, and it becomes apparent why the monument was set aside by President Clinton in 2000.

Despite its status as protected land, areas of the national monument are still at risk. A wildfire swept through much of the Fitzner/Eberhardt Arid Lands Ecology Reserve in 1997, and scientists expect it to take decades or much longer before the native grasses and sages recover.

68 McNary National Wildlife Refuge

Habitats: Shrub-steppe, lowland riparian, wetland, freshwater marsh, mudflat.

Specialty birds: Common Loon; American White Pelican; Tundra and Trumpeter Swans; Greater White-fronted Goose; Greater Scaup; Barrow's Goldeneye; Golden and Bald Eagles; Swainson's Hawk; Chukar; American Avocet; Black-necked Stilt; Solitary Sandpiper; Long-billed Curlew; Baird's and Pectoral Sandpipers; Wilson's and Red-necked Phalaropes; Bonaparte's Gull; Forster's Tern; Short-eared and Burrowing Owls; Vaux's Swift; Rufous Hummingbird; Red-naped Sapsucker; Hammond's and Dusky Flycatchers; Cassin's Vireo; Western Bluebird; Bohemian Waxwing.

Best times to bird: Year-round.

Trees are reflected in the waters of the Columbia River on the western edge of the McNary National Wildlife Refuge. The refuge provides critical habitat for migrating waterfowl that pass through the area each spring and fall.

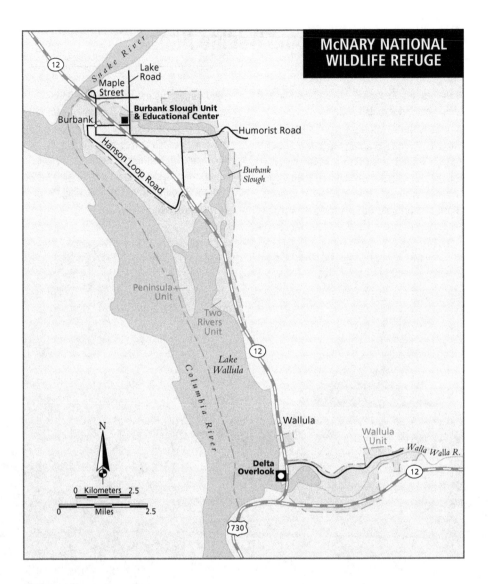

About the site:

Views of American White Pelicans and American Avocet in the summer and one of the largest congregations of migrating waterfowl in Washington in the fall and winter are two of the main draws of the McNary National Wildlife Refuge (NWR). Located near the confluence of the Snake and Columbia Rivers and spanning the shoreline in sections southward to the mouth of the Walla Walla River, McNary is a must-see site any time of the year.

Visitors to the McNary NWR are greeted by a wide range of habitats, from shrub-steppe uplands to sloughs and backwaters along the shores of the Columbia River on Lake Wallula that serve as bird habitat as well as habitat for chinook salmon. The refuge, which was originally set aside in 1956 as mitigation for the flooding caused by the McNary Dam, has grown in size during the years from its original 3,600 acres to today's size of more than 15,000 acres. Its sloughs, lakes, and the Columbia River can hold more than 100,000 waterfowl during migration, including as much as half of the Mallard population that migrates along the Pacific Flyway.

The best place to start bird-watching at McNary is along the shores of Burbank Slough and from a 1.9-mile trail at the refuge headquarters off Maple Street in Burbank. A viewing platform on the deck of the McNary Environmental Education Center offers the first glimpses of the bird diversity at the refuge. Look for quite a bit of waterfowl diversity on the Burbank Slough year-round, with American Coot, Redhead, and Canada Goose joined by Great Egret and Forster's Tern in summer, while Northern Shoveler, American Wigeon, Northern Pintail, and more join the floating and feeding flock in winter. The number of waterfowl at the refuge peaks around December.

To fully explore the Burbank portion of the refuge, walk along the interpretive trail and be sure to stop at the wheelchair-accessible viewing blind just a short distance from the refuge parking lot. As you walk along the trail, watching for sparrows, flycatchers, and warblers in the trees, keep an eye out for butterflies in the summer months. Monarch butterflies are common on the refuge, especially if you can find milkweed nearby.

An American White Pelican looks for food on a pond near the McNary National Wildlife Refuge office and visitor center.

Although the refuge's most obvious birding can be found near the education center, there is more bird diversity if you check some of the roadside sites with access to ponds and the banks of the Columbia River south of the main site along State Route 12. Look for the familiar blue goose markers that denote refuge entrances at pullouts along the highway and explore along the gravel access roads. The Two Rivers Unit offers views of the river as well as a Great Blue Heron rookery, and Black-crowned Night Heron are common as well.

The McNary NWR extends to the south all the way into Oregon, with the Wallula Unit encompassing the mouth of the Walla Walla River as the next-best birding opportunity in the Washington portion of the refuge. Just after SR 12 passes through the tiny town of Wallula, a nondescript access road between the highway and railroad tracks that are closer to the riverbank offers the best place to pull off the highway and scan the Walla Walla River delta for birds. The area is well-known for its diversity of gulls seen throughout the year and for the numbers of shorebirds that gather on the mudflats during the migration season, but be sure to bring your spotting scope since the birds are so far from the viewing site.

On the other side of the highway are additional bird-watching opportunities at Madame Dorion Memorial Park, a site that also offers primitive camping. Songbirds are common in the spring and summer months in the dense riparian foliage along the Walla Walla River, and during overnight visits in the campground we have seen Long-eared Owl and heard other owls calling. Also be on the lookout for Bank Swallows, which are commonly found here since they nest in burrows in the layers of silt deposits that can be seen in the park. Drive into the upland portions of the Wallula Unit for glimpses of shrub-steppe habitat and associated birds—Lark and Brewer's Sparrow, Horned Lark, and others.

McNary NWR ends in Oregon, where the State Line and Juniper Canyon Units add more bird diversity with habitat for Peregrine Falcon and other cliff-dwelling raptors. The Oregon portions of the refuge are in Umatilla County. If you continue exploring along the river's edge heading downstream, you will soon reach the Umatilla National Wildlife Refuge, which, along with the McNary NWR, is part of the Mid-Columbia River Refuges.

Other key birds: Horned, Pied-billed, and Western Grebes; Black-crowned Night Heron; Gadwall; Green-winged, Blue-winged, and Cinnamon Teals; American Wigeon; Northern Pintail; Northern Shoveler; Canvasback; Redhead; Ring-necked Duck; Lesser Scaup; Common Goldeneye; Bufflehead; Common and Hooded Mergansers; Ruddy Duck; Osprey; Rough-legged Hawk; Merlin; Prairie Falcon; Virginia Rail; Sora; Semipalmated Plover; Greater and Lesser Yellowlegs; Spotted Sandpiper; Dunlin; Semipalmated, Western, and Least Sandpipers; Long-billed Dowitcher; Wilson's Snipe; Ring-billed and California Gulls; Caspian Tern; Long-eared and Western Screech Owls; White-throated Swift; Downy Woodpecker; Western Wood-pewee; Willow Flycatcher; Say's Phoebe; Western and Eastern Kingbirds; Loggerhead and Northern Shrikes; Warbling Vireo; Bank Swallow; House, Bewick's, Rock, and Marsh Wrens; American Pipit; Orange-crowned, Townsend's, Yellow, MacGillivray's, and Wilson's

Warblers; Western Tanager; Chipping, Brewer's, Lark, Grasshopper, Fox, Savannah, Lincoln's, and Vesper Sparrows; Black-headed Grosbeak; Lazuli Bunting; Yellow-headed Blackbird; Bullock's Oriole; Red Crossbill; Evening Grosbeak.

Nearby opportunities: Sacajawea State Park is at the confluence of the Snake and Columbia Rivers, and Hood Park is nearby as well.

Directions: From SR 12 just south of the Snake River bridge, turn left at the refuge sign onto Maple Street. The wildlife refuge headquarters are at the end of the road.

DeLorme map grid: Page 39, C8.

Elevation: 365 feet.

Access: Wheelchair-accessible trails and restrooms.

Bathrooms: At the refuge headquarters.

Hazards: None.

Nearest food, gas, and lodging: Pasco.

Nearest camping: Hood Park or at the Madame Dorion Memorial Park for a more-rugged camping experience.

For more information: Check the refuge Web page at midcolumbiariver.fws.gov/mcnarypage .htm or the alternate page at refuges.fws.gov/ profiles/index.cfm?id=13520. Also check the page for the McNary National Wildlife Refuge Education Center at nwr.mcnary.wa.us.

THE WALLULA GAP

Although Lake Wallula is an artificial lake created by dams on the Columbia River, its presence near the McNary NWR is a reminder of the huge temporary lakes created again and again during the last ice age when the Missoula Floods swept through this area and formed backwaters upstream of the narrow geologic formation of Wallula Gap. The gap is formed by mountains on each side of the Columbia River that constricted the torrent of the Missoula Floods and forced unimaginable backwaters to form behind the gap before the waters could filter through the narrow opening.

You can see evidence of these ancient floods in silt deposits exposed by the roads in Madame Dorion Memorial Park. Look for areas in the park where the road cuts through something that looks like layers of sand. These silt deposits are favorites of Bank Swallows, since they can easily burrow into the sand and ancient mud to create their nest cavities.

69 Wawawai Canyon

Habitats: Lowland riparian, wetland, freshwater marsh, prairie.

Specialty birds: Barrow's Goldeneye; Golden and Bald Eagle; Swainson's Hawk; Chukar; Vaux's Swift; Black-chinned, Calliope, and Rufous Hummingbird; Red-naped Sapsucker; Hammond's, Dusky, and Pacific-slope Flycatcher; Cassin's Vireo; Pygmy Nuthatch; Western Bluebird; Bohemian Waxwing.

Best times to bird: Year-round.

The dark green trees and grasses at the base of Wawawai Canyon, alongside the Snake River, contrast with the dry grassland surrounding the canyon. The unique combination of habitats makes the canyon a worthwhile bird-watching destination.

About the site:

Wawawai County Park and the drive down Wawawai Canyon feature some of the best birding in the Pullman area. The route passes farm fields, orchards, and a steep riparian area along Wawawai Creek in the canyon before meeting the green oasis at the park, which offers a platform with views of wetland habitat at the head of Wawawai Bay as well as an upland interpretive walk that leaves the irrigated park grass behind for glimpses of native grasses and flowers on a hillside overlooking the park and campground.

The area at the foot of Wawawai Canyon served for centuries as a gathering place for Native American tribes. The name wawawai means "talk talk" or council grounds, and it is believed that tribes gathered near the site of the current park to fish, hunt, gather berries, and hold council among nations. Before the Snake River was dammed just downstream of the present county park, the foot of the canyon was the most bustling fruit-shipping and transportation center on the lower Snake River.

Today the area encompassed by the county park is a migrant trap and regular stopover for migrant birds as well as birds that nest and spend longer portions of the year in the canyon.

To start exploring this site, take Wawawai-Pullman Road off State Route 195, heading west and away from Pullman. The road winds through farm country, offering the chance to see blackbirds, sparrows, and both Swainson's and Red-tailed Hawks along the telephone poles and fence posts. After winding through the farming area at the edge of the Palouse, the road comes to a T with Wawawai Grade Road. Turn right to start the descent into the canyon.

The Wawawai Canyon offers brushy riparian habitat along the edges of a small stream that winds down the middle of the steep canyon. Watch the edge between the riparian area with its willow trees and shrubs and the grassy prairie area alongside it for birds moving between the two habitats. Also watch along power lines for kingbirds and American Kestrel. It's best to bird the canyon in the early morning, while birds are at their most active and when traffic is at a minimum. Pullouts along the road down the canyon are limited.

Once you reach the bottom of the canyon, turn right into Wawawai County Park and find a parking spot near the end of the lot. A trail departs the end of the parking lot, leading to a viewing platform with views over the wetland where Wawawai Creek empties into the small bay. This is the best place to look out over the water for waterfowl and over the wetland for wrens, sparrows, and other birds that prefer to skulk at the edges of dense vegetation. The park itself also offers dense vegetation, with willow, elderberry, cottonwood, locust, and a few fruit trees left over from the days when the park grounds were used by settlers. Within the park grounds you can see warblers and the occasional Northern Flicker, and if you watch the sky overhead, you may also spy a raptor riding thermals over the edges of the canyon or Bank Swallow looping through the sky. Depending on the sea-

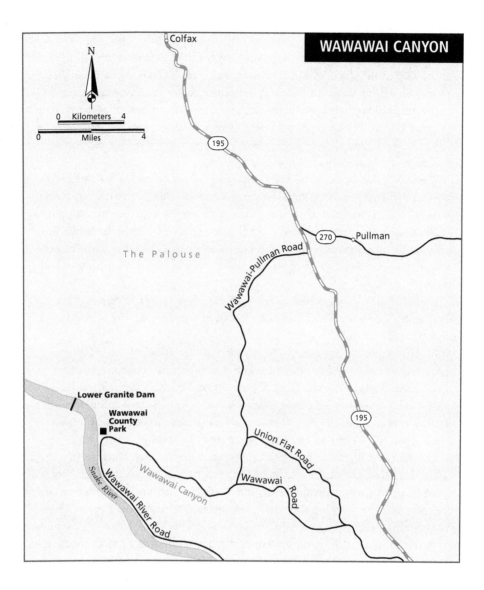

Colfax

N

0 Kilometers 4

0   Miles   4

195

The Palouse

270 Pullman

Wawawai-Pullman Road

195

Lower Granite Dam

Wawawai
County
■ Park

Union Flat Road

Snake River

Wawawai River Road

Wawawai Canyon

Wawawai Road

son, you could see Bald and Golden Eagles in the canyon, as well as Prairie Falcon. Bald Eagles are more common in winter.

After wandering through the park grounds, walk to the upper portion of the park, just past the bathrooms, to reach an interpretive trail that winds through the prairie habitat that is not kept green year-round by irrigation. This area of native grasses and plants holds birding potential, but it also is home in the spring to wildflowers such as desert paintbrush, shooting star, snapdragon skullcap, hound's-tongue, and others. For this reason, a spring visit to the park could yield not only migrants from the spring bird migration, but also spectacular flower displays along the interpretive trail and elsewhere in the canyon.

To make the most of your visit to Wawawai Canyon and to add more species for the site, be sure to drive the rest of the way down Wawawai Grade Road to check for waterfowl on the Snake River. The river runs slowly through the area, since it is dammed.

RIVER CORRIDORS AS WILDLIFE CORRIDORS

Wawawai Canyon bottoms out along the banks of the Snake River, making the small county park a prime location to find birds and butterflies that fly along the Snake River during their south-to-north migration in the spring and their north-to-south migration in the late summer and fall. Birds and butterflies use the low-elevation passages offered by the Snake River and other rivers both because of the habitat and foraging opportunities offered along the river edges and because they can take advantage of breezes that blow down the river corridor to speed them along their way. The Snake River is believed to be a corridor used by Monarch butterflies, among others.

Other key birds: Eared and Pied-billed Grebes; Gadwall; Green-winged, Blue-winged, and Cinnamon Teals; American Wigeon; Northern Pintail; Northern Shoveler; Canvasback; Redhead; Ring-necked Duck; Lesser Scaup; Common Goldeneye; Bufflehead; Common Merganser; Ruddy Duck; Osprey; Rough-legged Hawk; Prairie Falcon; Gray Partridge; Virginia Rail; Sora; Greater and Lesser Yellowlegs; Spotted Sandpiper; Long-billed Dowitcher; Wilson's Snipe; Long-eared Owl; Common Nighthawk; Common Poorwill; Olive-sided Flycatcher; Western Wood-Pewee; Willow Flycatcher; Say's Phoebe; Western and Eastern Kingbirds; Northern Shrike; Red-eyed and Warbling Vireos; Bank Swallow; House, Winter, Bewick's, Rock, Canyon, and Marsh Wrens; Swainson's Thrush; Gray Catbird; Orange-crowned, Yellow, MacGillivray's, and Wilson's Warblers; Yellow-breasted Chat; Western Tanager; Chipping, Brewer's, Lark, Grasshopper, Fox, Savannah, Lincoln's, and Vesper Sparrows; Black-headed Grosbeak; Lazuli Bunting; Yellow-headed Blackbird; Bullock's Oriole; Evening Grosbeak.

Nearby opportunities: Kamiak Butte County Park, Steptoe Butte State Park, and Steptoe Canyon also offer good birding.

Directions: From SR 195 driving south near Pullman, take a right onto Wawawai-Pullman Road just after the turnoff toward Pullman. Stay on Wawawai-Pullman Road until you reach the intersection with Wawawai Grade Road. Turn right onto Wawawai Grade Road and drive down the canyon to the county park.

DeLorme map grid: Page 57, C6.

Elevation: 800 feet.

Access: Wheelchair-accessible trails and restrooms in the county park.

Bathrooms: Inside Wawawai County Park.

Hazards: None.

Nearest food, gas, and lodging: Pullman.

Nearest camping: On-site in Wawawai County Park.

For more information: Check the Web page for Wawawai County Park at www.whitman county.org/Parks/Index_Pages/Wawawai.htm.

Tucannon River Valley

Habitats: Cliffs, mountain riparian, lowland riparian, wetland, freshwater marsh, mixed-coniferous forest.

Specialty birds: Bald and Golden Eagles; Northern Goshawk; Swainson's Hawk; Chukar; Northern Pygmy- and Short-eared Owls; Vaux's Swift; Black-chinned, Calliope, and Rufous Hummingbirds; Red-naped Sapsucker; Hammond's, Dusky, and Pacific-slope Flycatcher (Cordilleran type); Cassin's Vireo; Gray Jay; Western Bluebird; Gray-crowned Rosy-Finch; Pine Grosbeak.

Best times to bird: Summer and fall.

The Blue Mountains offer rugged, rocky habitat near the Washington–Oregon–Idaho borders. These mountains host some bird species whose ranges barely cross into Washington, such as Green-tailed Towhee.

About the site:

As one of the least-birded areas of the state, the Blue Mountains hold a lot of potential for bird-watchers willing to explore interesting habitat on their own. The Tucannon River Valley offers a good introduction to the Blue Mountains and its island of relatively damp, mountainous habitat in the far southeastern corner of the state. The habitat transitions from farm fields and gently rolling hills near U.S. Highway 12 to a riparian and then mountain-riparian area as the road follows the river into the heart of the mountains and into the William Wooten Wildlife Area. Throw in a few small lakes and ponds and the mixed-coniferous forest and you find a lot of birding potential here.

The drive up Tucannon Road starts at the farm fields on US 12. Telephone poles and power lines along the road offer glimpses of raptors, blackbirds, and kingbirds, and watch the sides of the road for Ring-necked Pheasant and Brewer's, Vesper, and Savannah Sparrows flitting among the tall grasses. Midway up the valley, be sure to stop and read the historical marker along the road where members of the Lewis and Clark Expedition had lunch during their trip back from the Pacific Ocean in 1806.

After passing through the tiny burg of Marengo, the road passes a series of farm fields before reaching the edges of the Wooten Wildlife Area, which covers nearly 12,000 acres right up to the edges of the Wenaha-Tucannon Wilderness and the Umatilla National Forest. Stick to the main road heading south into the mountains and start exploring the sides of the road just past the wildlife area headquarters, where Spring Lake is the first in a series of lakes that can hold waterfowl and other birds in the emergent vegetation along their edges and the trees surrounding the lakes. Wander through the camping sites in search of passerines and look in the brush for skulking sparrows. Repeat the same routine along each lake on the way down toward Camp Wooten State Park.

The habitat switches from typical riparian to mixed forest as the road reaches the state park. This opens the possibility of seeing many new birds—Red-naped Sapsucker, Winter Wren, and Swainson's and Hermit Thrushes. Also keep an eye out for owls. During one summer visit in another area of the Blue Mountains, near Ski Bluewood outside of Dayton, we watched a Long-eared Owl fly from one fir tree to another far up in the mountains. Be sure to scan the banks and center of the river as well, because quick-running mountain streams in the Blue Mountains can host American Dipper.

Tucannon Road continues into the mountains beyond Camp Wooten State Park, and it is worth driving to the end of the road to look for more birds and, if you visit on a sunny summer day, to check out the butterflies in the area. Drive at least as far as the Tucannon Campground, which offers easy walking to the riverbank as well as mixed-forest habitat. The higher you go into the Blue Mountains, the more new species you can encounter. Boreal Owls and isolated Green-tailed Towhees have been found by industrious birders who left the roads below and

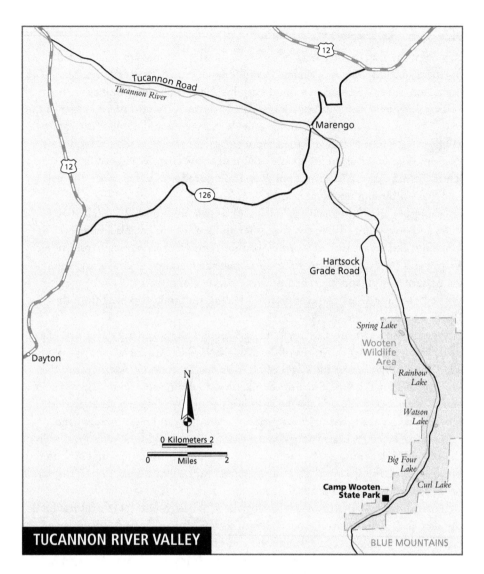

TUCANNON RIVER VALLEY

BLUE MOUNTAINS

ventured into the high forests. Meanwhile, careful examination of the riparian areas on the route back down from the Wooten Wildlife Area could lead to sightings of a controversial flycatcher, sometimes labeled as Cordilleran Flycatchers and other times labeled by experts in this part of the state such as Mike Denny, a field biologist for the U.S. Forest Service in the Umatilla National Forest, as either Western Flycatchers or Pacific-slope Flycatchers of a Cordilleran type. The reason for this confusion is that the only way to distinguish between a Pacific-slope and a Cordilleran Flycatchers is by listening for differences in their vocalizations. The problem with the flycatchers along the Tucannon River and in the Blue Mountains in general is that the same bird can emit a Pacific-slope call one moment and a Cordilleran call the next.

The best way to get more out of birding in the Blue Mountains is to visit the area in different seasons to see how the bird life and the natural world overall shifts from one season to the next. In January and February the fields along the Tucannon River host elk, and as the season shifts to spring watch for Wild Turkey in the wildlife area. Wildflowers are an attraction in May through early July, and bird diversity starts to peak with migrants moving through during that same time. The changing colors of leaves in the riparian areas along the river are an attraction in the fall, and in winter the raptors in the areas are a major attraction. You also may consider departing from Tucannon Road to drive up near Hatchery Ridge, where bighorn sheep often can be seen.

Other key birds: Hooded and Common Mergansers; Rough-legged Hawk; Merlin; Prairie Falcon; Gray Partridge; Ruffed Grouse; Wild Turkey; Spotted Sandpiper; Wilson's Snipe; Northern Saw-whet Owl; Common Nighthawk; Olive-sided Flycatcher; Western Wood-Pewee; Say's Phoebe; Western and Eastern Kingbirds; Northern Shrike; Warbling and Red-eyed Vireos; Bank Swallow; Mountain and Chestnut-backed Chickadees; House, Bewick's, Rock, and Canyon Wrens; American Dipper; Townsend's Solitaire; Veery; Swainson's, Hermit, and Varied Thrushes; Gray Catbird; Orange-crowned, Townsend's, Yellow, MacGillivray's, and Wilson's Warblers; Yellow-breasted Chat; Western Tanager; Chipping, Fox, Savannah, Lincoln's, and Vesper Sparrows; Black-headed Grosbeak; Lazuli Bunting; Bullock's Oriole; Cassin's Finch; Red Crossbill; Evening Grosbeak.

Nearby opportunities: More Blue Mountain birding can be found by driving up the road toward Ski Bluewood from Dayton, as well as by driving south of US 12 from Dixie toward Biscuit Ridge.

Directions: From US 12 northeast of Dayton, turn onto Tucannon Road and drive south to explore the river valley and climb into the Blue Mountains at the end of the road.

DeLorme map grid: Page 42, B3.

Elevation: 1,400 feet.

Access: None.

Bathrooms: At selected campsites along Tucannon Road.

Hazards: Rugged roads, heat.

Nearest food, gas, and lodging: Dayton or Pomeroy.

Nearest camping: Tucannon River Campground near the end of the road.

For more information: Check the Web page for the Wooten Wildlife Area at www.wdfw.wa.gov/lands/r1woot.htm.

THE BIRTHPLACE OF THE COLUMBIA BASIN

As you approach the Blue Mountains from the west, crossing the lower Columbia Basin, the mountains seem to rise out of nowhere, offering an oasis of habitat in the far southeastern corner of the state. The Blue Mountains sit at the center of what was once a huge system of volcanic dikes that erupted flood basalt that covered the Columbia Basin with hundreds of feet of lava, forming the basalt columns that were later eroded away by the Missoula Floods during the last ice age to create such formations as the Drumheller Channels found far to the northwest in the Columbia National

Wildlife Refuge. Flood basalt from the area of today's Blue Mountains erupted from the Grande Ronde volcano more than fifteen million years ago, and geologists estimate the volume of lava extruded at 149,000 cubic kilometers—enough to bury the continental United States under 12 meters of lava according to the VolcanoWorld Web site from the University of North Dakota (volcano.und.nodak.edu/vw.html).

As you look for birds in the Blue Mountains, be sure to pay attention to the layering effects of the lava flows that built this oasis that rises from the deserts of Washington, Idaho, and Oregon. And just try to imagine the huge pools of hot lava that oozed to the earth's surface over the span of about one million years. The Columbia River Flood Basalt Group, which includes the Grande Ronde floods as well as smaller floods from Picture Gorge, Wanapum, and the Saddle Mountains, created plateaus up to 3,500 meters in depth, eventually covering with a thick lava frosting the northeastern corner of Oregon, the entire Columbia Basin all the way north to the Okanogan, and the length of the Columbia River downstream to the Pacific Ocean.

Appendix A: Washington State Birds

The following is an annotated list of birds most commonly found in Washington. Each species is listed with its common name preceded by its family name, which is underlined at the top of each family of birds. Specialty birds are in **bold** type. Birds that are not common but that can still be seen on occasion in the state have their common names in *italics*. (W) denotes western Washington–only species. (E) denotes eastern Washington–only species.

Gavidae
Red-throated Loon
Pacific Loon
Arctic Loon
Common Loon Sites: 1, 2, 3, 4, 7, 8, 9, 10, 11, 12, 13, 14, 15, 16, 17, 19, 23, 24, 25, 26, 27, 28, 29, 30, 34, 35, 38, 53, 55, 56, 60, 64, 65, 68.
Yellow-billed Loon

Podicipedidae
Horned Grebe
Eared Grebe
Pied-billed Grebe
Red-necked Grebe
Clark's Grebe
Western Grebe

Diomedeidae
Short-tailed Albatross
Shy Albatross
Laysan Albatross
Black-footed Albatross

Procellariidae
Northern Fulmar
Murphy's Petrel
Mottled Petrel
Cook's Petrel
Buller's Shearwater
Pink-footed Shearwater
Flesh-footed Shearwater
Short-tailed Shearwater

Sooty Shearwater
Manx Shearwater

Hydrobatidae
Wilson's Storm-Petrel
Leach's Storm-Petrel
Fork-tailed Storm-Petrel

Sulidae
Blue-footed Booby

Pelicanidae
American White Pelican Sites: 43, 61, 64, 65, 66, 67, 68.
Brown Pelican Sites: 23, 24, 25, 27, 28, 29, 30.

Phalacrocoracidae
Pelagic Cormorant Sites: 1, 2, 3, 4, 7, 8, 9, 10, 11, 12, 13, 16, 17, 19, 23, 24, 25, 26, 27, 28, 29, 30.
Brandt's Cormorant Sites: 1, 2, 3, 4, 7, 8, 9, 10, 11, 12, 13, 16, 19, 23, 24, 25, 26, 27, 28, 29, 30.
Double-crested Cormorant

Ardeidae
American Bittern
Great Blue Heron
Great Egret Sites: 26, 28, 29, 32, 61, 64, 65, 66.
Snowy Egret
Little Blue Heron
Cattle Egret

Green Heron
Black-crowned Night Heron
Yellow-crowned Night Heron

Threskiornithidae
White-faced Ibis

Anatidae
Tundra Swan Sites: 10, 22, 29, 31, 32, 34, 46, 50, 54, 61, 63, 64, 65, 68.
Trumpeter Swan Sites: 10, 22, 29, 32, 54, 68.
Greater White-fronted Goose Sites: 2, 3, 8, 14, 15, 16, 19, 22, 23, 24, 25, 26, 27, 29, 31, 32, 38, 63, 68.
Snow Goose
Ross's Goose
Emperor Goose
Brant Sites: 2, 3, 4, 7, 8, 9, 11, 12, 18, 19, 29, 30, 31, 32.
Canada Goose
Wood Duck
Green-winged Teal
Falcated Duck
Mallard
Northern Pintail
Garganey
Blue-winged Teal
Cinnamon Teal
Northern Shoveler
Gadwall
Eurasian Wigeon
American Wigeon
Canvasback
Redhead
Ring-necked Duck
Tufted Duck
Greater Scaup Sites: 2, 3, 10, 11, 12, 13, 14, 15, 16, 18, 19, 20, 23, 26, 27, 29, 30, 31, 32, 34, 35, 38, 50, 51, 52, 55, 58, 60, 61, 64, 65, 68.
Lesser Scaup
Harlequin Duck Sites: 1, 2, 4, 7, 8, 9,

11, 12, 13, 16, 37.
Long-tailed Duck
Black Scoter
Surf Scoter
White-winged Scoter
Common Goldeneye
Barrow's Goldeneye Sites: 2, 3, 4, 7, 8, 9, 10, 11, 12, 13, 14, 15, 16, 17, 18, 19, 20, 23, 25, 26, 27, 34, 35, 38, 46, 49, 50, 51, 53, 54, 55, 56, 58, 60, 61, 63, 64, 65, 67, 68, 69.
Bufflehead
Hooded Merganser
Common Merganser
Red-breasted Merganser
Ruddy Duck

Cathartidae
Turkey Vulture

Accipitridae
Osprey
White-tailed Kite (W) Sites: 21, 22, 29, 31, 32.
Bald Eagle Sites: 1, 2, 3, 4, 5, 6, 7, 8, 9, 10, 11, 12, 13, 14, 15, 16, 17, 18, 19, 20, 21, 22, 23, 24, 25, 26, 27, 28, 29, 30, 31, 32, 33, 34, 35, 37, 38, 39, 40, 41, 42, 43, 44, 45, 48, 49, 50, 51, 52, 53, 54, 55, 56, 57, 58, 59, 60, 61, 63, 64, 65, 66, 67, 68, 69, 70.
Northern Harrier
Sharp-shinned Hawk
Cooper's Hawk
Northern Goshawk Sites: 5, 33, 34, 35, 36, 39, 41, 42, 43, 44, 45, 49, 52, 53, 54, 55, 58, 59, 62, 63, 70.
Red-shouldered Hawk (W)
Broad-winged Hawk
Swainson's Hawk Sites: 34, 39, 40, 42, 43, 46, 47, 48, 50, 52, 58, 59, 60, 61, 64, 65, 66, 67, 68, 69, 70.
Red-tailed Hawk

Ferruginous Hawk Sites: 46, 47, 48, 64, 65, 66, 67.

Rough-legged Hawk

Golden Eagle Sites: 5, 18, 34, 36, 38, 39, 40, 41, 42, 43, 45, 46, 47, 48, 50, 51, 52, 55, 56, 58, 59, 60, 61, 64, 65, 66, 67, 68, 69, 70.

Falconidae

American Kestrel

Merlin

Prairie Falcon

Peregrine Falcon Sites: 1, 2, 3, 4, 6, 7, 8, 9, 10, 11, 12, 13, 14, 15, 16, 18, 19, 20, 21, 22, 23, 24, 25, 26, 27, 28, 29, 30, 31, 32, 39, 40, 46, 47, 48, 52, 59, 60, 61, 66.

Gyrfalcon Sites: 8, 34, 55, 58, 59, 60, 65, 66.

Phasianidae

Chukar (E) Sites: 34, 35, 36, 39, 42, 43, 46, 47, 52, 59, 61, 65, 66, 67, 68, 69, 70.

Gray Partridge (E)

Ring-necked Pheasant

Ruffed Grouse

Spruce Grouse

Greater Sage Grouse (E)

Blue Grouse Sites: 1, 5, 33, 36, 39, 43, 44, 49, 53, 54, 55.

White-tailed Ptarmigan Sites: 33, 44.

Sharp-tailed Grouse (E) Site 59.

Wild Turkey

Odontophoridae

California Quail

Mountain Quail

Northern Bobwhite

Rallidae

Virginia Rail

Sora

American Coot

Gruidae

Sandhill Crane Sites: 19, 22, 32, 34, 50, 54, 58, 59, 61, 64, 65, 66.

Charadriidae

Black-bellied Plover Sites: 2, 3, 4, 7, 8, 9, 11, 16, 19, 22, 23, 24, 25, 27, 28, 29, 30, 31, 32, 65.

Pacific Golden-Plover Sites: 22, 25, 27.

American Golden-Plover Sites: 2, 3, 22, 27, 29.

Snowy Plover (W) Sites: 25, 29.

Semipalmated Plover

Killdeer

Mountain Plover

Eurasian Dotterel

Haematopodidae

Black Oystercatcher Sites: 1, 2, 3, 4.

Recruvirostridae

Black-necked Stilt Sites: 32, 60, 61, 64, 65, 68.

American Avocet Sites: 43, 58, 60, 61, 63, 64, 65, 68.

Scolopacidae

Greater Yellowlegs

Lesser Yellowlegs

Solitary Sandpiper Sites: 2, 3, 8, 9, 16, 19, 23, 25, 26, 27, 43, 58, 61, 65, 68.

Willet Sites: 22, 23, 24, 25, 29.

Wandering Tattler Sites: 23, 25, 30.

Spotted Sandpiper

Upland Sandpiper

Whimbrel

Long-billed Curlew Sites: 24, 25, 29, 34, 58, 60, 61, 64, 65, 68.

Hudsonian Godwit

Bar-tailed Godwit Site 28.

Marbled Godwit Sites: 23, 24, 25, 28, 29.

Ruddy Turnstone Sites: 1, 2, 3, 10, 28, 30.

Black Turnstone Sites: 1, 2, 3, 7, 11, 13, 19, 28, 29, 30.

Surfbird Sites: 2, 3, 7, 13, 30.

Red Knot Sites: 2, 23, 24, 25, 27, 28, 29.

Sanderling

Semipalmated Sandpiper

Western Sandpiper

Least Sandpiper

Baird's Sandpiper Sites: 2, 3, 16, 19, 23, 24, 25, 26, 27, 28, 29, 30, 43, 58, 60, 61, 64, 65, 68.

Pectoral Sandpiper Sites: 2, 8, 9, 16, 19, 23, 24, 25, 26, 27, 29, 30, 32, 43, 58, 60, 61, 64, 65, 68.

Sharp-tailed Sandpiper

Rock Sandpiper Sites: 1, 30.

Dunlin

Stilt Sandpiper

Buff-breasted Sandpiper

Ruff

Short-billed Dowitcher Sites: 2, 3, 8, 9, 19, 22, 23, 24, 25, 27, 29.

Long-billed Dowitcher

Wilson's Snipe

Wilson's Phalarope Sites: 32, 46, 54, 55, 58, 60, 61, 63, 64, 65, 68.

Red-necked Phalarope Sites: 2, 12, 16, 19, 23, 24, 25, 29, 46, 58, 60, 61, 63, 64, 65, 68.

Red Phalarope Sites: 2, 29.

Laridae

South Polar Skua

Pomarine Jaeger

Parasitic Jaeger

Long-tailed Jaeger

Franklin's Gull

Little Gull Sites: 12, 29.

Bonaparte's Gull Sites: 1, 2, 3, 4, 7, 8, 9, 10, 11, 12, 13, 16, 17, 18, 19, 22, 23, 24, 25, 26, 27, 28, 29, 30, 31, 32, 38, 61, 64, 65, 67, 68.

Heerman's Gull Sites: 1, 2, 3, 4, 7, 8, 9, 10, 11, 12, 13, 16, 23, 24, 25, 26, 27, 28, 29, 30.

Mew Gull Sites: 1, 2, 3, 4, 7, 8, 9, 10, 11, 12, 13, 14, 16, 17, 18, 19, 22, 23, 24, 25, 26, 27, 28, 29, 30, 31, 32, 38.

Ring-billed Gull

California Gull

Herring Gull Site 26.

Thayer's Gull Sites: 1, 2, 3, 8, 9, 11, 12, 16, 17, 19, 25, 28, 29, 30, 32.

Iceland Gull

Slaty-backed Gull

Western Gull Sites: 1, 2, 3, 4, 8, 9, 10, 11, 12, 13, 14, 15, 16, 17, 18, 19, 22, 23, 24, 25, 26, 27, 28, 29, 30, 32.

Glaucous-winged Gull

Glaucous Gull

Black-legged Kittiwake

Red-legged Kittiwake

Ross's Gull

Sabine's Gull

Caspian Tern

Elegant Tern

Common Tern Sites: 2, 3, 4, 11, 12, 16, 25, 29, 38.

Arctic Tern (W)

Forster's Tern (E) Sites: 61, 64, 65, 68.

Least Tern

Black Tern

Alcidae

Common Murre Sites: 1, 2, 3, 4, 7, 8, 9, 11, 12, 13, 16, 17, 19, 23, 25, 29, 30.

Thick-billed Murre

Pigeon Guillemot Sites: 1, 2, 3, 4, 7, 8, 9, 11, 12, 13, 16, 17, 19, 24, 25, 29, 30.

Marbled Murrelet Sites: 1, 2, 3, 4, 7, 8, 9, 11, 12, 13, 16, 19, 24, 25, 29.

Xantus's Murrelet
Ancient Murrelet Sites: 1, 2, 4, 12, 29.
Cassin's Auklet Site 4.
Parakeet Auklet
Rhinoceros Auklet Sites: 1, 2, 3, 4, 7, 8, 9, 11, 12, 13, 16, 17, 24, 25, 29.
Tufted Puffin Sites: 1, 2, 3, 4, 11.
Horned Puffin

Columbidae
Rock Pigeon
Band-tailed Pigeon (W) Sites: 2, 6, 7, 8, 9, 10, 11, 12, 14, 16, 18, 19, 20, 21, 22, 23, 26, 27, 28, 29, 30, 31, 32.
White-winged Dove
Mourning Dove

Tytonidae
Barn Owl

Strigidae
Flammulated Owl Sites: 39, 41, 43, 45, 53, 55.
Western Screech-Owl
Great Horned Owl
Snowy Owl Sites: 2, 29, 66.
Northern Hawk Owl
Northern Pygmy-Owl Sites: 1, 5, 6, 13, 16, 20, 21, 26, 32, 33, 34, 35, 36, 37, 39, 41, 43, 44, 45, 50, 51, 52, 53, 54, 55, 56, 57, 62, 63, 70.
Burrowing Owl Sites: 47, 48, 61, 64, 65, 66, 67, 68.
Spotted Owl Sites: 1, 29, 44.
Barred Owl
Great Gray Owl
Long-eared Owl
Short-eared Owl Sites: 2, 8, 10, 14, 19, 21, 22, 25, 26, 29, 30, 31, 32, 34, 46, 50, 51, 55, 59, 60, 61, 63, 64, 65, 66, 68, 70.
Boreal Owl
Northern Saw-whet Owl

Caprimulgidae
Common Nighthawk
Common Poorwill (E)

Apodidae
Black Swift Sites: 14, 33, 35, 36, 37, 38, 41, 44.
Vaux's Swift Sites: 2, 5, 7, 8, 9, 10, 11, 12, 13, 14, 15, 16, 18, 19, 20, 21, 22, 23, 24, 25, 26, 27, 28, 29, 30, 31, 32, 33, 34, 35, 36, 37, 38, 39, 40, 41, 42, 43, 44, 45, 46, 47, 48, 49, 53, 54, 55, 56, 58, 59, 68, 69, 70.
White-throated Swift (E)

Trochilidae
Black-chinned Hummingbird (E) Sites: 34, 35, 36, 37, 39, 40, 41, 42, 43, 45, 46, 50, 53, 54, 55, 56, 57, 58, 62, 63, 69, 70.
Anna's Hummingbird Sites: 1, 11, 12, 13, 14, 15, 16, 17, 18, 19, 22, 23, 24, 29, 37, 52.
Calliope Hummingbird (E) Sites: 34, 35, 36, 38, 39, 40, 41, 42, 43, 44, 45, 46, 50, 51, 52, 53, 54, 55, 56, 57, 58, 60, 62, 63, 65, 69, 70.
Rufous Hummingbird Sites: 1, 2, 5, 6, 7, 8, 9, 10, 11, 12, 13, 14, 15, 16, 17, 18, 19, 20, 21, 22, 23, 24, 26, 27, 28, 29, 30, 31, 32, 33, 34, 35, 36, 37, 38, 39, 40, 41, 42, 43, 44, 45, 46, 47, 48, 49, 50, 51, 52, 53, 54, 55, 56, 57, 58, 60, 62, 63, 65, 68, 69, 70.
Allen's Hummingbird

Alcedinidae
Belted Kingfisher

Picidae
Lewis's Woodpecker Sites: 34, 35, 36, 37, 38, 39, 40, 42, 43, 45, 46, 47, 50, 51, 52, 55, 56, 58, 60.
Acorn Woodpecker (E) Site 52.

Yellow-bellied Sapsucker

Red-naped Sapsucker Sites: 34, 35, 36, 37, 39, 40, 41, 43, 45, 50, 51, 52, 53, 54, 55, 56, 57, 58, 62, 63, 68, 69, 70.

Red-breasted Sapsucker Sites: 1, 6, 7, 9, 10, 11, 12, 13, 14, 15, 16, 17, 18, 19, 20, 21, 22, 23, 26, 29, 30, 31, 32, 33, 37, 38, 41, 44.

Williamson's Sapsucker Sites: 34, 36, 39, 41, 43, 45.

Downy Woodpecker

Hairy Woodpecker

White-headed Woodpecker Sites: 35, 36, 39, 41, 43, 45, 55.

Three-toed Woodpecker

Black-backed Woodpecker Sites: 35, 37, 39, 55.

Northern Flicker

Pileated Woodpecker Sites: 1, 2, 6, 7, 9, 10, 11, 12, 13, 14, 16, 17, 18, 19, 20, 21, 22, 23, 26, 29, 30, 31, 32, 33, 34, 35, 36, 37, 38, 39, 40, 41, 43, 44, 45, 47, 50, 51, 52, 53, 54, 55, 56, 57, 58, 62, 63.

Tyrannidae

Olive-sided Flycatcher

Western Wood-Pewee

Willow Flycatcher

Least Flycatcher Sites: 43, 63.

Hammond's Flycatcher Sites: 2, 6, 9, 11, 12, 16, 20, 29, 32, 33, 34, 35, 36, 37, 38, 39, 40, 41, 43, 45, 50, 51, 52, 53, 54, 55, 56, 57, 58, 62, 63, 68, 69, 70.

Dusky Flycatcher (E) Sites: 34, 35, 36, 39, 40, 41, 43, 47, 50, 51, 52, 54, 56, 58, 60, 61, 62, 63, 68, 69, 70.

Gray Flycatcher (E) Sites: 39, 40, 43, 50, 51, 58, 60.

Pacific-slope Flycatcher Sites: 1, 2, 5, 6, 7, 9, 11, 12, 13, 14, 16, 17, 18, 19,

20, 21, 26, 29, 30, 31, 32, 33, 34, 35, 36, 37, 39, 40, 41, 43, 44, 45, 50, 51, 52, 55, 56, 57, 58, 62, 63, 69, 70.

Black Phoebe (W)

Eastern Phoebe

Say's Phoebe

Vermillion Flycatcher

Ash-throated Flycatcher (E)

Tropical Kingbird

Western Kingbird

Eastern Kingbird

Scissor-tailed Flycatcher

Fork-tailed Flycatcher

Laniidae

Northern Shrike

Loggerhead Shrike

Vireonidae

Cassin's Vireo Sites: 9, 10, 11, 14, 19, 20, 21, 32, 34, 35, 36, 37, 38, 39, 40, 41, 43, 46, 47, 49, 50, 51, 52, 53, 54, 55, 56, 57, 58, 59, 60, 61, 62, 63, 64, 65, 66, 68, 69, 70.

Hutton's Vireo Sites: 1, 2, 6, 7, 9, 10, 11, 12, 13, 14, 15, 16, 18, 19, 20, 21, 22, 23, 26, 27, 28, 29, 30, 31, 32, 49.

Warbling Vireo

Red-eyed Vireo

Corvidae

Gray Jay Sites: 5, 33, 37, 39, 41, 44, 53, 55, 63, 70.

Steller's Jay

Blue Jay

Western Scrub-Jay (W)

Pinyon Jay

Clark's Nutcracker

Black-billed Magpie (E)

American Crow

Northwestern Crow Sites: 1, 2, 4, 7, 11, 12.

Common Raven

Alaudidae

Horned Lark

Hirundinidae
Purple Martin Sites: 14, 15, 16, 17, 18, 19, 26, 28, 31, 32.
Tree Swallow
Violet-green Swallow
Northern Rough-winged Swallow
Bank Swallow
Barn Swallow
Cliff Swallow

Paridae
Black-capped Chickadee
Mountain Chickadee
Chestnut-backed Chickadee
Boreal Chickadee

Aegithalidae
Bushtit

Certhiidae
Brown Creeper

Sittidae
Red-breasted Nuthatch
White-breasted Nuthatch
Pygmy Nuthatch Sites: 34, 37, 39, 43, 50, 55, 56, 57, 58, 59, 62, 63, 69.

Troglodytidae
Rock Wren
Canyon Wren (E)
Bewick's Wren
House Wren
Winter Wren
Marsh Wren

Cinclidae
American Dipper

Regulidae
Golden-crowned Kinglet
Ruby-crowned Kinglet

Sylviidae
Blue-gray Gnatcatcher

Turdidae
Western Bluebird Sites: 11, 21, 25, 26, 29, 34, 35, 36, 38, 39, 40, 41, 42, 43, 45, 46, 50, 51, 52, 55, 56, 57, 58, 59, 60, 62, 63, 66, 68, 69, 70.
Mountain Bluebird
Townsend's Solitaire
Veery (E)
Swainson's Thrush
Hermit Thrush
American Robin
Varied Thrush

Mimidae
Gray Catbird (E)
Northern Mockingbird
Sage Thrasher Sites: 39, 40, 42, 43, 46, 47, 58, 59, 60, 61, 64, 65, 66, 67.

Sturnidae
European Starling

Motacillidae
American Pipit

Bombycillidae
Bohemian Waxwing (E) Sites: 34, 35, 36, 55, 57, 58, 59, 62, 63, 68, 69.
Cedar Waxwing

Parulidae
Orange-crowned Warbler
Nashville Warbler
Yellow Warbler
Yellow-rumped Warbler
Black-throated Gray Warbler
Townsend's Warbler
Hermit Warbler (W) Sites: 20, 21.
Palm Warbler
Black and White Warbler
American Redstart
Ovenbird
Northern Waterthrush (E) Sites: 53, 55, 56.
MacGillivray's Warbler
Common Yellowthroat
Wilson's Warbler
Yellow-breasted Chat (E)

Thraupidae
Western Tanager

Emberizidae
Green-tailed Towhee (E)
Spotted Towhee
American Tree Sparrow
Chipping Sparrow
Clay-colored Sparrow
Brewer's Sparrow
Vesper Sparrow
Lark Sparrow (E)
Black-throated Sparrow
Sage Sparrow Sites: 40, 48, 59, 60, 61, 64, 65, 66, 67.
Lark Bunting
Savannah Sparrow
Grasshopper Sparrow (E)
Nelson's Sharp-tailed Sparrow
Fox Sparrow
Song Sparrow
Lincoln's Sparrow
Swamp Sparrow
White-throated Sparrow
Harris's Sparrow
White-crowned Sparrow
Golden-crowned Sparrow
Dark-eyed Junco
Lapland Longspur
Chestnut-collared Longspur
Rustic Bunting
Snow Bunting

Cardinalidae
Rose-breasted Grosbeak
Black-headed Gosbeak

Lazuli Bunting
Indigo Bunting

Icteridae
Bobolink
Red-winged Blackbird
Tri-colored Blackbird (E)
Western Meadowlark
Yellow-headed Blackbird
Rusty Blackbird
Brewer's Blackbird
Common Grackle
Brown-headed Cowbird
Bullock's Oriole

Fringillidae
Brambling
Gray-crowned Rosy-Finch Sites: 33, 34, 39, 41, 42, 44, 55, 59, 60, 70.
Pine Grosbeak Sites: 33, 37, 39, 41, 42, 44, 55, 70.
Purple Finch
Cassin's Finch
House Finch
Red Crossbill
White-winged Crossbill Site 55.
Common Redpoll Sites: 34, 58, 59, 63.
Hoary Redpoll
Pine Siskin
Lesser Goldfinch
American Goldfinch
Evening Grosbeak

Passeridae
House Sparrow

Bird species listed under the Federal Endangered Species List

Short-tailed Albatross (proposed)
Brown Pelican (endangered)
Aleutian Canada Goose (threatened)
Bald Eagle (threatened)
Snowy Plover (threatened)
Marbled Murrelet (threatened)
Spotted Owl (threatened)

U.S. Fish and Wildlife Service Species of Concern

Harlequin Duck
Northern Goshawk
Ferruginous Hawk
Greater Sage Grouse
Sharp-tailed Grouse
Burrowing Owl
Olive-sided Flycatcher
Loggerhead Shrike

Species listed as Threatened or Endangered by the Washington Fish and Wildlife Commission

American White Pelican (endangered)
Brown Pelican (endangered)
Aleutian Canada Goose (threatened)
Bald Eagle (threatened)
Ferruginous Hawk (threatened)
Sage Grouse (threatened)
Sharp-tailed Grouse (threatened)
Sandhill Crane (endangered)

Snowy Plover (endangered)
Upland Sandpiper (endangered)
Marbled Murrelet (threatened)
Spotted Owl (endangered)

Candidates for listing by the Washington Fish and Wildlife Commission

Common Loon
Short-tailed Albatross
Brandt's Cormorant
Northern Goshawk
Golden Eagle
Merlin
Common Murre
Cassin's Auklet
Tufted Puffin
Yellow-billed Cuckoo
Flammulated Owl
Burrowing Owl
Vaux's Swift
Lewis's Woodpecker
White-headed Woodpecker
Black-backed Woodpecker
Pileated Woodpecker
Horned Lark (streaked subspecies)
Purple Martin
White-breasted Nuthatch (Slender-billed subspecies)
Sage Thrasher
Loggerhead Shrike
Vesper Sparrow (Oregon subspecies)
Sage Sparr

★ Information courtesy of Audubon Washington, as found in *Important Bird Areas of Washington*.

Appendix B: Rare Bird Reporting

The following phone numbers allow you to dial in to check on rare bird sightings in each area covered by a particular rare-bird-reporting number, as well as a way to report your own sightings of rare birds.

Washington
Washington Ornithological Society
BirdBox (206) 281–9172.
Lower Columbia Basin (509)
627–2473.
Southeast Washington and Northern
Idaho (208) 882–6195.

Idaho
Southern Idaho (208) 236–3337.

Oregon
Oregon (503) 292–0661.

British Columbia
Nanaimo (250) 390–3029.
Okanagan (250) 491–7738.
Vancouver (604) 737–3074.
Victoria (250) 592–3381.

In addition to the bird-box phone systems above, you can also report rare bird sightings to the Washington Ornithological Society for review by the Washington Bird Records Committee. Just fill out the rare-bird-reporting form online at www.wos.org.

Appendix C: Glossary of Birding Terms

The following is a list of common bird-watching terms that are used throughout the text of this book. This is not meant to be an exhaustive list of birding terms, but rather an abbreviated list of common terms.

accidental. A term for a bird that is out of place and away from its normal migration or nesting range.

accipiter. Medium- to large-size hawks with long tails and short, rounded wings. These hawks are of the genus Accipiter. An example is the Sharp-shinned Hawk.

alcid. The family name for auklets, murres, puffins, and guillemots.

auricular patch. The area on a bird's head just below the eye, roughly corresponding to the cheek area on a human. This is one of the many birding field marks used to distinguish one species from another.

buteo. Large, soaring hawks with broad wings and broad tails. These hawks, such as the Red-tailed Hawk, are all from the genus Buteo.

coverts. Small feathers on a bird's wing or tail that cover the bases of the flight feathers.

crepuscular. Birds that are active at dusk. This is a term commonly used for species such as Short-eared Owls.

diurnal. Birds that are most active during the daytime.

emergent vegetation. This is a habitat term that describes the edges of wetlands and ponds where plants rise from below the water line, creating an inter-face between the open water habitat and land. A number of birds anchor their nests to emergent vegetation, such as Red-winged Blackbirds, Common Loon, and grebes.

field marks. A conspicuous marking, such as a wing bar or eye line or posture, that can help bird-watchers distinguish one species from another. Field marks also can include behaviors, such as tail twitches or the bobbing action of a Spotted Sandpiper.

irruptive. The periodic movement of numbers of a specific bird species outside of their normal range. An example of this is the periodic increase in the numbers of Snowy Owls that move south into Washington in years when the lemming supply is low in their normal range in the Canadian tundra.

lores. A common field mark denoting the area between the eye and the base of the upper bill.

malar. Another common field mark, this term refers to the area on a bird's head just below the eye and auricular areas.

migrant. This term denotes bird species that move each year between summer nesting areas and winter feeding areas.

molt. The term refers to the process by which birds regularly replace worn and damaged feathers with new feathers.

nocturnal. Birds that are most active during the night, such as many owl species.

passerine. This is a common term used for songbirds, or birds of the order Passeriformes.

pelagic. This term relates to birds that are normally seen near or on the ocean.

petagium. A term for the leading edge of the underwing, often cited for birds such as Red-tailed Hawks, which have a dark line on the leading edge of their underwings.

pishing. This is the practice of making a sound that approximates a bird call in order to urge birds to come out into the open to investigate, thereby giving you a better chance to look at them.

primaries. The largest outer wing feathers, also referred to as flight feathers.

raptor. Otherwise known as a bird of prey, such as a hawk, Bald Eagle, or Turkey Vulture.

resident. Birds that remain in a given area throughout the year.

scapulars. Feathers on the shoulder of a bird.

secondaries. Flight feathers that are closer to the bird's body than the primaries.

supercilium. An eye line above a bird's eye, somewhat like an eyebrow.

tertials. Referring to the innermost feathers on the upper side of the wing.

thermal. A patch of rising air or an updraft caused by heating and cooling of the earth's surface.

vagrant. A bird that has wandered outside of its normal migration or nesting range.

wing bar. Striping or barring on a bird's wings.

For much more information about common birding terminology, pick up a copy of *Birder's Dictionary,* by Randall T. Cox (Falcon Publishing Inc., 1996).

Appendix D: Resources

National Birding Organizations

American Birding Association
P.O. Box 6599
Colorado Springs, CO 80934
(719) 578–9703
www.americanbirding.org

Cornell Lab of Ornithology
159 Sapsucker Woods Road
Ithaca, NY 14850
(800) 843–BIRD (800) 843–2473
birds.cornell.edu

Falcon Research Group
P.O. Box 248
Bow, WA 98232
www.frg.org

HawkWatch International
1800 South West Temple
Suite 226
Salt Lake City, UT 84115
(800) 726–HAWK
www.hawkwatch.org

National Audubon Society
700 Broadway
New York, NY 10003
(212) 979–3000
www.audubon.org

Washington Birding Organizations

Washington Ornithological Society
(WOS)
P.O. Box 31783
Seattle, WA 98103
www.wos.org

Washington State Audubon Society
P.O. Box 462
Olympia, WA 98507-0462
(360) 786–8020
wa.audubon.org

Admiralty Audubon Society
P.O. Box 666
Port Townsend, WA 98368
(360) 385–0307
www.admiraltyaudubon.org

Black Hills Audubon Society
1063 Capitol Way South, Room 201
Olympia, WA 98501
(360) 352–7299
www.blackhillsaudubon.org

Blue Mountain Audubon Society
P.O. Box 1106
Walla Walla, WA 99362
www.bluemountainaudubon.org

Central Basin Audubon Society
(Moses Lake)
P.O. Box 86
Moses Lake, WA 98837
www.cbas.org

East Lake Washington Audubon
Society
P.O. Box 3115
Kirkland, WA 98083-3115
(425) 576–8805
www.elwas.org

Grays Harbor Audubon Society
P.O. Box 470
Montesano, WA 98563
(360) 495–3289
www.ghas.org

Kitsap Audubon Society
P.O. Box 961
Poulsbo, WA 98370
www.kitsapaudubon.org

Kittitas Audubon Society
P.O. Box 1443
Ellensburg, WA 98926
www.kittitasaudubon.org

Lower Columbia Basin Audubon
Society
P.O. Box 1900
Richland, WA 99352
(509) 588–4712

North Cascades Audubon Society
P.O. Box 5805
Bellingham, WA 98227-5805
www.northcascadesaudubon.org

North Central Washington Audubon
Society
P.O. Box 2934
Wenatchee, WA 98807
www.crcwnet.com/~ncwa

Olympic Peninsula Audubon Society
P.O. Box 502
Sequim, WA 98382
www.olympus.net/opas

Palouse Audubon Society
P.O. Box 3606—University Station
Moscow, ID 83843
www.palouseaudubon.org

Pilchuck Audubon Society
2829 Rockefeller
Everett, WA 98201
(425) 252–0926
www.pilchuckaudubon.org

Rainier Audubon Society (South King
County)
P.O. Box 778
Auburn, WA 98071
(253) 939–6411
www.rainieraudubon.org

San Juan Islands Audubon Society
P.O. Box 224
Deer Harbor, WA 98243
(360) 468–3068
www.sjiaudubon.org

Seattle Audubon Society
8050 35th Avenue NE
Seattle, WA 98115
(206) 523–4483
www.seattleaudubon.org

Skagit Audubon Society
P.O. Box 1101
Mount Vernon, WA 98273
(360) 424–9098
www.fidalgo.net/~audubon

Spokane Audubon Society
P.O. Box 9820
Spokane, WA 99209-9820
(509) 838–5828
www.spokaneaudubon.org

Tahoma Audubon Society (Tacoma)
2917 Morrison Road West
University Place, WA 98466
(253) 565–9278
www.tahomaaudubon.org

Vancouver Audubon Society
P.O. Box 1966
Vancouver, WA 98668-1966
clubs.homeearth.com/vas

Vashon/Maury Island Audubon Society
P.O. Box 838
Vashon, WA 98070
(206) 463–3153

Whidbey Audubon Society
P.O. Box 296
Langley, WA 98260
(360) 341–6387

Willapa Hills Audubon Society
P.O. Box 399
Longview, WA 98632
(360) 636–5461
www.willapahillsaudubon.org

Yakima Valley Audubon Society
P.O. Box 2823
Yakima, WA 98907
(509) 452–3260
www.yakimaaudubon.org

Books

A Birder's Guide to Coastal Washington, by Bob Morse (R.W. Morse Co., 2001).

A Birders Guide to Washington, edited by Hal Opperman (American Birding Association, 2003).

A Field Guide to the Cascades & Olympics, by Stephen R. Whitney (The Mountaineers, 1983).

A Guide to Bird Finding in Washington, by Terence Wahl and Dennis Paulson (Morris Publishing, 1991 edition).

Birder's Dictionary, by Randall T. Cox (Falcon Publishing Inc., 1996).

Birder's Guide to Washington, by Diann MacRae (Gulf Publishing Co., 1995).

The Birder's Handbook: A Field Guide to the Natural History of North American Birds, by Paul Ehrlich, David Dobkin, and Darryl Wheye (Simon and Schuster, Inc. 1988).

Birds of the Puget Sound Region, by Bob Morse, Tom Aversa, and Hal Opperman (R.W. Morse Co., 2003).

Brittle Stars & Mudbugs: An Uncommon Field Guide to Northwest Shorelines & Wetlands, by Patricia Lichen (Sasquatch Books, 2001).

The Butterflies of Cascadia, by Robert Michael Pyle (Seattle Audubon Society, 2002).

Fire, Faults, and Floods: A Road and Trail Guide Exploring the Origins of the Columbia River Basin, by Marge and Ted Mueller (University of Idaho Press, 1997).

Geology and Plant Life, by Arthur Kruckeberg (University of Washington Press, 2002).

Important Bird Areas of Washington, compiled by Tim Cullinan (Audubon Washington, 2001).

Lives of North American Birds, by Kenn Kaufman (Houghton Mifflin Co., 1996).

National Geographic Field Guide to the Birds of North America (National Geographic Society, 2002 edition)

The Natural History of Puget Sound Country, by Arthur Kruckeberg (University of Washington Press, 1991).

Northwest Arid Lands: An Introduction to the Columbia Basin Shrub-steppe, by Georganne O'Connor and Karen Wieda (Battelle Press, 2001).

Olympic National Park: A Natural History, by Tim McNulty (Sasquatch Books, 1996)

Passionate Slugs & Hollywood Frogs: An Uncommon Field Guide to Northwest Backyards, by Patricia Lichen (Sasquatch Book, 2001).

Plants of the Pacific Northwest Coast, by Jim Pojar and Andy MacKinnon (Lone Pine Publishing, 1994).

Rare Encounters with Ordinary Birds: Notes from a Northwest Year, by Lyanda Lynn Haupt (Sasquatch Books, 2001).

River-walking Songbirds & Singing Coyotes: An Uncommon Field Guide to Northwest Mountains, by Patricia Lichen (Sasquatch Books, 2001).

Roadside Geology of Washington, by David Alt and Donald Hyndman (Mountain Press Publishing Co., 1984).

Shorebirds of the Pacific Northwest, by Dennis Paulson (University of Washington Press, 1993).

Sibley's Birding Basics, by David Allen Sibley (Knopf, 2002).

The Sibley Guide to Bird Life & Behavior, by David Allen Sibley (Knopf, 2001).

The Sibley Guide to Birds, by David Allen Sibley (Knopf, 2000).

Wildflowers of the Olympics and Cascades, by Charles Stewart (Nature Education Enterprises, 1988).

E-mail lists and Web sites

The first place to check for updates and corrections to the text of this book is on the Web site www.birdingwashington.com. We offer a birding diary and periodic updates about some of the sites featured in this book on this Web site.

The emergence of the Internet as a bird-watching resource has been one of the biggest developments in the birding community during the last ten years. Below is information about a few of the most useful Internet resources for birding in Washington.

E-mail lists

Tweeters

With more than 1,000 readers, Tweeters is the most active e-mail list in Washington. Since it is hosted on the west side of the state at the University of Washington, the list tends to feature Western Washington reports more than the rest of the state. To subscribe to Tweeters visit www.scn.org/earth /tweeters. Dan Victor is the administrator for Tweeters, and he can be contacted at dcv@scn.org.

Inland Birders

Northern Idaho, Eastern Washington, and the Northeastern corner of Oregon are the focus on this list that is hosted at the University of Idaho. For details about the list check www.lists .uidaho.edu/mailman/listinfo/inland-nw-birders. Charles Swift is the administrator for the list, and he can be contacted at owner-inland-nw-birders@uidaho.edu.

BirdYak

Yakima County birders have their own e-mail list, and if you are interested in birding in this bird-rich part of the state, the list is a great resource. To subscribe, visit groups.yahoo.com/ group/birdyak. The BirdYak list administrator is Denny Grandstrand, and he can be contacted directly at osprey@nwinfo.net.

Oregon Birders On Line

This list is run by Greg Gillison, owner of thebirdguide.com. Subscription information and instructions are offered at www.oregonbirds.org. Gillison can be contacted directly at greg@thebirdguide.com.

Web sites

A number of Web sites serve as great resources in addition to any guidebooks you own, and the information they offer ranges from bird identification and distribution details to site guides.

Birdnotes.net

Track your bird lists for any site you visit and track what birds have been seen by others who use the Birdnotes system in that same location by setting up a free account at www.bird notes.net.

Birdweb.org

Stop at www.birdweb.org for details about which birds can be found in Washington, when, where, and much more. The relatively new site features photos of many species along with the most detailed distribution maps for Washington birds found anywhere online.

Bird checklist of the US/ Washington

Bird lists for a number of sites across the state are offered at www.npwrc .usgs.gov/resource/othrdata/chekbird/ r1/53.htm, the Washington state page from the excellent birding and biology information offered on the USGS page from the Northern Prairie Wildlife Research Center.

Christmas Bird Count Data

Investigate what birds have been seen during the annual Christmas Bird Counts, or CBCs as they are known, in your part of the state at audubon 2.org/birds/cbc/hr/count_table.html.

eBird.org

Keep your own yard or site lists on this Web site from the Cornell Lab of Ornithology at www.ebird.org.

Events

Skagit River Bald Eagle Festival

Typically held around the beginning of February, when the concentration of Bald Eagles along the Skagit River reaches its peak, the festival includes lectures, slide shows, cultural events, and birding guides stationed at viewpoints along the river. Check www .skagiteagle.org for current information.

Sandhill Crane Festival

Each year in late March thousands of bird-watchers migrate to Othello in the Columbia Basin to view thousands of Sandhill Cranes that roost and perform their mating dance. An annual festival marks the occasion with lectures, slide shows, book sales, and more at Othello High School. Check www.othello wa.com for more information.

Grays Harbor Shorebird Festival

Normally held near the end of April, when the spring migration reaches its peak in Grays Harbor, the annual shorebird festival offers lectures, shopping, food, and field trips. For details about this year's festival, check www.shorebirdfestival.com.

Leavenworth Spring Bird Festival

Held each year to coincide with International Migratory Bird Day, this festival features field trips, lectures, and guided bird walks on Blackbird Island and other important habitats around Leavenworth. Learn more at www .leavenworthspringbirdfest.com.

Bird Fest

Held in early October at the Ridgefield National Wildlife Refuge. Check the Web site at www.ridgefiel friends.org for more information.

Fall Festival of Foliage and Feathers

Held near the end of October in Walla Walla. The festival typically includes birding field trips and lectures. For more info, check www.downtown wallawalla.com/promotions/fall_ festval_foliage.htm.

Index

304, 305, 308, 320, 325, 330, 334, 335, 338, 343, 348, 350, 352, 358, 365; **Golden,** 4, 29, 37, 55, 56, 116, 184, 191, 193, 197, 198, 199, 207, 210, 214, 219, 221, 223, 227, 229, 236, 237, 240, 244, 247, 257, 262, 266, 269, 281, 286, 295, 298, 300, 301, 304, 305, 308, 325, 330, 333, 335, 338, 339, 343, 348, 350, 352, 359, 365

Egret, Cattle, 26, 357; **Great,** 4, 21, 24, 151, 160, 163, 165, 178, 308, 309, 325, 327, 328, 330, 335, 345, 357; **Snowy,** 357

F

Falcon, 193; **Peregrine,** 4, 7, 10, 22, 23, 29, 30, 32, 39, 43, 48, 49, 52, 60, 64, 66, 70, 74, 79, 81, 84, 86, 88, 91, 93, 96, 101, 106, 116, 120, 128, 131, 135, 136, 139, 141, 143, 147, 151, 155, 160, 163, 168, 173, 175, 178, 183, 210, 214, 216, 240, 247, 266, 300, 304, 308, 346, 359; **Prairie,** 29, 73, 213, 218, 226, 229, 230, 233, 235, 243, 244, 245, 250, 269, 303, 307, 311, 329, 333, 334, 337, 339, 341, 346, 350, 351, 355, 359; *See also* **Gyrfalcon**

Finch, 25, 237; **Cassin's,** 194, 197, 201, 205, 209, 213, 218, 222, 226, 231, 237, 239, 243, 260, 265, 269, 275, 280, 285, 293, 294, 303, 307, 324, 355, 364; **Gray-crowned, Rosy-,** 4, 9, 29, 184, 186, 187, 188, 210, 219, 223, 225, 232, 233, 281, 300, 301, 304, 352, 364; **House,** 5, 7, 26, 30, 364; **Purple,** 7, 47, 59, 69, 86, 91, 95, 99, 110, 119, 125, 130, 134, 137, 153, 167, 176, 183, 190, 205, 209, 235, 364; *See also* **Rosy-Finch**

Flicker, Northern, 5, 31, 139, 203, 349, 362

Flycatcher, 24, 27, 32, 45, 137, 139, 156–57, 184, 187, 211, 216, 259, 275, 317; **Ash-throated,** 245, 267, 269, 362; **Cordilleran,** 352, 354; **Dusky,** 4, 7, 191, 193, 195, 198, 210, 214, 219, 223, 227, 257, 262, 266, 277, 286, 295, 297, 304, 308, 315, 320, 321, 343, 348, 352, 362; **Fork-tailed,** 362; **Gray,** 4, 7, 210, 214, 227, 257, 262, 295, 297, 304, 321, 362; **Hammond's,** 4, 43, 60, 74, 84, 88, 106, 128, 178, 186, 191,

193, 195, 198, 202, 207, 210, 214, 219, 227, 236, 257, 262, 266, 272, 277, 281, 286, 290, 295, 297, 315, 320, 343, 348, 352, 362; **Least,** 4, 184, 227, 323, 362; **Olive-sided,** 47, 63, 69, 77, 82, 91, 104, 110, 114, 124, 130, 137, 153, 176, 190, 194, 197, 201, 205, 208, 209, 213, 221, 231, 239, 260, 265, 269, 285, 289, 294, 298, 319, 324, 351, 355, 362, 365; **Pacific-slope,** 4, 39, 43, 55, 60, 66, 74, 84, 88, 91, 93, 96, 100, 106, 111, 116, 120, 128, 131, 151, 163, 168, 173, 178, 186, 191, 193, 195, 198, 202, 203, 210, 214, 219, 227, 232, 236, 257, 262, 266, 281, 286, 290, 293, 295, 297, 304, 313, 315, 320, 348, 352, 354, 362; **Scissor-tailed,** 362; **Vermillion,** 362; **Western,** 354; **Willow,** 42, 47, 63, 69, 77, 82, 91, 97, 99, 104, 110, 119, 124, 130, 134, 137, 141, 153, 158, 167, 176, 183, 193, 194, 197, 201, 205, 209, 213, 221, 231, 255, 260, 265, 275, 280, 285, 289, 291, 294, 307, 324, 346, 351, 362; **Wilson's,** 319

Fulmar, Northern, 24, 34, 42, 47, 357

G

Gadwall, 47, 51, 77, 82, 91, 95, 99, 104, 114, 117, 119, 124, 130, 137, 141, 145, 150, 153, 158, 162, 176, 183, 194, 197, 209, 230, 243, 250, 260, 265, 269, 275, 280, 285, 289, 298, 307, 311, 323, 324, 328, 329, 331, 334, 337, 341, 346, 351, 358

Garganey, 358

Goose, 26, 68, 145, 153, 175, 182, 327; **Aleutian Canada,** 166, 175, 181, 365; **Cackling Canada,** 175, 181; **Canada,** 5, 17, 31, 32, 46, 98, 101, 118, 137, 165, 166, 175, 179, 181, 193, 207, 323, 334, 345, 358; **Dusky Canada,** 166, 175, 181; **Emperor,** 358; **Greater White-fronted,** 4, 32, 43, 48, 70, 96, 101, 106, 120, 135, 139, 151, 163, 173, 178, 182, 207, 320, 323, 334, 343, 358; **Ross's,** 358; **Snow,** 17, 73, 77, 80, 81, 82, 182, 183, 207, 323, 358

Gnatcatcher, Blue-gray, 227, 230, 363

Godwit, 145; **Bar-tailed,** 4, 160, 162, 359; **Hudsonian,** 162, 359; **Marbled,** 4, 139, 143, 147, 160, 162, 163, 359

79, 84, 88, 89, 93, 106, 139, 143, 147, 151, 155, 160, 163, 168, 360; **Herring,** 47, 51, 86, 91, 137, 141, 145, 150, 151, 153, 158, 162, 167, 183, 207, 289, 311, 329, 334, 337, 341, 360; **Iceland,** 360; **Little,** 4, 88, 89, 207, 360; **Mew,** 4, 39, 43, 45, 48, 52, 66, 70, 74, 79, 84, 88, 89, 93, 96, 106, 111, 116, 120, 135, 139, 143, 147, 151, 155, 160, 163, 168, 173, 178, 360; **Ring-billed,** 42, 47, 51, 69, 73, 77, 82, 86, 91, 95, 99, 104, 110, 114, 119, 124, 137, 141, 145, 150, 153, 158, 162, 167, 171, 176, 183, 194, 197, 209, 213, 218, 226, 230–31, 243, 250, 269, 289, 298, 311, 327, 329, 334, 337, 341, 346, 360; **Ross's,** 360; **Sabine's,** 34, 360; **Slaty-backed,** 360; **Thayer's,** 4, 39, 43, 45, 70, 74, 84, 88, 106, 111, 120, 147, 160, 163, 168, 178, 360; **Western,** 4, 39, 43, 45, 48, 52, 70, 74, 79, 84, 88, 93, 96, 101, 106, 111, 116, 120, 135, 139, 143, 147, 151, 155, 160, 163, 168, 178, 360
Gyrfalcon, 4, 70, 72, 82, 191, 282, 295, 298, 300, 301, 304, 359

H

Harrier, Northern, 5, 23, 26, 70, 76, 82, 99, 116, 121, 131, 133, 147, 174, 175, 179, 182, 193, 208, 250, 323, 328, 333, 358
Hawk, 279, 327; **Broad-winged,** 358; **Cooper's,** 5, 30, 58, 358; **Ferruginous,** 4, 27, 184, 240, 244, 247, 313, 325, 330, 335, 338, 339, 359, 365; **Red-shouldered,** 81, 126, 137, 181, 182, 183, 358; **Red-tailed,** 5, 7, 9, 30, 32, 82, 133, 179, 182, 199, 233, 237, 298, 300, 332, 349, 358; **Rough-legged,** 71, 73, 76, 77, 81, 82, 124, 137, 175, 176, 179, 182, 183, 213, 218, 235, 250, 265, 269, 280, 298, 301, 303, 307, 311, 329, 334, 341, 346, 351, 355, 359; **Sharp-skinned,** 5, 30, 97, 100, 358; **Swainson's,** 4, 184, 191, 210, 214, 223, 225, 227, 240, 244, 247, 250, 257, 266, 269, 295, 298, 300, 304, 308, 325, 330, 335, 338, 339, 343, 348, 349, 352, 358
Heron, 31, 326, 334; **Black-crowned Night-,** 82, 183, 209, 241, 243, 250, 311, 327, 328, 329, 333, 334, 341, 346, 358; **Great Blue,** 5, 22, 24, 49, 75, 79, 89, 116, 117–18, 122, 152, 175, 293, 327, 328, 346, 357; **Green,** 69, 82, 91, 97, 99, 104, 110, 114, 117, 119, 124, 130, 136, 137, 141, 153, 158, 167, 171, 175, 176, 181, 183, 358; **Little Blue,** 357; **Yellow-crowned Night-,** 358; *See also* **Night-Heron**
Hummingbird, 25, 86, 139, 141, 211, 275; **Allen's,** 361; **Anna's,** 4, 30, 70, 84, 88, 93, 96, 101, 106, 111, 116, 120, 135, 139, 163, 178, 361; **Black-chinned,** 4, 191, 193, 195, 198, 202, 210, 214, 219, 223, 227, 236, 240, 272, 277, 281, 286, 290, 295, 315, 320, 323, 348, 352, 361; **Calliope,** 4, 32, 191, 193, 195, 198, 202, 205, 207, 210, 214, 219, 223, 227, 229, 232, 236, 237, 240, 257, 262, 266, 272, 277, 281, 286, 290, 295, 304, 315, 317, 318, 320, 323, 330, 348, 352, 361; **Fur,** 257; **Rufous,** 4, 39, 43, 55, 60, 66, 70, 74, 79, 84, 88, 93, 96, 98, 101, 106, 111, 116, 120, 128, 131, 135, 139, 143, 151, 155, 160, 163, 168, 173, 178, 186, 191, 195, 198, 202, 203, 207, 210, 214, 219, 223, 227, 232, 236, 240, 244, 247, 252, 262, 266, 272, 277, 281, 286, 290, 295, 304, 315, 320, 323, 330, 343, 348, 352, 361

I

Ibis, White-faced, 334, 358

J

Jaeger, Long-tailed, 360; **Parasitic,** 34, 42, 47, 54, 64, 86, 89, 91, 110, 141, 145, 150, 167, 360; **Pomarine,** 34, 42, 167, 207, 360
Jay, 62; **Blue,** 362; **Gray,** 4, 27, 29, 55, 56, 186, 188, 202, 210, 219, 232, 272, 281, 320, 352, 362; **Pinyon,** 362; **Western, Scrub-,** 110, 134, 137, 153, 158, 176, 181, 183, 268, 362; **Steller's,** 5, 27, 181, 362; *See also* **Scrub-Jay**
Junco, Dark-eyed, 5, 9, 31, 32, 253, 364

K

Kestrel, American, 5, 174, 175, 213, 233, 237, 278, 279, 298, 328, 349, 359

298, 305, 307, 312, 319, 324, 328, 329, 332, 334, 337, 341, 346, 351, 355, 362

Pigeon, Band-tailed, 4, 43, 60, 66, 70, 74, 79, 84, 86, 88, 96, 106, 120, 121, 128, 131, 135, 139, 151, 155, 160, 163, 168, 173, 178, 361; **Rock,** 5, 361

Pintail, Northern, 22, 45, 47, 51, 73, 77, 82, 86, 99, 104, 110, 114, 119, 124, 136, 137, 141, 158, 167, 171, 176, 181, 183, 194, 197, 230, 243, 250, 260, 265, 269, 275, 280, 285, 289, 298, 307, 311, 324, 329, 334, 337, 341, 345, 346, 351, 358

Pipit, American, 25, 47, 59, 69, 73, 77, 86, 91, 99, 103, 104, 110, 124, 135, 137, 150, 153, 158, 167, 176, 183, 190, 194, 197, 209, 235, 307, 312, 346, 363

Plover, 23, 24, 333; **American, Golden-,** 4, 43, 45, 48, 135, 155, 163, 359; **Black-bellied,** 4, 43, 48, 52, 66, 70, 74, 84, 106, 120, 135, 136, 139, 143, 147, 155, 157, 160, 163, 168, 173, 178, 359; **Mountain,** 359; **Pacific, Golden-,** 4, 9, 135, 136, 147, 155, 359; **Semipalmated,** 51, 91, 124, 137, 141, 145, 148, 150, 167, 183, 323, 346, 359; **Snowy,** 4, 23, 147, 148, 163, 166, 359, 365; *See also* **Golden-Plover**

Poorwill, Common, 27, 29, 194, 197, 201, 213, 218, 226, 230, 231, 243, 245, 250, 285, 289, 298, 303, 312, 324, 329, 334, 337, 341, 351, 361

Ptarmigan, White-tailed, 4, 17, 25, 29, 184, 186, 187, 188, 232, 233, 359

Puffins, Horned, 361; **Tufted,** 4, 37, 39, 41, 43, 45, 48, 52, 53, 84, 89, 361, 365

Pygmy-Owl, Northern, 4, 39, 55, 60, 106, 128, 131, 151, 178, 186, 191, 195, 198, 202, 210, 219, 227, 232, 236, 257, 262, 266, 272, 277, 281, 286, 290, 315, 320, 352, 361

Q

Quail, California, 5, 45, 193, 203, 237, 359; **Mountain,** 359

R

Rail, Virginia, 32, 45, 69, 73, 77, 82, 91, 97, 99, 104, 110, 117, 119, 124, 130, 136, 137, 153, 157, 158, 167, 176, 181, 183, 194, 209, 213, 230, 243, 245, 250, 260, 265, 269, 285, 289, 294, 298, 305, 307, 311, 324, 329, 334, 337, 341, 346, 351, 359

Raven, Common, 5, 21, 25, 27, 29, 187, 190, 221, 305, 332, 362

Red Knot, 4, 43, 48, 139, 143, 147, 155, 157, 160, 163, 360

Redhead, 183, 194, 197, 209, 230, 243, 250, 260, 265, 269, 275, 280, 285, 289, 298, 307, 311, 321, 324, 328, 329, 331, 334, 337, 341, 345, 346, 351, 358

Redpoll, Common, 4, 32, 191, 270, 295, 300, 320, 323, 364; **Hoary,** 364

Redstart, American, 272, 275, 280, 285, 288, 289, 294, 321, 323, 324, 363

Robin, American, 5, 7, 8, 25, 363

Rosy-Finch, Gray-crowned, 4, 9, 29, 184, 186, 187, 188, 210, 219, 223, 225, 232, 233, 281, 300, 301, 304, 352, 364

Ruff, 360

S

Sanderling, 23, 47, 51, 54, 73, 77, 84, 86, 91, 110, 124, 141, 145, 150, 158, 162, 165, 167, 171, 360

Sandpiper, 24, 118, 175, 326, 333; **Baird's,** 4, 9, 16, 43, 45, 48, 106, 120, 122, 139, 143, 147, 151, 155, 160, 163, 168, 227, 230, 295, 304, 308, 323, 325, 327, 330, 343, 360; **Buff-breasted,** 360; **Least,** 8, 23, 47, 51, 73, 77, 86, 91, 104, 110, 124, 136, 137, 141, 145, 148, 150, 157, 158, 162, 165, 167, 171, 176, 182, 183, 230, 298, 307, 311, 324, 327, 329, 334, 346, 360; **Nelson's Sharp-tailed,** 360; **Pectoral,** 4, 9, 31, 43, 48, 70, 74, 91, 106, 120, 139, 143, 147, 151, 153, 155, 163, 168, 178, 227, 304, 308, 323, 325, 327, 330, 343, 360; **Rock,** 4, 23, 39, 168, 169, 360; **Semipalmated,** 47, 51, 145, 230, 346, 360; **Solitary,** 4, 43, 45, 70, 74, 106, 122, 141, 147, 151, 153, 155, 295, 308, 330, 343, 359; **Spotted,** 25, 51, 73, 77, 91, 95, 97, 99, 104, 109, 110, 124, 141, 150, 153, 158, 162, 167, 176, 183, 187, 188, 190,

About the Authors

Natalie McNair-Huff started bird-watching as a young child by watching the birds at her grandparents' feeders, on the beach during walks with her family in Gold Beach, Oregon, and in the Sonoran Desert, where she always liked to see Road Runners. She has lived in Washington since she was age six, when her family moved to Longview. She now lives in Tacoma, Washington, with her writing and business partner, and husband, Rob. She is the Webmaster of the Tahoma Audubon Society and, at the time of this publication, is serving as president along with Rob. When not birding or working, she likes to dig around in her organic garden, look for native plants, and work on restoration projects. She is most comfortable around "big water and big mountains," and frequent trips out of the city to see turtles, owls, and coyotes, among other creatures, keep her sane.

One of Rob McNair-Huff's first birding memories includes watching an American Kestrel kiting in the wind as it hunted over the open fields on his family's farm in Rochester, Washington. Rob now lives in Tacoma with his wife and writing partner, Natalie, and he is more likely to spy a Sharp-shinned Hawk diving into the shrubs in pursuit of a sparrow dinner outside the kitchen window. When he isn't driving around the state in search of new birding locations, Rob spends his time chasing butterflies, working with Western pond turtles, and serving as the Conservation Committee chair for the Tahoma Audubon Society. Rob writes an online nature journal called The Equinox Project at www.whiterabbits.com/weblog.html.

Rob and Natalie are the co-authors of *Insiders' Guide to the Olympic Peninsula* (The Globe Pequot Press, 2001), and Rob was the revision editor of the second edition of *Mountain Bike America: Washington* (The Globe Pequot Press, 2001).